A TOUCH OF PARADISE IN HELL

For Katrien

A Touch of Paradise in Hell

Talbot House, Poperinge – Every-Man's Sanctuary from the Trenches

Jan Louagie

Helion & Company Limited

Helion & Company Limited
26 Willow Road
Solihull
West Midlands
B91 1UE
England
Tel. 0121 705 3393
Fax 0121 711 4075
Email: info@helion.co.uk
Website: www.helion.co.uk
Twitter: @helionbooks
Visit our blog http://blog.helion.co.uk/

Published by Helion & Company 2015

Designed and typeset by Bookcraft Ltd, Stroud, Gloucestershire
Cover designed by Paul Hewitt, Battlefield Design (www.battlefield-design.co.uk)
Printed by Gutenberg Press Limited, Tarxien, Malta

Introduction and editorial text © Jan Louagie 2015
Images © as individually credited

Front cover: 'Toc H at Pop', drawing by J.W. Leighton, 1933, from the collection of Talbot House.
Rear cover: Charcoal preliminary sketch for oil painting 'The Conquerors' (Canadian War Museum),
presented to Talbot House by war artist Eric Kennington in 1931.

ISBN 978-1-910777-12-1

British Library Cataloguing-in-Publication Data.
A catalogue record for this book is available from the British Library.

For details of other military history titles published by Helion & Company Limited contact the
above address, or visit our website: http://www.helion.co.uk.

We always welcome receiving book proposals from prospective authors.

Contents

List of Illustrations   viii
List of Abbreviations   xiv
Acknowledgements   xviii
Introduction   xix

PART 1 – AN EVERY-MAN'S CLUB   **25**

PART 2 – A HOME FROM HOME   **228**

I   Realm of the Body   231
    1   From the Notice Board   232
       1.1   Matters Domestic   232
       1.2   Anecdotage   235
    2   Friendship's Corner   237
    3   'Wander into the Canteen…'   239
    4   'Come into the Garden and forget about the War'   242
    5   The Concert Hall   245
       5.1   Music and Drama   246
       5.2   Cinema   251
       5.3   Lectures, Debates and Discussion…   251
       5.4   'A little Treat for the Belgian Kiddies'   255
       5.5   Hannah, Protégée of Talbot House   259

II   Realm of the Heart and Mind   264
    1   'This is a Library, not a Dormitory!'   265
    2   Church Shop   267
    3   The Canadian Lounge   268
    4   The Chaplain's Room   269
    5   Writing-rooms   271
    6   The General's Bedroom   274

III Realm of the Soul   276
   1   The Chapel – 'the Shrine of the whole Salient'   277
   2   A Place of Worship   281
       2.1 Communion   281
       2.2 Baptism   286
       2.3 Confirmation   288
       2.4 A Call to Holy Orders   290
   3   A Place of Spiritual Refreshment, Strength and Guidance   291

PART 3 – A HOUSE OF PEOPLE   **298**

I   The Innkeeper – Capt. Leonard Browne   298

II   'The General', My Brave Old Batman – Rev. P.B. Clayton   303

III The Customers   309
   1   A Scrap of Memories by the Innkeeper   309
       1.1 L/Cpl. Archie Forrest – From Baptism to Death   311
       1.2 An Unknown Gunner – Requiem for a Friend   314
       1.3 Sgt. John Waller – On Eternal Leave   315
       1.4 Pte. John Henry – C.-in-C. of Billiards   318
       1.5 Capt. Cecil Rushton & Capt. Tom Le Mesurier – Chivalrous Knights 322
       1.6 General Sir Herbert Plumer – Sympathy for a Footslogger 324
       1.7 Major Harold Philby – Thoughtful for his Men   325
       1.8 Capt. Marshall Webb – A Tormented Spirit   326
   2. Some Reminiscences by Talbotousians   328
       2.1 "Him"   328
       2.2 Capt. Philip Gosse – Conspiracy for Good   330
       2.3 Sister Alison Macfie – A Memorable Visit   331
       2.4 Lt. John Nicholson – In Spite of Himself   336
       2.5 Rfm. Donald Cox – 'The Witness of a Wayfarer to Talbot House' 337

PART 4 – BEYOND THE WALLS   **340**

I   Slumming   340
   1   An Outpost of Talbot House – Major Hugh Higgon   340
   2   A Celestial Breakfast – Rev. P.B. Clayton   343
   3   A Pyx in Flanders – Rev. P.B. Clayton   345

II   Little Talbot House   349
   1   Introduction – Rev. P.B. Clayton   349
   2   Little Talbot House – Dr. C.J. Magrath, YMCA   351
   3   Memories – P.C.H.   352
   4   Dr. Charles Magrath, "the YMCA Hero of Ypres" – Barclay Baron 355

APPENDICES

I   Note on Talbot House – Rev. P.B. Clayton (11 June 1917)   358
II   Further Note on Talbot House – Major G.B. Bowes, Chairman
       (26 December 1917)   359
III   Talbot House Committee (October 1917)   360
IV   Report of Social Sub-Committee (28 August 1917)   361
V   Report of House Sub-Committee (29 August 1917)   362
VI   Report of Finance Sub-Committee (29 August 1917)   364
VII   Constitution of Committee of Management and Financial Instructions
       (26 January 1918)   365
VIII   Talbot House Constitution (30 January 1918)   367
IX   Talbot House Staff (June 1918)   369
X   Talbot House Canteen   370

Bibliography   375
Index   377

List of Illustrations

Isabel Clayton, Tubby's mother.	26
Rev. Neville Talbot.	26
Philip Byard Clayton.	26
General Sir Reginald May.	28
Gasthuisstraat (Rue de l'Hôpital), Poperinge. Future Talbot House is third house from the left.	28
Maurice and Alida Coevoet-Camerlynck.	28
The Carpenter's Bench.	31
Pte. Arthur Pettifer.	33
Reginald Clayton, Tubby's father.	33
Signboard.	37
Pte. Robert Bell.	37
Gilbert Talbot.	38
VI Division Christmas card, 1915.	40
'A' Company, 1st Bn Queen's Westminster Rifles, in the yard of their billets next door to Talbot House, in or about January 1916.	44
From album of Sister Alison Macfie, V.A.D.	49
As Deputy Chaplain-General, Gwynne was the beloved chief of all C. of E. BEF padres throughout the war. Tubby frequently referred to him as 'Bishop Greatheart'.	50
Page from the Talbot House Visitors' Book.	51
Part of the splendid hangings from the Bishop's Chapel at Southwark.	52
Sitting room at Little Hatchett.	54
Page from Guide *Militaire Anglais-Flamand* (Guides Plumon, Paris, 1915).	55
Shop nearly opposite Talbot House.	55
Guards and Canadians in the tea-room of Talbot House, 24 April 1916.	57
Château D'Hondt.	59
Nursing Sisters taking care of civilians at Château D'Hondt.	60
Emile de Laveleye.	60
Charcoal preliminary sketch for oil painting *The Conquerors* (Canadian War Museum), presented to Talbot House by war artist Eric Kennington in 1931.	63

The Chapel , etched by E. Charlton, from a sketch by L/Cpl. Lowman, Q.W.R., early 1916.   65

Portable harmonium brought back from leave in January 1916 by Major Edmund Street, 2nd Bn Sherwood Foresters.   67

Lt. Godfrey Gardner.   67

No. 16 General Hospital, Le Tréport.   70

Sketch from La Poupée Visitors' Book.   72

Ginger.   72

Extract from the Register of the Assistant Provost Marshal.   73

The Upper Room, 1916. Picture taken from the rafter-loft.   74

Tubby and the Talbot House staff in the garden, 24 April 1916. 'Gen' is seated on the extreme right, Sgt. George Godley on the left of Tubby.   74

Randall Davidson, Archbishop of Canterbury.   75

Edward, Prince of Wales.   77

Tubby at Little Hatchett.   81

Neville Talbot and the staff of Talbot House and The Officers' Club, June – July 1916. Sgt. George Godley on the left of Talbot.   85

Wooden grave marker of Gilbert Talbot, preserved in a beautifully decorated shrine in the Upper Room.   87

Leonard Browne.   92

Cpl. Jacob Bennett.   97

Rev. Edward ('Ted') Talbot (with cap) at a retreat at St. Eloi, 25 August 1918.   101

Drawing by Bandsman Erskine Williams.   109

The Clayton family. *From left to right:* Grace Butler (family friend), Nurse Elsie ('Nursie'), Ivy Frances (younger sister), Reginald (father), Philip ('Tubby'), Stuart (daughter of 'Jack', elder brother), Isabel (mother) with Hephzibah ('Heffy') the dog at her feet, Isobel ('Belle', elder sister), Beatrice ('Trixie', wife of Jack).   113

Perugino's Crucifixion - the altarpiece of the Upper Room.   115

Capt. Thomas David, 4th Bn Welch Regt., killed in action 27 July 1917, buried in Bard Cottage Cemetery (Ieper).   116

Harmonium, in use in the chapel and the concert hall (larger congregations). After the war it ended up with the British Army of the Rhine in Wiesbaden. It was brought back to England in 1927 by Rev. J. St. Clair Goldie and returned to Talbot House in 1930.   118

Officers and Senior NCOs, 141st Heavy Battery, R.G.A.   120

Sister Dorothea Macfie, V.A.D.   120

Sister Alison Macfie, V.A.D.   120

Children of Maurice and Alida Coevoet-Camerlynck. *From left to right:* Yvonne (1906), Roger (1908), Marie-Madeleine (1904) and Fernand 1910).   124

The Chaplain's Room, faithfully reconstructed in 2005.   125

Shelter, watercolour by Eric Kennington.   127

The orchestra of Talbot House in the garden.   129

Rev. Maurice Murray.   132

The Canadian Lounge, badly shaken by a shell burst in July 1917.   133

The beautiful old *prie-dieu* in the Upper Room bearing the names of Pte. William   135
    Locke, 133 Field Ambulance, and Pte. Kenneth Mayhew, 6 London Field
    Ambulance.

Tubby on leave at Little Hatchett.   138

Tubby addressing a congregation outside East Boldre Church.   138

Cpl. Herbert Hoptrough.   145

Postcard of the Upper Room with the times of daily services printed at the back;   149
    widely distributed and treasured by many.

Chinese labourer 18693 Song Xiufeng poses with Maurice, the son of photographer   150
    René Matton, in Proven.

"Great candlesticks made of bedposts stand sentinels of light above the worshippers."   154
    (P.B.C.)

Many 'Talbotousians' and their families donated presents for the children's party.   159

Sitting room at Little Hatchett.   163

Capt. E. Van Cutsem, Town Major of Poperinge.   167

 Lt.-Col. James Lee, Town Major of Ieper.   168

Rev. Pat Leonard.   170

The 'Wunny Wuns' troupe (11th Division Concert Party). Bandsman Erskine   176
    Williams, who had played in several concerts at Talbot House, is the soldier
    standing centre. He was recruited as their scene painter while they were at 'Pop'.

Civilians fleeing their homes.   182

Barclay Baron, who served the YMCA from its Headquarters at Poperinge.   183

Alida Camerlynck (wife of Maurice Coevoet) and her sister Marcelline seated, with   189
    their children and nanny (standing at the back), in the garden of 'Chalet Lutherean'
    (Lisieux) where they had fled to escape the war in the spring of 1918.

German army map of Proven, March 1918, showing La Lovie Château (map square   190
    6259) and the aerodrome (6258 & 6259). The supposed location of Dingley Dell is
    marked with an arrow.

Tubby, his sister-in-law Annie Blanch (née Nepean) and little Nancy ('Bubbles') at   193
    Little Hatchett, 1918.

Two simple wooden prayer-desks in the Upper Room, one bearing a plate in memory   195
    of 2nd Lt. Bernard Stenning.

Tubby was so attached to the hut in which he had lived at 'Dingley Dell' that after the   196
    war he had it transported to Little Hatchett, where it was put in the garden. It was
    returned to Poperinge in 1999 and now forms part of the Talbot House collection.

Going home, 1999.   199

Town Hall in Proven.   201

To the left: Hephzibah ('my delight is in her') or 'Heffy', the first of a long succession of   204
distinguished pets kept by Tubby. In April 1918 she gave birth to 'Kemmel', named
after the village that fell to the Germans in the same month. *To the right:* Bango, a
friend's dog.

A large audience of soldiers and a number of children watch 'The Balmorals', the 51st   207
Division Entertainment Party. (IWM)

Poperinghe Police Force 1918.   209

Charcoal preliminary sketch for oil painting *The Conquerors* (Canadian War Museum),   211
presented to Talbot House by war artist Eric Kennington in 1931.

The library in the front room.   213

Decorative painting on the door of the front room.   213

Shop in Casselstraat, Poperinge.   214

The 'Eighty Eights' Concert Party (88th Battery, R.G.A.) in the Talbot House garden.   219

George Upton-Robins.   220

Shelter, watercolour by Eric Kennington.   221

The Upper Room, pen drawing by Cyril Worsley, 1917.   225

Tubby bids farewell to the Coevoet family, February 1919.   226

Tubby's 'whizz-bang', a parody of the Army Field Postcard.   227

From the middle of the 18th century till 1911, the house was lived in by the Lebbe   230
family, hop merchants by trade and tradition in Poperinge. The glass panel of the
door separating the front from the back hall bears the engraved initials 'LV'. The 'L'
stands for Lebbe. The 'V' is uncertain. The wives of three generations of the Lebbe
family had a surname beginning with 'V': Van Isacker, Vantours and Vuylsteke.

Detail from the iron-grilled door.   231

The Pess-Optimist. Wot a life! No rest, no beer, no nothing. It's only us keeping so   236
cheerful as pulls us through.

Pte. Ralph Morris, 763 Area Employment Coy. (left) and Gnr. Cyril Mumford, 25   239
Siege Battery, R.G.A. Picture taken near Talbot House, December 1917.

Donald Hodge.   241

Herbert Hodge.   241

Talbot House from the garden, 24 April 1916. On the foreground, three Welsh   242
Guards; Pte. Pettifer sitting against the wall of the bath-house. The hole in the back
of the house caused by a German 5.9 inch shell has been boarded up.

A Corps band in the garden, 1917. Many regiments, including the British West Indies,   244
are represented – one by its mascot goat.

Cosmo Gordon Lang, Archbishop of York.   244

Lord Plumer, 1918.   247

L/Cpl. Arthur Burgess, 1/21 Bn London Regt., aka 'Titch'. Picture taken by Camille   247
Battheu.

Extract from Canteen Stock Book, February 1918.   250

Cpl. Charles Gethin.   251

The House staff entertain the British West Indies Regiment after a debate on 'The   253
   Colour Problem in the Empire'.

Marcel Leroy, who attended the party on St. Nicholas Day 1916.   256

Jeanne and Rachel Battheu. Rachel died in 1917.   257

Extract from Canteen Stock Book, December 1917   258

St. Nicholas Day Party, 6 December 1916. At the far right of the picture, Tubby   259
   Clayton with child on his shoulder.

Hannah Mitchell.   259

Samuel Giles, R.E. Signals Section, librarian at Talbot House.   267

One of the writing-rooms. Through the window one can see the entrance to the   272
   Concert Hall.

Lt.-Col. Archibald Buchanan-Dunlop.   273

Charcoal sketch by Eric Kennington.   274

Painting of the Upper Room by Kenneth Barfield, 1917, from which coloured post-   276
   cards were made that were freely distributed after services. Many 'Talbotousians'
   treasured these as souvenirs for the rest of their lives.

Major Henry Duncan Bentinck.   276

Crucifix presented by the 120th Railway Construction Company.   278

Silver wafer-box commemorating Rfm. Newton Gammon, Q.W.R.   278

The silver-gilt Chalice and Paten that were in constant use in the Chapel.   278

Oak carving of a kneeling monk, given by 18th Siege Battery in memory of Fitter   278
   Charles Payne.

The Westminster chimes struck on the gongs summoned worshippers to the Chapel.   282
   The order in which the four brass plates have to be struck is marked on the
   framework.

Rev. Julian Bickersteth.   289

Horace Manton Brown   290

The Earl of Cavan.   292

Rfm. Basil Lawrence.   293

Rev. A. Llewellyn Jones.   295

Drawing of Tubby, 1916.   299

The old General in war paint.   304

Watercolour of 'Pettifer's Den' on the 2nd floor of Talbot House.   308

'Gen' and Tubby, 1928.   309

Oak chair in memory of L/Cpl. Archie Forrest, given by his comrades of 'P' Special   312
   (Gas) Company.

War widows near Lijssenthoek Military Cemetery, Poperinge – Toc H/St. Barnabas   313
   Pilgrimage, March 1923.

Sgt. John Waller.   316

Guards and Canadians in the tea-room of Talbot House, 24 April 1916.   317

Billiard-table in the canteen, 1918.   318

Extract from the Register of the Assistant Provost Marshal.   320

Capt. Thomas Le Mesurier.   323

Grave of Capt. Cecil Rushton at Steenbrugge. After the war it was moved to Larch   323
    Wood, Zillebeke.

Major Harold Philby, 5 August 1914.   325

Tubby, 1915.   329

Execution post in the courtyard of Poperinge Town Hall. Eight men are known to   331
    have been executed here. Picture taken by Camille Battheu.

From left to right: Alison Macfie, R.A.S.M., Dorothea Macfie, at Couthove, April   333
    1917.

Sisters Mary Dorothy Allen and Ethel Webb-Johnson at Talbot House, April 1916.   335

Donald Cox.   337

Charcoal preliminary sketch for oil painting The Conquerors (Canadian War   339
    Museum), presented to Talbot House by war artist Eric Kennington in 1931.

This army map of 1916, 'won' from 162nd Heavy Battery, R.G.A., was put up in the   341
    hall of Talbot House. Thousands of muddy fingers left ever so many marks and still
    show the places most frequented by the troops. Ieper is completely worn away. The
    curved front line is clearly marked off, and also Poperinge, the most popular place of
    rest and relaxation, disappears under the dirty fingerprints.

141st Heavy Battery R.G.A., January 1918.   341

Ypres asylum, picture taken by Camille Battheu.   342

This Crucifix accompanied Tubby on his journeys to all parts of the front.   343

Charcoal preliminary sketch of a field kitchen by Eric Kennington.   344

Lt. Herbert Shiner, 1915.   346

Entrance to dugout, watercolour by Eric Kennington.   347

Drawing of Tubby's Pyx by Barclay Baron. It carries the inscription: "A Pyx for the   347
    great Gift of Love, from the poor of Beeston Street, Portsmouth, to the B.E.F. In
    constant use, 1915-1918, in Talbot House, Poperinghe."

Ypres Reservoir Cemetery with ruins of Ypres Prison in the background.   349

The Cellar Chapel, Little Talbot House, 1917.   353

Barclay Baron's billet at YMCA Headquarters, Poperinge.   356

Dr. Charles Magrath (centrally seated), Ypres, 1918.   357

List of Abbreviations

A.A. & Q.M.G.	Assistant Adjutant and Quartermaster-General
A.C.	Assistant Chaplain
A.C.G.	Assistant Chaplain-General
A.D.M.S.	Assistant Director of Medical Services
A.H.C.	Army Hospital Corps
A.H.Q.	Army Headquarters
A.I.F.	Australian Imperial Force
A/Lt.-Col.	Acting Lieutenant-Colonel
A.M.F.O.	Assistant Military Forwarding Officer
Amm. Col.	Ammunition Column
A.M.P.	Army Military Police
A.N.Z.A.C.	Australia & New Zealand Army Corps
A.P.	Armour Piercing
A.P.M.	Assistant Provost Marshal
A.P.O.	Army Post Office
A.R.O.D.	Army Railway Operating Department
A.S.C.	Army Service Corps
Attd.	Attending
A.V.C.	Army Veterinary Corps
B.C.-post	Battery Commanding post
Bde.	Brigade
B.E.F.	British Expeditionary Force
Bn	Battalion
Bty	Battery
B.W.I.	British West Indies
C.A.	Church Army
Capt.	Captain
C. in C.	Commander-in-Chief
C.C.S.	Casualty Clearing Station
C. of E.	Church of England
C.E.M.S.	Church of England Men's Society
C.F.	Chaplain to the Forces
C.M.S.	Church Missionary Society
C.S.M.	Company Sergeant Major

C.O.	Commanding Officer
Coy	Company
Cpl.	Corporal
C.R.	Captain Reverend
D.A.C.	Divisional Ammunition Column
D.A.C.G.	Deputy Assistant Chaplain-General
D.C.G.	Deputy Chaplain-General
D.C.M.	Distinguished Conduct Medal
D.D.M.S.	Deputy Director of Medical Services
Div.	Division
D.L.I.	Durham Light Infantry
D.N.O.	Directorate of Naval Ordnance
D.R.	Despatch Rider
D.S.C.	Distinguished Service Cross
D.S.O.	Distinguished Service Order
D.V.	Deo Volente (God being willing)
E.F.C.	Expeditionary Force Canteen
Exp.	Expeditionary
F.A.	Field Ambulance
F.A.N.Y.	First Aid Nursing Yeomanry
G.H.	General Hospital
G.H.Q.	General Headquarters
Gnr	Gunner
G.O.C.	General Officer Commanding
G.R.O.	General Routine Order
G.S.	General Service
H.A.	Heavy Artillery
H.A.C.	Honourable Artillery Company
H.E.	High Explosive
H.L.I.	Highland Light Infantry
H.O.	Headquarters Office
H.Q.	Headquarters
H.R.H.	His Royal Highness
I.B.	Infantry Brigade
Inf.	Infantry
K.O.S.B.	King's Own Scottish Borderers
K.O.Y.L.I.	King's Own Yorkshire Light Infantry
K.R.	King's Regulations
K.R.R.C.	King's Royal Rifle Corps
K.S.L.I.	King's Shropshire Light Infantry
L.A.C.	London Artillery Company
L/Cpl.	Lance Corporal
Lt.	Lieutenant
L.T.H.	Little Talbot House
L.R.B.	London Rifle Brigade

M.C.	Military Cross
M.F.P.	Military Foot Police
M.G.C.	Machine Gun Corps
M.M.	Military Medal
M.M.G.	Motor Machine Gunners
M.O.	Medical Officer
M.P.	Military Police
M.T.	Motor Transport
N.C.O.	Non-Commissioned Officer
N.Z.E.F.	New Zealand Expeditionary Forces
N.Z.R.	New Zealand Regiment
O.C.	Officer Commanding
	Officers' Club
O.O.	Operations Officer
O.R.	Other Ranks
P.B.	Permanent Base
P.B.C.	Philip Byard Clayton
P.B.I.	Poor Bloody Infantry
Plat	Platoon
Pnr	Pioneer
P.O.W.	Prisoner of War
Pte	Private
Q.	Quartermaster branch of General Staff
Q.A.I.M.N.S.R.	Queen Alexandra's Imperial Military Nurses Service Reserve
Q.E.D.	Quod Erat Demonstrandum ("which had to be demonstrated")
Q.M.G.	Quartermaster-General
Q.M.S.	Quartermaster-Sergeant
Q.W.R.	Queen's Westminster Rifles
R.A.F.	Royal Air Force
R.A.M.C.	Royal Army Medical Corps
R.A.P.	Regimental Aid Post
R.B.	Rifle Brigade
R.E.	Royal Engineers
Rev.	Reverend
R.F.A.	Royal Field Artillery
R.F.C.	Royal Flying Corps
Rfm	Rifleman
R.G.A.	Royal Garrison Artillery
Regt	Regiment
R.I.P.	Requiesce in pacem
R.M.S.	Regimental Mail Sergeant
R.N.A.S.	Royal Naval Air Service
R.O.D.	Royal Operating Department
R.P.O.	Regimental Post Office
	Regulating Petty Officer

R.R.C.	Royal Red Cross 1st Class
R.S.M.	Regimental Sergeant Major
R.T.O.	Railway Transport Officer
S.B.A.C.	Siege Battery Ammunition Column
S.C.F.	Senior Chaplain to the Forces
Sdr	Saddler (Mule Corps)
Sgt.	Sergeant
Sigs	Signallers
Spr	Sapper
Sqdn	Squadron
T.A.B.	Typhoid-paratyphoid A and B vaccine
T.H.	Talbot House
V.A.D.	Voluntary Aid Detachment
V.C.	Victoria Cross
W.A.A.F.	Women's Auxiliary Army Forces
Y.M.C.A.	Young Men's Christian Association

Acknowledgements

For this book I am greatly indebted to Ken Prideaux-Brune, son of a 'Talbotousian', for consistently giving me encouragement and advice. His superb knowledge of the English language has helped rid this manuscript of many errors. I very much appreciate his much-needed guidance.

I owe a particular thank you to my colleagues of the Administrative Council of the Talbot House Association, namely Christine Bostock, Noel Cornick, Bertin Deneire, William De Vloo, Roger Griffiths, Ian Hussein, Kurt Vangheluwe and Jean Whiteman, as well as the staff, for their support and kindness.

I would like to thank Duncan Rogers of Helion & Company for his enthusiasm and belief in the project. A particular thank you to Dr Michael LoCicero, commissioning editor, for his hard work to help produce this book.

My warmest thanks are due to my children, Simon, Dana and Yasmin, for once again indulging my incurable fascination with the First World War in general and Talbot House in particular, as I forever disappeared to my study to wrestle with this book.

Lastly, this project would not have been possible without the unfailing encouragement and love of my wife, Katrien, whom I first met at Talbot House 33 years ago and who, despite failing health, has been a constant source of inspiration, advice and good sense. She has always believed in me and my work for Talbot House. I dedicate this book to her.

Introduction

The visitor to the battlefields of Flanders perceives a gentle, peaceful countryside scattered with prosperous towns and villages. Although nature has reclaimed much of the wounded landscape of mud and shattered tree stumps, not all the scars of war have been healed. Pillboxes, trenches and water-filled craters hint at the horror which churned up these fields and destroyed communities. The memorials and the thousands upon thousands of gravestones are reminders of the sacrifice and slaughter that took place a hundred years ago.

For over four years, the city of Ieper (Ypres) was in the eye of the storm. To conceive a picture of the opposing forces, imagine the Salient as a giant bow, drawn back by some titanic archer before the arrow is released. Ieper was the arrowhead, Poperinge (Poperinghe) about eight miles to the west, the feather. Along the shaft passed hundreds of thousands of men destined to hold the line or be thrown into a sea of mud in a desperate effort to drive the enemy from the strategically important high ground. Over a quarter of a million of them never returned. Those who did, were often shattered in body and soul.

From early spring 1915, Poperinge, a peaceful little hop town, transformed into the nerve centre of the British sector. Its station was the railhead; its narrow streets were crammed with troops, artillery pieces on heavy carriages, ambulances, lorries and London buses bringing in fresh troops. The rural area around the town was transformed into an industrial hinterland with rest camps, workshops, ammunition dumps, training grounds, hospitals and airfields, intersected by new corduroy roads and light railways.

"Pop" was regarded as a haven. Here the battalions, resting after their turn in the trenches, enjoyed a hot tub in one of many divisional baths, sought their recreation and did their shopping. It still retained many civilian inhabitants. Others had sought greater comfort and safety in France, their place being largely taken by refugees from the uninhabitable parts of the Salient and from further afield. Ordinary industry was inevitably almost at a standstill, but a new and lucrative business had sprung up: supplying everything the troops required at extravagant prices. You could stroll from one shop window to another, and buy Cadbury's chocolate, Cooper's marmalade or a Swan pen, in addition to 'real Ypres lace' and a splendid range of souvenirs and other knick-knacks. You could order omelets and chips from old women who produced them in unprecedented quantities, spoke fluent though hideous-sounding English, and piled up small fortunes. Daunted by the prospect of battle, men sought solace in drinking, gambling and brothels. Estaminets, canteens, cafes and coffee-houses of all kinds flourished, offering so-called beer, *Cafe Cognac* or *vin blanc*. Officers could get a splendid dinner and a bottle of bubbly at 'Skindles' or 'A la Poupée' where they would be served by charming young "Ginger" and her two sisters. At Pop you could go to moving pictures featuring Charlie Chaplin or attend a sparkling musical show by 'The Fancies', a first-rate pierrot-troupe, and forget there was a war on.

Naturally, life in this bustling town also had its excesses. The Town Major, who had the general supervision of good order, tried to curb these with the help of the municipal authorities. Civilians were forbidden to sell beer without permission and estaminets reported for serving alcohol to troops at prohibited hours were placed out of bounds or closed down. Street patrols were deployed to prevent looting. Prostitution was managed to cut down the number of soldiers being infected with venereal disease. Soldiers were locked up in the town hall cells for drunkenness, fighting, theft, returning late to billets, absence without leave and resisting arrest. Civilians were arraigned on charges of infringing traffic regulations, moving about without passes, theft of British Army property, selling rum and espionage.

At times though, Poperinge could be hell. Crammed with troops, the town provided a tempting target for enemy artillery and aerial bombing thus inflicting military and civilian casualties, demolishing buildings and roads and starting fires. Moreover, if the wind blew from the east there was the threat of gas. On the façade of the town hall a large board was erected, indicating whether the wind was 'SAFE' or 'DANGEROUS'.

Casualty Clearing Stations were set up in the Poperinge area to tend the wounded and heal the sick. Remy Siding, located in the hamlet of Lijssenthoek just south of the town, developed into the largest hospital site in the Ypres Salient, a village in itself, with a total capacity of four thousand patients. Those who did not make it were buried in the adjacent cemetery, which expanded as the war progressed to some 11,000 graves. At *Hôpital Elisabeth* civilians who had been bombed out of their houses and children whose limbs had been shattered through playing with unexploded bombs, were looked after. Poperinge was also the place where courts-martial were convened. In 1916 the prison cells became death cells where men judged to be deserters and cowards spent their final agonising night before being shot at dawn in the courtyard of the town hall.

The manifold problems prompted the military authorities to make special efforts to provide recreation and relaxation for the men. In the summer of 1915 Lt.-Col. Reginald May, Quartermaster-General of 6th Division – billeted in Poperinge and vicinity – felt there was urgent need for a religious and social centre for officers and men. He approached the Senior Chaplain, the Rev. Neville Talbot, who took great pains to get the man he wanted for the job, the Rev. Philip Clayton, a chaplain from 16th Brigade, universally known as "Tubby". The Town Major introduced both men to Mr Maurice Coevoet, a wealthy banker and hop merchant, who in turn led them to his large, white house in Gasthuisstraat, which they agreed to rent. The original intention was to christen it Church House, but realising that such an uninspired name would frighten away the very men they wanted to attract, Col. May insisted, despite the protests of Neville Talbot, that it be called Talbot House. Neville in fact dedicated it to his younger brother Gilbert (a prime example of what became known as the "lost generation") who had been killed at Hooge in July 1915 whilst serving with 7th Rifle Brigade. In the army signallers' code of those days 'T' was Toc and the House, therefore, came to be known to everyone simply as "Toc H". Open day and night, it welcomed its first visitors on 11 December 1915. By day, it acted as a recreation centre; at night it transformed into a rest-house where officers and men coming and going by trains in the small hours could get supper, bed and breakfast. During the following months, its scope gradually extended far beyond the single Division and it became one of *the* institutions of the British Army. It was not an officers' club, nor was it a club for other ranks, and its life expectancy, like that of all who entered it, was very uncertain indeed. The signboard over the magnificent front door aptly indicated the character of the House: 'TALBOT HOUSE 1915 – ? EVERY MAN'S CLUB.'

The House was, in many parts, exactly like a private home, with genuine wallpaper, carpets, curtains, floor mats, delightful pictures, arm chairs with comfortable cushions and flowers planted in vases. Its floors catered to the many needs – body, mind and soul – of those who called it home away from home.

To step out of the street – and out of the war's madness – into a friendly, welcoming environment was bliss. The spirit of the place was denoted by an entrance sign pointing back to the door, "Pessimists, Way Out". Other notices were amicable and humorous: "If you are in the habit of spitting on the carpet at home, please spit here". The canteen, with a creaking old piano, brought one tea and cakes, popular songs and contagious laughter. There were wall maps of Britain, Canada and Australia hanging in the hall where men could identify their hometowns. In "Friendship's Corner" a man could add his name to a rendezvous list and discover where friends were stationed or whether there was anyone about who knew his town, village or lived in the next street. Gazing through the hall one could glimpse a well-kept garden where men were basking like lizards in the summer sun, nibbling a biscuit or dozing a little. In an adjoining hop store, which had been ingeniously turned into a cosy concert hall, you could enjoy a wide range of entertainment. On Saint Nicholas' Day, parties were hosted for the Poperinge children, and their joy and laughter when receiving chocolate and toys reminded you of your own children or siblings.

If one accepted the invitation to "Come upstairs and risk meeting the Chaplain" you ascended to the realm of the heart and mind. There was a library, crammed with books, and comfortable chairs where you could sit and read; losing yourself in another world and pretending that there had never been a war. To borrow a book you left your army cap in pawn. Across the landing was the writing room where pens, ink and paper invited you to drop a line to your darling Aggie, Mabel, etc. In the games' room, chess, draughts, billiards and ping-pong catered to a variety of tastes. On the door of Clayton's quarters was a sign deliberately misquoting Dante: "All rank abandon ye who enter here". Here generals and privates rubbed shoulders and the most unlikely friendships were forged. One was always welcome to join a cheery tea party, no matter how full the room was or, if need be, have a private conversation of a deeper kind with the chaplain. Upstairs again were two lecture-rooms. There you could take a class on public health or partake in a debate where the motion was "That this House is profoundly convinced that the war will be over this year".

Climbing another, steeper staircase, one arrived at a spacious loft that had been converted into a chapel. An old, worn carpenter's bench, discovered in a garden shed, provided the altar. Around it were many memorial gifts. Ornaments of exquisite taste were brought together to add to the homely beauty and serenity of this "Upper Room", which came to be known as "the Shrine of the whole Salient". Many were baptised and confirmed here; many made their first Communion here. Indeed, for many it was their first and last. Nevertheless, chapel attendance was never compulsory, yet if one did use it, it was recognised that the foundations of this house were in the roof. The services with the old chants and hymns helped one to face the unknown tomorrow. Here, away from the noise, squalor and death, one could find comfort, guidance, strength and refreshment for the soul.

But what was the secret of Talbot House? First and foremost, it had a remarkable atmosphere. Its whole raison d'être was to be a home away from home. It may only have been second best, but it was genuine. Inside one could find comfort and warmth, games and music, laughter and prayer. Here one was distracted by other things than war and the mind was free. Its comfort, however, went much deeper than mere cosiness. The house offered a welcome haven to all who entered. No matter how many newcomers had dropped on any given day, there was invariably someone there who seemed to be expecting you. At Talbot House you could strike up friendships with those you would never have met otherwise. Social background, personality, rank and creed seemed irrelevant. Moreover, as a "customer", you were given a voice in house maintenance and proceedings: "You will find yourself mending electric bells, tipping cues, mending lamps, or licking envelopes, before you know where your support line is. Can you sing; recite; act; conjure; debate; play chess; paint scenery; run a cinema? Even if you can't, it won't make any difference." Clearly, the place belonged to one in a home-like way, and depended on kindness in return. "Today's guest is tomorrow's host", was the one inflexible rule impressed upon all who crossed its threshold. One was reminded in no uncertain terms that what had been done for you today, was to be reciprocated for those that came tomorrow. "All this", wrote Lt. John Nicholson, a regular visitor, "helped you to feel that you were not just a cog in the machine of war but a person with likes and dislikes, a standard of comfort and, oddest of all, a mind".

And then there was the magnetic personality of the "innkeeper". It would be hard to imagine anyone less military-looking than Philip Clayton. Improperly dressed in breeches, puttees and faded blue blazer, he created around him an extraordinary atmosphere of hilarity. Concerts and debates showed him at his best, contributing rollicking songs or witty repartee. If Talbot House attracted and challenged because it was a cheerful place, it was the more serious things in life that held you there. Whether one had a grievance about the inequality of rations, leave or pay, or felt weary and fed up with the war, you could air it without being made to feel like a bore. Clayton took a genuine interest and care in one's welfare and was able to lift spirits and set you on your feet again.

Although the "life and soul" of Talbot House, Clayton's ministry was not confined within its walls. From time to time his customers invited him to repay their calls. He would take unpredictable journeys to all parts of the front, his faithful old batman at his heels, and paid regular visits to sections within his "parish", enquiring after their well-being, ministering to their needs and often holding Holy Communion under intense shell fire. These frequent visits to the danger zone were referred to by Tubby as "slumming". His earnest talks, full of humour and conveying a real understanding of the lives of his listeners, made his visits an event to be looked forward to. Everywhere his appearance acted like a tonic upon the men.

In the late autumn of 1917, a daughter-house was established in the cellar of a lace school on the Rijselstraat Ieper, the Rev. Ralph Goodwin in residence. An above ground room was fitted as a reading and writing room with piano in it. Beneath, in the so-called "catacombs" was a chapel, canteen, kitchen and sleeping billets. For five months Little Talbot House carried on in the same spirit as the Old House under increasingly dangerous conditions until its evacuation during the German spring 1918 offensive.

For three long years, full of incident both grave and gay, Talbot House served its unique clientele. At the end of the war the House was handed back to its original owner, its former patrons returning to families and careers disrupted or deferred by war. But Philip Clayton and a number of stalwarts dreamed of re-creating the spirit of Talbot House in peacetime. Thus a new Talbot House was established in London in 1920; others soon followed. Veterans who had known Talbot House came together spontaneously, not only in the UK, but throughout the

British Empire. They were inspired by a vision to keep alive the spirit of comradeship which united them during wartime, the legacy of which would be passed on to the post-war world. In this way they could honour the fallen, not by building memorials but by building a better world.

A hundred years on, Talbot House, now faithfully restored, has become a place of pilgrimage for a growing number of visitors, many of them as young as those who knew it during the Great War. Some even book overnight accommodations in order to experience that rare, intangible sensation of something genuinely good having arisen from the terrible bloodshed. Following the tradition that started in 1915, volunteer wardens greet visitors with a cup of tea in the former canteen. The magnificent garden is still an oasis of calm, and the chapel offers a haven of tranquility amid all the memories of death and destruction associated with a battlefield tour. A fascinating museum extension in the Concert Hall documents 'Life behind the lines' through an innovative giant photo album browsed by Tubby Clayton along with a fine recreation of a period concert party known as the 'Happy Hoppers', which transports visitors back in time with a sparkling musical show. Although Talbot House has improved in terms of offered facilities over the years, its essence remains the same: "Somewhere to find peace and quiet, or company and conversation, somewhere for silent reflection and contemplation or for lively and noisy gaiety, somewhere for spiritual renewal or for physical refreshment", as a regular visitor once put it. And so the spirit of Talbot House lives on in many places, through many people. Long may it continue!

A Kaleidoscope of Stories

The first part of this book, An Every-Man's Club, paints a graphic picture of Talbot House against the immense backdrop of the waste and horror of war, from its early beginnings at the end of 1915 till the private owner's return early in 1919. The ongoing thread is provided by a wide selection of Tubby's letters, the majority to his mother. These are supplemented with extracts from his diaries and other wartime writings, as well as letters and eyewitness accounts. Together they provide an intimate, vivid and complete picture of what life at the House was like. They provide a fascinating insight into the world of Tubby and his many soldier guests, their thoughts, visions, hopes and ideals. It is this litany of the human experience that provides the authentic history of Talbot House

In part two, 'A Home from Home', Tubby provides the reader with his personal warm welcome, after which he guides around Talbot House from the raucous gaiety of the canteen to the peace and serenity of the upstairs chapel. This "guided tour" is interspersed with the recollections of some 40 officers and other ranks relating how they experienced the unique atmosphere of this remarkable wartime haven.

In 'A House of People', the primary focus is on Tubby and his batman, Private Arthur Pettifer, the two permanent members of staff who for three long years, each punctuated by countless crises, were "glued together" at Talbot House. This is followed by a colourful collection of stories by the "innkeeper", each concerning a particular "customer" who, for one specific reason or another, stood out in his experience – not an easy thing to do, as at Talbot House "one sees practically everybody in the Salient at one time or another." Depicting an engaging variety of scenes and subject, these tales illustrate the spirit which manifested itself in this Emmaus Inn day by day. A number of 'Talbotousians' also have a tale to tell, five of whom relate a significant incident that will forever be associated with Talbot House and Tubby.

The final chapter takes us beyond the walls of the Old House. In a few poignant sketches it describes Tubby's visits to his frontline parishioners in what he described as "taking a whiff of the healthy T.H. gas to them". It portrays the comradeship of shared experiences, the excitements and the miseries and the triumph of the human spirit over unimaginable suffering. Some rare reminiscences of the short-lived and much-tested Ieper-based daughter-house complete the picture.

A fascinating selection of relevant documents, the majority produced at Talbot House during the war years, sheds further light on its early history, management and day-to-day workings.

Sources

Already during the war, handwritten and typescript copies of some of Tubby's letters circulated amongst his family and friends at home. Some were published in newspapers *(The Times)* and journals *(The Nutshell, The Challenge,* etc.). After the war, short extracts found their way into the *Toc H Journal* (1926) and a small number were reproduced in *Letters from Flanders* (1932). The correspondence confirms (and occasionally acts as a corrective) for what Tubby subsequently wrote, partly for the public record and partly as propaganda, in his popular post-war memoirs *Tales of Talbot House* (1919). This was followed by *Plain Tales from Flanders* (1929), which contained 16 separate stories. After the House had closed its doors, handwritten notices, printed cards, posters, pictures, bits of paper with anecdotes or stories relating to its history became the treasured possessions of Toc H Houses worldwide. Other memorabilia was preserved by Tubby at All Hallows, his parish church near the Tower in London. Moreover, scores of individuals, both soldier and civilian, maintained letters or other souvenirs related to their beloved Tubby. Since the reopening of Talbot House on 5 April 1931, a great many of these precious "relics" have returned "home". A large selection of these form the core of this book. My own research dates back more than 25 years and resulted in the voluminous *Talbot House, Poperinge – De Eerste Halte na de Hel* (First Stop After Hell) (1998), co-authored with my wife, Katrien. Since then a great deal of additional Material has been unearthed to find its way into this annotated English edition. Wherever possible the reminiscences of all these 'Talbotousians' have been linked to particular locations and events, so that this book can also serve as a "Talbot House guide" to the British sector of the Western Front.

Part 1

An Every-Man's Club

Philip Byard Clayton, affectionately known as 'Tubby', was working as a curate at St. Mary's in Portsea when the war broke out. In spring of 1915, at the age of 29, he was given a temporary commission as "Chaplain Fourth Class" and posted to the staff of No.16 General Hospital situated within a cliff-top Le Tréport hotel. In November, Bishop L. H. Gwynne, Deputy Chaplain-General, sent him, by special request, to the Ypres Salient to work under Neville Talbot, senior chaplain to 6th Division.[1] The divisional padres resided together in a "kind of wild west log-hut" in Dirty Bucket Camp, situated in a large wooded area between Elverdinge and Poperinge. Apart from his flock, "apparently to be some Buffs and Bedfords", Clayton was unsure what Talbot had in mind for him, but hoped "please God, to find better work to do than mere parades and funerals".[2]

Chaplains' Quarters
c/o 6th Division HQ
B.E.F.
Friday afternoon, 26 November 1915

Dearest Mater,
The winter sun is shining brightly, and one of the battalions I am responsible for is camped invitingly close, so I mustn't be long. But it's nice to write before the weekend begins. Tomorrow my other battalion is taking me in for the weekend, where they are resting. And I go down with sleeping sack, shaving soap etc. to them in the queer old caravan we call our own, and stop till Monday. This enables me to get to a multitude of little units in these parts for Sunday services – a Field Ambulance, an A.S.C. depot, a workshops place, another battalion hard by. In some measure the Sunday's work thus compensates for the lack of opportunities during the week.

---

1   Tubby was an old friend of Neville, whom he had known in his Oxford days. The former went to Exeter College in 1904 and gained a first class degree in theology; the latter went to Christ Church in 1903 and read *literae humaniores*, taking a second class degree in 1907.
2   P.B. Clayton, letter to his mother, 14 November 1915. Clayton was attached to the 1st Buffs and 8th Bedfordshire Regiment (16th Brigade).

Philip Byard Clayton.

Isabel Clayton, Tubby's mother.

Rev. Neville Talbot.

Talbot[3] is trying to get an empty house for me in the nearest town, where I can both live myself and start some kind of homely club for a few of the multitudes of troops who pass to and fro. I'm strongly in favour of this, as it's work I should be less of a duffer at than this bush brotherhood business, with its distracting distances. If it pans out, I shall want a lot of odd things like papers and pens and pictures (of the Pears' Annual type)[4] and shall also have a room for a Chapel which we badly need for Confirmation work as well as Celebrations. They are potting at some Bosche[5] aeroplanes while I sit here writing, but I'm too blasé already to find much amusement in getting a stiff neck watching.

Love to you all.

Your loving son,

Philip

*   *   *

Discovery of the House

It was plain that it was up to the chaplains to open a place of their own, an institutional church, to provide happiness for the men, and also, if possible, a hostel for officers going on leave. This trouble, like all our troubles, was taken to Colonel R.S. May, the "Q"[6] of the 6th Division. Aided wholeheartedly by him, we approached the Town Major,[7] who introduced us to M. Coevoet-Camerlynck,[8] a wealthy brewer of the town, who in turn led us to his great empty mansion, the back part of which previously had been struck by a shrapnel shell from the Pilckem Ridge[9]

3   Neville Stuart Talbot (1879-1943) was the second son of E.S. Talbot, a distinguished theologian and Bishop of Winchester (1911-1923). Commissioned into the Rifle Brigade, Neville saw active service in the Boer War of 1899-1902. However, in 1903, and by now a staff officer in South Africa, he chose to resign his commission in order to study at Oxford. He was ordained priest in 1909, when he was also elected chaplain of Balliol College, Oxford. Along with his brother, Edward Keble Talbot of the Community of the Resurrection, Neville was commissioned into the Army Chaplains' Department in August 1914. In October he welcomed his transfer from a Base Hospital at Rouen to the 17th Field Ambulance at Armentières, and in June 1915 he was moved to Poperinge to become senior chaplain of 6th Division.

4   A & F Pears, the famous British firm noted for their hand soap, issued a large format Christmas annual each year. It not only contained Christmas stories and advertisements, but also included presentation prints for framing.

5   Boche (alternative English spelling, Bosche): French pejorative slang for German.

6   Lt.-Col. Reginald S. May, as Assistant Adjutant and Quartermaster-General of 6th Division (15 February 1915 – 5 February 1916) was the Chief Administrative Officer of the Division. He would become the first Chairman of Toc H in 1919.

7   A staff officer having the general supervision of good order in an occupied city during military operations, the Town Major's office was responsible for billeting and sanitary arrangements, traffic control and the co-ordination between French or Belgian gendarmerie and the British Military Police when dealing with the civil population. The Poperinge Town Major at this time was Capt. E.H.D. Collins, Yorkshire Hussars.

8   The diary of the Town Major relates that a meeting took place on 29 November. Earlier that month, Maurice Coevoet (not a brewer but a banker and a hop merchant) moved with his wife, Alida Camerlynck, and four children to the reportedly safer village of Roesbrugge situated near the French frontier.

9   German howitzers constantly shelled Poperinge from the direction of Pilckem Ridge. The back walls of the houses in Gasthuisstraat (where Talbot House is situated) were in line with this gunfire.

General Sir Reginald May.

Maurice and Alida Coevoet-Camerlynck.

Gasthuisstraat (Rue de l'Hôpital), Poperinge. Future Talbot House is third house from the left.

direction. We accepted this tenancy joyfully at a rent which was subsequently fixed at 150 francs a month, undertaking as the conditions of our lease (1) to make the house weather-proof, and (2) to remove from the small front-room a large safe, which, on account of its immobility, had remained when all the other furniture had been taken away. Strong in the consciousness of the British Army at our backs, we made no bones about the conditions, but took over the house forthwith. Bowing the owner out, we started on our inspection of the premises. The large entrance hall was flanked on the left by a highly decorative drawing-room with a dingy dining-room beyond, and on the right by a small office, the staircase, and the kitchen. The conservatory beyond lay sideways along the whole breadth of the house at the back. It was in a bad plight, for the shrapnel had gashed its leaden roof and brought down the plaster ceiling in a melancholy ruin upon its tiled floor. The plate-glass was broken in all the windows, and the rain came in freely both sideways and from above. However, it's an ill shell that blows no one any good, and this had blown us a house which would otherwise have been occupied as a billet. Upstairs, on the first floor, reached by an elegant painted staircase in white and gold, was the landing, four bedrooms, and a dressing-room; on the second floor, a large landing, one huge nursery, and three small bedrooms; above this, reached by a difficult companion-ladder, a great hop-loft[10] covering the whole area of the house. One corner of this attic and the bedroom below it had been knocked out by a shell. We then descended to consider our other liability. The safe was in the little front office, and presented the appearance of a large brown painted cupboard against the wall. Neville gave it a friendly push, with no result whatever. My assistance made not the lightest difference. I stepped round the corner for the Bedfords. About sixteen of them came in an S.O.S. spirit. As many as could do so got near the safe and pushed perspiringly. The faintest sign of motion was now visible. Determined to see the matter through at once, lest it should breed in us some craven superstition, we suborned certain transport folk to send round their heaviest wagon and a team of mules. Meanwhile we got ropes round the safe, and some logs, as for launching a lifeboat. With sixteen men on the rope the safe fell forward on the rollers with a crash comparable only with the *coup de grâce* the Australian tunnellers gave to Hill 60.[11] Crowds gathered in the narrow street, and the waggon and mules made heavy weather of backing into the entrance of the house. Meanwhile we piloted the safe into the hall. The mules were taken out and led away that they might not see what they were doomed to draw. The back of the waggon was let down, the stoutest planks were laid leading up to it, and the drag-ropes were handed freely to all passers-by. Vaguely it was felt by all who had no precise knowledge of the situation that a successful tug would in some way shorten the war; and the traffic, now completely blocked, added those homely criticisms for which the British driver is justly notable.

The room situated at the northeast side of the house is still called the 5.9 Room after the 5.9" shell that struck there. The hole was boarded up, but – despite of its obvious German origin – it figured, to the tune of 2,000 francs, in the invoice for damages presented to Talbot House at the end of its occupancy!

10   The attic was never used to store or dry hops, but to dry out the washing hanging out on lines from wall to wall. The previous owners of the house, the Lebbe family, who were hop merchants, made use of their hopstore (the current Concert Hall) adjacent to the garden to dry hops.

11   In November 1916, 1st Australian Tunnelling Company took over the Hill 60 mining operations from the Canadians. Their task was to counter German attempts to locate and destroy the British charge galleries beneath. These were maintained until 7 June 1917, when they were fired along alomg with 17 other mines, at the start of the Battle of Messines (7–14 June).

Even the safe felt moved in its rocky heart, and, surrendering to the impulse of a hundred hands, found itself installed in the wagon. It was no time for hesitancy now. Pressing ten francs into the hands of the muleteers, we told them the desired destination and saw them and the safe no more.

(P.B. Clayton, Tales of Talbot House)

*   *   *

c/o 4th Labour Battalion R.E.
B.E.F.
S. Andrew's Day (30 November 1915)

My dear Nutshellites,[12]
…
I'm up to my eyes in – what do you think? – not gore, but scrubbing brushes; and my team of regimental housemaids will be parading again in a few minutes. As you may be at a loss to understand what housemaids, even if they belong to a fierce fighting Midland Battalion, have to do with the strategic situation on the Western Front, I had better explain myself. I am now (to cut a long story short) a substantial householder in a famous Belgian town. It's quite true that a few weeks ago a shell hit the house under the bonnet, so to speak, and that any fine day another may do likewise; but meanwhile the house from roof to cellar (a roomy one) is mine by the decree of the Town Major, and the sanction of its owner; and by the time the heavy footed housemaids have cleared away the debris of bricks and glass, and the N.C.O. in charge of them has mended the magnificent front door, and the R.E.'s (whose names are written in heaven) have shored up the wrecked gable, the house will be established as a port of call for Officers and men, and the creative comforts of the canteen will compensate for the perplexing presence of P.B.C. At this point the housemaids paraded, and I went out to fetch in a carpenter's bench from the other end of the wild overgrown garden, having it in my heart to make of this the Altar of the Carpenter in our little Chapel room. As we brought it down the garden, the Bosche sent the usual salvo of seven shells into the square, three of them being duds. Two lady-birds from the garden have travelled in on my tunic and are now reading this letter before publication. Blissful beings – they have never heard of 'whizz-bangs',[13] and 'cushy ones'[14] and salient.[15]
    … The whole life is thus strange and restless, full of incident, opportunity, and excitement; and yet, since there is nothing stable or normal with which to contrast it, there is in its very variations a monotony as universal as the mud. There is precious little glamour about modern

---

12 Former members of Tubby's Boys' Club "Company Brown" of St. Mary's, Portsea were linked together during active service by *The Nutshell* magazine.
13 British slang for German 77 mm field guns projectiles. Their flat trajectory and velocity greater than the speed of sound gave no warning to the intended victim/victims who heard the 'whizz' of the shell before the succeeding 'bang'.
14 Cushy: Happy or pleasant; a cushy wound was just serious enough to allow a brief escape from the trenches, whereas a Blighty wound was a serious but non-fatal wound often requiring hospitalization in Great Britain.
15 A position projecting into the enemy lines; the British position at Ypres was almost universally known as 'The Salient' throughout the BEF.

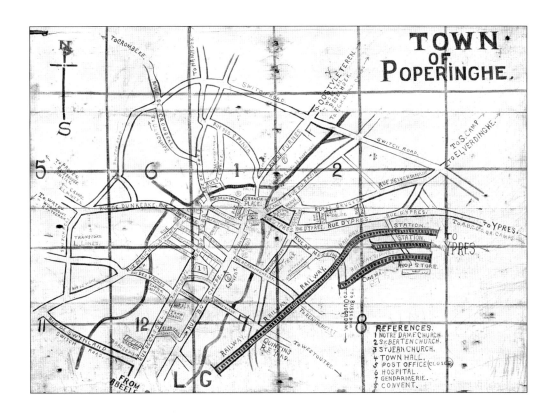

The Carpenter's Bench.

war seen on the spot; squalor is its means, and destruction its end. Everyone is homeless, and the homeless man is, for all his heroic cheerfulness, a most forlorn fellow. Letters and leave are the lode-stars of our existence, and it is not the defence of an abstract cause, but the defence of a particular red brick house, whether large or small, that nerves men to stand waist deep in water night after night, and play hide and seek with high explosives; this house is, for a foreigner's house, peculiarly homely in its atmosphere. We found quantities of broken toys in the cupboards yesterday, bricks, ninepins, dismembered dolls.

There is a large dovecot lying wrecked in the long grass of the garden, and in the stable two wooden horses and a doll's perambulator. While the same things on a larger human scale are everyday sights, these discoveries nearly moved the Corporal (whose home is at no more romantic spot than Southend on Sea) to open grief. It is perfectly true that a shell might to-morrow treat this or any other house here as a child in a tantrum treats a house of bricks; but there is no sorrow so piteous as a child's sorrow. God grant that this Christmas may be our last asunder.

…

Your brother,
Philip Clayton

*   *   *

Church Institute
c/o 4th Labour Battalion R.E.
B.E.F.
Wednesday, 1 December 1915

Dear Guv.,[16]
…
I am getting happier daily at my new job here, which is of the kind I more or less understand, i.e. being friendly to all comers, without any of the regimental business to bother me. Tomorrow, the Corps General,[17] a most exalted personage, comes to inspect the place: we have not much to show him at present, except one reading-room ready for action and a perfectly delightful Chapel.[18] We had only heard of his advent tonight, when it was too late to go and weed the garden. I shall be glad when he's come and gone, and the place is in full swing, i.e. by next week. It's an odd business turning into a kind of hotel-keeper, but plainly it's needed, and gives one a real chance of personal influence, so far as one has any to use. It's very jolly the way chaps already begin to drop in casually to play about, fix up the Chapel, hang up lamps, mend chairs, dust, brush and carpenter. I had tea tonight with some jolly military police. You can make your minds quite easy about me so long as I'm on this job – there is no danger whatever, and I shall laugh and grow fat and sleep warm. My only cares will be parochial, i.e. that I'm doing my job, and domestic – the ordering of an establishment with a staff of four servants. My own – Pettifer[19]

---

16 Tubby's father, Reginald Byard Buchanan Clayton (1845-1927).
17 Lt-Gen Sir John Lindsay Keir (1856-1937) GOC VI Corps.
18 The Chapel occupied the second floor landing at this time..
19 This letter contains the first mention of 239, Pte. Pettifer, A. 1st The Buffs, soon to be known as "The General" (or more commonly "Gen"). In November 1915 he had been instructed to report as

Pte. Arthur Pettifer.

Reginald Clayton, Tubby's father.

by name – is an old Buffs man of 28 years' service on and off, who knows nothing about a house except what he has gleaned from Mrs P. in Bethnal Green. The great difficulty is to prevent him "scrounging" in my interests. "Scrounging" is slang for borrowing without the owner's knowledge. He will retrieve anything like a faithful dog of that description. On Sunday, having overheard that I wanted a bit of carpet for the Chapel, he scrounged some from an empty house next door. When I pointed out to him that we could scarcely say our prayers on a carpet thus acquired, he suggested meekly that it would do equally well for the living-room. I felt quite a brute making him put it back.

...

What are the right things to plant in our garden? We have 5 nice little frames in a row, well-manured. Also a chunk of kitchen garden. I must get you to send me seeds, as none are obtainable here, so far as I can see; certainly not without a familiarity with Flemish. I want some spring vegetables, please.

Now I must go to bed. Much love, dear dad,
from your loving son,
Philip.

batman to Tubby at Chaplains' Quarters (Map reference A.30 central, Dirty Bucket Camp, between Poperinge and Elverdinge). At their first interview he frankly declared his total inability to meet an officer's domestic needs. He would, nonetheless, subsequently demonstrate a unique capacity in that direction. Pettifer remained on the permanent staff of Talbot House to the last. Following this, Tubby and "Gen" were never separated for any length of time until the latter's death in 1954.

*   *   *

Church Institute
c/o 4th Labour Battalion R.E.
B.E.F.
Monday, 9.30 a.m., 6 December 1915

Dearest Mater,

At last it looks like having a good yarn with you. I am comfortable, warm, and have just had a late breakfast, after a hard but happy day yesterday. I'm sitting in a beautiful room with a cosy fire – there's no carpet and the furniture is handmade and highly collapsible. My paper-block is resting on a little iron table from the lovely ruins of the garden. I have Belle's[20] slippers on my feet, and don't purpose getting into working rig yet awhile, as I have much to write before the post goes at midday. I won't forget Mrs Cooke; also Jack,[21] whose cigars turned up safely yesterday after much redirection – the stamps were torn off but the tin case saved the contents. They are a great joy and just in time to be really useful for propitiating Town Majors and such like. Please be careful that anything you send me is packed beyond all chance of damage. The pressure on the post is tremendous, and papers, labels etc. get torn to pieces. Practically no letters came through last week, but I got yours and one from H.B.C.[22] safely yesterday. Also 1000 cigarettes in tins from Players at Nottingham, with no clue to the noble donor. Now I had better explain what I am doing dans cette galère.[23] Talbot has given me the job of opening a kind of Church House here in a town full of troops, some permanent like police, signal companies, R.E.'s, R.A.M.C., A.S.C., etc. Others coming in and out on their way up. True the Bosche are less than ten miles away on three sides of us, and don't let us forget it from time to time. But, if they shell this place, one or other of their own billets gets a return of the compliment with interest from our "heavies";[24] so that the game is on the whole unprofitable from their point of view. I have written for the Nutshell a fairly full description of the house as we found it, so won't repeat it here. It is a beautiful house with a lovely garden – I wish I had the guv. to take this on – full of standard roses, pergolas, wall-fruit, chicken-run. I'm going to get together a little batch of amateur gardeners to run the garden in spare time – it will be a peaceful recreation, much appreciated, and I'm anxious to have the place in apple-pie order. After the voluntary service last night (held in a music hall)[25] about forty men came round with me and went over the house, which was great fun and made them quite keen on it all. We have an inaugural Concert on Sunday night, and on Sunday morning at 11.15 the first Celebration in our Chapel (a big landing on the second floor). There is room for fifty or sixty,

20   Tubby's elder sister, Isobel.
21   Tubby's elder brother, Reginald John 'Jack', who was married to Beatrice Dickens, granddaughter of
       Charles Dickens.
22   Tubby's younger brother, Hugh Byard Clayton.
23   In this galley.
24   Heavy Batteries.
25   A reference to 'The Fancies' – the 6th Division concert hall in the Ieperstraat, Poperinge – where "a
       first-rate pierrot troupe" of the same name provided amusement for officers and men. Among the
       artists were, according to Tubby, "two Belgian ladies known respectively as Lanoline and Vaseline,
       who could neither sing nor dance, but at least added a touch of feminity". On Sunday nights the hall
       was utilized for church services.

OORLOG 1914-16...   38. POPERINGHE — Engelsche troepen op de markt
Uitgever: Sansen-Vanneste, Poperinghe
Troupes anglaises sur la Grand'Place
British troops

and I hope we shall have it full. Celebrations out here have nearly always to be regardless of the fasting rule, owing to exigencies of work. Meanwhile as I write, a stream of traffic like that of Fleet Street passes slowly – staff cars, motor-cyclists, lorries, waggons, horsemen, ambulances, soldiers of all sorts and descriptions, Furniture of refugees who can stand it no longer (probably when the real risk is all over) tied on precariously, like the old Tinware cart from Lymington. I covet those chairs and tables greatly. Meanwhile, odd papers, books, and a Lord Wimsey[26] from time to time will be a real help. The men here are grateful for the simplest kindness shewn to them personally: a cup of cocoa and a Belgian bun do not lack their reward. I've got a bit of a cold myself through coming to live in a house again, I suppose. I'll certainly search for Dr. Gosse[27] – it should be possible to find him in VI Div.

... My Christmas promises well, please God. One of my battalions has asked me to Celebrate for them just behind the line (they are out resting for the present) and then we have great festivities here on Christmas evening, with "Box and Cox"[28] acted by some men in the Mobile Vets, i.e. the horse hospital chaps who gave me lunch yesterday.

Your loving son,

Philip

26 Lord Peter Wimsey is a fictional character in a series of detective novels and short stories by Dorothy L. Sayers (1893-1957), in which he solves mysteries, usually murders. Wimsey is an archetype for the British gentleman detective.
27 Dr. Philip Gosse and Tubby saw a good deal of each other before the war. Their New Forest homes were only a few miles distant at the time.
28 A one act farce (1847) by John M. Morton, about two men, named Box and Cox, renting the same room, one occupying it by day and one by night without either's knowing about the other.

*   *   *

Talbot House
c/o 4th Labour Batt. R.E.
B.E.F.
Wednesday morning 3.30 a.m., 15 December 1915

Dearest Mater,

Rather an unusual hour for letter writing even for me, but I am not sleepy and the fire is very comfortable. Besides I owe you a letter, and I love writing to you. So here goes.

A good deal has happened since last week. You will note in the first place that the name of the house has changed for the better – this was a command from Divisional H.Q., and has been carried out in spite of Talbot's protests. I am glad as a Junior Chaplain to find that there are men so resolute in high command that they can impose their will on the Senior Chaplain. Moreover, he deserves it, and his name is one to conjure with on all sides. Secondly, the house is now open in two departments out of three. The men's part accommodating about a hundred for reading, writing and arithmetic, opened on Saturday, with a singsong, at which I sang the guv's ditty about "sixteen blades and a corkscrew."

On Sunday our little Chapel was full for the Celebration at 11.15, and there is every promise of it being the centre of real work and worship among the men coming and going through here. I am very happy and hopeful about all this. It is work I more or less understand, and does not involve any regimental red tape.

Another sphere of the house's work accounts for my being up tonight. I have just sent my two weary travellers[29] to bed, after soup and biscuits, and they will have excellent breakfasts in the morning before they go on their way rejoicing. This is the opening of our divisional rest-house, to which Officers coming and going by trains in the small hours can come and get supper, bed and breakfast. Tonight, being the first time, I went up to the station with the very nice night-orderly – I now control a staff of three men under an N.C.O.[30] besides my own, Pettifer – and rescued these two from a cold night in the waiting-room (so called). We can accommodate twelve, and shall have the house full every night a week hence, when it is known. Both were profoundly grateful, and were nearly moved to tears by the carpet slippers awaiting them.

The third department of the house – the Officers' Clubroom – is not ready yet, but will be, I hope, in a few days – and all this within a few miles of the German lines.

---

29   The two 'hostellers' left their names and comments in the Visitors' Book. They were Lt. Col. J.C.W. Connell, 6/K.O.S.B., D.S.O.("Many thanks for all your kindness.") and Lt. H.S. Price, Queen's Westminster Rifles ("Thank you for the most comfortable bed and an excellent breakfast."). For the Visitors' Book, see p. 274.

30   They may have been dispatched to Talbot House through the good offices of the Rev. Neville Talbot. One has been identified as Pte. Robert William Bell ('B' Company, 17th F.A.) by his grandson during a visit to Talbot House in 2000. Bell's personal memoirs relate his involvement in the early days of Talbot House, speaking very warmly of its importance to him when a young soldier. On 19 March 1916, the attached R.A.M.C. staff were withdrawn to their units when the 6th Division were sent further back for a rest period of one month. They were replaced by Coldstream Guards under Sgt. Godley.

Signboard.

Pte. Robert Bell.

I should like to go on now, and write about ten pages of gratitude for the glorious gifts in tin boxes – I took some of the peppermints tonight and shared them with the RTO – and all my letters, parcels, papers, etc. which are at last finding me in a steady stream, just when most needed. But I can't particularize now, as I have a lot to do tomorrow, or rather today. In chief, I have a lorry to board at 10 a.m. and go up and hunt for a man in a Battery, who does not know me from Adam, but is believed to have a piano up his sleeve, which I propose to relieve him of.[31] So now I shall turn in for several hours. I'm very fit, very happy, very busy, very comfortable, very safe and very sleepy.

Your loving son,

Philip

*   *   *

---

31   The "man in a battery" was Lt. Robinson, 47th Battery and the piano was duly secured. According to Tubby "the piano was very good indeed, and even in old age, after three years of constant strumming, retained its tone. Moreover, it had learnt things. If you so much as sat down before it in 1918, it played 'A little grey home in the West' without further action on your part."

Gilbert Talbot.

Name of the House

I have not yet explained the House's name. It was Colonel May's doing entirely, and nothing delighted me more than to find that Neville also was a man under authority. We had, after many wild suggestions, agreed on some tame and non-committal title, and having contrived six feet of stretched canvas, were busy on the first letter of "Church House," when Colonel May arrived and announced that the House should be closed there and then if we did not call it Talbot House.[32] Despite Neville's protest, the name was fixed forthwith. It had about it the homely flavour of a village inn, and for its deeper note there was the thought of the commemoration of Gilbert Talbot, whose grave in Sanctuary Wood held the body of one who would have been to English public life what Rupert Brooke began to be to English letters.[33]

(P.B. Clayton, *Tales of Talbot House*)

32   In a letter to Barclay Baron (editor Toc H Journal) dated 9 May 1943, R.S. May wrote: "I stopped my car, went in and told Neville that such a sign would frighten away the very men he wanted to attract. I did not mind what the house was called so long as it was not called "Church House" and suggested he should call it after his own name. He did so, but really dedicated it to his brother of whose death I was ignorant."

33   Lt. Gilbert Talbot, Rifle Brigade was killed at Hooge (Zillebeke) on the afternoon of 30 July 1915 whilst leading a counter-attack in the immediate aftermath of the first *Flammenwerfer* attack against British troops. Two days later, after dusk, Neville crawled out through the dead and found Gilbert's body. Removing his cap-badge and other personal items he gave his brother the benediction. On 7 August he saw the body brought in by some men of the East Yorkshire Regiment and buried it at Sanctuary Wood. Gilbert was educated at Winchester and Christ Church, Oxford, where he was President of the Union and a formidable debater. Few if any contemporaries doubted that a fine career in politics lay ahead of him. Gilbert was a Tory and a particular devotee of Arthur Balfour, the former conservative prime minister (1902-05) and subsequent coalition government foreign secretary (1915-16).

R.I.P.
Lt. Gilbert W.L. Talbot, 7 Rifle Brigade

Son of the Right Rev. the Lord Bishop of Winchester and the Hon. Mrs E.S. Talbot,
Farnham Castle, Surrey
Brother of the Rev. Neville Talbot, Senior Chaplain 6th Division and of the Rev. Edward
Talbot, Senior Chaplain 8th Division

30 July 1915 – Age 23 – Sanctuary Wood Cemetery (Zillebeke), I.G.1

*   *   *

Talbot House
c/o 4th Labour Batt. R.E.
Monday, 20 December 1915

Dearest Mater,

I'm afraid this scribble is likely to be my Christmas letter to you; a very poor return for all the splendid parcels, letters and oddments which are pouring in on me. But we had anything but a quiet weekend – a very vexatious strafe which broke out at odd intervals by day and night: with the result that what with shelling of the town in the small hours, a crowd in the Field Ambulance, and funerals, writing has been disturbed and sleeping likewise.[34]

Dear Bates, one of the six padres of the Division,[35] got his leg broken about five minutes after he left us yesterday morning, rescuing a small child from a beastly aeroplane bomb; he's quite all right, but it's a two months' job, so we are very shorthanded for Christmas. My round of services on Sunday takes me out of the town to units in the neighbourhood, so I was, as usual, well out of the way of the excitement. But it's an unpleasant proceeding at best, though we did not need our cellars. However, the cads got more than they gave, and things are quiet again now.

Some magnificent parcels have come, from you, and Belle, and Nancy,[36] and Mrs Fry.[37] Also I had the forethought to get Christmas carols in stock, and we had a carol practice last night with a crowded choir in the men's recreation room. It is extraordinary how the meaning of Christmas grips and holds us out here. For example, on Friday, an unknown R.E. Sergeant-Major came right away down, not because he knew me, but because he had heard that I had a

---

34   The Diary of the Town Major states that more than 200 shells landed on the town during 19–20 December. Civilians: 5 killed, 14 wounded. British military: 10 killed, 22 wounded.

35   Rev. Harold R. Bates was retained at the old chaplains' headquarters to continue his pioneering work with Church Army Huts. The other five were Rev. J. Reid ("adopted" by the Queen's Westminsters), Rev. Hamer (with the Durham Light Infantry), Wheeler (2nd York and Lancashire Regiment), Rev. Kinloch-Jones (71st Infantry Brigade) and Rev. P. B. Clayton.

36   Wife of Tubby's brother Hugh.

37   The Fry family were prominent chocolate manufacturers (J.S. Fry & Sons, Bristol). Mrs Fry, with whose wounded gardener Tubby had struck up a friendship in hospital, posted large quantities of parcels to Talbot House throughout the war. For example, in January 1918: "Magnificent parcel of woolies including chocolate and beautiful warm leather gloves from Mrs Fry, together with cocoa for nearly 1 000 men…"

VI Division Christmas card, 1915.

copy of Christmas carols with music. This he begged to be allowed to borrow, in order that one of his men might copy the score, and others the words; so that they might not be carol-less in the exposed position where they are stationed when the day of day comes. He was as good as his word, and returned the book this morning by a messenger.

Our programme for Christmas is quite tentative as yet, but on Christmas Eve we have, in the dear little Chapel, Festal Evensong at 6 p.m., followed by a Celebration at 6.30 p.m. for those on duty by night. On Christmas we have no Parade Services, but only Celebrations everywhere; and in the afternoon and evening I have thrown open the house for a regular old-fashioned romp. The divisional train has supplied a huge Christmas tree, which Nancy's parcel will decorate grandly; and what with singing and games of all sorts, I hope for a really happy Christmas for us all, please God.

If possible, I shall go up and Celebrate for my regiments just behind the line in the early morning.

These outlines will give you some idea of what I shall be doing on Friday and Saturday so that we may be in touch thus, as in all other ways.

I shall be thinking of the quiet Christmas at Hatchett,[38] when old guv. proposing as always the toast of the absent. Now I must, however reluctantly send this off, if it is to catch tonight's post. But I'll try and write more tomorrow on the off chance of its reaching you in time.

---

38   The Claytons settled at Beaulieu in New Forest in 1905. The house, Little Hatchett, was built on the lines of an Australian bungalow. It had a large garden and faced the forest.

Much love dearest Mater to you and to all the family circles. May God grant that next Christmas tide may find us together and in times of peace among men.

Your ever loving son,

Philip Clayton

*   *   *

4th Lab. Batt. R.E.
Sunday 1 pm, 26 December 1915

Dearest Mater,

I am disgusted with myself for only writing once last week, and that such a poor letter for Christmas. So I'll slip in a line or two while waiting for Hamer (my fellow-padre and one of the best) to come in to lunch. We've had a glorious Christmas, so far as any could be away from home. I didn't get really homesick at all until yesterday evening at about 9 p.m. when all our guests had departed, and after a tremendous day. Hamer and I began comparing notes on home while we waited for supper. His mother is 80, and a widow, and with neither son nor daughter to make her less lonely.

Now let's see. What a fearful lot there is I should like to say! The incidents of war, I suppose come first, though I don't know why they should.

We had a highly unpleasant weekend before Christmas – I imagine the idea was to get the "strafing" over before the parcel-post came in on both sides. I was taking a Service with the Labour Battalion when it started; we were at the second verse of "Rock of Ages"; the Adjutant dashed out and in again to signal to the Colonel that the Parade should be at once dismissed, but the old Navvies wouldn't budge until they finished their hymn; as one of them said afterwards to me: "If we were going to be hit, we'd better be singing hymns than hiding!" The business went on intermittently all day and both nights, so that it was rather a sleepless weekend. My dear old Pettifer of the Buffs takes command on these occasions, being exceeding war-wise like Aylward,[39] and orders the garrison off the upper floors when things are getting hot. But it all quieted down again on Tuesday, and not a shell has come into the town since. Yesterday, all was peace except a little anti-aircraft shooting. We had a lot of visitors at all times of the day and night last week, Officers and men almost collapsing with that devilish gas; all their buttons and cigarette-cases green with it. But the new helmets are magnificent.[40]

Now, let us put the war on one side, and come to the house itself and domestic problems. We are really getting along swimmingly, and the place is in full swing; the old shell hole covered with boards and blankets, and little pieces of holly stuck in the shrapnel holes in the walls. I am

---

39   Samkin Aylward is one of the main characters in *The White Company*, a historical novel by Arthur Conan Doyle (1859-1930). Set during the Hundred Years War, Aylward is an elite archer who spent most of his life as a soldier. His excellent archery skills, hardy constitution, sense of humour and good fortune saw him through many battles.

40   Holding the line between Frezenberg and Boesinghe, VI Corps (6th Division and 49th Division) experienced the first enemy phosgene attack before dawn on 19 December. A combined total of 1,069 gas casualties (120 of them fatal) were sustained by both formations, three-quarters of the combined losses by 49th Division.

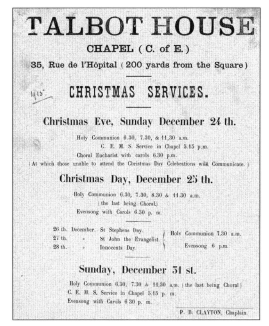

writing at a dining-room table of my own design, the top being the floor boards of a small tent, covered with wall-paper. The piano is going full tilt (or lilt) all day long, but I want some more popular song books – old English songs, etc. I must write to Nancy for them – she has been perfectly splendid – I never had such parcels.

Last week the A.D.M.S. came round on a tour of sanitary inspection. As luck would have it, he popped his head into the kitchen and asked "How many dish-cloths have you got?" Unfortunately, the question was answered by a simple and truthful R.A.M.C. man (who has now left us under a cloud): "Please sir, we wipes up with the wrappings off the parcels, sir. "I nearly had a fit outside, but tried to pull myself together when the great man came out and said, "Very extraordinary about your dish-cloths." I said blithely, "Oh! that will be all right, sir. We are sending to – for some tomorrow." "How many?" I hadn't the least idea, so I replied, "Oh a dozen, I expect." To which he replied severely, "You must have six dozen and boil them every night." However, when we found the price of them out here is 1 fr.50 each, we got only a dozen after all. If you can get me another dozen at a reasonable price, we shall be thankful, as about three hundred people have cocoa etc. here every day. Now for Christmas.

The Chapel on the landing is simply splendid – everyone has put in time, taste, and trouble to make it as perfect as possible. The only disadvantage is that it will only hold fifty at the outside.

We hold Evensong there daily at 7.15 with a Congregation of about ten. Celebrations on Saints' days etc., but if we can get the huge attic licensed by the R.E.'s to carry the weight of numbers, we shall move our Church up there.

On Christmas Eve we had an early Celebration for a company of Q.W.R.'s who were going up the trenches for Christmas. In the evening we had Festal Evensong, followed by a Celebration for night duty men; both were well attended, but there were no communicants that night – the natural feeling against making one's Communion at night is very strongly felt here; and those for whom I had intended it, got off and came yesterday morning.

Three chaps rigged up a glorious little Crib with lint, cotton wool, and a Christmas star Nancy sent by divine chance. Then an electrician rigged up a tiny lamp off a dry battery to shine down from the top of the cane – they burnt it all down once after two days work, trying to fix a candle – and it stood on a bamboo plant stand discovered in the garden and draped, beside the Carpenter's bench Altar. We had the Church furnished well with joyful guests at 7 and at 8, and again at 11.30, both yesterday and today; among unexpected pleasures being the quiet coming of the Town Major at 8 a.m., who had not previously been at all sympathetic.

Yesterday afternoon and evening, Hamer and I kept "open house", an extremely cheap business; tea from the billet next door, halfpenny buns, a lot of odd cake, and some holly from Charlton[41] at Boldre (not for consumption); from 3 – 5 a Concert; then tea – the Corporal tells me that 270 men had some sort of tea, including a couple of Belgian soldiers; then Evensong (that was when one felt the inadequacy of the Chapel); then conjuring by a policeman from Portsmouth, and more songs, and carols till 8.30, and a little bit of a dance after that. It was a huge success, and chap after chap said that they didn't think it possible to have spent so happy a Christmas away from home. I am really overjoyed with the opportunities of it all here, and no longer regret the Hospital.[42]

Once again, even this long letter is all about myself, but I know you understand and forgive. It is not because I do not think of you. Home, and especially you, mother, are simply so bound up with me that it seems absurd to try and write about it. How I longed for a sight of you all yesterday evening. All I could do was to try and help others to bear their own homesickness as best we could together. I am sure you would not have me home, if there are here these chances of service. Much love to you all, then, and to you above all. He will watch between us while we are absent one from another.

Your son,
Philip

* * *

'Talbotousians' in first Phosgene Attack

On December 19, four days after the House was opened, the company of the Westminsters which had just gone up into the support at Potijze, having had their Christmas party, and crackers to boot, in Talbot House the day before, met a crisis characteristically. That night a gas attack and a heavy bombardment broke suddenly on our local lines. Things looked quite dirty, and a message got through to the company in support to hold not only their support line but the Potijze Road itself. For the latter task seven men were all that could be spared. Five of

---

41 Edward Charlton, a Boldre friend and neighbour of Tubby, was a member of the Royal Society of Painter-Etchers. When, in early 1916, L./Cpl. Lowman of the 1/16th Queen's Westminsters drew a first sketch of the Upper Room, Tubby posted it to Charlton who made an etching of it. It went to the Society of St. Peter and St. Paul for reproduction on a series of cards along with the times of the daily services, which hung in billets throughout the Salient.

42 Tubby having first arrived in France during spring of 1915, was assigned staff chaplain of No. 16 General Hospital, Le Tréport.

'A' Company, 1st Bn Queen's Westminster Rifles, in the yard of their billets next door to Talbot House, in or about January 1916.

these crouched on the road itself, with one in the ditch each side. Beyond their rifles they had one machine-gun, which they trained to sweep the road. They wore stuffy P.H. helmets with good cause, for that night the gas cloud travelled further back than Vlamertinghe. Here comes the inimitable Westminster touch. They wore on the top of their masks their paper caps out of the Christmas crackers, and one rifleman insisted on brandishing a toy water-pistol, which he was at pains to fill at an adjacent shell-hole. This I heard at 2 a.m. on the 23rd, when a company that had been badly cut up came down to rest next door, waking the sleeping street with their indomitable "Rogerum".[43]

(P.B. Clayton, *Tales of Talbot House*)

R.I.P.
1/16 London Regiment (Queen's Westminster Rifles) – 19 December 1915

Rfm. Frederick H. Browne, Age 24
Lijssenthoek Military Cemetery (Poperinge), II.D.25

Sgt. John H.T. Corlett, Age 23
Ypres Reservoir Cemetery, I.B.71

---

43 "Rogerum" is a minstrel song version of the Parable of Dives and Lazarus. Dick Horne, of the Q.W.R. transport, made it famous at 'The Fancies', the Divisional Concert Hall. According to Tubby, "its magnificently onomatopoeic chorus lifted the feet of thousands of marching men of the 6th Division along the pavé or out of the mud and clay".

L.Cpl. Frederick S. Doggett, Age 22
Ypres Reservoir Cemetery, I.B.70

Rfm. Herbert G. Edwards
Ypres Reservoir Cemetery, I.B.68

Rfm. Horace A. Glover, Age 20
Potijze Burial Ground Cemetery (Ieper), N.12

Rfm. George C. Hinde
Ypres Reservoir Cemetery, I.B.72

Rfm. Edgar G. Lewis, Age 32
Potijze Burial Ground Cemetery, O.11

Rfm. Harold D. Rogers, Age 23
Lijssenthoek Military Cemetery, IV.A. 23A

Rfm. James W. Wootton, Age 25
Potijze Burial Ground Cemetery, O.12

*   *   *

Talbot House
4th Lab. Batt.
Tuesday 4 p.m., 11 January 1916

Dearest Mater,
There are one or two boys coming in to tea in a few minutes, so this won't be a long letter. As a matter of fact, I'm confined to the house at present by an episode which had both its ridiculous and its painful side. About a week ago I had a party of Q.W.R. stretcherbearers in. They are a glorious set of people, and had a very thin time of it with the gas attack on the 19th. Anyhow the French teapot refused to pour. No hatpins available, so the leader of them, called Tiny – he is about as big as Neville Talbot – said "just blow down the spout, padre, it's the only way." I did so too heartily with the result that the lid came off and the hot tea leaves all up my cheek. It was frightfully funny at the time, but the burn has not cut up rusty, and I have a bit of a swelling which the Labour Battalion M.O. has in hand; it is bandaged by the R.A.M.C. Corporal who is my chief of staff (that's the best of these wonderful R.A.M.C. men), but for a day or so it means keeping inside Talbot House.

However, I'm getting a lot of things straight meanwhile, and my letters done.

The House is going swimmingly, and I'm thoroughly happy with it. I hope to get 24 hours at no. 16 by the end of the month, and leave home in February all being well.

All your letters and the great parcel with its multifarious surprises – everything from dish-clothes to a jack in the box purse arrived safely this afternoon. The House is going well finan-cially – it cost 1500 francs to start with and we have made over 1000 profit in 3 weeks towards paying off the Church Army[44] loan etc. I've written today to John Barker asking about a regular supply of cold meat pies such as you used to get, as the great difficulty is to have food nearly at all times of the day and night. Over 100 officers have stayed here, and it's most interesting meeting them thus. With all my innate prejudice against the Class. I am most struck by their courtesy and goodness of the quiet downright kind. It's a delight to be able to do anything like this for them.

As for the men, they are quite wonderful. One is always unearthing something splendid. Just after Christmas, we had some gorgeous Yorkshire fellows into one of our huts, "drunken but not with wine," and the form their humour took was, on entrance, "three cheers for the Kaiser!" which was given with ironical enthusiasm.

What can the Gates of Hell prevail against this?

Here comes an R.A.M.C. boy, who works with the doctor of the Labour Battalion. Don't worry about my silly scald – it's only a trifle. Think of leave in February!

Your loving son,

Philip

*   *   *

The Royal Navy at Talbot House
In January 1916, when the Ypres Salient was at its worst under the winter rains, stagnant water stood almost everywhere. The ordinary drainage had been damaged by mines and shelling, and the pumping station was out of action. At this appropriate moment "Comic Cuts" (the unofficial name among the troops for Corps Headquarters' Routine Orders) announced that the Royal Navy were on their way to pay a visit to the Salient. This information was received with cheers! Soon afterwards an R.N. Party made its appearance. To our regret they did not bring their ships! They told us they had come as visitors, and that they were commissioned to return to their respective stations in the Home Fleet after a week or more of fun in Flanders. When they got back they would be given orders to tell what they had seen of trench warfare.[45]

My own Division – the 6th – became their hosts, and for lack of other accommodation they were billeted in Talbot House. During my time as Curate of St. Mary's, Portsea, I had been in close touch with H.M. Ships and Dockyard life. Therefore, to some extent, I knew a little of their ways and outlook.

The 6th Division ran a raid for them, in which our guests decided to partake. As often in a raid, some awkward moments had to be faced by unexpected means. Thus a machine gun crew was knocked out, but their gun not seriously damaged. A Petty Officer, whose post of vantage was near the spot where this distress occurred, forgot, in his excitement, the injunction that he was nothing more than a spectator. He and a Leading Hand and a junior rating rallied round the gun, got it to work, causing thereby a widespread irritation in the Bosch Lines. The Petty

---

44   An organization of ordinary people under the authority of the Church of England who assisted local church officers with society assistance, esp. with those less fortunate. The Church Army was very active among the troops throughout the conflict, staffing some 2,000 canteens and recreation centres.

45   Men of the 63rd (Royal Naval) Division visited Talbot House in the late summer and autumn of 1917. From 26 October to 10 November 1917, this formation fought in the Second Battle of Passchendaele.

Officer received, to his surprise, the D.C.M. (more popularly known as "Don't Call Monday"). He must have been the earliest R.N. rating to win this soldierly reward in Flanders.

(P.B. Clayton)

*   *   *

Talbot House
Monday, 17 January 1916

Dearest Mater,

I felt towards the end of last week as if I were never going to get time to write to you again! Now I have time to spare, as I've got my old periodic go of malaria, that has come round so regularly three or four times a year. I know it better than the doctors who however have the whip hand this time and have confined me to bed for 48 hours. I worked happily through yesterday, so must not kick against the pricks today. It's not the least serious, and will probably get me a 48 hours' holiday at Le Tréport before the end of the week. Neville is coming himself to be O.C. Talbot House for a few days, which will be excellent for everyone. Meanwhile Pettifer and the R.A.M.C. staff have been coming up all the morning to wash me, or comb my hair, or generally spoil me.

At this moment my C.E.M.S.[46] Secretary, Corporal Ashdown, R.A.M.C., looked in with a semi-professional eye. We have collected a goodly list of C.E.M.S. men here now – over fifty have signed the roll on the notice board, and we meet every Sunday at 5 for tea and business to be followed by our evening service at 6 p.m. This Service is growing rapidly – in fact we were crowded out last night. I wasn't up to taking it, so Reid took it for me and excellently well too.

Some things are really encouraging. During the week a certain R.G.A. colonel called one morning – (I was out, I try to get a bit of visiting done in the mornings: it makes all the difference) – and left a delightful note asking for a regular Sunday service for his battery. The trouble is that batteries are not really in any Division, so sometimes get left padre-less. Anyhow, they sent a big car for me yesterday afternoon, and I had one of the best services possible in a place where we could not stand upright. This was my first real visit to a battery headquarters, which for obvious reasons have few visitors. Batteries themselves have none! This introduction led to another, and on our way back I was given an equally warm welcome by the O.C. battery transport, whose men had not had a padre near them since they came to France! It is these odd units that form my peculiar Parish.

I'm afraid you'll find this letter very difficult to read. This is the result of being in bed. You needn't worry the least about this silly old temperature. It will go as quickly as it came, and if I get to no. 16 for a night or so, I shall rejoice at the opportunity of seeing the folk there again. Meanwhile, I am entitled to leave home any time after Feb. 10th. But all being well, I shall wait till the last week in Feb., so as to be there for the real birthday.[47] I hear from the Vicar today that

---

46   The Church of England Men's Society was formed in 1899 by Frederick Temple, Archbishop of Canterbury. It was intended to be the educational, social and representative arm of the Church of England. Adapting to local circumstances, it expanded rapidly in local parishes. Members were expected to contribute something for the good of the community.

47   1916 was a leap year. Tubby's mother celebrated her birthday on 29 February.

dear Paddy is dying[48] – it is heartbreaking not to see him again now, but it is only a question of waiting for the great Reunion. A year ago I should have felt it much more acutely, but now one gets so used to the idea of death that one comes to realize, as Edmund Street,[49] a brave man, said to me yesterday, that death is far from being the worst thing that can happen to a man.

This letter has been scrawled during many interruptions from sympathetic inquirers of various units, and now I must really close it down with much love to my dear mother and the household at large.

Your loving son,
Philip

*   *   *

10th C.C.S.[50]
Thursday, 20 January 1916

Dearest Mater,
In an hour or two I shall be travelling in luxury on one of those beautiful Red Cross trains, to Boulogne or (if luck favours me to Tréport) for a little change and rest. There's nothing at all wrong bar the ridiculous old temperature, which refuses to go down, unless I go down to the Base somewhere.

I hope it won't be more than a week, and unless they press it I shan't come home. It would spoil my leave for your birthday. I've written to H.B.C. who will find out with MO 5[51] sagacity what's the no. of my residence.

Your loving son,
Philip

48   Boy Shipwright Frank A. Padfield of H.M.S. *Victory* died on 20 January 1916 and is buried in Portsmouth (Kingston) Cemetery, Taylor's, 3.32.
49   This letter contains the first mention of Major Edmund Street, 2nd Sherwood Foresters (Notts & Derby Regiment), whom Tubby later described as "one of the earliest and deepest friends of Talbot House". Street was with the party who, after Evensong at the Divisional Concert Hall ('The Fancies') on 5 December, came round with Tubby to explore the House. Early in January, Street brought over a portable harmonium from Great Britain as a gift for Talbot House. The subsequent Sunday excursions of this so-called "groan-box" are mentioned in Tubby's later correspondence.
50   In June-July 1915 the British established No. 10 Casualty Clearing Station at the hamlet of Lijssenthoek just south of Poperinge. The farm of Remi Quaghebeur (whose buildings remain to this day) was the ideal site for a field hospital – a few miles behind the front, but out of extreme range of most German artillery. Situated next to the Poperinge-Hazebrouck railway line, the main communication line, it was between the rear echelon Allied military bases and the forward area. By late 1916, there were four CCSs at Remy Siding, scattered over a staggering 125 acres and with a maximum capacity of some 4,000 beds. With 10,784 graves, Lijssenthoek Military Cemetery is the third largest Commonwealth cemetery in the world.
51   Tubby's brother, Hugh Byard Clayton, worked for the Security Service, a subsection of the War Office Directorate of Military Operations, Section 5 (MO5).

Poperinghe 1920 - Cemetery " Remy " Kerkhof.
Ingang naar het Gasthuis en het Kerkhof.
Intrance to the hospital and the Cemetery.
Entrée vers l'hôpital et le Cimetière.

Thank guv. for his amusing card. Honestly, there's no cause for anxiety. My only longing is to get back to work now, and you in Feb.

   PBC

*   *   *

14 General Hospital Boulogne
Officers' Quarters
Monday morning, 24 January 1916

Dearest Mater,
I'm to be allowed to dress this afternoon, and sit around as large as life. This is today's news, and at this rate of progress, I calculate I may after all get back to work before the end of the war!

Mornings in hospital are always rather uncanny. Here they wake you, apparently, shortly after midnight and give you tea, then someone comes in and washes you, and before you have time to settle down to sleep again, two people come in and make your bed. Then a man comes in and polishes the floor, then a V.A.D. (whose husband is D.D.M.S. 5th Army!) dusts, then someone else takes your temperature (whether you have any or not),

From album of Sister Alison Macfie, V.A.D.

then the V.A.D. reappears with a bowl of lovely yellow gorse. By this time there are some signs of daylight, and just as you are settling down for a nap, in comes breakfast, followed by a barber, followed by the doctor on his morning rounds. One needs a splendid constitution to stand the strain of being sick in a hospital like this. They feed you on egg-flips about four times an hour and stand over you while you drain them to their soapy dregs.

… What a funny scrap of a letter! But that's the best of writing every day. I can make up for it tomorrow!

I thought of you all a lot yesterday, and the long journeys to Church. Did the guv. go to Beaulieu in the evening? Too wintery for Sunday evening walks yet. What book are you reading aloud?

Your son,
Philip

*   *   *

From Neville Talbot to Tubby
T.H. (business as usual)
25 January 1916

My dear Tubby,
I can't say how glad I was to get your letter and to gather that you are really likely to arise and shine here again. We are, as it were, carrying on with oil lamps, the electric light having gone out. There are so many things I might tell you of, but you know the scatterating effects of residence here.

But first, I have written to Gwynne to say that no fresh electric plant is needed but that I was keeping this exceeding round hole open for its truly proper peg.

… The inspired Scotswoman keeps pouring things in – 15 bales arrived – beds, chairs, curtains, tablecloths, cutlery, China, cashboxes, etc. etc. and I don't know what. I try as well as I can to fill the shoes of your "beautiful" feet.

There was rather a crise on Sunday tea-time when old Nick[52] and Brigade Major requiring tea upstairs and I downstairs with 3 men (C.E.M.S. rather went up the spout) the kitchen grappled at 5.15 p.m. with the situation of having its own tea. Corpl. Bradshaw handed in with the cash at 10 p.m. and written ultimatum of resignation – but

As Deputy Chaplain-General, Gwynne was the beloved chief of all C. of E. BEF padres throughout the war. Tubby frequently referred to him as 'Bishop Greatheart'.

52   Brigadier-General C.L. Nicholson, O.C. of 16th Infantry Brigade (6th Division)

neither he nor I have referred to it since. The Wednesday Service came off – and last night a lovely Concert – and the Sunday night service was as full as possible, with Nick in the royal box. I haven't coped with the attic yet – but long to. I wish the house were bigger. I am getting more small tables and shall make the 1st landing into another men's room.

May came in yesterday to say that he had heard that our charges were excessive – but I expounded – and have since asked all comers and have had no confirmation. If I can ever cope with accounts I can see whether we could reduce expenses for 6th Division – but you and Bates must be repaid. An aeroplane dropped a bomb at midnight up the street on Sunday night. Much fuss since about light showing at night. Grand debate tomorrow on "Should the parsons fight?" I send on letters – have opened parcels including galumpshous pork (v. big pig) pie.

…

Ever affectionately
N.S. Talbot

*   *   *

On 1 February Tubby returned to Talbot House.
c/o 4th Labour Batt. R.E.
B.E.F.
3 February 1916

Dearest Mater,
Things here are in full swing again: ten officers in last night, going on leave, and ten sad ones this morning returning. All, sad and merry, requiring beds and breakfasts. The last has just finished, paid his 5 francs and gone. They are a very nice lot, and well repay trouble. Over two hundred have stopped here since Dec. 20th! Then there is the men's side of things. Some five hundred use the Recreation and Writing rooms every day. We have moved the Chapel into the attic, which makes a perfectly beautiful Church, with hangings from the Bishop's Chapel at Southwark.[53] We have a daily Celebration at 7.15 which means I am getting to bed earlier, and a faithful few are beginning to come in regularly. Evensong at 7.15 at night is well attended.

… It is one of the many joys of the place that one sees practically everybody in the Salient at one time or another.

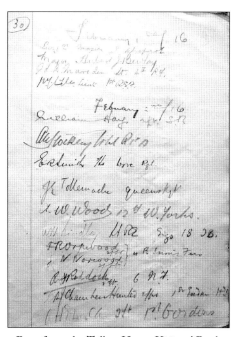

Page from the Talbot House Visitors' Book.

---

53   As Bishop of Winchester, previously Bishop of Southwark (1905-11), Edward Stuart Talbot, father of Neville and Gilbert, had sent to Poperinge the beautiful hangings, embroidered with lilies, of his private Chapel to surround the Carpenter's Bench. The new Chapel in the attic was first used on Sunday 6 February when a Confirmation Service took place, led by Bishop Gwynne.

Finance is going well, and out of a/cs covering 1800 francs for last month, I was only 15 centimes out. We can now practically pay off all our debts on the house. A Taube[54] over the town this morning may mean shelling this afternoon – this is the only disadvantage of these beautiful spring days. Zepps seem to be perfectly beastly in England; I hope they don't choose Feb. 29th for a visit, or I shall get "the wind up" as we say out here. A very jolly debate last night in which Women's Suffrage[55] was heavily defeated in a crowded house.

Much love.

Philip

Parrott & James have now a regular order for 2 pies a week!

* * *

How the "Upper Room" came into being

For the first fortnight, the Chapel of Talbot House was on the floor below the attic. It was Padre Crisford, of the L.R.B., who insisted on its exaltation to the big hoploft above. The difficulty of this step lay in the fact that one wall of this attic had been holed by a shell; and even when this damage was repaired, the R.E.'s entered their caveat against the soundness of the floor. There ensued a series of consultations which grew gloomier in ascending ratio of rank. First, two London sappers danced on

Part of the splendid hangings from the Bishop's Chapel at Southwark.

it, and assured us cheerily that it would stand anything. So far so good. But the lance-corporal in charge of them shook his head with the pregnant pessimism of Lord Burleigh[56] himself. An appeal was lodged with the sergeant over him, who expressed the gravest doubts. Next, the lieutenant immediately concerned tapped and condemned the joists. His captain came in one day, and verbally countersigned this adverse verdict. The major of the Field Company trod

---

54   Literally 'dove'. At the outbreak of war this monoplane was the principal scout of the German Army air service.

55   On 6 February 1918 , the Representation of the People Act was passed, enfranchising women over the age of 30 who met minimum property qualifications. Thus approximately 8.4 million women gained the vote. In November 1918, the Eligibility of Women Act was passed, allowing women to be elected into Parliament. The Representation of the People Act 1928 extended the voting franchise to all women over the age of 21, thus granting women the vote on the same terms as men.

56   William Cecil, 1st Baron Burghley (1520-1598). Chief advisor of Queen Elizabeth I for most of her reign and known for his pessimism. He created a highly capable intelligence service that was responsible for the discovery of a number of plots to replace Elizabeth with Mary Stuart, Queen of Scots.

as delicately as Agag,[57] and left us a prey to an hourly expectation of spontaneous collapse. In despair, we appealed to Colonel Tannet-Walker, who, after personal inspection, had the details of the floor worked out and presented in triplicate, proving conclusively that the attic was wholly unsafe. After this we asked no more questions, but opened the Chapel therein without more ado.

(P.B. Clayton, *Tales of Talbot House*)

* * *

Talbot House
Tuesday, 8 February 1916

Dearest Mater,
You will probably have had a wire from H.B.C. by now telling you of my change of plans. I am coming home on leave at once, crossing tomorrow Wednesday. I have still got a certain amount of malaria hanging about me, and the doctor insists that it's no good trying to pick up here. Hence I anticipate your dear birthday, and come home for a real rest and holiday. I shall get Hugh and Nancy to take me in for a day or so and then come to Hatchett, and be spoiled. If I don't eat more than I do at present, I shan't be much of an expense; but probably a few inhalations of forest air will make me as hungry as a lion in the zoo.

Neville, who is as good as any brother (and I know what brothers can be) is taking over the helm here once again. There's nothing really wrong with me – only just a holiday on the cheap.

Much love,
Philip

* * *

From the Visitors' Book, Little Hatchett
PBC returns to Hatchett to spend the last week end of sick leave at home, and to be on the spot for the great 29th, a day as distinguished as the Division that bears that number. The previous weekend was at Portsea via Farnham[58] (on the Bishop's birthday), with Ivy[59] as chauffeuse. Then 3 days at Wells returning via Mrs Fry at Bristol & Uncle Horace[60] at Oxford & Cecil Rushton.[61] Babs administers a tonic 3 times a day, & whiskey in moments of excitement, when the parcels are being opened. The paper man pedals up past the remains of the snow-man, and Verdun is

---

57   Agag, King of the Amalekites was attacked by King Saul after the former ambushed the Israelite army, in other words, the former had deployed against the enemy undetected.
58   Farnham Castle was the residence of the Bishop of Winchester, Edward Stuart Talbot.
59   Tubby's younger sister.
60   Canon Horace Ernest Clayton was Vicar of St Mary Magdalen, Oxford, and Hon. Canon of Christ Church. It was after Philip Clayton went up to Exeter College in 1905 that he earned the nickname 'Tubby Junior' in deference to his uncle, who was generally known as 'Tubby Clayton'. Weighing some 24 stone (6 lbs), the latter was much more deserving of the name. Uncle Horace also gave P.B.C. a communion set which Tubby used during his time at No. 16 General Hospital and Talbot House.
61   Tubby's closest friend since preparatory school (Colet Court, London).

Sitting room at Little Hatchett.

what Mrs Malaprop calls "the sinecure of all eyes".[62] Everybody else brushes the snow off the drive, and occasionally (when it's wet enough) we go for family walks to get up a fresh appetite for whole-meal scones & chocolate cake. But Poperinghe & Talbot House are a-calling, and on Friday I recross the channel (has it two 'lls' or one?). The roars will be out next time, together with the lupins & "the whiteflowered elder".

(P.B.C.)

*   *   *

c/o 4th Labour Batt. R.E.
10 March 1916

Dearest Mater,
I'm just off shopping, a queer proceeding in this neighbourhood, requiring a knowledge of French and Flemish, and most useful of all, Tommy's Polapuk.[63] And after all the shopping is accomplished there is the fearful business of getting the stuff home. No shops send anything – at least if they do, it is always brought by engaging young ladies who scandalise the staff

62   Mrs Malaprop is a character from Richard Sheridan's play *The Rivals* (1775) and frequently misused similar sounding words to great comic effect (*malapropisms*, cp French *mal à propos*). What Mrs Malaprop (or Tubby…) meant to say was "cynosure", i.e. the centre of attention. In other words the papers were full of the Verdun fighting. On 21 February 1916 the Germans had attacked the French fortress town in great strength. The battle would continue for the remainder of the year.
63   Army slang.

22 —

Shoping

To buy	Koopen
To ask for	Vragen naar...
To order	Bestellen, vergen
To take away	wegnemen, wegdragen
To pay	Betalen
To sell	Verkoopen
Take me to	Breng mij naar...
I want to buy	Ik wil koopen
Show me	Toon mij
It is too small	Het is te klein
It is too big	Het is te groot
How much is it ?	Hoeveel is 't ?
It is to expensive	Het kost te veel
What is the size of this ?	Hoe groot is dit ?
I want to buy this	Ik wil dit koopen
How much does the whole cost ?	Hoeveel kost alles samen ?
What is this ?	Wat is dit ?
Have you nothing better ?	Hebt gij niets beters ?
Have you nothing cheaper ?	Hebt gij niets goed-kooper ?
I shall take this ; this will do	Ik zal dit nemen ; dit is goed
Will you make a parcel ?	Wilt gij een pakje maken ?
There is my address|	Hier is mijn adres

Page from Guide *Militaire Anglais-Flamand* (Guides Plumon, Paris, 1915).

Shop nearly opposite Talbot House.

by sitting in the hall and waiting for M. le Capitaine. If, on the other hand, I carry it home myself, I infringe all Army Orders. Yesterday morning I did so, and ran the gauntlet of the early morning streets with an oil stove – not as good as yours – and a miscellaneous parcel of tools. Of course I met, besides many painfully respectful Tommies, a party of Guards who gave me a paralysing "eyes right!" I could only gasp and hurry on.[64]

Two of the Staff – both day orderlies – are on the sick list, which makes the household very short-handed. And I have great fears that all the Staff will be recalled to their Ambulance, when the Division goes into rest; in which case Pettifer and I shall hold the fort together; though we can and shall have to get new hands, it won't be the same thing for the time.

Neville, I fear, is going to leave us altogether. He has offered himself as a Chaplain to our prisoners in Germany, and will probably be accepted. The sacrifice is almost as great for us as for him.[65]

---

64 Tubby also refers to the oil stove incident in his *Tales of Talbot House*: "Ultimately I became so nervous of these ordeals that I walked only by night in the Guards' area, and then said "Friend" hurriedly in the dark to the buttresses of the church."

65 Neville's plan did not Materialize. On 25 March Bishop Gwynne wrote to Bishop Talbot: "There must be many in England who could be easily spared, and are capable of doing excellent work

Meanwhile all goes well – no shelling of the town for several days – I touch wood – and the House crammed from morning to night, and Services growing in attendance steadily.

Tomorrow, the D.C.G. is bringing Lord Salisbury[66] here to tea – I only hope he'll clear out before the singsong at 6.30, or still better, perform.

We had a glorious concert for the six footers[67] last night.

Much love,

Philip

*   *   *

Talbot House
Monday, 20 March 1916

Dearest Mater,

I've treated you very badly lately but it's nothing to my other debts in correspondence: e.g. the poor Nutshell … But short of sitting up at night, which I am determined not to do, I have had literally no time. In a week or so, I hope to be straighter and freer. My real trouble is the fluctuations of my Staff; though the Brass Hats[68] are very kind in every way, I can't get another permanent Staff yet, and with a household continually changing, and at the same time a house full to overflowing, both of officers and men, I have to keep at it pretty hard myself, and scarcely ever get into my parish for visiting. However, I've now written to Bishop Gwynne and asked for a really permanent staff, if he can get it for me. Meanwhile the great Division to which I was originally going has instead come to me, and I get a stiff neck craning up to talk to them. They are wonderful folk, and by no means as unapproachable from my point of view as I feared; though of course they are not malleable like the young Army. I have a company of the best next door, who simply live in Talbot House, and I am officially their Chaplain for the time being. Really my status is quite odd – as I'm more of a Garrison Chaplain than anything else, subject to no Division. All my old friends are back at rest; so there's new ground waiting fallow all round, as soon as I can get time to tackle it.

Meanwhile, the garden looms large in my projects – a Badminton Court in the kitchen garden for Officers, and the repainting of the summer house for their dedication; and weeding and pruning everywhere. The town is very peaceful at present, our friends having apparently need of their long range guns at Verdun. Aeroplanes came over this morning and had a fight while

amongst English prisoners; but there are very few as well qualified by soldier's training and experience of work amongst men as he is – to influence our fighting men in this great crisis. He is a real asset in the fighting power of the men of his Division – in addition to his God-given powers of making men Christian."

66   James Edward Hubert Gascoyne-Cecil, 4th Marquess of Salisbury (1861-1947), the eldest son of former Prime Minister Robert Gascoyne-Cecil, was a Conservative Member of Parliament and in 1903 succeeded his father in the House of Lords of which he eventually became the Leader. In 1922 he became a Trustee of Toc H by Royal Charter.

67   Reference to the height requirement for new Guards recruits. At the start of the war, the elite status of the Guards meant they were inundated with recruits and the height requirement was raised. It was lowered later in the war in order to get the replacement recruits.

68   Army slang for high-ranking military officers.

Guards and Canadians in the tea-room of Talbot House, 24 April 1916.

I was shaving, but dropped nothing. The weather is perfect, and the wall fruit trees and roses need a lot of wisdom that is beyond me. How I wish I had the guv. to supervise these hulking Welsh and Irishmen. The Band is coming into the garden as soon as we have got it straight, every afternoon more or less, so we shall be cheerier than ever. My old Div. Headquarters gave me a second piano before they left, so I have now one going in the men's room, another in the officers', and two gramophones! These with the Band in the garden, and the harmonium in the Chapel, are calculated to attract notice to the House!

   Have you a good tip for making lemonade in large quantities? I can get lemons, but we have to boil the water, and have not too much in any case. Three Brass Hats, the glorious remnants of my own folk, blew in for lunch on Saturday; but a Parrot and James' pie was ready for them. Good Services yesterday, quite a crowd of Officers of all sorts; the Chapel is really amazingly beautiful. Now I must go and tackle the garden, which I think and hope is going to be not only a great delight to my guests, but also a great source of recreation for me. All about myself again! Love to all.

   Your son,
   Philip

A jolly boy from Manor Road, Portsmouth, one of my own and oldest, Charlie Payne,[69] found me out on Friday – he is with a Battery to which I am now appointed Chaplain! Such a joy to see him! The first I have seen in 10 months out there.

---

69   For Charlie's death, see letter for 25 September 1917.

* * *

Talbot House
Friday, 24 March 1916

Dearest Mater,

Life is easing down a bit, and we are rejoicing in our immunity from the daily ration of shells in the town, owing to "Percy"[70] being temporarily indisposed. Either someone has hit his little railway line so that he can't take his constitutional, or he has gone for a star turn down South. Anyhow, he's no loss. Meanwhile the shops open up gaily amid the battered houses, and sell anything they can, mainly a beer which is the colour and constituency of bath-water, and floral postcards of coloured silk, in which the soul of Tommy takes high delight.

I had a very touching experience on Wednesday, of the kind that really helps one. The day before, while I was helping to try and reduce our wilderness into something like the garden it once was, an Abbé accompanied by a Belgian Officer came to call. The purpose of their visit was to ask me to officiate at the funeral of a Belgian artillery man, who had been killed the night before, and who was believed to be an English Churchman.[71]

On Wednesday afternoon, in the pouring rain, I went, accompanied by Sergt. Newton of the Coldstream (who has been lent to me as Chief of Staff temporarily, while awaiting his Commission (– a very fine fellow, an ex-Church Army Captain, and student at S. Boniface, Warminster)). We arrived in good time at the Belgian Hospital, and opening the main door found ourselves at once in the Chapel – the hall of the ex-château.[72] Here lay the coffin under the Belgian flag. Behind it, a beautiful kind of Lenten veil screened the sanctuary, whether to guard it from our unorthodoxy or as a seasonal hanging I could not judge and did not ask. I robed in the Matron's room, which had flowers and pictures and a general air of sweetness and light so strange after the usual billets, and then returned to the Chapel to find it full of Belgian soldiers in their metal hats; about twenty Officers and the Matron and two Sisters were also there on the steps facing me. Here I took the first part of the Prayer Book service slowly, trying so to inflect it that it should not sound meaningless to those who knew no English. Then we passed out through the great doors into the pouring rain, and proceeded on our journey to the

70   "Percy" was a German long-range railway gun.
71   Emile Robert Edouard de Laveleye (°2 June 1880, Liège) served in the 7th Belgian Field Artillery (fighting in support of the British forces from May 1915 to May 1917) and acted as liaison officer between the Belgian and British armies. He was the son of Edouard, a Belgian nobleman, and Florence Wheeler (Hastings, UK). In 1912 he married Dora-Mabel Newchurch in Victoria, British Columbia (Canada). He was killed in action at St. Eloi on 20 March 1916. After the war, his youngest sister, Gladys, became a member of the Toc H Women's Association Brussels branch. The Lamp of the Magnificat (symbol of the movement) held by this branch, was dedicated to Emile and now resides at Talbot House.
72   This château, named after its owner, Mr D'Hondt, justice of the peace, was situated along Deken De Bolaan, Poperinge. It was used as a clearing hospital for soldiers (during the 1st and 2nd Battles of Ypres) and civilians (from January 1915 – primarily for typhoid patients). There was a special ward for the 7th Belgian Field Artillery. Burials took place in the adjacent garden until the beginning of May 1915 by which time it was completely full (Poperinghe Old Military Cemetery). The castle was pulled down after the war, and a great number of its decorative stones were used as facade embellishments to nearby homes (no. 45-55).

Château D'Hondt.

Military Cemetery which lies half a mile out of the town, and is half Belgian half British.[73] Six bearers carried the coffin, and the whole congregation followed regardless of the rain. Arrived at the place, which was looking its worst, the coffin was set down at the shallow end of the long trench in which the Belgians bury their dead side by side. I began the second part of the Service, but paused after the "Suffer us not for any pains of death to fall from thee." It was well I did so, as otherwise we should have missed an incident that I shall never forget. The Commandant of the Battery stepped forward, and with bare head began to speak in slow and simple French. I never heard a speech that moved me more. From first to last it was addressed to the dead man, and had a ring of patriotism and pathos that I could not attempt to reproduce. In effect, it was an exhortation to confidence and quiet courage, "that the qualities which he had shown in life so well, might still sustain his soul." "Take heart, 'cher camarade', the cause in which you have given your life shall not be lost. 'La force barbare' shall be thrust back whence it came. Never fear concerning that. Perhaps, again the thought of her you love, of the two little ones,

73   *Cimetière Militaire No.2* (further down the road from *Château D'Hondt*) was established by the French at the end of April 1915. In June it was taken over by the British (*Poperinghe New Military Cemetery*). Between July 1915 and March 1916, eight Belgians, all serving in the 7th Belgian Field Artillery Regiment, including de Laveleye, were interred there. On 20 May his body was exhumed, put in a lead coffin and placed within the Lebbe family vault in the Communal Cemetery. Coincidentally, since the mid-18th century until 1910, a branch of that family resided in what would become Talbot House.

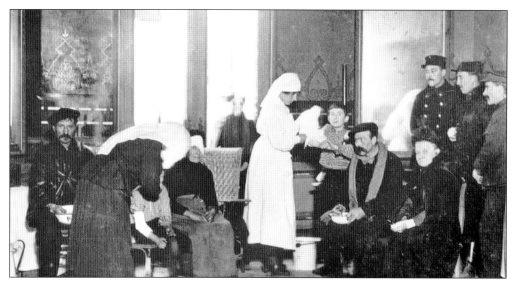

Nursing Sisters taking care of civilians at Château D'Hondt.

and of 'l'un qui vient' is grieving you. Have no fear, dear comrade, so long as one of us is left, they shall not want for aught. And you for your part, who passed the gate of death, would bid us also be of good cheer, and go back to the guns you served so well, knowing that, come life or death, there lies beyond a glorious future for our country and for all who suffer in the one great cause."

This précis is a poor travesty of the real words; I shall always remember the pathos of the 'écoutez vous?' interjected from time to time, and the tone in which 'la force barbare' was said. After this, I completed my part of the Service, saying the Pater Noster in the hope that some might catch a familiar word even in the English pronunciation of Latin. Then, in place of our bugle call, with its weird grandeur of the missing note, each Officer from the General downwards stepped forward, one by one, and put a spadeful of earth on the Coffin, now lying in its shallow grave. I walked back

Emile de Laveleye.

with the Matron, who told me something of the story. It was one of those numberless stories of private sacrifice which the war has to its credit. He, a Belgian nobleman by birth, had in his childhood and boyhood lived in England, and had joined there our own Church. From England he had gone to Canada, where the outbreak of war found him prosperous and happily married. Even there he had felt the call of the little country he had only seen with child-eyes; and, selling his estate, brought his wife and children to London, where he left them. For more than a year he had served as a volunteer in this Belgian battery, spending his leave in England, where his wife was living on the slender capital created by the sale of the Canadian estate. She, poor lady, expects another child in a few weeks' time, and their friends did not know whether to break the news or not. I offered, of course, to write to her, but the Matron told me that it would be wiser to wait awhile. Then, she said, with a sad smile, "Please do so. My only son was killed last autumn, and I know how a few details help one at such a time."[74]

As I came along, I felt two simple emotions, the first was concerning this stranger and his story; and the wonderful way in which our own Church was there to gather its adopted son to itself at the last. But the dominant impression was that left by the Commandant's speech. How truly and how simply the French and the Belgians understand the issues of it all, the urgency of the need, the greatness of the cause.

I must not write more now; but it seemed good to get this down on paper before the incident melts into a memory only. I am fit and happy, and see lots of real work developing, which is what I want. Your letters are full of all I want so much to hear, though I reply so little.

Much love to you all.

Your loving son,

Philip

R.I.P.
Emile Robert Edouard de Laveleye
Adjutant, 7th Belgian Field Artillery
20 March 1916 – Age 35 – initially buried in Poperinghe New Military Cemetery

*   *   *

On March 30th the Welsh Guards sang at 6 p.m., and at 9 p.m. (when all troops were in billets); the Town Police came in to see the place was empty, and stopped to make it full.

(P.B. Clayton, diary 1916)

*   *   *

Talbot House
Saturday, 1 April 1916

Dearest Mater,
I look forward to mothering Sunday tomorrow, and a really happy busy day. Let me sketch my programme: -

---

74 Tubby's letter of 24 March was published in *The Times* and handwritten copies circulated amongst his relatives and friends at home. On 19 April, Tubby requested his mother also to send a copy to de Laveleye's widow, whose address he had managed to get hold of, in the hope that it would bring her a little comfort at Easter time.

8 a.m., I shall probably attend the Celebration here and assist a fellow Chaplain who was at
    Portsea for the Mission – Harold Hubbard will be Celebrant and all the Corps people,
    including probably Cavan,[75] will be there.
9.30 a.m., a small parade of one company of a Labour Battalion here; they are great pals of mine
    and have lent me an excellent L. Corporal who has been working day by day in the garden
    for weeks past.
10.30 a.m., a full parade of another Labour Battalion, my old one.
11.30 a.m., Choral Celebration.
12.30, lunch (with some rhubarb out of the garden).
1 p.m., start in car for a siege battery (where Charlie Payne of Portsea is!)
2 p.m., service there, and harmonium carried in car.
3.15 p.m., another siege battery.
5.30 p.m., service at Corps Headquarters.
6.30 p.m., Evening Service here.

It sounds a jolly day; and I shall try and talk about mothering Sunday most of the time.

Neville came on Jumbo,[76] and was splendid. Now that the town is so peaceful, the owner is
exhibiting a desire to return to his house,[77] so I am in the old position of having to hope for a
little shelling to keep him quiet!

Many thanks for Punch. Who is it who sends me the Illustrated London News from Smiths?
I suspect Nancy. It is a great acquisition. Now I must try and get things straight for tomorrow,
before tea. Who do you think is coming? Why, a jolly corporal who was a Confirmation candidate of mine at No. 16 in September. He came and discovered me yesterday, and yesterday
evening another link with No. 16 turned up in the person of a young lieutenant, who I knew
well there as an R.A.M.C. orderly.

Good afternoon to my own dear mother. I wish I could send you a simnel cake, with some
violets! But neither one nor the other grows here. However you know what I do send you

Your loving son,
Philip

PS a jolly receipt for lemonade came from Mrs Davies. I'll try and write her a line soon.
PBC

*   *   *

75   Frederick Rudolf Lambart (1865-1946), 10th Earl of Cavan, GOC XIV Corps. Cavan was Tubby's
     2nd cousin and his mother Tubby's godmother, so lieutenant general and priest very close. Indeed, the
     former became a regular visitor and staunch supporter of Talbot House. He also wrote the foreword
     to Tubby's *Tales* (1919) and when Toc H was launched became its Vice-President.
76   Neville often paid flying visits to Talbot House. On one occasion, he proposed to stable his giant
     chestnut horse Jumbo in the garden aviary. A soldier encountering rider and horse on the moonlit
     street was heard to exclaim: "Blimey, camels in Flanders!" Neville was 6 ft. 4.5 in. tall.
77   On 31 March, the Town Major remarked: "An enquiry is held at this office. AA QMG Guards Div.,
     Capt Talbot & owner of soldiers club. Arrangements will probably be made for a new lease as neither
     party like the present one."

Talbot House
Wednesday night, 5 April 1916

Dearest Mater,
I enclose a cheque for £ 2 to cover my
debt for pyjamas and a little over. I want
a knitted black tie please, a new one for
Easter. Otherwise I have no pressing
needs.

Today I lunched with Cavan at Corps
Headquarters, a great honour; and no
one could have been kinder. He talked
most affectionately of you and asked me
to send you his greetings. He also talked
a lot of Seymour, Alec, and George
Robbins,[78] and of Aunt Addie's accident,
and Uncle Fred.

He is going out of his way to do me
kindnesses; especially he is securing for
me, by personal application on his part,
two R.A.M.C. boys I greatly need on
my staff here. One, Victor Hamblin of
Mirfield[79] who I got to know and be
fond of while his ambulance was in these
parts, and secondly Cecil Vokings[80]
from No. 16 Gen. Hos., my right-hand
man there: with these and Pettifer, my
anxieties about the staff should be in a
fair way of ending. This is far more than
I ever hoped for, and makes the future
very bright.

Charcoal preliminary sketch for oil painting *The
Conquerors* (Canadian War Museum), presented to
Talbot House by war artist Eric Kennington in 1931.

78 Tubby's first cousin, Capt. George Upton-Robins 3rd Bn East Yorkshire Regiment, was fatally gassed
    at Hill 60 on 5 May 1915. In October/November 1918, Tubby spent a few days trying to locate
    Upton-Robins' grave (see p 220).
79 Victor Hambling left the College of the Resurrection at Mirfield on 31 July 1915 "to help with the
    war effort". He acted as "chapel housemaid and tea-maid" from June 1916 when Neville Talbot took
    over Talbot House in Tubby's absence. Taken ill the following July, he was sent to rest camp and
    transferred to an RAMC unit stationed Far East. Unhappy with this assignment, he vainly wrote
    "frenzied appeals" to Neville to intervene for his return to Talbot House.
80 Cecil Vokins' friendship with Tubby began in May 1915 at Le Tréport. Unable to get on with Rev
    Bullock, one of Tubby's replacements in the summer of 1916, he was posted back to No. 16 General
    Hospital. In January 1917, Bishop Gwynne appointed him to the Talbot House staff once more,
    where he served till the end of the war. He was in charge of the Library, the Chapel and Chaplains'
    Shop. After the war he joined Toc H and helped compile a register of Foundation Members, i.e.
    those using Talbot House during the conflict.

Sunday was a great day and all my nine services went well. As I left one heavy battery in the afternoon, they started firing again, and as I was at the time only about twenty yards from the nose of the gun (pointing of course almost vertically) I got the full benefit of the performance, and nearly fell out of the car. The harmonium came to pieces, but this was not due to fright on its part so much as the roughness of the roads. However, some jolly Signaller boys mended it for me on Monday.

All goes very well, and I am thoroughly happy in my work, far more than I deserve to be.

Much love,

Your son,

Philip

PS 1000 excellent cigarettes from the guv. Many thanks.

PS also a box of small paper handkerchiefs as advertised in Church Times, for use as Purificatus

*   *   *

Wrestling with a Beast of a Harmonium

Fatty (one of the Corps Signals officers) has been very busy these days trying to get the harmonium at the 'Toc Aitch' (as it is pronounced) club into order.

"Look here, Wallah," he said, "if you know about the insides of a piano, don't be lazy; come along and give me a hand with that wretched harmonium."

...

Up in the big attic is the chapel. It is there that Fatty and I have wrestled with that devil of a harmonium.

...

Yesterday was one of those muggy, damp days which make life a misery. So, not feeling virtuous, instead of censoring letters I went for a walk and met Fatty in his little Singer. He took me into Pop. to have a cup of tea together. What happened was that he went to wrestle with that beast of a Toc H harmonium. A couple of hours later he was still wrestling and I was minus tea. So I left him to it and returned to do the letters. I always did think harmoniums were inventions of the devil.

(Diary of 2nd Lt. G.Ll.-W., aka Corps Cyclist Wallah, 1916)

*   *   *

On April 7th the tea-pot brought together Lord Cavan (Corps Commander), Captain Headley of North Riding Heavy Battery, Lieut. T.A. Officer and six most noble men of the Royal Horse Guards, who were looking round for the war.

(P.B. Clayton Diary 1916)

*   *   *

Talbot House
Monday, 10 April 1916

Dearest Mater,
Life is very happy; I'm amazingly fit, no sign
of fever or other ill: and really the work is a
joy such as few can have at present. The little
Church is getting known and loved, and folk
turn to it naturally, e.g. this afternoon an utter
stranger, an Officer in – , came in and asked
shyly if he might go up to the Chapel and be
quiet. I, in response, asked if I could be of any
help if I went up to him there. He accepted
gladly, and after a little time I followed him.
It turned out he had just had news of his
father's death at home. The news had been
delayed in reaching him owing to his regiment moving, and the funeral was to be at 3
this afternoon. So at 3 in the Chapel I held
the Burial Service, with a quiet congregation
of one: and he went back to his regiment I
think with his sorrow somewhat assuaged.

Yesterday's Services were full of joy and
promise. The Chapel is really needed, and
since we scrubbed and whitewashed it last
week is amazingly beautiful. Nancy's flowers
came just in time for Sunday, and we have
made stained glass windows out of a roll of
Sunday school pictures sent by Mrs Cooke.

The Chapel , etched by E. Charlton, from a sketch
by L/Cpl. Lowman, Q.W.R., early 1916.

Jack's second box of cigars and the guv's magnificent gift are both safely arrived, and a great
standby.
    Your son,
    much love,
    Philip

Neville has wired accepting my invitation to take the Three Hours here. I hope it is not too
ambitious to try and hold it seven miles from the line! PBC

*   *   *

I think our first Easter is worthy of note, lampers of the most lovely cut flowers arrived from
England, and a band of willing workers with artistic tastes made the Chapel the most beautiful
spot in Europe. On Easter Day the sun shone and men muttered God is good. Bang! and still
another, somebody hurt, a woman wounded and a child killed. Not long ago I saw them smile.
            (Pte. George Lubbock, R.A.M.C., Server and Sacristan of the Upper Room)

*   *   *

Easter Day, 1916, I shall always regard as the happiest of my ministry.

(P.B. Clayton, Tales of Talbot House)

*   *   *

Talbot House
Easter Monday, 24 April 1916

Dearest Mater,

It is 9.15 p.m. I am alone, and have just finished supper and my post-prandial canteen accounts with Sergt. Godley,[81] my senior N.C.O. and Chief of Staff. This always ends up with a gossip, as he is a most delightful fellow. I only wish I could keep him. However, when the two beloved boys come whom Cavan is moving mountains to secure for me, these and Pettifer will hold the fort whoever comes and goes.

It is the first night I have been alone for a week, as Gardner,[82] a Lieut. in my old Division, was living with me last week, and has today rejoined his regiment. He was a really jolly fellow, and an amazingly good musician, so that his presence at our little groan-box in the organ loft all last week has been of the greatest value.

We had quite a wonderful week – thirty or so at Evensong every night, and about fifty at Neville's Three Hours (including Cavan), and on Saturday the Chapel was transformed into the most perfect place of worship in Belgium. Mrs Coevoet-Camerlynck had left a roll of crepe behind, which draped the Altar on Good Friday. On Saturday flowers poured in from home, and a lovely Frontal came to order from Holy Cross Court, Hayward's Heath. So everything for Easter was exceedingly magnifical. And Easter Day was worth it. We had about 270 Communicants, the Divisional General, most of the Staff, Brigadiers, Colonels, Bandsmen, Signallers, Railway Men, R.A.M.C., A.S.C., M.T., R.E.'s (including dear Bert Potter of Portsea), Infantry, Motor Machine Gunners, Heavy Gunners, Amm. Col. men, armourers, Army Ordnance men, Red Cross folk, and even a Sergt. of the A.V.C. If the Chapel floor had collapsed at 8, 9.30 or 11.30 (as it ought to have done by all laws of gravity) practically every branch of the Army here would

81   Battle of Mons veteran Sgt George Godley (1885-1954), 1st Bn Coldstream Guards, was assigned to the staff at Talbot House while completing his hospital convalescence following treatment in Britain for wounds sustained during the Battle of Loos. He remained in charge of the staff till the end of June, having made a major contribution to the well-being of the House. Tubby wrote in his *Tales* " ... nor, in domestic matters, were the floors ever so spotless, the lamps so well trimmed, or the garden so neat, as under the regime of Sergeant Godley." When the Guards left for the Somme, Neville Talbot managed to keep Godley at the newly opened Officers' Club (see p. 71), but he was eventually called back at the beginning of August to replace heavy losses. After the war, Godley joined Toc H and became President of Toc H Brighton.

82   2nd Lt. Godfrey Gardner, 9th Bn Suffolk Regt., son of a professor of music, was educated at the Royal Academy of Music and a member and organist of the Royal Philharmonic Society. Organist at Holy Trinity Church, Paddington and St Giles, Cripplegate, London, he joined the 1/16th Queen's Westminster Rifles on 1st September 1914, obtaining a commission in the Suffolk Regiment on 14th December 1914. Dispatched to the front in October 1915, he arranged various entertainments for the men. Killed in action on 13 Sept. 1916 (age 34) whilst leading his men at Ginchy, he is commemorated on the Thiepval Memorial.

TALBOT HOUSE
CHAPEL (C. of E.)

EASTER MCMXVI
35 Rue de l'Hôpital (200 yds. from Square)

Portable harmonium brought back from leave in
January 1916 by Major Edmund Street, 2nd Bn
Sherwood Foresters.

have had its representative in the common
ruin! The 11.30 Service I shall always
remember, as indeed I think will all those
who were there – about a hundred, half of
whom had returned to give thanks for their
Communion earlier. We sang Merbecke[83]
and Easter hymns all through, and the real
reverence of all was most marked. I had help
at 6.30, 7, and 8, but was alone for 9.30,
and 11.30, except for Servers in uniform.
But no one found the Service too long, I
am certain. Believe me, the old Church
isn't half as moribund as some folk seem to
think; and the reality of Churchmanship
among the Canadians is a most significant
and inspiring fact.

83   John Merbecke (c. 1510 – c. 1585)
     was the composer of one of the most
     popular musical settings for the Anglican
     Communion service.

Lt. Godfrey Gardner.

The Offertory totalled £10, which is divided between the Convent of the Holy Cross (for the Frontal, etc.) and the Prisoners of War Fund. As the result of our Lenten Offertories, another £10 has gone to the Waifs and Strays.[84] Before the 11.30 Service ended, the Colonel of a Brigade of Heavy Artillery was waiting for Gardner and the harmonium and myself. We lunched with him at his Headquarters, some miles out – such a jolly party – and then held the Easter Service there; thence at 3 p.m. we went up to a Battery I had not visited before (I vary my suburban existence every Sunday afternoon by Battery Services), and although the Boche was making the roads unpleasant, succeeded in reaching the spot.[85] A Boche plane however evidently thought the folded harmonium a suspicious object, as it hung overhead, so that we had to wait for an hour in a sandbagged retreat while they shelled the field on our left with great gusto. Then we got to our ruined stable, and had a fine service. We then had tea and after another delay from a similar cause, got safely home just in time for Evensong. The moment I reached Talbot House, Pettifer told me that one of our old night-orderlies, a splendid R.A.M.C. fellow, had been badly hit and wanted to see me that night in the Casualty Clearing Station. So I wrote a desperate chit to the C.O. Motor Machine Gunners, who had been at Communion in the morning, asking for a cycle car at 8 p.m. Then we had a glorious Evensong, with the Chapel recklessly overfull again, after which I swallowed some coffee and climbed into the place behind where the machine gun should be, and tilted down the road full pitch to the C.C.S. We couldn't find the turning off to it, so I left the sidecar with its jolly Scotch driver to solace himself with one of Jack's precious cigars, and proceeded along a railway line I knew would bring me to it. Here I found that my way was obstructed by an empty goods train, which took it into its head to have a particularly bulging wagon at the very spot where it crossed a trestle bridge over a slow and smelly stream. I therefore had to crawl in my fur coat under the wagon along the track across the open sleepers, hoping meanwhile that no one would try shunting the train. No one did, and I emerged safely, found the C.C.S., knocked up an R.A.M.C. captain I knew there, found the boy in his own ward doing well, in spite of a bit of shrapnel through his lung. I re-emerged into the night, retraced my steps, negotiated the bridge again, found my cycle car, and whirled back to a late and glorious supper of soup and tinned sausages. After which I subsequently retired to bed. Quite a jolly Easter day of the right kind.

Today I have been slacking. We had four Communicants all right at 7.15 a.m.; after breakfast, I did the accounts all the morning, superintended the photographing (by special permit) of the garden, house and Chapel all the afternoon, walked down to another C.C.S. for tea with a dear old friend from No. 16 who is Matron, saw the boy (still going well) on my way back; then boarded an empty train going my way and called on various units on my road back from the station, to Evensong here at 7.15 p.m. Since then, nothing but supper, the Sergt., and this scribble.

Tomorrow, I hope to take all our Easter flowers to the British Cemetery here, and have a Confirmation Class at 6 p.m. Otherwise another slack day.

Everyone is amazingly nice, and I'm really happy and thoroughly thankful to be where I am.

---

84   Known today as The Children's Society, The Waifs and Strays Society, a charity allied to the Church of England, was founded in the late 19th century to establish children's' homes as an alternative to workhouses and orphanages. The offertory to the Waifs and Strays provided over three years "more than the yearly maintenance" of one little girl, Hannah Mitchell, the unseen adopted child of Talbot House. For Hannah's story, see p. 259.

85   The battery position was situated at Fantasia Farm between Brielen and Elverdinghe.

Much love, dearest Mater; I'm afraid this letter is all about myself again, but that can't be helped.

Your son,

Philip

*   *   *

It was night-orderly Aubrey Colwill who got severely wounded in the shoulder by a splinter of a shell which burst in the garden. He was taken to No. 17 C.C.S. Remy Siding.[86] Tubby wrote the following letter to Aubrey's sister following a visit to the patient:

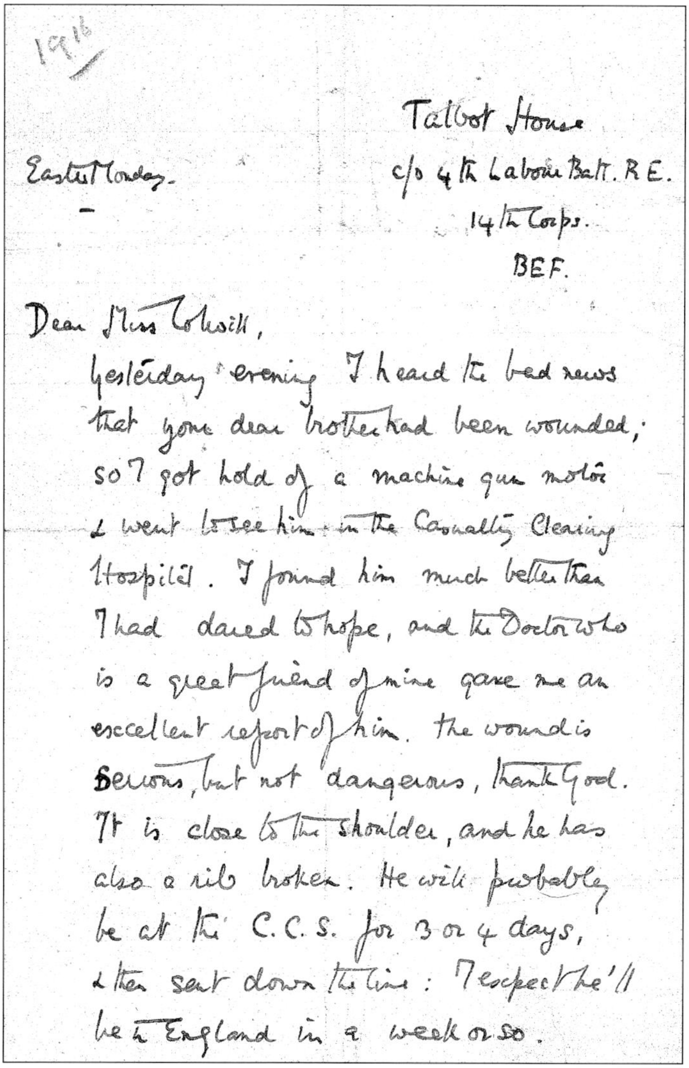

> 1916
>
> Easter Monday.
> —
>
>   Talbot House
>   c/o 4th Labour Batt. R.E.
>   14th Corps.
>   BEF.
>
> Dear Miss Colwill,
>   Yesterday evening I heard the bad news that your dear brother had been wounded; so I got hold of a machine gun motor & went to see him in the Casualty Clearing Hospital. I found him much better than I had dared to hope, and the Doctor who is a great friend of mine gave me an excellent report of him. The wound is serious, but not dangerous, thank God. It is close to the shoulder, and he has also a rib broken. He will probably be at the C.C.S. for 3 or 4 days, & then sent down the line: I expect he'll be in England in a week or so.

* * *

Talbot House
Saturday, 6 May 1916

Dearest Mater,

Only a word or two now. Neville is back from leave and we are coping with the big problem of extending Talbot House into an adjoining House; he to run the Officers' Club,[87] and I the men's. We went yesterday to a Conference of the Army at[88] – where Talbot House of the present was highly recommended, and the extension approved.

Both my boys secured for me permanently by Cavan's kindness – Cecil Vokins from No. 16 G.H. and Victor Hamblin of Mirfield from a F.A. – have arrived. The rest of my delightful staff will, I fear, move with their Division soon.

On Wednesday I am going for two days to revisit No. 16 G.H., a long journey but a great joy. And in June, I find I am entitled to two weeks' leave, my year as a C.F. being completed in a few weeks now. This is great news, and I must simply do my part in getting the new work started here before I come.

Now I'm off to lunch with some jolly Motor Machine Gunners and superintend the erection of a little altar in their field for a Celebration in the open air there tomorrow. Your letters all to the good.

Love to all.
Your son
Philip

No. 16 General Hospital, Le Tréport.

87   The Town Major remarked on 18 May: "Corps commander arranges 43 Rue Hopital to be an officers' club." Talbot House was situated at no. 35.

88   The Conference was held at Second Army HQ, Cassel. Tubby recounted this experience as follows: "The Army Commander [General Sir Herbert Plumer] took us in hand for an hour or more, explaining much of which the civilian clergy, hurriedly commissioned, were naturally ignorant; then passed on to illuminating hints, full of sagacity and salted with dry humour. He touched upon the choice of hymns and of familiar tunes, the reading of the Lesson, the topics for short sermons, modes of prayer, the way to gain facilities for worship. Then came some wider notes – life in the Mess, visiting in billets and in the line, courage and tact and sympathy."

* * *

The Officers' Club

"The adjoining House", occupied by "A" Mess of the Guards Division, became the Officers' Club, run by Rev. Neville Talbot. On 11 June 1917 he wrote the following note concerning its recent past:

In May 1916 I received orders from A.C.G. II Army to go to XIV Corps H.Q. as chaplain to Corps Troops & to extend Talbot House into an Officers' Club. The Club was opened in June 1916. Subscriptions and loans were drawn from the three Divisions of the XIV Corps viz: Guards, VIth and XXth, also from Talbot House and from the Church Army. Some assistance in the way of staff, furniture, and cutlery was derived from Talbot House. During the winter 1915-16 Talbot House had acted as a night rest-house for officers and had paid its way with money thus obtained. Talbot House was in a measure the parent of the Officers' Club.

In August 1916 the XIV Corps moved to the Somme and the Club was handed over to the VIIIth Corps, and the Rev. C.S. Ensell D.A.C.G. of the VIIIth Corps took charge. The Club repaid all loans but not subscriptions.

I started and managed the Club with the help of a Committee consisting of one Staff Officer from each Division and the Town Major of Poperinghe.

Subsequently, to meet the manifold problems of catering etc., in view of the tremendous concentration in 1917, the Officers' Club was handed over to E.F.C., who maintained it until the evacuation in the spring of the following year.

Shortly after the war the well-known Skindles Hotel was opened in this building. It claimed to be "the best hotel in the Salient, homelike, with electric light, bathrooms and central heating", and was used extensively by pilgrims.

POPERINGHE – Hôtel Skindles

Officers Only

Apart from the clubs operated by the Army, there were also officers only restaurants and hostels run by civilians. Writing of this situation in December 1915, Tubby observed:

Two of the four chief restaurants were already in full swing, the best, cheapest, and oldest, being *The British Officers' Hostel* in the Rue de Boeschepe. Very much second came *A la Poupée*, behind a shop in the Square, where the thirteen-year-old schoolgirl "Ginger" had already established her fame.[89] Any defects in the cuisine or in the quality of the champagne were more than compensated by the honour of being chosen as her partner in the exhibition dance which she gave with the utmost decorum as the evening drew on. *Skindle's*[90] was not yet in being, so far as I can remember, nor the ill-fated *Cyril's*.[91]

(P.B. Clayton, *Tales of Talbot House*)

Sketch from La Poupée Visitors' Book.

Ginger.

89   The establishment was run by Mr and Mrs Cossey and their three daughters. The youngest, Eliane, was a most attractive red-haired girl, a feature that quickly gave her the nickname 'Ginger'. Of this famous officer haven it was said that more champagne corks popped during the war than shells fell on Poperinge.

90   Originally known as the *Hôtel de la Bourse du Houblon*, the name was too difficult for its clientele. Undeterred, a Rifle Brigade officer christened it 'Skindles' after a well-known riverside hotel in Maidenhead. This Flemish Skindles relocated to the Officers' Club, the extension of Talbot House, in 1919.

91   Run by Ieper refugees Cyriel Vermeulen and spouse, the restaurant was destroyed by a direct hit in March 1918. For this incident, see p. 171.

Office No.	Date of Letter.	From whom received or if emanating from the Office, by whom sent.	Sender's No.	SUBJECT.
P.R. 960/282.	P.M. 19.10.17	Fifth Army	P.2.P 10/88	LOST. From "LA POUPÉE" Restaurant. Wallet containing 2000 Francs.

Extract from the Register of the Assistant Provost Marshal.

*   *   *

The pictures of the house and garden[92] which Tubby referred to in his Easter Monday letter were posted to Neville Talbot's parents, who had provided the beautiful hangings for the chapel. On 10th May, Mrs Talbot sent a warm letter of thanks to Tubby from the Old Government House Hotel on the Isle of Guernsey where she was staying:

My Dear Mr Clayton,

    It was a delightful little envelope full of photographs which you sent of THE Chapel. Do tell Neville that we have got them; it will be some consolation to his disappointment that we had not bought the rather expensive etching from the artist,[93] – and we can well replace in imagination the effect of our dear old Kennington hangings as to colour. I think I shall have to send you in return for the photographs a fine lot of flowers when I get back to Farnham on the 23rd. I love the feeling of that Chapel more than most things.

    ....

    I hope you'll get all right my grateful thanks for the Chapel photographs & the Group with yourself in the middle.

    It is dark & grey here today, but warmer & a welcome change for high chill winds. Tomorrow I hope for a blazing sun. We are only 12 miles from Brittany now I wish we could get over & make our way across to you! But the greatest vigilance goes on our passports here, and the little islands have slowly awoken to the fact that Germans & spies are everywhere.

    I hope you are feeling well and not getting tired.

    Yours very sincerely,

    Lavinia Talbot

*   *   *

92   These pictures are reproduced on p.57 (tea-room), p.74 (staff and chapel), p. 242 (garden) and p. 317 (tea-room).

93   See note 41.

The Upper Room, 1916. Picture taken from the rafter-loft.

Tubby and the Talbot House staff in the garden, 24 April 1916. 'Gen' is seated on the extreme right, Sgt. George Godley on the left of Tubby.

May 17th – Archbishop of Canterbury visits Toc H[94]
(Diary Cpl. Len Ashdown, R.A.M.C.)

Last Wednesday the Chaplains of the Army gathered
at Poperinghe to meet His Grace of Canterbury. It
was an historic occasion, and we were a very motley
crew, Chaplains in the wideawakes of sunny Australia,
and the khaki twill of the tropics, Chaplains in steel
helmets who have never seen the front line, Chaplains
garbed in kilt and sporran, Chaplains with beards and
Chaplains without, all met to pay homage to the great
man. He, noble man, was gracious to us all, though
he must have thought that his suit of sober black was
peculiarly out of place at such a fancy dress ball!

The proceedings commenced with the inevitable
Conference, held luckily out of doors so that the flag-
ging interest of the weaker brethren found food for
thought in the glory of nature and the skill of our
airmen.

When all were exhausted, even the most perse-
vering of the hot-air brigade, the Senior Chaplains
of each Division were presented to his Grace the
Archprelate. Our Senior was on leave so I deputised

Randall Davidson, Archbishop of
Canterbury.

for him. It was a tense moment fraught with potential greatness when hand grasped hand, and
eye met eye. Words were superfluous. I must say I liked the old man and was much impressed.
He seemed less of the diplomat and more of the Father in God than I had expected.

(The Revd Pat Leonard, Chaplain to the 8th Bn King's Own Royal Lancaster Regt.,
letter of 22 May 1916)[95]

*   *   *

Friday, 19 May 1916

Dearest Mater,
Pettifer is waiting for the post, so I must hurry. All here goes well, except for one great sorrow
in the death of Major Philby, D.S.O. He was and is a great friend of mine, and a great hero of
the true and quiet kind. A shy and gentle man, amazingly brave, and as thoughtful of his men
as if they were his brothers. They simply loved him.[96]

94   Randall Thomas Davidson, Archbishop of Canterbury 1903-1928. He became President of the newly
     founded Toc H in 1920, and in 1922 offered Clayton the vicarage of All Hallows-by-the-Tower
     (London), which has since been the Guild Church of Toc H.
95   Leonard, J. & Leonard-Johnson, P., *The Fighting Padre, Letters from the Trenches 1915-1918 of Pat
     Leonard DSO*, p. 74.
96   For Major Philby's story: see p. 325.

On Wednesday the Archbishop confirmed four of his men (the Sergt. who got the D.C.M. was one of them),[97] and about two hours after he was killed in front of the front line. It was by his special arrangement that they were left with transport lines for their Confirmation Classes, while the regiment went up. The eventful Wednesday was a great success here, about 150 Chaplains gathering in the garden and having talk, tea, and Service. After they had gone, we had the Confirmation of 37 Candidates. Cantuar was perfectly delightful, and as simple as a Mission preacher with them.

I kept most of my chaps – 10 of them out of 14 – here the night by special leave. They slept in the garden, after a wonderful little preparation service late at night, and there were about 20 at their First Communion at 7.15 a.m. on Thursday.

Now we are trying to get Neville's new House in order – it's a splendid place and only four doors away. It's badly wanted – I had 76 Officers on my hands last night – over 50 for breakfast – the Staff are almost off their legs. But it all emphasises the need of the new house.

Much love,
Philip BC

R.I.P.
Harold P. Philby
Major, 2nd Bn York and Lancaster Regiment
17 May 1916 – Age 28 – Hop Store Cemetery (Vlamertinge), I.A.16

*   *   *

Wednesday, 24 May 1916
a CCS

Dearest Mater
My old "thorn in the flesh" – the malaria business – has suddenly laid me by the leg again, and after finishing a fine Sunday at Talbot House, I collapsed with annoying suddenness, and am now here for a few hours, en route as last Feb., I expect, for No.14 General at Wimereux. They say it'll take at least a fortnight. The most miserable part of this miserable business is that dear Neville was just wading into his new work, and now will be left with all mine to do as well. I wish you would write to him and apologise for the broken-reediness of Tubby.

I think you'll be safe to write to 14 G.H. & I shall long to hear.

Your loving son,
Philip

*   *   *

97   The four men were Sgt. David Thomas Hazelhurst, Cpl. John Hollies, L/Cpl. James Field and Pte. James Arthur Wyard. The first three survived the war. Wyard died on 20 May 1918, age 27, and is buried in Ipswich Old Cemetery (Suffolk, UK).

May 24th – Prince of Wales visits Toc H[98]
(Diary Cpl. Len Ashdown, R.A.M.C.)

I am very proud to share with a few here this evening an early friendship at Oxford with Gilbert Talbot, whose father and brother stand beside me and after whom Talbot House was first named. I share with hundreds here, and thousands more that you represent, an affectionate remembrance of the Old House in 'Pop' … I am sure that none of us who remember the Old House will ever forget it.

(Edward, Prince of Wales, Toc H Birthday Festival, 15.12.1922)

*   *   *

Edward, Prince of Wales.

98   In September 1915, Edward, Prince of Wales, was appointed to the staff of Major-General Lord Cavan. It was under the auspices of the latter as GOC Guards Division and GOC XIV Corps that he served for most of the remaining period of the war. It was Cavan who brought the Prince to Talbot House. On one occasion he left his name on the Communicants' Roll. On another, he presented the House with a large Belgian painting of peasants in a field praying for the souls of the fallen, the latter appearing ghost-like in the sky above. The Prince became the Patron of the newly-founded Toc H in 1921. At its first Birthday Festival in 1922, he donated the "Prince's Lamp" to the movement. From this 'parent' lamp of all others, the lamps of the new Toc H branches all over the world were to be lit for many years to come.

14 Gen. Hosp.
Thursday, 25 May 1916

Dearest Mater,
As I prophesied, the hospital train repeated the history of my February escapade and brought me to the same floor, almost the same room, in the same hospital looking out towards Folkestone. The sisters have changed, and some of the orderlies, but the doctor is the same and plunged into a discussion of the first volumes of Gibbon[99] at the point where we had broken off before.

The malaria is rapidly declining, but unfortunately, I've got a bit of an extra and rather a painful one in an acute dose of 'shingles', a rotten kind of inflammation along my right side. It apparently has no known cause, except the general run-downedness; which is the more queer as I felt as fit as a fiddle till Sunday night. There's not the slightest danger attached to it, but I'm afraid it may take some time. Meanwhile the doctor is so pleased with it that he's gone to get the photographer! It's an ill wind, etc.

I'm afraid the whole business will be another 3 wasted weeks, during which Neville will have to cope single handed. The one clear fact is that when I do go back, it will be to only half of Talbot House – the men's half; and Neville taking the Officers in the new house will give me a real chance of taking things easily.

Much love to all,
Your own son,
Philip

*   *   *

From Neville Talbot to Tubby
29 May 1916

Dear Tubby
It's very late and I'm doggers but I am glad to hear from you. Daylight is showing all round. I'm off to buy things tomorrow. I wish I had a clearer idea of what you had ordered. I'm sending on your letter now that I know where you are.

The staff will have to go sooner or later but I am fighting for Godley and Kirkland.

We had beastly shelling yesterday (Sunday).[100] I was up at Elverdinghe with H.A. A high explosive landed in garden just opposite men's latrine – house spattered – a Canadian mortally wounded in hall – a bit driven through your folding doors and through window on street. Hambling had the wind up – he has gone on leave. Must go to bed.

Bless you
N.S. Talbot

---

99   Edward Gibbon (1737-1794) was an English historian and MP. His most important work, *The History of the Decline and Fall of the Roman Empire*, was published in six volumes between 1776 and 1788. This celebrated work is known for the quality and irony of its prose, its use of primary sources, and its open criticism of organised religion.
100 On 28 May 1916, the Town Major's diary states: "4.15 p.m. to 4.50 p.m.: Bombardment – 2 guns – about 36 shells; casualties 2 O.R. killed – 15 O.R. wounded – 2 Belgian soldiers wounded, 6 civilians wounded."

R.I.P.
A Canadian Soldier
Known unto God
28 May 1916 – mortally wounded at Talbot House

* * *

From Arthur Pettifer to Tubby
Arthur Pettifer, B.E.F.
1 June 1916

Dear Mr Clayton,
In answer to your most welcome letter, Mr Talbot, myself and all the staff are overjoyed to hear you are going on so nicely and they all send their love to you and are just dying to see you back again, but please allow me to tell you to be quite contented looking at the sea – that will do you a lot of good. The lads will hold the fort all right until you come back. Bombing as you speak about was not much. I have sent book, ties and pin, and also a photo of the old General in war paint. Sergt. Godley has returned from leave and enjoyed himself immensely and sends kind regards to you. The wife and children send their love to you, and they have heard from Miss Clayton,[101] and when she comes back to London they are going to tea. But I think you and me will have our tea in P.O.P. …
  I remain,
  Yours sincerely,
  General

* * *

No sooner ensconced in Talbot House than an aeroplane dropped bombs blowing in windows.
(Capt. C.W. Bayne-Jardine, 81st Battery, R.F.A., diary 1 June 1916)

* * *

14 General Hospital
Saturday, 10 June 1916

Dearest Mater,
I got a charming letter from Anderson the S.C.F. of 2nd Army last night, to say he had seen Bishop Gwynne and they had decided between them I wasn't fit to go back to Pop yet. So they proposed to give me temporary work somewhere here. This is of course a fearful blow for me, and also I know for Neville. I have written to ask that the sentence may be revoked, but doubt its being done. I have also asked that if they won't let me go back yet, I may be allowed to take my fortnight due at the end of my years' service, and come home for the rest of June from my discharge here next week. This is more probable, and if it works I may be home by Saturday next. Don't alter any plans of going to London etc. for me, as it's quite uncertain still for a few days.

---

101 Tubby's elder sister, Isobel, who had a flat in London.

Your loving son
(in haste to catch post)
Philip

*   *   *

Officers' Club
Boulogne-sur-Mer
Tuesday, 13 June 1916

Dearest Mater,
I got discharged (from hospital, not the Army) this afternoon, and am going back to Talbot House tonight for 36 hours, just to get some kit, and arrange various things with N.S.T. After that I return here, take duty on Sunday, as they are very shorthanded, and come across on Monday's boat all being well. I shall be home till July 2nd, all being well.
    Excuse this horrible nib.
    A great joy to be out of jail.
    Your loving son,
    Philip

I'm travelling up with poor old Mellish V.C.[102] tonight; what an awful holiday he had! We shall sleep at T.H. in the early morning.

*   *   *

Last Supper
In January I had discovered a most valuable ornament in an old Hop Store in the Rue d'Ypres in Poperinghe – a great oaken carving of the "Last Supper". It was said to have been in a private collection in a house in Ypres and brought to Poperinghe for safety. It came presumably from some Flemish Church, and dates, I understand, probably from the early 18th century. It is a fine though unfinished workmanship. I purchased it from the *avocat* of Mr. Flamand of Ypres on 16 June for the nominal sum of 75 francs on the understanding that it was to remain always in the Chapel of Talbot House. So anxious were we for its safety that I brought it home with me on leave, carrying it in my sleeping bag and valise, and it was deposited in the War Chapel at St. Mary's Portsea.[103]
                                                                                                    (P.B. Clayton)

102 Rev Edward Noel Mellish (1880-1962). Attached to the 4th Bn Royal Fusiliers; first chaplain VC; awarded for bravery at St Eloi in March 1916.
103 Tubby was a curate there. Following the war, the 'Last Supper', together with the other furniture from the Upper Room, was placed in the Chapel at Toc H Mark I, London. In 1930, after Lord Wakefield of Hythe had purchased and donated the property to the newly founded Talbot House Association, the carving was returned, finding a permanent place on the renewed second floor landing where the chapel was originally located during the first eight weeks of Talbot House's life. Why the carving was never finished remains unknown. Did the artist leave his creation unfinished because of turbulent times? Did he deliberately leave it in its 'embryonic state'? Did he come to an untimely end?

*   *   *

From Tubby's mother to Arthur Pettifer
Little Hatchett,
East Boldre,
Brockenhurst
June 1916

Dear Pettifer
I want to send you a word about my son.
He looks well & is cheerful & I am sure
we owe much of this to you & I want to
thank you. He is having a really good time.
His brother from the War Office is here
& they have capital times together. He is
now out with his dear dog for a walk in the
forest. He often tells us about you & your
dangerous walks together. I am sending
you a pipe which I hope you will like.
Yours very gratefully & wishing you every
blessing & your family at home
    Isabel Byard Clayton

*   *   *

Tubby at Little Hatchett.

From Neville Talbot to Tubby
Officers' Club
23 June 1916

My Dear Tub.
Things are going there is no doubt.

Plumer lunched today … a very proper & kindly old man. Haig was hereabouts, but he didn't look in. Had better have a sign out – 'A good pull up for Generals & Red Tabs'.

Shall have clearly to pay T.H. a good deal for things we have taken. Have tried religiously to keep a list of it all. If you see or think of any other good garden game… roll on.

Tubby, I am afraid you are in for 2 months at Boulogne. I had a distinctly stuffy letter from Anderson in answer to a long one of mine – the letter = orders is orders.

Bullock hasn't moved in yet from P[roven] but will… He has moved in to the old Officers writing room[104] – a good move I think. He is a good fellow & will I've no doubt effect things. It was amusing to hear him say as a new comer that the General was "quite allright". What an outrage on our ancient sanctities.

The officers latrine at T.H. is offensive in the heat. Am closing it down. 1st consignment of Cox's vegetables[105] coming up tonight. Such a good evensong tonight. Your works live on & we'll keep the homefires burning.

Ever most affectionately.
N.S. Talbot

* * *

June 28
Little Hatchetts
Dear Pettifer
I wanted to send 2 pipes
& 2 hankies by my son but
he was too lazy! So here
they are with my best thanks
for your unceasing care of
him. P.S. he told us of
~~the Pulpit & by the~~
table.
Thank you many times
& may the God of the True
bring you home safely
to Old Blighty once
more in peace
Isabel Byard Clayton

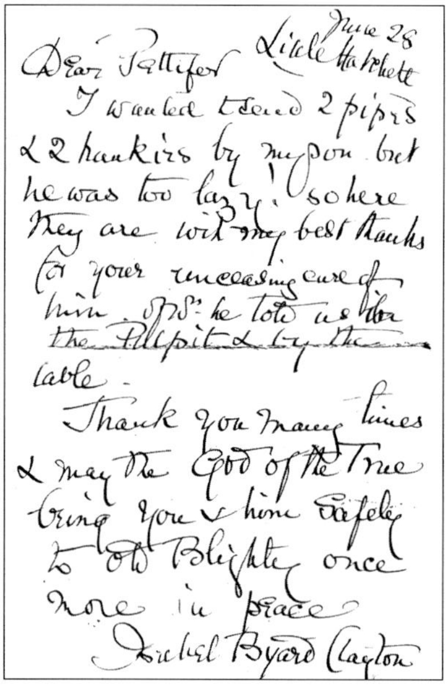

104 A first-floor room vacated by the creation of the Officers' Club.
105 Cox's Boulogne, commissioned to ship vegetables to the Officers' Club.

*   *   *

British Officers' Club
Boulogne
3 July 1916

Dearest Mater,
Just to tell you of my prospects. The A.C.'s Dept. still sling with cruel kindness to the belief that I need rest and change, and therefore for a month or so to come I am to be Chaplain to No. 7 Stationary Hospital, a big hotel which overlooks the harbour here. It is entirely an Officers' hospital – a queer irony of fate – but has had two splendid Chaplains up till now so I find everything built up already, and a really nice M.O.'s mess, and Sisters Staff. So I must just learn 'therewith to be content' as the school patron saint says and try and keep things going after a fashion. Severe as the disappointment is, and the separation for the time from Neville, it's plainly the time for hospital work rather than recreation places.
   Therefore No. 7 Stationary Hospital or c/o A.C.G.'s office, Boulogne will find me equally well as an address. I'm much more cheerful about it, now that I've seen the hospital, the personnel, and moreover the convoys coming in. What I really dreaded was enforced idleness. I'm also Chaplain to the Red Cross Society here, among whom there are many interesting folk.
   Now to bed,
   Your loving son,
   Philip

*   *   *

From Neville Talbot to Tubby
12 July 16

My Very Dear Tubby,
They have been shelling this place horridly for the last two days – 2 officers killed in the square – but the two houses survive.[106] If they go on, it will play the deuce with the Club – at the same time on coming back from Yps today where I had been RGA-ing[107] I kept wondering whether I should find everything kaput & instead found our luscious dinner going on Savoy wise with a band in the garden.
   I feel exceedingly miserable about you – all the more that I am afraid everything has come about through an unwise phrase of mine in a letter to the Bishop wherein I expressed a doubt as to whether this place & you did agree as to health – but it was never in my mind that you'd be hung up in this maddening manner. … In fact I should certainly tell the Bishop that I wouldn't go on here unless you can take up again the work you have made.

---

106 The Diary of the Town Major records that on 12 July alone some 150 shells landed on the town.
       Casualties – killed: 2 officers and 6 other ranks; wounded: 1 officer, 15 other ranks and 1 civilian.
       Much damage caused to property.
107 Visiting heavy batteries in action.

OORLOG 1914-1916

42. POPERINGHE — Engelsche troepen op de Londensche Autobussen ingebracht
Troupes anglaises emmenées sur les Autobus Londoniens
British troops brought in London autobusses

My people strongly want me to take the fortnight to which I am entitled as recontractor on August 21st – that suits my father & it would be a very great gain if you could be back in the saddle before then, & I shall work for that. Meanwhile souls are souls even at Boulogne.

… The General is very unhappy about you, and is not I fear quite sure that I have really tried to get you back. Don't come and take your things away – there is no need. Bullock is getting things under way a bit, an N.C.O.'s room[108] prospers, but I don't feel that the place is loved. The maps of Canada & British Isles look superb in the hall. Our (the Club) billiard table has arrived. I rather wish you had included its legs,[109] they would have been only a flea bite of extra weight – the weight of the table is vast & I don't know how to get it up our stairs. The T.H. table hasn't turned up yet. But the station & environs just now is 'no place for boys'[110] as my late R.B. Colonel would say.

The elaborate hammock has arrived, but some pigs sat on it in fours and the bars of the upright have been horridly bent.

A wind fall has come at my request to Talbot House – some mysterious South African garrison found having 500 fr. to dispose of – & I said 'thank you, Billiard Table'. We shall be alright about finance … face Fritz & his souvenirs. My brother has been into the very jaws of things at La Boiselle.[111]

Well Tubby… hold on. Do nothing rash & remember we stand or fall together. …

Ever very affectionately,

N.S. Talbot

*   *   *

108 Required by Guards Division.
109 Tubby had ordered a table only, to rest on an ordinary table.
110 Poperinge station was under heavy shelling at that time.
111 Rev. Edward Keble Talbot, M.C., Senior Chaplain 8th Division. When 3rd Corps (incl. 8th Division) of the 4th Army attacked the German line at Ovillers and La Boisselle on 1 July 1916, they were facing formidable opposition.

19 July 1916

Dearest Mater,

…

Pop. is having a very bad time indeed – nearly a week's continual bombardment, and the town is now virtually closed down. I've not heard from Neville again, and am rather anxious about him, the Staff, and the dear old house. Not to mention all my belongings there![112]

    Your loving son,

    Philip

* * *

From Neville Talbot to Tubby
c/o 4th Labour Bn R.E.
B.E.F.
24 July 1916

My Dear Tubby

It is hard to write freely under the censorship. Everything is in flux. T.H. is at present pretty well a desert owing to absence from troops billetted here. We must simply await developments. I think that if quiet continues things will fill up again. Bullock is off on leave in a day or two but I can keep my eye on T.H. for the present.

    The Club is reviving, & if my opposite number in the crowd which is succeeding your relative's[113] plays up, I can hand it & T.H. over to him. But of course the staff at the Club will have to change entirely. Godley & Co. are going to be claimed & the remainder are actually off tomorrow. I shall simply say nothing about Pettifer, whom I think his Division has forgotten – & he will I hope remain at T.H. for your return (I

Neville Talbot and the staff of Talbot House and The Officers' Club, June – July 1916. Sgt. George Godley on the left of Talbot.

112 Tubby was particularly worried about the Font and the Communion Set. The Font, which had been used for his own Christening, was sent out by his mother to No. 16 General Hospital and then came with him to Poperinge. The Communion Set was a present from his Uncle Horace.

113 Tubby's second cousin, the Earl of Cavan (GOC XIV Corps). Both houses were taken over by VIII Corps, Rev. C.S. Ensell, DACG moving in.

shan't move I suppose for a fortnight). I don't feel really well again yet & everybody is rather miserable.

...

Ever yours,
N.S. Talbot

*   *   *

From Neville Talbot to Tubby
26 July 1916

Dearest Tubby
Your letter just in. It is a very beastly situation. I don't know how to better it. The order for me to move with all the rest came from your relative. I suppose I have to comply. I shall stay here till I can hand over this show properly to the successors to my crowd.

I hope that Bishop Gwynne's promise to me to let you back to TH at the end of August will hold good. It is foul the disruption of everything... but there is the house and the men are coming back to it bit by bit now and I believe you ought to take it up again for another winter campaign.

I am afraid you will be cursing me over the bills. Can you crown all your excellencies by sorting things out?

I am anxious that you shouldn't be out of pocket over everything. My sister has got £ 35 collected for Talbot House – for the moment I've told her to hang on to it. There is plenty of money at T.H. but I summon you to let me know how much should go to refund you. Well goodbye.

Ever affectionately,
N.S. Talbot

*   *   *

From Neville Talbot to Tubby
30 July 1916 – anniversary of Gilbert's death

Dearest Tubby
I have written a last testimony to the Bishop. I can't do more. ... There is the House – it is full again of men. It calls for you. You ought to do it – it's what you are made for. If health disallows then hand it to another for good. The present situation – Johnston for Bullock for you – is intolerable for all concerned.[114]

---

114 Rev. Bullock having gone on leave, Rev. Johnston replaced him. In the following weeks, Neville made several vehement appeals to Bishop Gwynne to allow Tubby back "to rescue Talbot House from being merely a coffee bar with papers and draughts" ... "The hordes of homeless lads crowded in billets," he wrote, "want a homey place with a friend at home to them and a quiet and beautiful place to worship in. It is qualitative, intensive, personal work that is needed." Tubby was eventually allowed to take up his old job in early October 1916.

The difficulty is the rush of things. I lost some of my chosen staff and have had very poor replacements and with changing conditions prevalent everything has been rather a nightmare. … You mustn't mind about me. Cavan insists. … There is the House – you made it – it's what you can do. It is full of men again. You owe them a great 2nd campaign there. I don't know how long I shall be here. I have somehow to hand over to the new Corps.

N.S. Talbot

Voks hangs on and I do hope that the Buffs have forgotten the General.

* * *

From Neville Talbot to Tubby
2 August 1916

Ever hourly desired Tubby
I am just off up to Sanctuary Wood to see if I can find any traces of Gilbert's Grave before I go. It will take a little getting at – but I have all a night and the willing help of Canadian staff people. The site was fought over and is now I think just behind our line.

Ensell, my opposite number in the new crush has arrived – old, Tubby, and a little generally on the ebb. But his General[115] wants him to take over the Club and as his General is full of uncaged energy he has to take it on. I have had no answer yet from the Bishop about you and haven't much hope. As things are, everyone has promised me that you come back on Sept. 4th.

I want to say this – if you do come back be very Christian and cooperate as much as you can with the Divisional Chaplain who has troops in the town. He ought to have a room where he can see folk … and I think you ought to take away all ground for the feeling that TH is for other chaplains like a YMCA show in the sense that 'their men' go there and they can't get at them.

What a ragged end to our cooperation: be very good and pray for me and we'll start something in those promised other cities beyond the veil.

… I shan't get away before Sunday so I think if you answer to 4/Lab. Bt it would get.

Ever yours affectionately,
N.S. Talbot

* * *

Wooden grave marker of Gilbert Talbot, preserved in a beautifully decorated shrine in the Upper Room.

115   Lt.-Gen. Sir Aylmer Hunter-Weston (1864-1940) GOC VIII Corps.

Whilst at No. 7 Stationary Hospital, Tubby also received a letter from his closest friend, Capt. Cecil Rushton of No. 8 Squadron RFC. He had flown during the initial stages of the Battle of the Somme and narrowly escaped death following a crash.

No. 8 Squadron
R.F.C.
2 August 1916

Dear old thing,
Why, oh why, did I not know you were in Boulogne? I passed through last week on my way back from leave, and had no idea you were there. I may say at once that I do *not* fire at infantry from 100 feet as insinuated in your letter. I have only had one day of low altitude flying, and that will last me some little time. I think I told you that we had a smash some weeks ago and broke every single part of the machine except the tail and the rudder, and were not in the least hurt, or even shaken. It was a million to one escape as we fell a thousand feet on to the ground – otherwise no excitements, and rather slack just now. I do a little work in the office here for the C.O. as well as flying, as I hate hanging about doing nothing when there is nothing doing in the air.
     Do write if you get any time.
     Yours ever,
     Cecil Rushton

*   *   *

From Neville Talbot to Tubby
7 August 1916

Dearest Tubby,
I am handing over all right. It's bound to be a Corps to Corps business and you will find Ensell entrenched – but I have baptized him with streams of your praises and you will always be welcome I'm sure. Ensell is a very good fellow… responsive to younger energy – an unmistake-able gent. He'll chat away with officers well. He is Rev C.S.E. O.C. c/o 4th Lab etc. etc.
     I am afraid the House is again pretty empty but your substitutes seem to have no idea of friendly tea parties. We have had no more shells. …
     I go off by the early train on Thursday morning with the remainder of the staff – tho' I might get a car. … I am hoping operations permitting to go on leave on August 21 – I am entitled to a fortnight on signing on again. If I do go we must meet at B[oulogne] & I'll try and let you know when I pass through. My last appeal to Gwynne has failed. So nothing now will be done here before September. Bless you – you know my address XIV Corps HQrs.
     Ever yours
     N.S. Talbot

*   *   *

From Arthur Pettifer to Tubby
239 A. Pettifer, B.E.F.
12 August 1916

My Dear Sir,
Don't be alarmed, the old General is still alive and kicking. I think it is almost time I answered your letter, don't you? Never mind, you are a long way from me and cannot hit me – Ah, ah! Well, myself and young Vok are very pleased you are coming back soon. You can bet we shall be pleased to see you again. Of course you know there has been a great change to both houses since you left us. Sergt. Godley and his men have left us, also Mr Talbot, and Mr Talbot told me he had a very hard struggle with my Colonel to keep me. Fancy you coming back and finding me in the trenches, once more popping at the boshes! Old Fritz has not sent us any iron rations over for four weeks now, he generally pays a visit about every six weeks, so I suppose we can soon look out for him. I feel sorry you are so lonely there. Never mind, it is a long way to Tipperary, I mean a long lane that has no turning. Sergt. Godley and the lads all wished to be remembered to you before they went. Myself and young Vok send our love to you and don't forget when you come back – to bed early. Will see that you don't get knocked up again in a hurry.
Will close now with love from the old General.[116]

*   *   *

7th Stationary Hospital
20 August 1916,
Sunday after tea

Dearest Mater,
…
I enclose more letters from Neville, which you will see make the situation still more perplexing. Talbot House with Neville no longer in the neighbourhood loses much of its attractiveness.[117] I shall just wait and do what I'm told as best I can. One can't expect everything as one would like it during a war! Probably I was enjoying my life too much, a wicked thing to do out here; and this is a just nemesis. Anyhow, I've settled down quietly and happily here, and like the job. This morning, after a record number of Communicants in various wards, besides the 6.30 and seven Celebrations, I wasn't altogether sorry that both parades had to be cancelled. I went for a long walk on the breakwater, made friends with a young M.F.P. (Military Foot Police) who had been gassed at Loos, and watched the Boulonnais sabbath-breakers trying to catch fish.
   Now I must write some letters for patients, and then a Confirmation Class for 2 wounded officers, and a short Evensong for the Red Cross at 7 p.m. So you'll forgive short letter. Otherwise I would dilate on the fishing, for the guv's amusement.
   Love to all,
   Philip B.C.

---

116 This document does not contain a single punctuation mark. For a contemporary depiction of Pettifer's 'agony of composition', see p. 307.
117 Tubby later described it as "a spiritual failure, merely becoming an E.F. Canteen Officers' Club".

*   *   *

7 Stationary Hospital
Monday, 28 August 1916

Dearest Mater,
When I got down to the office this morning, I found my transfer back to Talbot House had come through, and I return thither in high spirits on Thursday. I've enjoyed my time here, especially the last month of it, since I found my feet, but it's altogether too cushy a spot to settle down in, while the war is on. The work is ideal for a more than middle-aged man, but I feel ashamed to be here, now that I'm as fit as a fiddle again. Of course, I shall miss Neville terribly, but 'c'est la guerre', and I'll try and carry on without him. Pettifer and Vokins are friends worth having, and not a few of the lightly-wounded here belong to them parts and are back there again. Indeed, I travel up with one ex-patient, a great friend of mine, on Thursday. So all is merry and bright. Incidentally, I shall now get leave before Christmas, all being well, which I shouldn't get down here. Please see that my address alters accordingly c/o 4th Labour Batt. R.E. as before.
    Your very fit, cheerful, and loving son,
    Philip

P.S. There are now several Hampshire units in the neighbourhood of Talbot House, so I hope to have a point of contact that way.

*   *   *

Talbot House,
c/o 4th Labour Batt. R.E.
Monday, 4 September 1916

Dearest Mater,
I reached here on Saturday, and saw my first two old friends out of the window before the train stopped – two M.F. Police who waved encouragingly. Pettifer was on the platform; he is my great stand-by. I came down to the Officers' Club and found Ensell (Talbot's successor) who was extraordinarily nice. There is still however a difficulty over Talbot House, as the 29th Div. are short of a chaplain, so for the time being I'm going to the 87th Brigade, and go up the line this afternoon, taking Pettifer of course with me. We shall live in a cellar for a week, and be as happy as kings. …
    I shall think of you all in all your doings. I'll write more from up beyond.
    Your son with much love,
    Philip.

*   *   *

Thursday night, 7 September 1916

Dearest Mater,

As I was foolish enough to tell you yesterday of my prospective trip this morning, I had better write and relieve any anxiousness I might have raised. I went right round, beyond water sandbags and cheerful North countrymen. I saw less of war than I see in T.H. Not a shot was fired from the other side anywhere in our neighbourhood, and I had several charming views over the top, which, as in Bruce Bairnsfather,[118] presented a dreary enough landscape. The war seems a very onesided business just here at present, and apart from the fact that one lives in a cellar protected by the ruins of the house above it, there's not much that is romantic. The place is an utter contrast in this aspect to its condition when I saw it just ten months ago, when one ran risks anywhere in its neighbourhood. One can now go country walks in broad daylight along fields and lanes to the East, where before the boldest travellers only walked in bye-ways. The cellar shakes as I write, but only with the detonations of our own busy big guns. In short, the Hun is a very chastened creature; and not the man he was. Probably he still has some kicks left in him, and things may be nasty again; but never as they once were; I am greatly attracted by the fascination of it all, and wish I could tranfer Talbot House in lots to the locality – there would be lots to be done with it hereabouts. I stumbled tonight on a dear old friend – a bobby who like myself was here last autumn and has just come back. Alas! his old pal – and a great friend of mine – was killed near Talbot House on Sunday, with his leave papers in his pocket, and his banns called for the third time at home. What precise position they will give me permanently is still undecided, but next week will probably see it settled. Meanwhile, I'm quite happy and very fit.
  Much love,
  Philip B.C.

Stuart[119] would love this house – Pettifer climbed what's left of the staircase today and found a Flemish Bible in the wreck of what was once a bedroom floor.

R.I.P.

Oliver C. Haines
L/Cpl., Corps of Military Police (Foot Branch)
3 September 1916 – Age 22 – Poperinghe New Military Cemetery, II.G.9

---

118 Humour contributed to the maintenance of troop morale. This concept appears to have been grasped by the British high command. Lt. Bruce Bairnsfather (1st Bn Royal Warwickshire Regiment), who arrived at the Ploegsteert Wood sector in November 1914, was the greatest soldier-cartoonist of the war. His best-known character was "Old Bill", a simple soldier with a magnificent walrus moustache.
119 Tubby's niece, daughter of his elder brother 'Jack'.

Oliver Haines and his pal, Harold Cook, had signed the Visitors' Book at Talbot House on 21 December 1915 with the following poem:

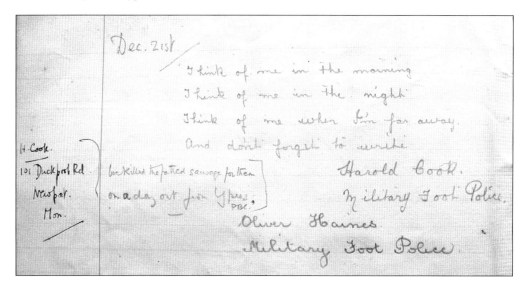

*   *   *

Talbot House
c/o A.P.O. S.4
20 September 1916

Dearest Mater,

I can't even now write the letter you deserve, but just send my love and the new more direct address; the other will now only find me more slowly.

I've just come back from dinner with Cavan's successor, who thanks to Neville knew all about me, and was most unaccountably kind and eager to help in all sorts of ways. This of course makes the outlook particularly rosy for the winter work, and Neville Talbot's successor at the Club is also one of the kindest and most excellent Regulars I have met. A third and intimate friend is Captain Browne, a doctor attached to the Railway Troops

Leonard Browne.

in my parish, who has much time to spare, and who comes in every morning to read the Acts[120] with me and then do the house accounts.[121]

So I am blessed with more help than I deserve in every way. The House is going quietly but very well; and my new units are quite delightful.

I'll write more fully in a day or so; but mustn't stipulate.

Your loving son,

Philip

*   *   *

Sunday 1 October 1916
6.30 p.m.: service. Preacher: Rev. P.B. Clayton.
Choir first instituted, & Psalm & Vesper Hymns introduced
(Register of Services)

*   *   *

Talbot House
c/o 4th Labour Batt. RE
Wednesday, 4 October 1916

Dearest Mater,

I'm back here for the afternoon, waiting for Anderson, the A.C.G., who I think and hope is going to set matters right about my permanent job here. I find the house full to overflowing of goodfellows, many fellow-countrymen of my own, who are I think going to be really fine Material for work among.

Meanwhile, after Anderson has come, I shall board a lorry to the half way town, and then walk back to Pettifer and the cellar. Tomorrow the Major of the regiment I am temporarily with is going kindly to take me round the trenches to have a look at the lads. Everything is very quiet in these parts.

I hope to be back working here in about a week's time. Stick to this address.

Your loving son,

Philip

*   *   *

---

120 Richard Belward Rackham, *The Acts of the Apostles*, London, Methuen, 1904. The volume still in the Talbot House library. After obtaining a First in Theology at Oxford in 1909, Tubby became a research student at the Deanery of Westminster. There he met Rackham, a brilliant New Testament scholar, who convinced him to take holy orders.

121 "Browno" acted as Talbot House treasurer from September 1916 to August 1917 when he was invalided home. It was he who invented the famous motto over the door of the Chaplain's Room which ran: "All rank abandon ye who enter here." He also played a large part in running the CEMS branch, from which many men registered as ordination candidates. Back in Great Britain, Browne became a valuable ally to the Army Ordination Candidates scheme and from 1919 onwards played a prominent role in the Toc H movement. In 1930 he became a member of the Old House Committee and acted as a financial administrator during the renovation works to accommodate pilgrimages.

Talbot House
A.P.O. S.4
Wednesday, 11 October 1916

Dearest Mater,
I must again content myself with a word or so only, as it's late; and a rigid time for bed must be kept, if I'm going to do what I want to do here this winter. Thanks to Macmillan, the Ordinands scheme has made great progress, and a memorandum we drew up between us is now in the hands of the Archbishop for distribution and action at home.[122] Some of my best candidates have been killed on the Somme, but I suppose that that is only another and higher form of Ordination.

I spent Monday night with Gwynne, who was perfectly charming; and I feel that, please God, this House is going to do some good work between now and Christmas. The keenness of the Church life is simply overwhelming. I've another jolly bunch of Confirmation candidates in preparation now.

Tomorrow night I spend as usual – every Thursday – with my dear R.G.A. folk, who are really splendid – a service at 6.30, a Cinema at 8 (a baby Pathescope I have borrowed) and a Celebration early next morning, before I come back here again.

I expect to come on leave in November, please.
Much love,
Your son,
Philip

*   *   *

"Talbot House, B.E.F."
A.P.O. S.4
Saturday, 14 October 1916

Dearest Mater,
All the post seems out of joint. I got your last two letters yesterday and today in reversed order. All goes very well here. We have got a big billet facing on the garden for our new big Church,[123] but are going to keep the old attic Church intact for Celebrations. Also kind fairies are putting in electric light all over the house, which makes an enormous difference to one's comfort and labour.

---

122 Rev John Macmillan, formerly chaplain to the Archbishop of Canterbury, served as a padre on Bishop Gwynne's staff at St. Omer, where he acted as a liaison between Davidson and Gwynne. By 1916 the issue of vocations to the Anglican ministry became one of real concern. Many ordination students had joined the forces during 1914-15. In April 1915 *The Challenge* published an article calling for mass recruitment from the armed forces for the ministry. Tubby was amongst the first to make this vision a reality. Some two hundred officers and men put their names on the roll at Talbot House.

123 The need for a space that could house larger congregations became pressing especially as Tubby intended to strike a blow for the National Mission to be held at Talbot House from 9 December onwards. A doorway was eventually knocked through the end wall of the neighbour's hopstore and an entrance staircase constructed. The new Church Hall was opened on Sunday 3 December. The service was attended by 205 men.

I may be home about 10th all being well, but must let National Mission[124] here over-rule my personal predilections as to date.

   Your loving son,
   Philip

* * *

Sunday 15 October 1916
3 p.m.: Confirmation. Preacher: Archbishop of Perth.[125]
(Register of Services)

* * *

Talbot House
A.P.O. S.4
Wednesday, 18 October 1916

Dearest Mater,
Past 11 p.m. so bed looms large, after a long, happy and I hope useful day.
   The House very full, and jolly. Tonight there sleep here besides the normal Staff:

1.   2 Officers' servants going on leave;
2.   2 Officers' servants not going on leave;
3.   An old Australian, who came and gave himself up to me as a deserter, and for whom the escort has not yet come – a sad case; his only thought is for his old mother.[126]
4.   2 R.E. boys sick, and sent here to convalesce by the O.C. of their unit. One is my organist, and the other my choirmaster.

All these are now between blankets, and I must follow their example.
   Much love,
   Philip

---

124 Launched in autumn 1916, "The National Mission of Repentence and Hope" was a Church of England attempt to respond to the spiritual needs of the wartime population. It was also intended as a powerful reply to a number of prominent critics who argued that the established church was not rising to the demands of the national crisis.

125 Charles O.L. Riley, Anglican Chaplain-General of the Australian Imperial Force. In the autumn of 1916 he visited the Western Front. On the return voyage his troopship SS *Ivernia* was torpedoed amidships in the Mediterranean, resulting in 130 deaths. Riley lost everything but his clothing ferrying a lifeboat of 50 survivors to an approaching trawler.

126 According to Philip Gosse, MO 69th Field Ambulance (23rd Division) "it was nothing extraordinary for a deserter to go to Clayton, for he was the recognised friend and confessor of all soldiers who were down on their luck or in need of help or advice." That very same morning, at dawn, 28-year-old Pte. Albert Botfield (9th South Staffordshire Regiment) was executed for cowardice in the courtyard of Poperinge Town Hall. A few weeks after this letter was written, Tubby would visit Gosse to discuss what should be done about a shell-shocked lad who had deserted and come to Talbot House. See p. 330.

*   *   *

From Neville Talbot to Tubby
Headquarters Reserve Army
20 October 1916

Dear Tubby,
Just arrived here – feel a very new boy.[127] I saw Dawkins go through my Dressing Station, not I thought mortally hit – broken thigh – but very exhausted. Go forth Christian Soul! Is Gardner[128] killed too? O dear! …
    So glad about Talbot H. religious prosperity.
    I must somehow get to Pop.
    Ever affectionately,
    N.S. Talbot

    Be good about bed
    Love to the General

R.I.P.
Godfrey D. Gardner
2/Lt., 9 Suffolk Regiment
13 September 1916 – Age 34 – Thiepval Memorial, Pier and Face 1 C and 2 A

Guy S. Dawkins
2/Lt., 2 Scots Guards
25 September 1916 – Age 27 – La Neuville British Cemetery (Corbie), II.F.18

*   *   *

Memories of Cpl. Jacob Bennett and Lt. Guy Dawkins, 2nd Scots Guards
Cpl. Jacob Bennett came with his Platoon Officer, Lt. Guy Dawkins, to their Communion at Talbot House whenever the 2nd Scots Guards were back from the line. Both men had the loveliest characters. The day after they were out of the line, Lt. Dawkins, who held the L.A.C. Championship for "Putting the Weight", and was at the same time no mean organist, used to walk up to Cpl. Bennett, and the following colloquy ensued:

Lt. Dawkins: "Corporal Bennett!"
Cpl. Bennett: "Sir?"
Lt. Dawkins (quietly):   "I'm going to Talbot House tomorrow morning early. Would you like to come with me?"

---

127 Talbot had just been appointed assistant chaplain-general to Reserve or Fifth Army (GOC General
    Sir Hubert Gough).
128 According to Tubby, he played the groanbox "divinely" in the Upper Room at Easter. See 24 April
    1916 correspondence.

(then fortissimo, as other Guardsmen passed): "STAND TO ATTENTION WHEN AN OFFICER IS SPEAKING TO YOU!"

(quietly): "Are you coming, Cpl. Bennett?"

Cpl. Bennett: "Yes, Sir."

They came and knelt together in the Upper Room.

Guy Dawkins died of wounds on the Somme. When I say "died of wounds", I exaggerate. Rather he died of heartbreak. The Corporal wept for him. He loved him like a father his son.

(P.B. Clayton)

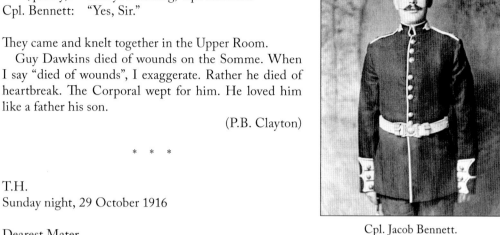

Cpl. Jacob Bennett.

*   *   *

T.H.

Sunday night, 29 October 1916

Dearest Mater,

A very good day here, and now at 10 p.m. to bed with a jolly week ahead. And the week after, all being well, I shall be home on leave. I should think on Tuesday night 7th November until the following Thursday. If it were not for the National Mission at Portsea, I should not think it right to come.

Much love,

Philip

*   *   *

Thursday night, 16 November 1916

In the semi darkness of a train somewhere

Dearest Mater,

A very peaceful crossing, and several old friends on the boat. One, the O.C. of the H.A. Group I used to be Chaplain to last spring, gave me a lift in his car up to the border, and now I go the last piece in a train. So that by great good luck I shall get in by about 10 p.m. and get a good night's rest, instead of a dreadful railway journey, in the small hours. This makes a lot of difference to my outlook. We had a glorious drive, though it was bitterly cold. But coffee, and subsequently some dinner on the station here, has made a new man of me, and I return to T.H. full of vim and vigour. I'm only distressed that I saw so little of you dear folk, "my ain folk."[129] Next time I think I shall just come to Hatchett and stay there, and the primroses will be out.

Your loving son,

Philip

129 Tubby was less than two days at home. He subsequently visited Portsea and was recalled prematurely.

*   *   *

T.H.
Tuesday , 21 November 1916

Dearest Mater,
Your dear letter reached me yesterday – in bed. No need to be alarmed. It was only the Prussian procedure of the Poperinghian Dr. Browne, who discovered I'd got a suspicion of fever and sent me to bed forthwith, stationing Pettifer on guard as with a flaming sword at the door so that I couldn't see anyone. Browne's a thorough fellow; and this morning the temperature's simply scared out of me, but I shall take a day or two easy meanwhile.I caught a chill coming up from Boulogne that bitter night, endless standing about for about four hours next morning while the law's delays took their course. Everybody was very apologetic at two days loss of leave for five minutes evidence – the result I haven't yet heard. T.H. is very flourishing, full to the brim, and a lot of the good wine of the keen boys' club kind of being infused the duller water of the casual passer-by. Not that any of them are really dull, only some of them have got out of the way of sparkling. The Corps Commander[130] came in on Sunday (of all awkward days) but was very nice to make up for it. Here comes Browne! = 10 a.m. when the post goes also.

*   *   *

Saturday, 25 November 1916

Dearest Mater,
In order to throw off the cold or touch of flu or whatever it was, Ensell and Browne between them have insisted on my taking the weekend off, and I am till Monday an inmate of a queer little Corps Rest Station in a village a few miles back. It's rather dull, but not without the usefulness of idleness, in that my letters are getting straighter already.

I shall return to T.H. on Monday, and buckle down to the Mission preparation. One realises from the gratitude with which fellow inmates accept a place far less comfortable than my ordinary life at T.H., what a sybarite life of luxury I normally lead, compared to everyone else.

No need to be in the least worried about me, but please send me a bottle of Byards, please!
Much love,
Your son,
Philip Clayton

*   *   *

Sunday 3 December 1916
6.30 p.m. – New Church Hall opened. Attendance: 205. Preacher: Rev. C.S. Ensell
(Register of Services)

130 Lt.-Gen. Sir Aylmer Hunter-Weston.

* * *

All our saints are with Christ, which is far better – dear Street of the Sherwoords the last I have heard of.

(Neville Talbot to Tubby, letter of 25 October 1916)

Talbot House, A.P.O. S.4, B.E.F.
5 December 1916

Dear Mrs Street
I need scarcely say that I am one of those to whom the life of Major Street was, and always will be, an inspiration that his heroic death only crowns. I had, during my time with the Sixth Division, not a few opportunities of getting to know him well, and his friendship is a thing for which I shall always thank God. Often he has been to the Sacrament in the tiny Church of which I enclose a picture. Indeed, his help and sympathy were largely instrumental in the beginning of Talbot House. It was for us that he brought back that little portable harmonium from leave last winter, and now both he and Lieut. Gardner of the Suffolks, who played it, are in the nearer presence of Him whose true servants they always were. I cannot say how deeply I felt his loss. It was to me like the death of a great-hearted elder brother; but I know well that your sorrow, while far more poignant than that of any other, is yet full of a quiet pride and joy, for both his life and death were alike examples to us all. We remember him daily here before God, with a peaceful thankfulness.
   Yours sincerely,
   P.B. Clayton

R.I.P.
Edmund R. Street
Major, 2 Sherwood Foresters (Notts and Derby Regiment)
15 October 1916 – Age 40 – Grove Town Cemetery (Méaulte, Fr.), I.B.7

* * *

Talbot House, A.P.O. S.4
11 December 1916

Dearest Mater,
I write to you between Jack's birthday and my own, and on the first weekday of our Mission. I'm not certain how old it will make me, and don't much care. A year less or more seems a very minor matter at present ... Dr. Browne may have to go home soon through ill health, but I hope and trust not. Meanwhile the Mission goes well, and Ted Talbot is a real joy. He has a kind of charismatic gift which delights us all, and is one of those happy Christians who really enjoys his religion. I enclose a notice which will help you to follow our doings. The Corps Commander came to the Officers' service on Sunday, which was otherwise badly attended, and was "exceedingly polite" as Gilbert[131] says, about the usefulness of the House, which is now indeed at its zenith of prosperity.

We hope to have a party for Belgian children under 10 (about 30 of them) in the new hall after Christmas.[132]

Last Friday I had an amusing hour or so on my way back from my R.G.A. people, as I found a detachment of them, Cockneys under a town-bred officer, trying to remove the big branch of an old apple-tree which fouled the back line sighting of the guns. We wanted the guv. then badly. After much ineffectual sawing and pulling, I took the law and saw into my own hands, clomb the tree and thanks to my left-handedness, succeeded in sawing where they had failed. One up to the Padre!

I take Ted up this week, with great pride and joy.

Much love, dearest Mater,

Your son,

Philip

* * *

The National Mission
The Mission will be held in Talbot House, Poperinghe, from Dec. 9th – Dec. 17th inclusive.

The Messenger will be the Rev. E.K. Talbot, M.C., of the Community of the Resurrection, Senior Chaplain, 8th Division.

The Service at Talbot House will be as follows:
Dec. 9th, Saturday, 6 p.m. Welcome of the Missioner, and introductory address.

131 From the chorus of Gilbert & Sullivan's "My Gallant Crew, Good Morning".
132 See 'A little treat for the Belgian Kiddies', p. 255.

Rev. Edward ('Ted') Talbot (with cap) at a retreat at St. Eloi, 25 August 1918.

Dec. 10th, Sunday
   6.30 a.m., 7.30 a.m., 11.30 a.m.: Holy Communion, the last being Choral.
   2.30 p.m. Service for Officers
   5.15 p.m. C.E.M.S. Service
   6.30 p.m. Evening Service in the new Church Hall
Dec. 11th – 16th, Monday – Saturday
   Daily Celebration at 7.30 a.m.
   Mission Service each evening at 6 p.m.
Dec. 17th, Sunday
   6.30 a.m., 7.30 a.m., 11.30 a.m.: Holy Communion, the last being Choral.
   2.00 p.m. Confirmation, by Bishop Gwynne, D.C.G.
   5.15 p.m. C.E.M.S. Service
   6.30 p.m. Thanksgiving Service

Units in het neighbourhood of Poperinghe will be given special facilities for attending the Services.
   Corps units further afield will be visited at various centres by the Messenger.
   C.S. Ensell,
   S.C.F. VIIIth Corps

*   *   *

Officers' Club
9 a.m.
Monday, 18 December 1916

Dearest Mater,
As I didn't succeed in writing to you last night after evensong (I had a couple of boys in to supper – a plate of Symington soup, a tin of fruit, Oliver biscuits and cocoa) I am writing here in luxury after breakfast. It is only 6 doors away, and I have generally two meals a day here for which I pay *en pension* 4 fr., having no *menage* of my own at T.H., but on most days I am out a good deal, and get free food from the units upon whom I descend. It's not often that I sit in the Club as now, and look at your four beautiful colour prints on the wall. I wonder if the grateful Bros. with the mysterious patent process would ever stamp up some more samples of their handiwork for T.H.? We had a good day yesterday, but I in common with everyone else have a cold, cough and such like, so it was rather more of an effort and less of a joy to me personally than usual. To-day I go 5 miles on a lorry or bicycle or anything handy to take service for a bright little bunch of police up the line – this is now a regular Monday fixture. I'll just jot down my week's programme, for your amusement and reference. It's much the same each week:

Sunday.
Celebrations at 6.30, 7.30 a.m.
Service with Artillery workshops 9.15 a.m.
Morning service at T.H. (chiefly Signal school) 10.30.
Eucharist with hymns 11.30.
Bible Class 3 p.m.
C.E.M.S. social meeting 4.45 p.m.
Men's Prayer meeting 5.15 p.m.
Evensong 6.30 p.m.

Monday.
Celebration 7.30 a.m. (2 each weekday)
2 p.m. Police Service. If I get up early enough, I visit a battery section beforehand, and lunch with them or Winterbotham.
Return to T.H. for tea with various men.
Evensong 6 p.m.
6.30 p.m. Lecture (lantern) by S.C.F. of a neighbouring division on China to-night.

Tuesday.
At home during the day till after Evensong.
5.30 p.m. Whist-drive in T.H. Go up to Anti-aircraft service at 7 p.m. and stop to dinner, returning 10 p.m.

Wednesday.
At home all day, plus various visiting of local units.
After Evensong, a men's debate on Industrial Conscription – i.e. munition workers in khaki at soldiers' pay. Last week in crowded House (i.e. about 200) the motion carried that "the war would be over by August."[133]

Thursday.
I leave T.H. early in afternoon, Battery section (Advanced) service at 5 p.m. Another at Battery H.Q. after a mile's walk between them, at 7 p.m. Dinner and sleep there.

Friday.
Celebration at Battery H.Q. at 8 a.m. Breakfast afterwards. Service with some Field Survey folk at 11 a.m.
Lunch with them or elsewhere.
Service with bobbies in – at 3 p.m. catch a lift home.
Service at T.H. 6 p.m.
Shakespeare reading (a group of about 15 keen folk) at 6.30 p.m.

Saturday.
At home mostly. C.E.M.S. meeting for discussion of Ordination proposals 6.30 p.m.

Each week I have little festivities for various units in the neighbourhood. E.g. on Tuesday this week 8 boys from St. Albans and Wheathampstead way in to tea, and a Serg.-Major of Police in to supper on Wednesday.

So the world wags.

Each week of course also brings its deeper work – interviews, confessions, and other opportunities of which I am not worthy. It's a happy life, isn't it?

The Munitions explosion in London[134] sounds very grim; but if the world will go mad, it must expect to suffer. The whole business sometimes seems sheer insanity on a huge scale. It's queer to see Bosche prisoners trotting about round here in their red forage caps, looking eminently pleased with themselves. I wonder if Talbot House will be moved to Brussels by the end of the year?

Snow still all over the ground here, and a hard frost has held for a week-end now; which makes journeying a brisker business.

I hope to get leave in the end of February, if not before; and shall lie low at Hatchett, if you can provide me with a few sunny days, please. I look forward passionately to the spring-time, and yet dread the holocaust of suffering it must bring. But anything is better for the men than stagnation.

Now I must return to T.H. to get the day's work in hand.

Much love to you, dearest mother, and to all,

Your son,

Philip

* * *

---

133 See Notice p. 252.
134 After the declaration of war, new factories were set up to dramatically increase the production of explosives. A great number of munition workers (mostly women) died in explosions at work and there were many minor accidents.

Talbot House
Tuesday, 19 December 1916

Dearest Mater,

I'm sitting cosily in my room – the warmest in the town – while it snows outside. And before a few youngsters troop in to tea, I'll just get a word of quiet with you.

The Mission has been really good, and is not likely to be transitory in its effects. All the services were on the whole well attended, and Ted was a great joy to us all. He went off yesterday with Waggett who had been Missioner to a neighbouring Division.

(Same evening. 11 p.m.) A few lines more before I turn in. My dear Corporal Stagg has just finished putting our Christmas Crib into the alcove on the staircase, and fitting it with electric light. It is simply a box fitted with a cardboard stable, and the little statuettes of the Holy Family we had last year, together with a lamb, ox and ass from a toyshop in Dunkirk. But it looks bewitching. The minds of four of us – Pettifer, the two Q.W.R.'s[135] and myself, go back to the 19th Dec. last year, the night of the awful gas attack, when the Q.W.R.'s were in the front line, and Pettifer and I together here in a stricken house; all night the town was being shelled, and the wounded coming down. What a lot we have all to be thankful for!

I suppose we are the only four together now here, whose friendship dates from then. The Q.W.R.'s had just built our Chapel which is now famous up and down the B.E.F. and the House has a year of preservation and usefulness to praise God for. So we know that all things work together for good to them that love Him.

My Christmas Day promises to be very happy: after four celebrations here, I go up in the afternoon to my dear Heavies for Christmas services, and Christmas dinner. I sleep there the night, and return here after a Boxing Day Celebration for the forward section in the following afternoon.

On Friday next, 22nd I spend a night at G.H.Q., with the Bishop, who took one Confirmation here on Sunday – over 200 candidates in our new Church Hall (these came partly from various Divisions, some from T.H. itself.)

Now I must to bed.
Much love.
Your son,
Philip Clayton

*   *   *

'A Historic Visit'
On 25th December Fred Burrow and myself stopped a motor lorry somewhere in (not Blighty) and proceeded to a certain celebrated house, known as TALBOT HOUSE. Arriving there quicker than we antisaped (sic), and finding nobody at home we divested ourselves of our hats

---

135 Rfm Ronald Brewster and Cpl Herbert Stagg, 1/16th Queen's Westminster Rifles. Billeted in the storehouse next door, both had been involved in transforming the attic into Chapel in January 1916. Following participation in the Battle of the Somme, they returned north to recuperate in an entrenching battalion. At the behest of their CO., they were attached to the House staff until fit to rejoin their regiment. Brewster was called back in July 1917; Stagg in September of that year.

and coats and lit up two fat cigars. We had been sitting down for about an hour, when a noise outside the door, told us that the one and only P.B.C. had arrived.

We then had the greatest joy in taking part in the little service of "Holy Communion" . Afterwards we once more entered the ROOM (which by the way reminded us of the library in the vicarage.) Now came the awful problem of dinner (or rather lunch). Can you imagine P.B.C., F.B., H.C.H. and another nice chap, sitting at a round table in an excellent restaurant, eating and talking at the same time. I shall never forget that four course lunch, what with the soup then the crab and -, then the substantials, followed by the cheese, nuts, oranges, and cigars, I must remark that F.B. was a little shy at first, but he soon became his old self especially towards the round up of the cheese and cigars. At last we came out of this sort of place, and thence back to the house. Towards the end of the day, we had a little game between ourselves (you know those little games don't you). After tea we dressed for a motor tour. Yes we (Fred and myself) had a jolly little run. When we finally reached our destination, great difficulty was experienced in getting out of the car. Books, boxes of crackers, had been packed in the car on top of us, as P.B.C. was going on one of his many excursions to cheer up the tommies who could not get near to such a nice place as TALBOT HOUSE. Well, to finish up, Fred and I must admit that the 25th was the best day so far, that we had spent away in a foreign country.

Cpl. H.C. Hoptrough
Alias The Mighty Atom.[136]

R.I.P.

Frederick G. Burrow
Corporal, 15 Hampshire Regiment
1 August 1917 – Wijtschaete Military Cemetery, VI.D.8

Herbert C. Hoptrough
Corporal, 15 Hampshire Regiment
20 September 1917 – Age 21 – Tyne Cot Memorial (Passendale), Pnl. 88 to 90 and 162

* * *

From Edward Talbot to Tubby
H.Q. 8th Division
29 December 1916

My Dear Tubby
Xmas agenda have postponed any intention of writing. I want to say how much I loved being with you at Pop and breathing the air of Talbot House – the only place on the Front which has kinship with Bethlehem. I only wish I had been able to help your flock better. I was myself in one of the spiritual 'pockets' into which my soul sinks at times, & I fear sadly that it affected my ministrations. As a matter of fact something was wrong with me physically which has broken

---

136 Published in *The Nutshell*, No.10, spring 1917, p.10.

out since in blotches & blains. However all that is self-conscious and I am really grateful for having been with you and with the splendid fellows you have gathered round you. It has been a great stimulus to one's ordinary work.

I hope you had a blessed Xmas & that the Belgian party went with a roar.[137] Give my love to Ensell – and oh! by the way – I feasted grossly & frequently at the Club without paying a farthing. Do let me know how much I owe & I will send a cheque.

Bless you, Tubby
Yours affectionately
E.K. Talbot

On 31 December 1916, Rev. E.K. Talbot sent the following letter to fellow members of the Mirfield Community of the Resurrection:

I have been having an interesting bit of experience – going up for 10 days to the northern-most Army to conduct a "Mission" in connection with the National Mission. I had a continuous mission each evening at Talbot House, an institution called after my brother, now run by Clayton, of Portsea, much the most Christian institution on the British Front. It is really refreshing to get into an atmosphere entirely disinfected of khaki and saturated with really evangelic brother-hood and joy. They have got a heavenly chapel, and there we had our mission, which at Clayton's request was on the "personal religion' line and not "national" though this had to come in. The men were mostly those of good-will, some very keen – and I think it was a help. ...

*   *   *

Talbot House,
B.E.F.
Thursday, 4 January, 1917

Dearest Mater,
...
I'm waiting for a friendly lift by some Archibald[138] Officers which will bring me near my beloved parishioners of Thursday – Friday. Normally the Corps lend me a car, but today they haven't got one to spare – this is their first failure – so others come to aid. This is always my experience, it seems, nowadays. Every one helps.

Dr Browne is unfortunately leaving here on Monday, as half of his folk are living now nearly 20 miles away; and he must attend to them. This will be a great loss to us both, as he loves the House, and has been a splendid partner for the last 4 months. The excellence of the C.E.M.S. Branch owes much to him. But we hope to see him occasionally.

The recreational party seems to have been a "succes fou", and the Christmas which makes others happy is the only one worth having nowadays. We had a wonderful evening here last night, when Anderson, the A.C.G. of the Army, brought to T.H. all his set of Ponting's films of

137 Tubby planned a party for Belgian children in the new hall after Christmas. See 'A little treat for the Belgian Kiddies', p. 255.
138 Anti-Aircraft battery.

the South Pole Expedition,[139] and also a 'movie' of the Christmas Carol. I don't think men were ever so breathlessly interested before. Now I must get ready for the long long trail – yet (to mix quotations) – the trail that is always new.[140]

Much love, dearest mother

Philip B.C.

*   *   *

T.H.

A.P.O., S.4.,

Tuesday, 9 January 1917

Dearest Mater,

I'm sorry I've been so remiss about writing, but no news is good news of the Church here, as it is of the Church in the New Testament. We had the best Sunday on record on 1st after Epiphany, over 80 Communicants: which is good for a normal Sunday, isn't it? when you remember that practically each one has to make a struggle and sacrifice to get there at all. The 11.30 Celebration has an atmosphere of reverence that I have never experienced anywhere else. Besides this, I now have a 10.30 morning service here (instead of in a neighbouring Camp). This is easier for me, and better for the boys concerned, who are the Corps Signal Instruction School – 200 of the brightest and best youngsters, picked out to learn improvements in signalling – a school term being two months; so that I really get a chance with them of taking a continuous course of teaching, Sunday by Sunday, which they don't seem to resent. In the afternoon I went up to – in a side-car, one of my dear police having been killed. He made his Christmas Communion here on Christmas eve, at night, and in his diary wrote that he felt through it nearer to his wife and children than ever since he came out. It is hard on them. They live in Newcastle, and I wrote yesterday, so I don't neglect others as much as I do you. Then I came back to find dear Browne (who is *not* moving, thank goodness) running the crowded C.E.M.S. tea, and – best of all – 5 Portsea boys assembled for the first time! Then our prayer meeting, at which there were over 30, and finally our Evening Service with over 200. So all is indeed well.

The Bosche is very much more lively of late, but has left Pop alone, thank goodness; the only other misfortune of war is that Harrison of my Archibalds has been rather badly hit. I see a lot of Fatty Winterbotham, his adjutant, and like him immensely. … Margaret Pantin's[141] books have not yet arrived, but are awaited with great eagerness. We are on our beam ends till they come.

Your loving son,

Philip

---

139 Herbert Ponting was the Scott Terra Nova expedition (1910-13) photographer and cinematographer. It was in this capacity that he captured some of the most enduring images of the heroic age of Antarctic exploration. He was also one of the first men to use a portable film camera in Antarctica. This primitive device, known as the cinematograph, could capture short film sequences.

140 A mixture of quotations from the popular song *There's a Long, Long Trail A-Winding* and Rudyard Kipling's poem *The Long Trail* ("Pull out, pull out, on the Long Trail-the trail that is always new!").

141 The Pantins were acquaintances of the Claytons. They also acted as a host family for Canadian soldiers on leave in England.

* * *

Talbot House
Sunday night, 14 January, 1917
10.15 p.m.

Dearest Mater,

I'm sitting with my feet on the stove, which is trying to digest some stuff sold as coal, but in reality more like black brick dust – however Pettifer is going on the scrounge tomorrow,[142] so all will be well. It's best to write to you now before I turn in, as I have a full week ahead, as well as behind. Bert Potter, the last of those who came in after service, has just left to go back to his Railway truck. I've had several other Portsea boys in lately, which is good. Also Alec Paterson,[143] best of all men.

We've had a good Sunday – really inspiring services at 11.30 and 5.15 (the men's prayer meeting) at which about 50 were present, with about 10 taking part, the little address given by a sapper, and the lesson read by another. But I won't tell you about another Sunday, not that I fear re-iterating it to you; but that it would be more generally amusing to tell you of my weekdays, for a change.

The sorrow of the week has been the death from wounds of the young O.C. of my Anti-Aircraft folk, who was wounded by a Bosche bomb on Friday week. On Tuesday I went up to his section for evening service, and stopped to dinner with Winterbotham afterwards. On Wednesday, we had an amusing debate here on – "that the House is in favour of the taxation of bachelors." A house of about 200 men rejected this proposal, much to my relief. This Wednesday the subject is that "this House is convinced the war will be over by August." I don't think!

On Thursday I went up to my dear Heavies, and found them in the thick of things more or less; I had a lantern service with the forward section, and then walked back in the pitch dark to the centre section and thence to their headquarters, avoiding with difficulty a number of new pitfalls dug by Bosche shells the previous afternoon. After service, and dinner, I begged to be allowed to go with the O.C. to get in the way during the putting of some guns in some new positions. Previously I had rather shared the Infantry's view that 60 pounders are a "cushy" job. But when we had wrestled with them awful things in the mud from 10 p.m. to 2 a.m. (they weren't finally in position till 5.45 a.m.) I began to think differently. I never met such senseless heavy nightmares – it was only a question of shifting them 20 ft. from where the horses had drawn them, but it meant lifting wheel after wheel with jacks and levers, and getting planks under them to present their entire submergence in the mud. As an irresponsible bystander, it was amusing, if chilly – it snowed the whole time. Next morning I had a Celebration at 8.30

---

142 For a humorous account of Pettifer scrounging coal: see p. 305.
143 Having been wounded three times, Capt. Alexander Paterson, 22nd London Regiment, was attached
        to a divisional school of Instruction in the vicinity of Poperinge. Enlisting at the outbreak of war,
        he rose through the ranks to a commission. He was mentioned in dispatches, awarded the Military
        Cross and recommended (twice) for the VC. The spirit of friendship fostered at Talbot House across
        social and denominational boundaries inspired Paterson, Rev. Dick Sheppard of St Martin-in-the-
        Fields and Tubby to set out what became known as the 'Four Points of the Compass', i.e. the ideals of
        Fellowship, Service, Fair-mindedness and the Kingdom of God, that would form the basis of the Toc
        H movement in 1920. Paterson served as first chairman from 1922-24.

The oompah - oompah section

Drawing by Bandsman Erskine Williams.

a.m., a concession to late hours, and then walked up with the O.C. across country to a château where I had a service with some delightful folk – 17 men and a Sergeant – who afterwards gave me a bully beef dinner. Thence to my dear Police, with another service at 3 p.m., and after tea with them they stopped a passing motor bus – think of it! – a genuine, if somewhat war-worn motor bus – which landed me back here at 5.45 p.m. in time for evensong. On Saturday I made up for my exertions by having breakfast in bed, and had the joy in the afternoon of welcoming Vokins – my old ally from No.16 Gen. Hosp. – whom the Bishop has again got for me onto the staff of Toc H. He was sent back to No. 16 when I was ill in the summer. It makes all the difference to have him here.

Another letter all about myself, but I know you don't resent that – it's not because I don't think of home, as you know.

…

Goodnight dearest Mater,
Your loving son,
Philip

R.I.P.

George C. Harrison
Lieutenant, 6th Anti Aircraft Battery, 24th Heavy Artillery Group, Royal Artillery
10 January 1917 – Lijssenthoek Military Cemetery, IX.B.19

*   *   *

From Major Herbert Shiner to Tubby
Somewhere near the War
Saturday
27 January 1917

My Dear Revd Clayton,
I was simply delighted to have your cheery note and always my best thanks for congrats. I am so glad that we (the H-army!) have not succeeded in turning you into a red tape respecter.

I will have a guide to help you along to my new abode. I only wish I could send a car or something. Do you ever attempt the noble animal? If so I could always send you a horse. If you could only add us to your list of services I should be grateful for we have no regular Padre here but I know the amount of ground you cover and do not want you to be put to any serious inconvenience. However more of this when we meet.

Yrs very Sincerely
H. Shiner[144]

P.S. I have been trying to imagine you looking awed, but up to the present moment my fertile imagination has not produced the picture!!

*   *   *

Talbot House
1 February 1917

My dearest Mater,
…
Ensell went on long leave yesterday, and I have to hold on to both our jobs for his three weeks of absence. Probably he'll motor over and see you sometime. He's a dear, but rather old for the big job here; which for the time being devolves entirely on me. However, I'll do my best, and as usual happy and much helped by everyone. …

Another magnificent case of 600 cigars from Jack to-day – I took 100 down to Col. Kiddle at 7 Stationary yesterday, when I went for the joy of the ride so far with Ensell, to see him off. Another box goes up to the gunners to-night with me in half an hour's time or so, together with three of your lovely pictures – the two Greuze's[145] and another – for the Officer's Mess, that have been so good to me. This as a reward well won, since they are one of the few messes that have not plastered their walls with vulgarities out of "La Vie Parisienne".

---

144 Major Herbert Shiner was promoted CO 154th Southampton Territorial Heavy Battery in July 1916 and remained its C.O. for the remainder of the war, receiving the DSO and MC. Prior to this he was CO 141st East Ham Heavy Battery. Visiting the front line area at least once a week to minister to what he called his 'forward flock', Tubby became attached, quite unofficially and by chance, to both batteries, which Shiner later described as "the *really* first branches of Toc H in the Ypres Salient". 'Shi' became the first warden of Toc H Mark I (i.e. 'Talbot House London') in May 1920 and was subsequently appointed Vice-President of Toc H.

145 Jean-Baptiste Greuze (1725-1805). French artist specializing in portraits, religious scenes and depictions of everyday life.

I may write badly – worse than ever – for a few weeks – but you will understand, and I shall I hope be home at the end of February. ... More on Sunday night, I hope,

Much love,

Philip.

*   *   *

T.H.

7 February 1917

Dearest Mater,

I was too sleepy by the time Sunday night came to do any writing, even to you. And Monday was like a little Sunday on its own – a workshops (H.A.) service in the morning, followed by a long excursion north in the mid-day on a Motor Machine Gun side-car to visit some outlying posts. (What can one do for 250 men, split up in groups of 7 over a 15 mile area?) Then in the afternoon the same quaint conveyance again; a call at one place I go to every Friday to pick up a little harmonium, then across to Major Shiner (whose letter I sent you), and the Southampton Battery. Arrived there at H.Q. late as usual, had tea, during which the motor got stone cold – its driver also having tea, afterwards we pulled and pushed the beastly thing till at last it unfroze, and got going again. Then a journey up forward to a ruined village I have never visited before, and after many adventures, we at last arrived at our destination – a forward gun section, where we had a topping service, one of the best I ever remember; so grateful were they that their Officer concluded the proceedings by making a speech of thanks from them all, a most irregular but moving little corollary to a Padre's visit. Then folk talk about men not wanting religion – the men who really know what the War is have a different tale to tell. Only it must be real religion – have you read Neville's book,[146] just out. I'll send you a copy, if you like. Anyhow, I then got into the side-car again, the engine kept warm meanwhile by my coat and muffler, and came back to Battery H.Q. where we had another topping Service, and then dinner, and I slept like a top in the mess room on a lovely bed they had manufactured especially for my benefit, a beautiful little stove fire made of an oil drum glowing away most of the night. I got up lazily in the morning about 8.30, (usually I am bathing at 7 a.m.) and we had a Celebration in the same room at 10 a.m. with about 20 Communicants, including the Major and Adjutant and Sergeant Major. After this, I lounged about and talked to men, and got in the way generally, and had my hair cut by the Batttery barber (who comes from a saloon below Bar) and finally made off on foot about midday. I walked to H.A. Headquarters, whence a keen young Etonian Lieut. had several times come down to T.H.[147] He brought me back home in a car, and we lunched together, and swore an eternal friendship, so to speak. (He came in again later to make his Confession). Then tea with a few bright spirits, and after 6 p.m. Evensong, another journey in a box car this time to Winterbotham's folk. Service there at 7 p.m. and dinner afterwards with some Siege folk who

---

146 In his short but insightful book, *Thoughts on Religion at the Front*, Neville Talbot wrote with great candour of the barrier that inevitably existed between chaplains and the men to whom they were trying to minister. He also dwelt on the difficulty of focusing on religion in an environment in which God seemed distinctly absent. E. Madigan, *Faith under Fire*, p.130 & p.174.

147 2nd Lt. Leslie A. Dent, R.F.A., X Corps, H.A.

share their mess. Home here at 10 p.m., and bed. Celebration this morning at 7.30. To-day and Friday night – Monday morning are at present my only times in T.H. which however goes on just as well without me.

Now young Blomeley[148] (who shares with Browne the doing of our House accounts) another keen officer – is waiting to take me out to Lunch – so I must shut down.

Much love to all you dearest of dear folk, and above all to you, Mother o'mine,

Philip.

* * *

T.H.
Monday, 12 February, 1917

Dearest Mater,
A quietish day at last, so I'm writing a line before I go up to a Div. H.Q. which has kindly asked me to lunch. I should have had two services this morning, but both washed out owing to pressure of work. A Confirmation interview at 3 p.m. and various people to tea, followed by Evensong at 6 p.m., and a lecture (by someone else) at 6.30 complete an easy stay at home day.

Yesterday was the reverse. 4 Celebrations (one at Corps H.Q.), 3 Parade Services – one Bible Class, a crowd to tea, a Prayer Meeting and CEMS admission at 5.15, and then a long journey by car to a jolly R.F.C. Squadron where I stayed to Supper, returning at 10 p.m. to be greeted with the information that upstairs there was an officer who had come a hundred miles to see me. I couldn't conceive that such a person existed, so was amazed to find in my easy chair Lieut. Frank Wilkins, R.F.C., ex S. Mary's Co., who had flown up from down South, and had lost his way.

10 p.m. Monday. The dear thing (who I hadn't seen for two years) had some cocoa with me (Pettifer with his usual talent had already got him some dinner) and slept at the Club. And this morning we had a Celebration together, with him as Server (he was training at S. Augustine's before the War); then breakfast, and then having two calls to make in that direction I walked down with him to the camp where his plane was waiting him; and he sailed off from there quite happily. He says he has found a lot of R.F.C. men down South, who know Little Hatchett well,[149] and think of it most gratefully. Beyond this, on Saturday evening a L./Cpl. walked into my room who was an old Bible Class boy from Fifth Street, and yesterday Harry Murley and Stan Pead came in (two of of my most intimate boys of Camp days, whom I haven't seen for two years nearly). Lastly, this afternoon, as I was walking up to lunch at Div. H.Q. a Sergeant Major of R.F.A. stopped me in the road, and discovered himself to be one who had cebrospinal meningitis at 16 General Hospital eighteen months ago! These happy meetings are, please God,

148   2nd Lt. Cyril Blomeley, A.S.C., No. 3 Coy, 39th Divisional Train. See his letter of 14 April 1918.
149   An airfield was constructed next to East Boldre, Tubby's home village, in 1910. A flying school resided there for two years before the field reverted to quiet grazing land. In 1914 one of the school's hangars was taken over by the RFC. By 1915, the demand for pilots was so great that a training school, called 'RFC Beaulieu' was built on the same area. In early 1916, a plane crashed in the garden of Little Hatchett. Pilots were made very welcome at Tubby's home and quite a number of them signed the visitors' book.

only a foretaste of what is in store for us, when it's all over; as I'm now convinced it will be by the autumn.

…

Much love. I do love you all so!

Your son,

Philip.

*   *   *

24 February 1917

Dearest Mater,

I shan't be coming on leave till Monday week, i.e. Monday, 5th March. I could come on Wednesday the 28th, but should lose two days, which isn't worth it, as you have no real birthday this year! Ensell is back, and highly pleased with his visit to you.

Don't bother about writing again, unless it's easy. I hope to see you on Wednesday the 7th, i.e., I shan't catch the boat till Tuesday 6th, and then sleep at H.B.C.'s or Belle's.

All going very well and happily.

Much love,

Philip

*   *   *

From the Visitors' Book, Little Hatchett

March 7 – 15

A very delightful time with our dear Padre and son. With every trust to meet again here, he is gone to Poperinghe via London.

(Tubby's mother)

The Clayton family. *From left to right:* Grace Butler (family friend), Nurse Elsie ('Nursie'), Ivy Frances (younger sister), Reginald (father), Philip ('Tubby'), Stuart (daughter of 'Jack', elder brother), Isabel (mother) with Hephzibah ('Heffy') the dog at her feet, Isobel ('Belle', elder sister), Beatrice ('Trixie', wife of Jack).

*   *   *

T.H.
Saturday, 17 March 1917
After leave.

Dearest Mater,
Just a word or two before lunch, which is waiting, to tell you of my safe crossing and rapid transit up the line. Nothing eventful on the journey across: a lot of newcomers on the boat, who said great things and no doubt dreamed great dreams as they came in sight of Cape Gris-Nez. I'm not without my dreams, but they are not warlike ones.

An R.F.C. tender wafted us half way up here, and an Archibald for the rest of the way, so I was in T.H. 11½ hours after I left London. Pretty good for war-time! And a big tea at Cassel on the way. All well here, and T.H. very clean and neat to welcome me. Lots of work ahead, I see, but this is as I want it.

What a lovely day this must be at Hatchett, but it couldn't be happier than the days I had at home.

Your loving son,
Philip B.C.
Love and blessing to Joyce for the Confirmation Day.

*   *   *

T.H.
1 April 1917

Dearest Mater,
I enclose Holy Week card, so that you can follow and sympathise.

All well here – splendid services today. We have raised over £ 18 for Waifs and Strays during Lent, and have thus adopted one child – Hannah Mitchell – as the T.H. child for a year.[150] One boy gave me 30/- he had saved to spend on a leave which never came, and another tonight 5 francs (half of a prize for the best kept horse in his battery) so H. Mitchell has found a warm place in their hearts.

A very busy week ahead, but full of joy of service. I shan't write much till after Easter now. Much love.

Your son
Philip

TALBOT HOUSE CHAPEL

HOLY WEEK & EASTER, 1917

PALM SUNDAY (APRIL 1ST)
Holy Communion, 6.30, 7.30 a.m.   Bible Class . . 3 p.m.
Morning Service . 10.30 ,,   C.E.M.S. Meeting, 4.45 ,,
Holy Eucharist . 11.30 ,,   Evensong . 6.30 ,,

MONDAY
TUESDAY } Holy Communion . . . 7.30 a.m.
WEDNESDAY } Evensong, with Address . 6 p.m.
THURSDAY . } AND Story of the Cross.

Also on MAUNDY THURSDAY: Celebration of
Holy Communion, 6.45 p.m.
(For those on morning duty.)

GOOD FRIDAY
Litany and Ante Communion . . . . 7.30 a.m.
Morning Prayer . . . . . 10.30 ,,
3 Hours' Devotion . . . . 12-3 p.m.
Conducted by
Mission Service and Selections from "The } 6.30 ,,
Crucifixion" (Stainer) . . . . . }

EASTER EVEN.
Holy Communion . . . . . 7.30 a.m.
Evensong and Preparation . . . 6 p.m.

EASTER DAY
Celebrations of Holy Communion at
5.30, 6, 6.30, 7.30, 8.15, 10.30
Choral Eucharist . . . . . 11.30 a.m.
Festal Evensong . . . . . 6.30 p.m.

---

150 For Hannah's story, see p. 259.

* * *

6 April 1917 – Good Friday – 6.30 p.m. – Preacher: Rev. P.B. Clayton – Lantern Service with selections from "The Crucifixion". Hall packed. Soloists: Sgt. Davey, Rfmn Brewster, Sapper Thornton.

(Register of Services)

Perugino's Crucifixion - the altarpiece of the Upper Room.

* * *

T.H.
11 April 1917

Dearest Mater,

I have only a few minutes to spare, and cannot now write the account of our glorious Easter I wanted to – but I don't think the memory of it will fade with waiting. I had about 480 Communicants, single-handed at Talbot House (except at 6.30 when I served to a padre, whose brother, killed on the Somme, had signed the Communicants' Roll for that service last Easter).

In the afternoon I started again, and had Celebrations at Battery positions and elsewhere, an Evensong at Kite Balloon Section, and Evensong at T.H., and an evening Celebration for some 40 men who had been on duty in the morning. This made 14 services during the day, which kept me from stagnation. Yesterday, I had another Easter with Major Shiner and, except for the fact that an S.O.S. went up just as I got there, and service was impossible till 10 p.m., all was excellent. A happy Celebration in the morning, after which I walked across in an April snowstorm to arrange for two subalterns and a Sergeant Major (who are anxious to be confirmed) to come down to-day to T.H., but when at last I got home, I found a wire waiting to say that Bishop Gwynne is ill – so had to cancel all this.

Ensell goes to the Chaplains' School to-day, so I am left with double job for a week, but on Friday 20th I go there myself for the day to take the Quiet Day as best I can. I'm rather shy of this, with Chaplains as congregation, but hope to pull through somehow. I wish there was more time in life for writing to you, and also to others, but there isn't; and I know you would rather I kept fit and did my job than sit up to write letters about it all.

Much love to you, dearest Mater,
Philip B.C.

Capt. Thomas David, 4th Bn Welch Regt., killed in action 27 July 1917, buried in Bard Cottage Cemetery (Ieper).

*   *   *

T.H.
Thursday morning, 26 April 1917

Dearest Mater,
As I haven't written a decent letter for ages, here goes at last for something less scrappy than usual.

… It's a bit too late now to describe Easter day, which remains however a monument of eminence in the history of T.H. What is it, I wonder, which suddenly vitalises the multitude of Churchmen for 24 hours in the year? Would that the secret of it could be applied to every Sunday with the same fruitfulness.

The Chapel looked perfectly divine, flowers everywhere, from Setley and elsewhere, a new altar-cloth worked (unknown to me) by the sister of an R.E. friend of more than a year's standing. Cecilia's surplice also made a great difference, and is perfectly beautiful. I wish I could write to her about it, but the time is not yet.

I scrounged an organist from a neighbouring Territorial Band, so that we had hymns 134, 135, 140 in continual succession. More and more officers and men flocked in, so that the landing and stairs below the Upper Room were crowded with their waiting until the Service before was completed. This went on from 5.30 – 8.30 without a break. I had about five minutes for a cup of tea – and then – (at this point of arrival of Vokings with the post, including a case of cigars from Jack which is just in the nick of time, …) – 9.30, 10.30, and 11.30 at the last of which we sang Merbecke with great joy. Then a hurried meal, and a car to Y. where there more Celebrations, returning at 5.15 to find an R.F.C. tender waiting for Evensong with a Kite Balloon Section; Evensong here after that (simply crowded out), and a Celebration afterwards for some 40 on day duty. Then Laus Deo,[151] and so to bed. I never had a harder or happier day.

… On Monday this week I went to Major Shiner's as usual. The Bosche had a new balloon up and was shelling the road, so far as I could judge, by which I should normally go. So I trod like Agag delicately, and cut across the fields; when I rejoined the road, I could scarcely recognise it – just a chain of shell holes. The first people I came across were two gunners relaying the wires, who told me what had been happening all the afternoon. No casualties, fortunately, and no guns damaged, in spite of it all. But the place looked like the surface of the moon through a telescope. The gramophone in the Officer's Mess got a direct hit on it, and the place where I was going to sleep was simply one yawning gulf of wreckage. So we built a wigwam with canvas round the waterwheel of the farmhouse nearby, and camped there happily enough. My lantern, a Communion box (which I had left there) were both smothered in brickdust but unhurt, and the grimmest thing was that the old farmer had died a natural death on Sunday (having refused to leave his farm in which he was born) and as he lay dead in bed, a shell blew in the side of the house and wounded the corpse. His poor old wife meanwhile refused to leave him and just huddled up crouching and untouched against the further wall. We thought she would be almost maddened by it, but strangely enough she was thankful, saying that she was so glad it had happened after his death, as the destruction of the farm would have broken his heart. The place

151 Latin translation: "Praise be to God".

Harmonium, in use in the chapel and the concert hall (larger congregations). After the war it ended up with the British Army of the Rhine in Wiesbaden. It was brought back to England in 1927 by Rev. J. St. Clair Goldie and returned to Talbot House in 1930.

where we were going to have service was badly wrecked, greatly to the distress of the boys, who had got it spick and span that morning; but we cleaned it up as best we could, and had lantern service on 23rd Psalm – I always tell them about the guv's love of the Psalms – and a comic lecture on Andorra[152] afterwards. Then I went off to bed, Major Shiner insisting, in a place made draughty by a shell splinter through the wall a few hours before, and slept soundly while the boys worked most of the night.

We had a beautiful Celebration in the morning, with about 16 Communicants. This afternoon I start once again for my weekly night out further north … Another visitor – this time a Signals Cpt. who used six months ago to be stationed here, and has several times been over to see me, and found me out. So glad I was in this time, as he came in from six miles away, and is a real old friend.[153]

Now, dearest Mater, I must close down.

When you go into Lymington again, stop please at the little cutter's shop on the left side of the hill … and get me another packet of Durham Duplex Razor blades. I will repay.

Much love,

Philip B.C.

* * *

Talbot House
Tuesday, 1 May 1917

Dearest Mater,

All well and going strong. I went for a long ambulance ride this morning with Captain Browne to visit the various railway troops, fixed up a new Sunday service for some 500 R.Es. who haven't had one for 1½ years! and bought a kitchen stove in a lovely old French town,[154] which gave one an idea of what Y[pres]. was like before the earthquake.

This afternoon, I have a garden party – tea for two nurses, who turned up in Church last Sunday night, creating a furore in the hearts of those who haven't seen an English lady for a year and more.[155] So I'm having a select party to meet them, two from each unit in the neighbourhood, a Colonel, a Major, Captain, and all the rest N.C.Os and men. Also 23 of Higgon's gunners,[156] who have just finished a long job, and are having a day off.

Fortunately food supply here is not seriously restricted as yet, so one can go ahead blithely.

Will you ask Miss Pantin whether yet another box of books is possible. …

Real summer suddenly today – spring seems to have washed out. Visitors just in!

Much love,

Your son,

Philip

---

152 Tubby once walked across the Pyrenees into Andorra in 1914.
153 Capt. Marshall W.T. Webb, Royal Engineers – Signals 6th Division. For Webb's tragic story, see p. 326.
154 Bergues.
155 Cousins Alison and Dorothea Macfie, VAD, who at that time were assigned to Hôpital Elizabeth, a small Belgian hospital near Château Couthove in the village of Proven. Tubby later described this party as "a great occasion – an epoch in the House's history".
156 Major L. Hugh Higgon was the C.O. of 141st East Ham Heavy Battery.

*   *   *

We were the special guests at a tea-party in the garden, when most of the others present were weary gunners straight out of the line.

(Alison Macfie, V.A.D.)

Sister Dorothea Macfie, V.A.D.

Sister Alison Macfie, V.A.D.

Officers and Senior NCOs, 141st Heavy Battery, R.G.A.

*   *   *

Talbot House,
Monday, 7 May 1917

Dearest Mater,
Your delightful letter, the Challenge,[157] and various enclosures arrived on Saturday... The Chapel is becoming quite a storehouse of little memorials of very gallant gentlemen. Two weeks ago the Australian Tunnellers lost several Officers who had made their Easter Communion here,[158] and they are to make some memorial candlesticks that witness "may live in brass" of them. A young Lieut. in a Kent Regiment who made his Confession and Communion here at Easter was designing the candlesticks, and yesterday, as I was in the vestry before 11.30 a.m. Celebration, his great friend came to me, much moved, with the news that he had been killed the night before, dying very nobly. A patrol from his battalion had been out, and on its return spotted; he had then gone out to bring in a wounded sergeant, and had done so successfully, but on going out again for another wounded man, himself was killed. It is a great responsibility – the greatest in life – to find oneself the last minister to the souls of men like this. The war is waking up round here – quite like old times. A general Boche strafe of the back areas, including a few for this town, both the last two nights. But I was too tired to lie awake listening to it. Once or twice I was woken by crashes in the neighbourhood, but quickly slept again. Somehow there's something ludicrous in heavy jam jars hurtling through space. More and more I feel that the war is not one of shells and bayonets, but entirely a question of character. What remains to be seen is whether the character on our side (with all its vices and defects) is not nearer to God's aspirations for the ideal citizenship of His Kingdom on earth than that of the fellows on the other side. The one anxiety among the men here is, can England stand shortage of supplies patiently and bravely, as the Boche has done for these two years? If she can, then victory, and all that it means for the good of the future world, is clearly with us. I don't quite know why I'm writing on these great matters, which are too high for me. But "them's my sentiments." To-night to Shiner again.
    Much love,
    Your son,
    Philip

R.I.P.
1st Coy, Australian Tunnelling Corps – 25 April 1917

Capt. Wilfred P. Avery
Poperinghe New Military Cemetery, I.E1.2

---

157 First published 1 May 1914, *The Challenge* was a weekly Church of England newspaper 'with a difference'. From the very beginning Tubby had been a contributor and, after the war, it continued as a valuable organ through which to express Toc H ideals.
158 Three officers and seven men perished in a Hill 60 tunnel accident on 25 April 1917. They were preparing an explosive charge in "D" left gallery when it prematurely exploded. The bodies were recovered three days later.

2nd Lt. Glyndwr D. Evans, Age 33
Railway Dugouts Burial Ground (Zillebeke), VII.G.33

Lt. Arthur E. Tandy, Age 25
Poperinghe New Military Cemetery, I.E1.1

Daniel A. Hodges
2/Lt., 3 Royal West Kent Regiment (Queen's Own)
5 May 1917 – Age 25 – Oosttaverne Wood Cemetery (Wijtschate), I.H.14

*   *   *

Talbot House
15 May 1917

Dearest Mater,
My letter a day late this week, but your Sunday one has not come yet, so we're quits! I've had a very lazy time since Wednesday, as my throat went groggy with a touch of temperature so Browne packed me off to bed and mounted guard over me. Ensell did my work on Sunday, and as they will spoil me, I'm falling into the humour of it, and had breakfast in bed both yesterday and to-day.

Dear Higgon and his folk are going back to the coast for a spell, so (joy of joys) I'm going with them for a few days next week, to swim and so forth, starting on Monday, and returning here for Whitsuntide. This will do me a lot of good, and not interfere with work more than necessary. Forgive this scrap – the postman is waiting at the door to take it.

Much love – don't worry in the least about me
Yours as always,
Philip

*   *   *

As from – Talbot House,[159]
A.P.O. Section 4.
B.E.F.
May 24th, 1917

My dear Squirrels,
I understand this *Nutshell* is going to be especially worth while your cracking. Personally, my contribution will be a lazy one, as I'm sitting in a rocking chair outside the drawing room windows of a beautiful château by the sea. The only sign of the times visible is that the lawn has been dug up for a vegetable garden, leaving only two large beds full of forgetmenots. The garden is fringed with budding roses and flowering lilacs, while behind them great chestnuts

---

159 See *The Nutshell*, No.11, Summer 1917, p.3-4.

and beeches in their early glory provide a perfect minstrels' gallery for the birds. Two days here are rejuvenating me. Yesterday we bathed en masse, and I shouldn't be surprised if I put a toe in again to-day. To-morrow, back to sterner things, the thought of which seems an impossible nightmare in this paradise. You must understand that a beloved battery, after more than a year's hard work and more than their share of trouble too, pulled out at last for a few days' rest, and came here to get it. A three days' trek brought them down; I wish I could have travelled with them, for they seem to have had an amusing journey. One night, for instance, after a long day's march, they arrived unexpectedly at the wrong village. This was no one's fault – if you will have two places of the same name within ten miles of one another you must expect such things. However, the Mayor was more than equal to the occasion. I wonder how an English village would have coped with a sudden invasion of 300 tired men and nearly the same number of weary horses – a column of dust 800 yards long? But *Monsieur le Maire* simply revelled in the crisis. Not only did he billet them all most comfortably and judiciously in the twinkling of an eye, but he organised an impromptu civic reception – lilac branches and children – and made a great speech, in which he welcomed them in the name of *la belle France*, and informed them that no English troops had come through the village since the battle of Cressy. Furthermore, the men had a new laid egg apiece for breakfast in the morning, a very practical interpretation of the entente. A truly great people – the French! Now the gunners are cheerily busy building a shingle road down the cliff on to the sands, where they boot and saddle daily, and perform surprising evolutions on an incoming tide to the admiration of shrimps and starfish. What Napoleon, who lay near here for some time, with his army of invasion, would say to this whirligig of history, I tremble to think. Anyhow, it's quite the best thing that has come my way in the last two years, and I'm thankful for it. We had a Celebration this morning in the woods, not quite such a perfect Church as in the old Camp of 1913,[160] but very wonderful all the same. To-night we have an evening service on the beach at 7 p.m. Come, if you can!

Tomorrow I leave at 8.30 a.m. to have a service in a very different place in the afternoon. But oh! it is good to find that after all, the grass is still green, the sky blue, the sea still musical, and the cliffs over yonder still white. Napoleon never longed to abolish that strip of dark water half so earnestly as we do now. But until our task is accomplished, our exile must continue. Then and not till then, can there be a homecoming for us in earnest, with no return tickets.

Yours always,
Philip Clayton

*   *   *

---

160 Tubby, then a curate at Portsea, organized a fortnight's parish youth camp in the New Forest – "simple forest House of God" – during summer 1913.

Rousbrugge, 29 May 1917

Reverend Father,
We have received with pleasure the beautiful Christmas souvenirs, for which I would like to thank you sincerely on behalf of my sister, my little brothers and myself. We shall keep them as a souvenir of you. Kindly accept this picture as a souvenir of us.
   Reverend Father, please accept our hearfelt thanks.
Marie-Madeleine Coevoet[161]

Children of Maurice and Alida Coevoet-Camerlynck. *From left to right*: Yvonne (1906), Roger (1908), Marie-Madeleine (1904) and Fernand 1910).

*   *   *

161 Marie-Madeleine (b. 1904) is the eldest daughter of Maurice and Alida Coevoet-Camerlynck. The family were in residence at Roesbrugge, a village close to the French border. Correspondence translated from French.

R.I.P.
H.F. Pike
Gunner, Royal Garrison Artillery, 290th Siege Battery
30 May 1917 – Age 33 – Vlamertinghe Military Cemetery, VII.C.15

*   *   *

Talbot House
Monday, 5 June 1917

Dearest Mater,
Your delightful letter has just come.

… The Boche is pretty active, but the House remains beautiful and serene. I go to Shiner's to-night. All very happy and hopeful. Services here rather small yesterday, owing to shelly morning on the outskirts.

I have moved my room to the coolest room in the house, looking out on a lovely roof garden we are concocting with easy chairs, hammocks, etc., where I sleep in the open all night, and benefit much thereby. Stagg and Brewster both on long-deserved leave. I shall probably come in a month or so, all being well, please.

…

Much love to you all,
Your son,
Philip

The Chaplain's Room, faithfully reconstructed in 2005.

*   *   *

18 June 1917

Dearest Mater,

Another broiling day here – it has been 90° in the shade two days running already! I am, however, fit and well, thank goodness, and taking life quietly.

The garden is lovely, full of roses, but very dry; and the grass, covered with khaki in a somnolent state, very brown without them. A number of last year's friends have been dropping in lately – all one really needs to do here is to sit still and work, and friends new and old arrive without seeking. Two members of the Parish Church choir have turned up in fine fettle.

Higgon's and Shiner's lot have both been having rather a bad time of it; but I suppose you can't have war without casualties, which isn't much comfort. Curiously enough, the gunners have suffered more than the infantry this time, on the whole.[162]

I had a rather rough journey with Pettifer on Friday and Saturday last. We reached our first objective – some flash-spotting folk – thanks to a lift in an R.F.C. tender (they are the most hospitable knights-errant possible on the road) at about 10.30 a.m. After half an hour we wanted to leave, but the Boche was meanwhile dropping H.E. of a heavy type on nothing in particular across the road. So though our journey to Shiner lay in that direction we decided to go forward a bit and then walk across well under the Niagara Falls, so to speak. The next trouble was that after we had crossed a couple of fields he suddenly burst an air-crump high in front of us. So we got down hastily into an old trench (of the early British 1914 neolithic type) and read about the air-raid punctuated with shrapnel bursts for half an hour. Shrapnel is queer stuff. Long after the burst, just when you are tempted to peer round like Bairnsfather's men and say "Where did that one go?"[163] you suddenly become aware of twigs and branches from the trees above being lopped off by invisible knives, and you cuddle down again under the traverse of the trench, and wish the tin hat was ten times as big.

After some time wasted here, we proceeded (no one ever "goes" anywhere in the Army). An erstwhile lovely lane, punctuated with ruined farms, stray dumps of ammunition, large guns, and big shell holes.

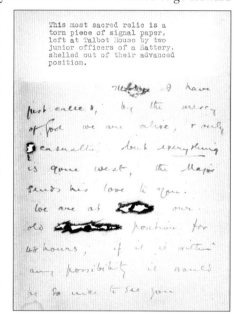

This most sacred relic is a torn piece of signal paper, left at Talbot House by two junior officers of a Battery, shelled out of their advanced position.

---

162   The British dealt their first blow in what was the great Flanders offensive on 7 June 1917. From Hill 60 to Ploegsteert Wood, they detonated 19 underground mines. Hundreds of Germans were killed or buried alive and, according to contemporary reports, the reverberations were felt as far away as London and Paris.

163   Bairnfather's first cartoon, "Where did that one go to?" was published in the popular magazine *The Bystander* in January 1915.

Shelter, watercolour by Eric Kennington.

A wayside stream a little further on, clear and cool for Flanders; with more men and guns; a nasty dusty cross roads with the ruins of a large *estaminet*, a dead mule or two (last night's transport); and a scrawl of chalk on a broken shutter "No beer sold here." Past this corner without lingering, we proceeded on our way across a broad wooden gun and lorry track (costing in all, one would think about 6*d.* on the income tax), and came on some of Higgon's boys on a working party putting up telephone wires for travellers to trip over. Then rows and rows of deserted and battered gun positions, the survivors having moved forward with the push. Light railways everywhere, which are marvellously useful, and so easily mended when shelled that it's not really worth shelling them, and R.F.A. ammunition spent, unexpended, stored, scattered, on all hands. A weedy piece of canal, a crazy be-sandbagged farm, a few clumps of what once were trees, and then our destination. Shiner has moved now, further forward again since Friday, and I am purposely altering a lot of details, so I don't think this letter is in any way indiscreet.

Imagine, therefore, living in holes scooped out of the railway embankment before the line reaches Brockenhurst Station – at Lyndhurst Road lives an enemy with effective guns who fires along the line whenever minded. Here I had some lunch with the subalterns, the Major being out reconnoitring, and then trotted along to the men. Sitting in the hedge with them, we were rudely disturbed by a heavy burst overhead, and tumbled helter-skelter into the nearest dug-out – not a very capacious place. Half a dozen more separate bursts, and then a salvo of three (which was beastly). So I had some hymn sheets in my pocket, and passed them down inwards, the subaltern and myself sharing the entrance. Here we sang "Hold the fort" rather appropriately, and had quite a jolly service, though I found preaching rather difficult, accompanied as it was by two menacing roars growing nearer and nearer, followed by terrific crashes, like an express train in a grand cinema collision. Meanwhile, I tried to tell the invisible audience what the words "the Kingdom of God" really mean. The service and the shelling ended together, and when we went out of the doorway, the first thing we found was the body of a dear young signaller lying quite quietly half under a semicircle of corrugated iron, which formed his sleeping place. He was the Major's clerk, a splendid fellow in every way, 6 months married. Apparently, he had been coming to lie down and sleep under cover, and the last burst of shrapnel must have caught him about 5 yards from the entrance to the dug-out. He must have dropped without a cry, being hit twice through the head, and made some convulsive movement towards his little house by which he fell. This discovery was terrible; it was so utterly unexpected, for though they have had several casualties we thought no one had been caught this time. He was a most popular man, and the officer in charge quite broke down, for which I liked him all the better.

At last the Major got back after a bad journey, and took the news as only a soldier and a Christian could. So then under a neighbouring corrugated cupola, I held a Confirmation Class for a few of the boys, promising to admit them the next day to Communion, as their Confirmation long overdue was still impossible for the time – not the Bishop's fault. We ought to have a Bishop with each of the Armies.

Then Pettifer and myself went by a byway to the dear bobbies in[164] – and picked up a few extra congregation from some infantry I knew hard by. At 8 p.m. we left them and threw ourselves on Higgon's kindness for supper and sleep. We were royally welcomed in a house with one wall only, and slept like tops, in spite of a good deal of strafe in the near neighbourhood. After early breakfast, we started off again for Shiner's, and I had a wonderful Celebration there at 9.30 a.m. with absolutely nothing of ornament except an old surplice, a stole, and the Pix that Miss Becket gave me from the folk in Beeston Street.[165] One or two of the regular Communicants could not leave their posts – there were about 15 of us – so I Reserved to Communicate them afterwards. When finally I was Communicating two signallers in among the bushes, as the Wafer actually lay in their hands, a heavy burst of shrapnel came as it seemed right overhead; but though the bushes were full of flying pieces none of us was touched, not (curiously enough) even frightened. It was the most extraordinary experience of the Peace of God I have ever known. Subsequently, Pettifer and I went on our way home, leaving these dear fellows to their task. They will have moved to a safer place by this Friday, so you need not be in the least anxious about me. I should not write all this, if I thought it would worry you. Besides, if I were not a Chaplain, I should have been a combatant, and killed long ago.

As soon as I can find someone to take over here for a bit, I shall put in for the leave Neville wants me to take, and come and rest at home.

Much love,
Philip

R.I.P.

W.H. Hall
Gunner, Royal Field Artillery, 189th Brigade
15 June 1917 – Railway Dugouts Burial Ground (Transport Farm), Zillebeke, VII.B.6/18

* * *

164 The Military Police resided in a series of dugouts beneath Ieper Prison.
165 The Pix was a welcome gift from Portsea parishioners.

T.H.
Thursday night, 21 June 1917

Dearest Mater,
A very happy week, thank you, with lots of bright folk rolling in. Tonight I expected to go up to a Battery, but the lift failed to eventuate – not my fault. So I thought of you, and a word to wipe out my rather gory letter of Monday. We had a topping concert yesterday evening for a little R.E. Coy., who had never had any kindness shown them in their life before. I never knew folk so grateful. And in the middle of things in walked Lowman, the Q.W.R. signaller who drew the sketch of the Chapel 15 months ago, now on his way for a Commission with a well won Military Medal. Lots of old friends turning up, and the House simply buzzing with manifold activities. To-morrow some walking exercise to Higgon's and Shiner's etc., and back on Saturday afternoon to preside at a lecture, after lunch with Colonel Hutchinson of my old H.A. Group on the return journey.
    Pettifer my trusty comrade,
    Much love,
    Philip

The orchestra of Talbot House in the garden.

*   *   *

Sunday 24 June 1917
11.30 a.m. – Parts of Merbecke – Officiant: P.B. Clayton – No. of Com.: 35 – In old chapel – "So thou liftest thy divine petition" from Crucifixion, sung by soloists Pte. Morley and Rfm Brewster.

(Register of Services)

*   *   *

T.H.
Sunday night, 8 July 1917

Dearest Mater,
All going well here. I had my usual journey on Friday-Saturday with Pettifer, and am slightly deaf in consequence, as things were very noisy. But the harvest is plenteous.

Upstairs, as I write, I hear the sleepy chatter of yen gunners from Shiner's Battery, whom he very kindly allowed down to-night for the service, and to return after the Confirmation to-morrow afternoon. We have two motor buses plying up and down collecting candidates at various places, bringing them here and returning them at night.[166] Meanwhile, a happy house party of nearly 20 of my chaps hold the fort. We had a wonderful baptism of a Bombardier to-night in Evensong, which was packed. So the harvest grows, in spite of all the difficulty. Neville dashed in a few moments ago, saw them wrapped up in curtains, etc., in lieu of blankets, and chuckled, and fled off again in his car. He will, of course, be here to-morrow. Tea for 80 or so is rather a tall order, but can, I think, be wangled somehow.

Much love,
Your son,
Philip

*   *   *

From Rfm. Ronald Brewster to Tubby
10 July 1917

Dear Mr Clayton
Please excuse the general aspect and roughness of this letter, but being now a soldier and not a dweller in a house of recreation yclept[167] "Talbot" things are a trifle different. I am now well in it again. It is something to be thankful for that the Regiment is out resting and not in the line, it takes the edge off considerably.[168] It seems most strange to be back at the old routine again; physical drill at seven in the road, route marching, rifle manual and all the other delights invented to bring the B.E.F. up to a pitch of training never reached before, are not as nice as they might be, after a long season at a "home from home". But I make the best of it, and in company with another old stager also combed out, the flag of hope is left flying. This is being written in an old French barn, quite the usual kind of affair, but the pond outside is about the limit. Mater has taken my return quite well, but I know she does not like it. It is a great help to me to know that she is one who can really get definite help from her religion. I used to think once that those people were few and far between, but since being at Talbot House, and coming into contact with so many people, I have changed my views. I gave Capt. Price your letter, and

---

166 One of the confirmation candidates was L/Cpl. Archie Forrest. For Archie's story, see p. 311.
167 Middle English for called, named.
168 The 1/16th Queen's Westminster Rifles (169th Brigade, 56th (London) Division) came out of the line weak in numbers following the Battles of Arras. Brought up to strength by drafts, it underwent a thorough course of training from May to July before participating in the Third Battle of Ypres.

he was most kind to me. I have got my Commission papers in, and waiting the signature of the Commanding Officer. I mentioned that the Rev. N.S. Talbot would put in a word for me, and if he is approached at all, you will now understand why. I understand it takes quite a long time to get home now, so I must possess my soul in patience, and quietly carry on. My period at Talbot House has done me a lot of good, it has given me assurance in things I put my hand to, & the influence of the Chapel has given me a latent power to bear things quietly, while before I was inclined to grouse and criticise. I should love to be back with you now, and I rather envy Stagg, but in quite a nice way. Do you find Vokins good? I am afraid he will want a little nursing. Goodbye now, the light is getting very dim, candles are being lit and the boys are preparing for bed (such as it is) and I must do the same. Please do not forget me in your prayers.

Yours sincerely,
Ronald Brewster

P.S. Stagg will give you my address and please write me when you can.

*   *   *

23 July 1917

Dearest Mater,
To-day has been a great day in T.H., the Archbishop of York,[169] looking unrecognisably old, has been here all day. A great Eucharist this morning, with more than 120 Chaplains. A Conference after Lunch, at which Neville put me on to try and rub in the Ordinands question. Had at 6.30 a great mess meeting in the garden of men, men, men. Lang was very good, but fearfully worn out, and will be more so by the time he has finished his trip.

Neville came up with me on my rounds on Friday, and slept at Higgon's etc. We got badly shelled, and had a miniature gas attack; it was great to have him. I can't say what his friendship and help mean to me. Meanwhile, I enclose the Church Offertory of Sunday towards the Hants Prisoners' of War Fund, of which you sent me the circular. I told the congregations what I meant to send it to, and they stumped up twice as much as usual. Please get a receipt sent me pro forma.

I shan't come on leave now till August anyhow, if then. But am very fit and happy, so don't worry.

Gwynne came to tea to-day, and was delightful, and Macmillan also, who is back with him.

Sorry letters are so scrappy for the moment, but I won't sit up late, even to write to you, and I write practically to no one else.

Much love, dearest Mater,
Your son,
Philip

---

169 Cosmo Gordon Lang, Archbishop of York 1908-1928.

One of those present at the Chaplains Conference was Rev. Maurice Murray, 12th Royal Sussex Regiment. He made the following entry in his diary:

Monday July 23rd: Very hot again all day. Went to Poperinghe on my bicycle to Talbot House at 10.30 for Celebration. The Archbishop of York celebrated and gave an address on the words: "The hour is come. Glorify (vindicate) me that I may vindicate them." 110 communicants, all padres of 5th Army and "Allied Trades" such as Church Army, Y.M.C.A. workers. An interval at 12.15 to 12.30. At 12.30 Intercessions taken (inaudibly) by the Archbishop. Lunch at various places in the town such as Skindles, Cyrils, etc. … Conference at 2. The Bishop of Khartoum there this time. Neville Talbot very much in evidence during day and Clayton's arrangements good. The Archbishop asked several questions but we all got rather discussive, including the Archbishop himself. Still, it was all very friendly and nice and did us good to meet and compare notes. Our Divisional padres met at Cyril's Restaurant for tea and Crawley sketched out the arrangements and where we were all to be in the advance or "the push". Crawley drew a plan showing us our jobs. I am to be in an R.A.P. in the front line so feel a bit honoured, but we all take our turns for such jobs later if not hit. I went back to the deserted Talbot House Garden and wrote this up and rested and tried to get cool. The fug in those restaurants is simply awful. "Home" to C. Camp.

Rev. Maurice Murray.

*   *   *

"We've got a good T.H. Committee together now."

(P.B.C., letter to his mother, 29 July 1917)

From the Minutes of the First Talbot House Committee Meeting, 26 July 1917

Sub-Committee
Resolved that there be four Sub-Committees: House, Canteen, Social and Finance.

Staff
The existing staff consists of 5 O.R.s reduced from nine, the four withdrawn not having been replaced.
Resolved
that XVIII Corps be asked to supply five additional men to the staff.
that women be employed temporarily as necessary for "spring cleaning" and daily cleaning between the hrs of 6.30 and 9.30 a.m.

Transport
Resolved
that it is essential that separate motor transport be placed at the disposal of Talbot House at least once a week for purchasing canteen stores.
that XVIII Corps be asked to provide a hand-cart or loan continuously for fetching local purchases.

Supper Bar
Resolved that in view of the increasing profits and the large amount of work requiring to be done immediately, the question of starting a supper bar be postponed for the present.

*   *   *

T.H.
Tuesday, 31 July 1917

Dearest Mater,
I'm hors de combat – and there's a good deal of combat going on[170] – for a day or so with my periodical thorn in the flesh – fever.

Rather a rotten moment to get it – but I've got into the way of real-ising that whatever happens turns out best in the end: "All things working together for good", e.g. yesterday afternoon the Boche put a 6 inch into the house next door,

The Canadian Lounge, badly shaken by a shell burst in July 1917.

170 The preliminary bombardment for the Flanders offensive commenced on 16 July 1917; the infantry emerged from their trenches fifteen days later on 31 July. The Third Battle of Ypres had begun.

while I was in bed here. Five yards higher on its ten mile journey, and T.H. would have come down with a run.[171]

As it was the verandah outside my window black with smoke and alive with lath and plaster; but only one boy was wounded, and he only slightly. This is just possibly the last time the Boche will ever be able to shell Poperinghe. I shall be up and about again I hope by to-morrow, and able to do my various jobs.

I forgot to tell you the story of "Jacko" the magpie, who is now sitting with his head on one side on the window ledge. Two weeks ago when I went up to Dain's Battery[172] which was then situated in some reserve trenches, I found Jacko sitting calmly on the parapet eating bully beef. He belonged, I discovered, to a Herts Lc/Cpl., who was caretaker in chief of this piece of strong post. What was our mutual amazement when the man turned out to be Olivia's ex-Scoutmaster from Whealhampstead,[173] so refusing all recompense, he gave me the magpie for T.H. which it now adorns. It lives mainly on collarstuds and pen-nibs so far as I can make out, and is a great addition to the amenities of the place.

If the advance goes on, the problem of moving T.H. will require coping with, as I don't want to be left too far behind.

Now the post is going, so I must close,

Much love to all,

Philip.

*   *   *

NOTICE
Our Animal Kingdom
Have you been formally introduced to –

Kitten, one, white, camouflaged. Belgique by parentage, but British (as the catechism says) by adoption and grace. It enjoys the war enormously, and is far too busy getting dirty to have time to spare for getting clean. It has a limited but vivacious repertoire of performances and has betrayed several Scotsmen into forgetting themselves so far as to smile.

The Love Birds. Their names "Hunter" and "Bunter"[174] are, as Sam Weller said of the sausage, "wropt in mystery".[175] Hunter is plain in appearance; Bunter is spot. They came from Boulogne in a five-ton lorry, and do nothing in particular, but do it very well.

---

171 About this narrow shave, see also P.B.C.'s letter of 6 August 1917 and 'The Canadian Lounge', p. 268.
172 Capt. Dain, 2/ic to Major Higgon, 141st Heavy Battery.
173 Olivia was Tubby's first cousin.
174 "Hunter-Bunter" was the nickname of Lt.-Gen. Sir Aylmer Hunter-Weston (GOC VIII Corps, MP), in whose area Poperinge then lay. He was a frequent visitor to Talbot House. After the war Hunter-Bunter became Chairman of the House of Commons Group of Toc H, which at its peak numbered 78 members.
175 Cockney Samuel Weller is servant to Mr Pickwick, the main character in *The Pickwick Papers*, the first novel by Charles Dickens. Weller often quoted contemporaries in a humorous way, making fun of established clichés and proverbs by demonstrating their veracity or impropriety in certain situations, especially when taken too literally.

The Jackpie or Magdaw. His name is Jacko; and his diet bully beef and collar studs. He came from a reserve trench at Elverdinghe: we clipped his wings on arrival, since when he flies much better than before. No! we decline to slit his tongue, in the hope that he will talk articulately. He talks Welsh perfectly at present.

*   *   *

3 August 1917

Dearest Mater

Jacko has walked off with my fountain pen and hidden it somewhere, so I'm writing with a little baby stylo that Jack once gave me.

I'm going up with big brother Neville again to-day, for the day only, returning late to-night. Last time I took him up I nearly got him gassed, but that's another story. The weather is indescribable, and the Clerk of the Weather is obviously a pro German.[176] But it can't be helped. No, the pen won't write – so I revert to the ink-dipping business. I'm so glad you were pleased with P. of W. money. I can send more from time to time, if a help. Your letters lately have been better than ever, while mine have been worse.

I have a lot of leave due to me, but shan't try and get any yet, provided I keep fit, as I can't go on leave while all my best friends go over – and under. Two of my dearest parishioners – a R.A.M.C. boy, and an R.F.A. Lieut. were killed last week; not that I think the word "killed" means much in such cases. But it's beastly shaking hands with boys who come in to say "well goodbye, Padre, in case I don't come through", and some have such clear premonitions of death.

… How is Heffy? Cause her to wag her tail, and give her Jacko's love. I haven't got it. I doubt if he has any affection in him, except for collarstuds and fountain pens.

Now I must pack and wait for Neville,

Much love,

Philip

The beautiful old *prie-dieu* in the Upper Room bearing the names of Pte. William Locke, 133 Field Ambulance, and Pte. Kenneth Mayhew, 6 London Field Ambulance.

CHRISTIAN CRESWELL CARVER

176 The summer of 1917 was the wettest in living memory, West Flanders experiencing an aberrational rainfall that stalled the great British offensive throughout August.

R.I.P.
Christian C. Carver[177]
Lt., "A" Battery, 83 Brigade, Royal Field Artillery
23 July 1917- Age 20 – Lijssenthoek Military Cemetery, XIII.B.22

William W. Locke[178]
Private, 133 Field Ambulance, R.A.M.C.
25 July 1917 – Age 23 – Gwalia Cemetery (Poperinge), I.E.8

* * *

T.H.
6 August 1917

Dearest Mater,
All bright and shining here; the town gets a dose of shelling on most days, but not enough to interfere with business as usual. I had a very interesting journey to Shiner's on Friday – such a long way off now – right in the old Bosche front line, where a few of their Gargantuan dug-outs survive on the lips of the huge old craters.

Neville takes over T.H. from me on Fridays, which is excellent from every point of view. The House is packed as never before, and Services, etc., claim for their full attendances. I enclose a letter from the children of Coevoet-Camerlynck, the landlord of the House, thanking for the toys I got them. It would be delightful if Stuart wrote to Madeleine at Rousbrugge (no further address needed).[179]

We are trying to start a supper room here – much needed to compete with the estaminets, but I'm not going to serve tables myself.

Please tell Jack this week that his cigars have again come, and are as welcome as ever. I can't be too grateful for them. A letter also, and a mended pipe from Nancy.

This is only a pot-boiling letter.
Love to all,
Philip.

* * *

T.H.
Monday, 6 August 1917

Dearest Mater,
Your beautiful tin boxful arrived safely last night, and I ate most of Stuart's sweets in early bed, while gunfire shook the surrounding scenery.

---

177 Carver died of wounds received on 15 July when his battery dugout at Zillebeke Lake suffered a direct hit. An antique copy of "The Poems of Robert Browning" inscribed with Carver's name was discovered by an Australian soldier who added his inscription: "Found today 30th October 1917 during the Passchendaele strike in a blown in dugout on the left of Hill 60".
178 In the Upper Room a beautiful old *prie-dieu* bears the name of William Wellings Locke.
179 Stuart (b.1902) was the daughter of Tubby's elder brother 'Jack'. For Marie-Madeleine see note 162.

We had a narrow shave for the House on Monday last about 7 p.m. when a 9.5 landed in the little house next door, and blew it to bits. Fortunately the folk who live there were out, or they would have lived there no longer. Several chunks came into the Library wall, two boys were blown out of hammocks, one other was slightly wounded, about 50 lying about in the garden were rudely awakened, the place filled with smoke and plaster: but by a miracle no serious damage was done. Another 5 yards higher on a 15 mile flight, and T.H. would have gone west with a hundred casualties at best. Laus Deo!

The lavender is a little droopified, but smells sweet all over the place, and is certainly a touch of home. Alas! Jacko has vanished, and hidden my fountain pen before he went. We had a very good Sunday yesterday, with about 150 Communicants, and the Evensong crowded out. Dear Timothy Rees of Mirfield preached, most wonderfully. Here comes Yorky for the post!

Much love to all.

Philip.

*   *   *

T.H.
10 p.m., 12 August, 1917

Dearest Mater,

Sunday night, after a long day, and Major Bowes and a subaltern from Shiner's named Dodd (who is having a night off here) are chatting on the verandah outside. So I mustn't delay long rejoicing them. Bowes[180] is now President of T.H. Committee, and a very good fellow. Dodd is a dear, and sleeping in my bed to-night – sheets! – while I sleep in the fleabag of Andorra fame in the garden summer-house.

If I don't write now, I shan't break silence till Wednesday, as I have Macmillan to-morrow night, and a Confirmation on Tuesday.[181] I am quite fit again, and up to scratch. Batteries are having rather a stiff time, not unnaturally. The books from Portsea haven't yet come; I wait eagerly for them. Books are what I want most. On the other hand, money is rolling in, and we are financially recuperated; while the canteen is rather enlarged and renovated, and will almost pay for the House on its own. Services quite good, as usual, and some very jolly Confirmation candidates. We had another Baptism this morning in the old Winton Font. I don't see much chance of getting away at present, as it's hard to get a substitute here, and also unsympathetic while other folk are being killed. However, I shall manage it when and how I can. Neville is a pillar of fire in the darkness of this present world.

Much love
Philip

*   *   *

---

180 Major George Brimley Bowes (2/1st Bn Cambridgeshire Regiment) was Chairman of the Talbot House Committee, remaining so until early 1918. In private life he was a bookseller in Cambridge. In December 1917 he wrote a note on Talbot House, see appendix II. In 1921 Bowes founded and chaired the Cambridge branch of Toc H.
181 Rev. Julian Bickersteth, M.C., Senior Chaplain 56th (London) Division, wrote about this service in a correspondence with his mother: see p. 289.

It was such a blessed relief to get away from the noise and sordidness to that little chapel up in the roof of Talbot House …

(Rifleman N.N., 2nd L.R.B., on his birthday, 26th August 1917)

*   *   *

From the Visitors' Book, Little Hatchett
1-10 September [1917]
PBC never could write with a J nib, but since Jacko stole his fountain pen just before he (PBC) came home on leave, he must record his sentiments with a J, or depart in silence. He hasn't done much writing during these days of bliss, although the mater's stamps are so readily scrounged. The weather has been excellent on the whole, with just enough wettitude to make the barometer an interesting study. Captain Wilson gave him a lift to Gosport on Monday 3rd, otherwise tennis, boating in G.J.'s boat, and swimming in the pond have occupied most waking moments apart from meals – such delicious things – and one long continuous munching of apples. Now back to la guerre; T.H. awaits its publican.

(P.B.C.)

Tubby on leave at Little Hatchett.

Tubby addressing a congregation outside East Boldre Church.

*   *   *

From Leonard Browne to Tubby
Crait House,
Carr Bridge,
INVERNESS-SHIRE
11 September 1917

My dear Tubby,
… The Medical Board at Wandsworth marked me permanently unfit for General Service. They only discharge you "if you are nearly dead" … (But in any case I can do the Registrar job for the Ordination Scheme when I get settled down.)

It seems ages since I left Pop probably because I have been to so many places since on my way to England. I do wish you were here so that I could see you and touch you and talk to you. I am rather Talbot House sick. I feel as if I could never worship in a place unless everyone was in khaki. I suppose I shall get over that in time, but women in church are rather a trial at present.

I can't say all the things I feel about you and T.H. My feelings are too deep for expression. But I can say that my friendship work with you has been one of the happiest experiences I have ever had. The great thing is that the friendship is only at the end of its first year – may it go on for many more. Perhaps we may be able to work together too – I hope so. I feel that my words are very meagre and inadequate to the occasion but you can fill in the gaps for you understand me well enough.

Good night. God bless you.

It *does* feel queer to be *writing* to you.

Wednesday morning.
Give my love to Big Brother.[182] I thought of T.H. a lot on Sunday though I did not know whether you would be back there by then. I wondered how the great problem of Hall or Garden would be settled without me.[183]

…

Yours ever,
Leonard F. Browne

*   *   *

Talbot House,
15 September 1917

Dearest Mater,
My good friend, the Gunner,[184] is helping me to write to you on Saturday night, so that in spite of the prodigious pressure at the present moment, you shan't fail to get something in the nature

---

182 Rev. Neville Talbot.
183 The Sunday evening service became too large for the Upper Room.
184 Gunner C.S. Pease, 141 Heavy Battery.

of a week end letter, the last I fear he will be able to do, as he is recalled to his Battery, and leaves me again desolate.

The House is absolutely crammed from morning till night. Yesterday we took 450 Francs in penny cups of tea,[185] with only about 20 broken mugs to do it with, and we long for the arrival of the Southampton china, as crockery is unpurchaseable anywhere here. Meanwhile the higher side of the House is also tremendously strong, stronger perhaps than I have ever known it, and I don't really know how we are going to get a tithe of the people in to Church to-morrow who want to come. Neville returns to-night and is preaching for me to-morrow night, otherwise I should not be writing, even to you.

I want you to go and buy that other bed post please, and take it also to the saw mill, and get them to treat it exactly like the others, except that it is not to have the candlestick fixture at the top, but the small round or square table head, so that we can put the dear old font properly and safely on it. If the candlesticks are ready, as I hope they are, please see that they are being sent off without delay. This is the zenith of Talbot House, and I want everything to be at its best, please God. I am extraordinarily fit myself, and enjoying my high pressure with a childish delight, asking nothing better, and being profoundly thankful for health and strength. It is indeed good to be here.

Sunday night – Some two hundred and thirty Communicants during the day, and about 500 at Evensong in the garden, to which N.S.T. failed to arrive; I preached extempore!

Much love,
Philip

*   *   *

In a letter home, dated 17 September 1917, L/Cpl. William G. Stone, R.E., recorded a deplorable incident that occurred at the House:

A piece of Communion plate was stolen from the chapel, which is always left open for private prayer. It is of great personal and intrinsic value and a reward of 150 francs is offered for its recovery. Wasn't it a mean and wicked thing to do?

Tubby remarked afterwards that he "had the greatest difficulty in preventing the mounting of a guard upon the holy place".

R.I.P.
William G. Stone
2nd Cpl., 25th Signal Coy., Royal Engineers
23 October 1918 – Age 22 – Cross Roads Cemetery (Fontaine-au-Bois, France), I.C.21

*   *   *

185 This amounts to approximately 4,150 cups of tea.

Talbot House
19 September 1917

My dear Browno,

I am sitting in a Wicker chair, which ill supports my weight, smoking a fat cigar, very much at my ease, and Gunner Pease of old 141 is helping this lame duck over his literary stiles.

There is an enormous amount to report to you, especially in view of your beloved letter, so before I lose Pease on Saturday, the report shall be made, though please don't imagine that I shall ever live up to letter writing, on this scale, when he is gone.

I had an extraordinarily health giving leave, swimming about in Hatchett Pond in pursuit of toy boats most of the morning, and playing Tennis with surprising agility for a man of my weight and years, during the afternoon. … I waited in vain to hear from you before I came back, but suspected that there had been a hitch somewhere, and still hoped against hope to find you in Talbot House on my return. I spent the night at No. 7 Stationary on my way up, or rather half the night, as I got a Car outside the "Folkestone" at 11.30 p.m. which landed me here just as dear old Pettifer was giving me up for the night. The situation that I discovered next day, certainly required a healthy constitution to withstand. A chapter of tragedies, accidents and such like had befallen the dear House in the course of 10 days, such as to leave us on our beam ends. To start with Stagg as an A man was returned on the third day of my Leave to his Regiment, by nefarious demands of the Entrenching Battalion, and in spite of all that the gallant Major[186] could do. I told you that as soon as your protective hand was withdrawn, these things would begin to happen. I heard from Stagg two or three days ago, who told me that when he reached the Westminsters the C.O. wanted to know the grounds of complaint on which he had been dismissed from Talbot House, where he had been left to maintain forever the Q.W.R. tradition. Of course, I have written to the C.O. – whom fortunately I knew as a Subaltern – and pointed out that the boot was very much on the other leg, and that it was we who were not worthy of him, asking at the same time, that he should be again medically examined, and if found unfit, that consent should be given to an attempt on our part to get him back. I am afraid, however, that from what Stagg says, his opportunity for a Commission has gone by, for the time being, so that he has lost by being here, in that sense.

The next tragedy concerned Pettifer, who was solemnly ordered also to report to his Regiment. When we protested that he had been unfit, the reply was, that he had never been marked 'P.B.',[187] and should not be so marked unless he went down to the Base, apparently on the prin-ciple that Doctors elsewhere, were not fit to express an opinion, so he too, has gone for the time being at least, though as he was accompanied by a request secured by Neville from the Army Commander himself, that Private Pettifer should be, if possible, returned to duty here – I still have hopes that he has not gone forever.

The third tragedy was that Corporal H. was arrested that same evening as a Deserter of 16 months standing.[188] I can't put the whole sad story on paper, but it was not cold feet, so far as I can make out. He had been apparently posted as Wounded and Missing, and took advantage of this to separate himself from a rather grim wife in Australia.

---

186 Major Bowes, chairman of the Talbot House Committee.
187 'Permanent Base' men were unfit for front line duty. Some were assigned to base camps whilst others were attached to labour units.
188 For Pte. John Henry's story: see p. 318.

The fourth tragedy was that, apparently, the thief of the two Offertories grew bolder, and on the second Sunday before I got back, stole that beautiful and very valuable silver gilt Wafer Box from the Credence table.

The fifth tragedy was that there was no water whatever and the sixth that there was practically no Staff. – This to greet me in a single day, rather knocked me endwise, but I have tried to carry out the principles that Donald Hankey[189] says so few Padres carry out, and not worry over-much. Things now are very much straighter. The gallant Major has really turned up trumps, and we have for the moment an enormous Staff of 14 headed by the nice Sergeant, a borrowed Coldstream Corporal and a L/Corpl. to boot, and under their command any amount of industrious apprentices in the shape of Scotchmen and Irishmen, who I don't think can read and write, and certainly cannot speak any formal English. However, if they cannot read, the Library will still have some room for visitors, and if they cannot write I shan't have to censor their letters.

Meanwhile, the House is clean, everyone is working pretty hard. Vokins is happier than I have seen him for a long time, in charge now, only of the Library, the Chapel and the Chaplains' Shop,[190] which we are now opening. The nice Captain Kidd of the R.E.'s is coming on to the Committee as Treasurer, and I have much to be thankful for.

I look forward, therefore, to the future, with altogether undimmed confidence. The Laycock-Evans combination[191] is another great asset, and everybody all round are as kind as they can be. I am losing dear Higgon and Dain and their families, but I cannot grudge their going to quieter things,[192] and as things stand at present, it may be a blessing in disguise, as it is quite plain that I cannot now expect to be able to get out of the House for very much. The number of people in the House has grown almost past conception. We took 450 francs in cups of tea alone, on Monday, and that, with our comical array of battered china, as instruments. People stream in to my Room, from morning till night, on various errands at an incredibly accelerated rate, from that of a few weeks ago, and it is difficult to keep first things first. This morning we had 60 at 7.30 and 50 (mainly Dain's Gunners) at a special Celebration at 11 a.m., and this evening the Chapel was full up for Even Song, including a mysterious old Colonel with blue tabs.[193] A quaint little Subaltern from your 268 Company came in to tea to-day (with a party of boys,

---

189 Donald Hankey was a soldier-journalist who wrote influential articles for *The Spectator* and *The Westminster Gazette* until his death in action on 12 October 1916. His writings were posthumously published in a popular volume entitled *A Student in Arms* (his pen name). E. Madigan, *Faith under Fire*, p.267.

190 For Chaplains' Shop or Church Shop, see p. 267.

191 Sapper Frederick Laycock, 5th Army signals and Private Eddie Evans, 14 Royal Welch Fusiliers, were staff members. The latter was also a member of the Social Sub-Committee and was with Talbot House as late as Christmas 1918. The former was a member of the House and Canteen Sub-Committees.

192 141st Battery was relieved and went into rest camp at the village of Noordpeene to the west of Cassel after the Battle of Menin Road Ridge (20-25 September 1917). Whilst there, Major Higgon, who had been unwell for some time, was invalided to the base. Capt. Dain also left the Battery.

193 The "Colonel" was Geoffrey Cecil Twisleton-Wykeham-Fiennes, 18th Baron Saye and Sele (1858 -1937). He was stationed as an Area Commandant at St.-Jan-ter-Biezen, west of Poperinge. He had fought in the Anglo-Zulu War of 1879 as a Captain in the Royal Scots Fusiliers. Appointed honorary regimental colonel in 1907. He succeeded his father and took up a seat on the Liberal benches in the House of Lords that same year. From 1912 to 1915 he served under Prime Minister H.H. Asquith as Comptroller of the Household. In November 1919 he became a member of the first Executive Committee of Toc H. He resided at Broughton Castle, the family seat near Banbury in Oxfordshire.

and an R.A.M.C. Major from Heaven knows where) and afterwards distinguished himself by standing on a broken chair and mending an electric light over the piano, amid loud applause. Someone scrounged my pliers that he was using for the task, but it is quite in keeping with the best traditions of the House that "Sam Brownes"[194] should mend electric lights, that "non-Sam Brownes" may see by them.

… I saw the D.C.G. on the Leave Boat, who was very keen that you should undertake the keeping of the Register of Candidates in England, and the corresponding with them, and I hope and trust that this arrangement will be made.

Candidates are simply pouring in here, that is to say two or three every day, and we simply must know where we stand, and that right soon.

I really must not, even with Pease's help, write more to you now.

Yours always,

Philip

*   *   *

Memories of Lord Saye and Sele

Lord Saye and Sele, eager as any schoolboy, arrived in Poperinghe in the ominous spring of 1917. We had heard rumours that some dug-out colonels were coming out as area commandants, to double the parts of viceroy and house agent, each with a hamlet as his capital. Four colonels came. The senior of the party was one whose name, whose character, whose sense of fun, whose habits of devotion, were unlike anything we had conjectured. His curious name caused trouble early on. A Poperinghe policeman saluted, stopped him, and asked him for his pass, which he produced. The M.F.P. was utterly confounded. "Excuse me, sir, but which of these two gentlemen are you?"

As time went on every one came to know him or to be glad he was about the place. Titles were not uncommon in the Salient; but liberal colonels, given to conversation with everybody in a British uniform, bordered on the exceptional. Full colonels could be awkward customers. Most men in crowns and stars could only be at ease with their own battalion. Yet this old man – as he seemed to us – behaved as if it was a treat to meet a stranger, a pleasure to fix up a billet for him, a privilege to crack a joke with him; you might imagine that he had no object in the world but to become a friend – and that was true. Need we wonder that St. Jan ter Biezen began to gain a popularity for troops sent back to "rest" – as it was called – and that the Colonel's modest room, a Belgian parlour crammed with unsafe chairs, knick-knacks , bijouterie, and religious oleographs was much frequented by the passer-by.

---

194 A Sam Browne belt is a wide belt, usually leather, which is supported by a strap extending diagonally over the right shoulder; primarily worn by officers and warrant officers.

In Talbot House the white moustache was famous. Here was a man whose whimsical philosophy lightened the War, relieved the general tension, hearkened with zest, replied with homely wisdom, and brightened every room he visited. But there was one room he knew best of all. This was the hoploft, which had been transformed into the throne-room of the Carpenter. Here Saye and Sele needed no introduction. A four-mile walk on an unpleasant road, blocked by the traffic of the Salient, and by no means immune from hostile attention, was nothing to this very firm old colonel, who never broke his fast before Communion and would not stay for breakfast afterwards. St. Jan ter Biezen will not readily forget its English squire, "Milor le Commendant." Nor will the stairs he climbed in Talbot House, the loft he loved, the Carpenter's Bench before which he knelt, discard the memory of his fidelity.

(P.B. Clayton)

*   *   *

24 September, 1917
Monday 9 a.m.

Dearest Mater,
Again only a card for the moment, written between early Service and waiting for breakfast. I arranged to go out to breakfast with an infantry captain, who came to service yesterday. And while I wait for him, I am munching Jack's nut sweets, which are just the thing to start a Monday on.

All goes well here, except that moonlit nights are providing us with a regular Boch's benefit of air-raids; distinctly pretty when at a safe distance, but – after two nights of it, I feel glad I don't live in London. The Old House comes off practically soot free every time. Bombs are worse than shelling; however it's not without its humorous side; though in order really to enjoy it we still need the return of Pettifer.

To-day Shiner entrains with all his happy crew; they are coming to a Celebration this morning, if possible; and N.S.T. and I went up yesterday afternoon, and had a farewell Service with them. This leaves me stript of all three old friends, but there's plenty still to be done.

Yesterday our harvest festival was good, all bombs considered. The Chapel looked lovely, and the fruit, etc., contributed by the men is going to the Field Ambulance.

Now this fellow still hasn't come, so I must get breakfast and start work; especially as Pettifer's understudy is yearning to clean my room.

Hurry along the photographs please. The carpets from Southton have come and are beautiful; but not the candlesticks yet.

Much love,
Philip

*   *   *

Talbot House,
A.P.O., S4, B.E.F.
25 September 1917

My dear old Boys,[195]
I know you will understand why this letter is even more behind-hand than usual. It has partly been a question of time, as I have been busier in the last two months, than ever in my life before; partly because I have not had the heart to get it written.

For more than two years on land, our Brotherhood has been wonderfully immune from loss. Not, I think, that we were behind hand in our contribution to the Army, though naturally the Sea came first with us; and our first loss was Harry Adams, of the "Formidable".

On land, our contingent in France grew slowly; Bert Potter alone represented us, in the Great Retreat, then gradually the new Armies came out. The next year, strangely enough, we paid no price out here, but at home the wonderful Frank Padfield who, more than any of us welded Fred Burrow into the Club life, died after a long painful illness, heroically borne.

Fred Burrow and Bertie Hoptrough spent both Christmas and Easter Day with me. Harry Townley brought along Charlie Grant. Syd Nagle came in with a friend to tea, and Harold Salter. Charlie Payne after a year's absence from these parts, came back with his big gun, and sought me out like the true brother he always was. Frank Gales even slept in my room, two nights on rest. Fred Jeffrey was close at hand. Stan Nancarrow and Harry Benham reinforced our Sunday evening choir in the true Portsea spirit.[196] Of these Fred Burrow, Charlie Payne, Charlie Grant and Syd Nagle have died in action. Fred Jeffrey and Frank Gales have been badly wounded, the first I fear, beyond recovery.

Cpl. Herbert Hoptrough.

I last saw Fred standing like a model of young manhood, with his shirt off, washing at the door of a hut. I had gone miles out of my way to find him, and how thankful I am now, that I did. Of his death I have only few details as yet, and indeed one can scarcely expect more at a time when every tick of the clock means a brave man's life. I am going to try and find his grave, as soon as I can, but though one of my Batteries fires over the place, it is as yet, impossible to reach in daylight. So Frank Padfield and Fred Burrow are together again. Charlie Payne, through his apprenticeship at Woolwich, was not so well known as these to the Club as a whole, but I think he was the first boy I really knew in Portsmouth. I looked forward to his rare holidays tremendously. He was full of happiness and uprightness of both kinds. As he grew up, and especially since he came out here, his character deepened splendidly, and, in his Section, and indeed through the whole of his Battery, he stood in his own quiet decisive way for whatever things are noble, and whatever things are pure. He was killed like Fred Burrow, instantaneously, and last Monday I stood before the Cross that marks his grave, with the Section on either side, to thank God for the example of his life, and to pray for the comfort for his folk at home.[197]

Now, my Brothers, I must stop. This is a sad letter but a very proud one, and while I do not feel, that I can write about anything else alongside these things, I am quite sure that neither Fred or Charlie nor any of them, would wish the *Nutshell* to be gloomy for their sakes. One has seen enough of death by now, to feel very certain that it is more a question of being frightened than being hurt; terribly sad, it is true, for the homes, but in no way a disaster to the individual soul.

…

Yours always,
Philip Clayton

The Nutshell also published the following letter extract by Cpl. Bert Hoptrough, H.Q. Signallers, 15th Hants:

I can truthfully say that I have not been in a position to write lately for I have had a busy time. I simply cannot explain how I feel about Fred, but I know you will understand. We joined up practically together and have been together for the greater part of our 15 months in France, so please express my real grief. Remember me to all in Club and Class.

Editor's Note:
Just before going to press we hear of the death in action of Bert Hoptrough, Fred Burrow's great and constant friend. They were always together in club and class; they joined up together and only a few weeks separated them in their death.

R.I.P.
Frederick G. Burrow
Corporal, 15 Hampshire Regiment
1 August 1917 – Wijtschaete Military Cemetery, VI.D.8

Charles W. Grant
Rifleman, 8 London Regiment (Post Office Rifles)
13 July 1917 – Age 20 – Oak Dump Cemetery (Voormezele), J.5

Herbert C. Hoptrough
Corporal, 15 Hampshire Regiment
20 September 1917 – Age 21 – Tyne Cot Memorial (Passendale), Pnl. 88 to 90 and 162

---

197 On that occasion the Battery gave Tubby a wooden carving of a monk, found in the ruins of Vélu (Somme), which Charlie had brought all the way up for the Chapel of Talbot House, where it still rests.

Sidney E. Nagle
Rifleman, 1/21 London Regiment (First Surrey Rifles)
7 June 1917 – Ypres (Menin Gate) Memorial, Panel 54

Charles M. Payne
Fitter, 18th Siege Battery, Royal Garrison Artillery
9 September 1917 – Age 22 – Duhallow A.D.S. Cemetery (Ieper), VI.C.6

*   *   *

THE DISPENSARY
Newcastle-on-Tyne
2 October 1917

My dear Tubular One,
I got your letter on Friday and it nearly made me weep.
… Neither you nor I were surprised about Corporal Henry. I remember you mentioning your suspicions months ago. But we were content to let sleeping dogs lie. I only hope Henry will not suffer from our failure to make proper enquiries about him. In spite of the cloud he is under I must say I like him. It is a good thing he is an Australian and cannot be shot.
I was particularly sorry to hear about Stagg because I might possibly have been able to prevent that catastrophe if I had been on the spot. But I expect by now you have brought the authorities to heel in a thoroughly repentant frame of mind.
Pettifer's return seemed almost assured at the time you wrote so I did not agitate myself about him. One of the principal duties of the Treasurer would seem to have been to certify that no useful man was fit for any form of active service other than helping to run T.H.
Your letter fortunately ended happily or I should probably by now have deserted to the Front and burst in upon you. T.H. has a wonderful way of pulling through the most hopeless muddles. But it is usually more by luck than good management.
I quite realise that your correspondence in my direction will not be very profuse in days to come. Indeed I was quite surprised to hear from you as soon as I did. But two or three lines without any padding will be advisable occasionally to keep me in touch with "things as they are".
I do miss the T.H. services frightfully. It is very hard to worship in a congregation mainly composed of women after being entirely with men and they in khaki.
Au Revoir,
Yours ever,
Leonard F. Browne

*   *   *

Sunday, 7 October 1917, 9.45 a.m.

Dearest Mater,
A most wicked time to start writing, just when I should be getting under way for the morning services, but I feel I must send you a line by this post to promise a letter by the next.
I'm very shorthanded, Vokins being on leave, Pettifer still unreturned, etc., and it's always my home letters that are a barometer of pressure upon my life.

I'm well and happy; and very rich in good friends and helpers. *Laus Deo.* I'll try to write again to-night.

Sunday night

I don't think I shall get much written before I drop off to sleep, but must hold to my promise of this morning. A quiet Sunday, the weather being absolutely awful, and prohibiting a full house. Winter is plainly upon us again. What a pity we couldn't have had a week or so more fine weather, it would have shortened the war tremendously. As it is, all has gone more than well lately, and everyone is full of high spirits about it, except the miserable people over yonder. We still get shelled and bombed a bit, but it's a back area business only, and with all my batteries shifted to quieter places, I have no adventures at present, and rather miss them.

Yesterday I borrowed a sidecar and went visiting the outlying parish: I fetched up for tea with a dear old man who at 68 years of age walks in here most Sunday mornings at 7.30 a.m. from two miles or more out for Service. This is Lord Saye and Sele (a quaint name) an old Colonel, who docs Area Commandant of a populous district. When he first arrived here, a M.F.P. asked for his pass, and then scratched his head as he read it, and said "Excuse me, Sir, but which of these gentlemen are you?" He is quite one of the most charming old men I have ever come across.

This week (on Friday) I go to St. Omer to take a Quiet Day for Chaplains again. Hooper's brother (a Captain in the R.G.A.) played the organ at our service tonight.

Much love,

Philip

* * *

Cutcliffe and I attended a most enjoyable service in the chapel of Talbot House. The chaplain who has an artistic taste has made quite a fine chapel out of the loft. The floor is covered with carpet, rather a pretty chandelier in the centre, while the light is supplied by candles which gives the room an Eastern effect. Hymn books and books of music for the psalms etc. are provided, and a harmonium supplies the tunes etc. The parson gave a fine address in a very sincere manner. I think this is the most enjoyable service I have attended out here.

Fritz over, bomb dropping during the service.

(Sapper Percy Room, R.E., F.F. Cable Section, diary, 14 October 1917)

* * *

24 October 1917

Dearest Mater,

Not long to write this wet morning, as I have much to do before I set out to fetch Canon B.K. Cunningham from the C.A. Hut where he was taking a Quiet Day yesterday, and set him on his homeward road.[198] And this before a funeral at 11.30! And my Sergeant i/c the House ill with a very bad cough etc.

---

198 Bertram Keir Cunningham (1871-1944) was recognized as the leading clerical trainer of his day. Founder of the Farnham Hostel and mentor of an elite band of clergy known as 'the Farnham Brotherhood', he was the principal of the Chaplains' School of Instruction which had opened at St.

Postcard of the Upper Room with the times of daily services printed at the back; widely distributed and treasured by many.

One thing to the good. Thanks to Neville, I have now old Pettifer back for duration this time, I think: entrenched behind masses of typewritten authority. This makes all the difference to me. I had a very nice time at D.C.G.'s again last Friday at a Conference with Neville: only the writing work it all opens up is beyond my time limits at present without sitting up all night, which I steadfastly refuse to do. They want various pamphlets and papers to be written by me, but unless I can lock myself up somewhere for a week or so, I see no chance. Last Sunday was most gorgeous, as some grand old Londons came in and flooded everything. About 250 Communicants, and the Chapel filled to suffocation for two evening services with folk clamouring down below to get in. Rather good for men to find they can't find room in a Church sometimes! It puts a new light on the situation of religion!

Much love,

Philip

*   *   *

Omer in February 1917. Michael Snape, *The Back Parts of War: the YMCA Memoirs and Letters of Barclay Baron, 1915 to 1919* (Woodbridge: Boydell Press, 2009), p.246.

From Mrs Pettifer to Tubby
12 Ravenscroft St.
Hackney Rd
E2
25 October 1917

Dear Mr Clayton
Many thanks for sending me Postal Order and also for your kindness to my husband. I was more than thankful when I heard that he was back with you again and I hope he will be able to help with you till this dreadful struggle is over. I must now close with wishing you every success and a safe return.

I remain Yours Respectfully
Mrs Pettifer

*   *   *

Sunday night, 28 October 1917

Dearest Mater,
I think I had better make a push and write to you now, as to-morrow morning I have a Confirmation Class among other things, and I shall infallibly miss the post if I delay. Major Bowes is back from leave, and this will relieve me a little of house problems – coal, oil, etc. (we had a bomb on our electric light plant).[199] The House itself goes wonderfully. To-day's Services were not quite so full as last Sunday's, but 100 or so Communicants isn't bad, all things considered, and Evensong and Sung Litany went well to-night.

Many old Canadian friends have turned up after a year's absence, and I can't make up my mind whether I like them more than the Australians. The weekday Evensong has been amazing this week, averaging nearly a hundred a night. All sorts of folk come in. I had two British West Indian Sergeants at Communion the other day, and two Chinese at Evensong during the week.

…

Much love,
Philip

Chinese labourer 18693 Song Xiufeng poses with Maurice, the son of photographer René Matton, in Proven.

199 The electric light engine was successively struck by two shells and an aerial bomb within two months.

* * *

30.10.17

My dear Browno,

I never thought you would get another letter from me; not because I have quarrelled with you, but because the combination of my natural indolence and the amazing busyness of this present life militate against anything of the kind. However, "the darkest hour always comes etc.",[200] and the dawn in this case is our old and mutual friend Sgt. McInnes who, being himself about twice as busy as I shall ever be, has volunteered to cope with my bad debts in correspondence. Laus Deo.

There is an amazing amount to tell you of various kinds. The most interesting things of course cannot be said owing to the Censor, but you will be happy at least to know that T.H. still stands fairly firm – a bomb on the electric light and another in the garden being our only military events up to now. The House meanwhile in its work flourishes amazingly, with old friends of more than a year ago coming back to it and new friends being continually added. Here again I cannot specify too minutely but must leave it for you to conjecture. Week-day Evensong now-a-days seldom falls below fifty, and last week, on Monday night, achieved the record of a hundred and sixty. There were last Sunday over a hundred Communicants, and on the Sunday previous over two hundred and fifty, but of course the population is not stable like it used to be, and many of the best depart to be no more seen. The Chapel is looking better than ever, thanks to various new gifts, and the Library now contains I suppose nearly a thousand books.

The staff question is still a series of crises. I have got Pettifer back with extraordinary difficulty and thanks mainly to Big Brother, but the counter-attack develops tomorrow in the medical examination of Vokins who, I fear, will be lost to me. You will, I know, be glad to hear that he has changed completely for the better recently, and for the last two months has been more than his old self, being worth his weight in gold. Otherwise, with the exception of Jimmy,[201] there is no one of the old brigade on the staff. A nice broken-down pioneer sergeant has taken the place of Stagg, but has not filled it, though he is good at some things, e.g. discipline etc., where Stagg was not. Five hard-working P.B. men, one of whom can read and write, (the rest being Irishmen) keep the house clean, but naturally do not understand it. A nice and pious Corporal, borrowed from a Battery, keeps the Chapel beautifully clean but has no grey matter in his head whatever. To these were added until today a couple of young gentlemen awaiting their Commissions, who for general incompetence and an outrageous opinion of their own importance are I hope an example in the history of Cadet Schools. One, who was supposed to have been running the Library, terminated his period of office last night by going to bed with the key thereof, and leaving me at midnight, while an air-raid was in progress, to discover the lamp and the stove both left alight behind the locked door!

The Committee meanwhile goes along pretty well. It has a highly comic side, which I only wish I had you to share with me. Kidd, your successor, presides over a great store of shekels and is really delightful, but unfortunately he is very shy of the men. We have more money than we

---

200 Proverb attributed to Thomas Fuller (1608-1661): "The darkest hour always comes before the dawn."
201 Staff cook Pte. Jimmy Moorhouse, 762 Area Employment Company.

know what to do with, and they won't let me 'blow' it, but spend hours of priceless time debating whether the two reserve funds, one of which must not be touched under any circumstances whatever, shall contain 6,000 or 7,000 francs, and whether this shall be called Reserve Capital or Reserve Fund! However, thanks to Bowes being on leave at the last Committee meeting, I managed to extract 2,000 francs which I spent on stoves and lamps and chairs and tin-tacks, bringing back my spoils in a lorry.

I must not now go further with this description, except to tell you of a boy who came in yesterday desirous of being Confirmed.

(The remainder of the letter is lost)

*   *   *

Talbot House,
5 November 1917

Dearest Mater,
A very old friend of mine, Sergt. McInnes, has come most gallantly to my rescue in the matter of letters, and so I can sit in a rocking chair, eating an apple (not one of yours) and talk to you quite happily for ten minutes without lifting a finger. Neither your apples nor the candlesticks have yet put in an appearance, but the china mugs came on Saturday and are a great success, only one of the gross being broken in spite of the tremendously rough journey. I am sending you in a few days a cheque to cover both these and the candlesticks, with much gratitude from the Committee for your help.

All goes well here and the dark nights render dreams more peaceful, if paraffin more scarce. Our electric light is still unrepaired. Apparently what is needed now is a resistance coil, electricity, like the British Constitution, being only at its best when it has something tough to shove up against. …

Much love,
Philip

*   *   *

NOTICE
Owing to the descent of a meteorite upon the electric lighting plant, the House is temporarily reduced to the oil and grease expedients of a bygone age. In regard to the former, gentlemen will please desist from turning the wick upwards, as the augmentation of the illumination thus secured is extremely temporary, and results in a soot bath and a cracked chimney. In regard to the latter, remember what Shakespeare says about its illuminant attractiveness, and please draw the blinds.[202]

*   *   *

---

202 Possibly a reference to Shakespeare's Othello, Act 5, scene 2, in which Othello, enraged and hurt, enters the bedroom of his sleeping wife Desdemona with a lit candle in his hand. He states that he is going to "Put out the light, and then put out the light", i.e. blow out the candle and then smother her to death. Before he lets in Emilia, his wife's maidservant, he draws the bed-curtains.

Talbot House,
5 November 1917

My dear Willy and Arthur,[203]
Thank you so much for your letter and please thank Mother for hers too. It makes all the difference to my happiness to have your Daddy back with me again, and I hope and trust we shall be together now till the end of the war. I will try and get him home to you as near Christmas as possible, but you mustn't be too disappointed if it doesn't exactly fit in. I am sure whatever time he does get home to you will be the right time for you. He will get a fortnight now instead of only 10 days.

   Yours affectionately,
   Philip Clayton

*   *   *

From the minutes of the Talbot House Committee meeting, 10 November 1917

House
Rev. P.B. Clayton proposed, Major Bowes seconded that improvements be made to small room on ground floor and that small room on first floor[204] be converted into an officers rest room. The necessary expenditure being authorized.

Advanced Talbot House
Resolved that Major Bowes be authorized to serve on Joint Committee for advanced Talbot House Ypres.

Social
Proposed by Major Bowes, seconded by Sapper Laycock that two parties be given to Belgian children on 6th December and 1st January at approximate cost of 250 francs. Details to be left to Social Sub-Committee.

Christmas
Resolved that Social Sub-Committee discuss details for Christmas parties etc.

General
Proposed by Major Rugg, seconded by Rev. P.B. Clayton "That this house be opened to British soldiers only". Amendment proposed by Major Bowes, seconded by Sapper Laycock that "white" be inserted after "opened to". Amendment was lost and original proposition carried.

*   *   *

203 Arthur (b.1907) and William (b.1909) were the sons of Pte. Pettifer, Tubby's batman.
204 I.e. the General's Bedroom: see p. 274.

12 November 1917

Dear Mr Clayton
Thank you for your nice present what you sent. Arthur and I hope you are quite well and also my daddy. I hope you are having fine weather. Dear Mr Clayton I hope you can let my daddy come home for christmas as mum and me and arthur would be glad to see him.
    I must close now with love from
    Willy

*   *   *

13/ 11/17

Dear mr Clayton
I hope you are quite well and in the best of health and thank you for your kind letter and nice Present which we receive quite safe Dear mr Clayton will you give my love to my daddy.

    I must close now with love from

    arthur and mum

*   *   *

Talbot House,
A.P.O. S.4,
14.11.17

Dearest Mater,
Grand old Sergt. McInnes and myself are settling down to strafe a week's accumulation of letters beside some bad debts, and the first shall be to you, as I promised last night. Since I then wrote a great event has happened. The candlesticks

"Great candlesticks made of bedposts stand sentinels of light above the worshippers." (P.B.C.)

have arrived, and are perfectly gorgeous. They fit the Chapel most wonderfully, and so does the Font Stand. Did I tell you in my letter last night that on Monday evening four B.W.I.'s, i.e. native troops, had been baptized with it before the Confirmation next day? I was wondering whether in Queensland it was ever used for the baptism of Kanakas.[205] If the cheque sent does not cover all our financial indebtedness, I rely on you to let me know. We took over Little Talbot House yesterday, and a very nice fellow-Chaplain named Goodwin is in charge of it for the present.[206] I hope its work will be as happy as that of the Mother-House, but shall probably not move up there myself until after Christmas. Meanwhile we are able to spare a good deal from the accumulation of the furniture, etc., here, to help fit it up. Water and gas are already laid on! …

*   *   *

Talbot House,
A.P.O., S4,
B.E.F.
22 November 1917

My dear Nutshellites[207]
Here am I with my feet on the stove, burning the leather off the soles of my slippers, and otherwise in the lap of luxury, ready to talk to you regardless of the fact that it is already past midnight. Probably some of you have already had occasion to notice an extraordinary change for the better both in my handwriting and in the volume of my correspondence. This is due to the exceeding kindness of an old friend of mine, a Sergeant in the Intelligence, who finds time somehow to spend the best part of two nights a week here typing faster than I can talk. The result is that for the first time during the last three years I am not frightfully behindhand with letters, and those of you who I have given up writing in despair had better please forgive the past and try once more and see what happens this time.

The tidings of Bertie Hoptrough's death only reached me after my letter had at last gone in to the Autumn *Nutshell*. I am sure, in a way, that his own choice would have been to die as he had lived side by side with Fred; and irreplaceable as they both are to us we must not grudge them to the higher service to which they have been called. We shall never forget them, and in those dark moments of despondency, when all the stars seem out, the example of their lives, their loyalty, their friendship, will shine the clearer. … News of many other old boys have reached me directly or indirectly. Will Ridoutt, I fear, was dangerously hit near here about a month ago. Bombardier Percy Hannam sang for me delightfully last night and while he was doing so in the big tea room, which is a kind of rough Day Nursery to the House where several thousand cups of tea go the right way down each afternoon, in walked Driver Ernie Williams. That is one of the chief delights of this place: that you wake every morning with the certain knowledge that

---

205 A Kanaka is a South Sea Islander, primarily one transported to Australia as a labourer in the 19th and early 20th centuries. The Font was used for Tubby's own Christening in December 1885.
206 The Rev Ralph Jonathan Goodwin served as curate of St Luke's, City Hill, Enfield prior to joining the Army Chaplains' Department.
207 *The Nutshell*, No.13, Christmas 1917, p.3-4.

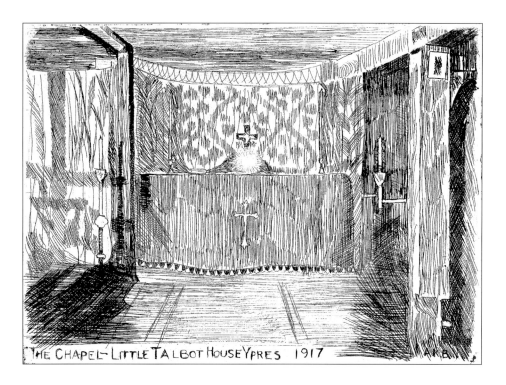

THE CHAPEL – LITTLE TALBOT HOUSE YPRES 1917

one or two old friends will roll in before the lights go out. By the same token, Harold Pridham had turned up to tea that same afternoon.

I must now enlist your sympathies on behalf of Little Talbot House, which is now open in a cellar 10 miles from here. I must not describe the site too accurately, as a Periodical so widely circulated and well-informed may come within the purview of the Bosch Intelligence. Suffice it to say therefore that the cellar is admirably appoined, water being continuously and gas occasionally laid on. It has been tremendous fun starting this advanced post, which at present is in the capable hands of a North Country Chaplain whom I hope to relieve for alternate weeks during the Winter. We are getting rather too far behind the line here to be of immediate service to the principal sufferers, the P.B.I. (poor bally infantry) though the old House has never been more crowded than it is at present. The new House above the cellar is somewhat sketchy for the time being, but is rent free, and by the time the R.E.'s have done with it, provided Fritz's pneumatic gun has done with it also, all will soon be merry and bright. A few paper streamers strung across the rafters, a lot of whitewash, and a little levelling of the floors, and we shall keep Christmas there in that spirit of happy make-believe at which the British Army excels. For make-believe, when it is a matter of anticipation and not merely of recollection, is a powerful stimulent indeed. It is part of the age-long ceremonies of the Passover that the household should repeat these words: – "This year slaves, but the next year free; this year exiles, the next year in Jerusalem." And while we have said this kind of thing in every Christmas *Nutshell*, it has not been with much conviction. But this time we really mean it, so we must make-believe once more to be ready for the Real thing in 1918. Not that Christmas itself is ever a failure. We may feel anxious beforehand, but with the first line of the first Carol our doubts are dispelled.

… I sometimes feel I should apologise for the growing sobriety of these letters. Partly it is due to the prosy expanse of middle age which is now upon me; but partly also, it answers a growing note of seriousness in your letters to me.

… War is also an ageing profession. Not only as the flower of a nation's youth killed, but youthfulness itself perishes. Even the children forget their games, and the boys' faces grow old before their time. Here too Christmas comes to awaken the child-heart in us all.

The post orderly has been waiting half-an-hour already, so I must stop, with an extra handshake all round for the Day Itself, and may every one be where we should be in twelve months' time, the Bosch in Boschland, the Belgiques here, and you and I in the neighbourhood of the Chocolate Co.

Yours always,
Philip Clayton

William A. Ridoutt
Lieutenant, 7 Bn Durham Light Infantry
19 February 1919 – Age 27 – Portsmouth (Kingston) Cemetery, Pink's.2. Last.

* * *

NOTICE
Little Talbot House
The Sunday Services yesterday, the first Sunday in the new Chapel, were simply crowded out; and this week the House starts its social side, on the traditional lines. If duty (or pleasure) takes you that way, walk along the Rue de Lille, or the right of the Cloth Hall, and 150 yards up on the left, you will find our daughter House.

Magazines etc. go on from this House, so the better they are used here, the better for the boys up yonder.

Gifts of magazines, games, etc. for them may be left here, to be sent up.

26/11/17. P.B.C.

* * *

27 November 1917

Dearest Mater,
You won't get much of a letter I fear with a pen, as I'm getting lazy when reduced to such a primitive instrument. But McInnes hasn't yet got here, so I'd better send a line like this to make certain.

I enclose a delightful slip from Magrath,[208] my oldest friend now in Y (apart from the Town Major). You'll be glad to hear that Little T.H. is going very strong there under a delightful fellow Chaplain called Goodwin. We are working hand in glove, and I hope to go up early tomorrow with another lorry load of goods, tea-stuff, stoves, and a ragtime piano.

---

208 In the ancient lock room, deep within the bowels of the Lille Gate at Ieper, Dr. Charles Magrath, a schoolmaster from Sheffield ran an unusual YMCA canteen. He was instrumental in the start of Little Talbot House. For his account, see p. 351.

The House here grows more and more perfect. I have a volunteer party of Canadian carpenters doing wonders day by day – real bright boys. The English are dull dogs by comparison.

Much love,
Philip

*   *   *

From Ronald Brewster to Tubby
45, Elmwood Road,
Herne Hill,
London S.E.
10.12.1917

Dear Mr Clayton,
You will notice by the address that I am home again. After three days of the Cambrai battle and in the morning at 5.45 a.m. I received my movement order to proceed to England on commission. It could not possibly have come at a better time, and although in a way I did not like leaving the boys to it, it seemed to me to be direct deliverance, especially as I was the only one out of six waiting, who received the order. It was a great thing for Herbert[209] and I, and I know you will think so too, that we were together for half an hour before the attack developed, as by a strange chance the left of his company rested on the right of ours, and we both happened to be on the flanks. I am sure we both gained help from each other's society, and the bulk of our conversation centred round Talbot House and yourself. I have written to him to-day, and I pray God that he is still alright.

… I trust Talbot House will have a good Xmas, and that the Belgian Kiddies will have their little treat.[210] Goodbye now. Mother and I both join in wishing you as happy a Xmas as is possible under the circumstances. Write me soon if you have time.

Yours sincerely,
Ronald Brewster

*   *   *

12 December 1917

Dearest Mater,
I write on my birthday from an easy chair a few miles back from Talbot House, in fact in an Officers' Rest Station. What brought me here was that on Saturday I got another touch of the old fever, which only lasted till Monday, since when I've been normal though slightly pulled down. So the doctor wants to try and get to the bottom of these periodic attacks, and sent me here for a day or two's rest, and also to have my blood tested for malaria.

T.H. is in good hands meanwhile, and everyone extremely kind, so I have no anxieties, and am rather enjoying a bit of laziness. If they offer it to me, I may go down to the coast or to Paris for a few days' change to get fit before Christmas, which will be exacting in proportion to its excellencies.

---

209 Herbert Stagg, former staff member of Talbot House.
210 Reference to the children's party planned for New Year's Day.

Many 'Talbotousians' and their families donated presents for the children's party.

CHURCH ARMY OPEN TO ALL

Church Army Recreation Hut
ON ACTIVE SERVICE
WITH · THE · BRITISH · EXPEDITIONARY · FORCE

I enclose a copy of our beautiful Christmas Card, of which 2,000 are now on their way to those whose names are on our Communicants' Roll.[211] The sending out of these and the Children's party and all the letters of thanks for some 50 parcels of presents and ordinary work, really rather put the lid on last week, so the temperature mayn't have been malarious after all! Anyhow it's plain sailing now till about the middle of January when I propose to put in for leave.

I'm afraid the next few months are going to be very hard on the boys, the Boche very strong and fierce, thanks to Russian impotence;[212] but we shall weather the storm with God's help. And I feel more and more convinced as the time goes on that we must go on too. I should not relish the task of going to the women in black at home and saying, "It was all a mistake. There was no need for him to have died at all."

A very nice set of officers in here with me, but it's not far enough away from T.H. to be a change of air as well as a rest. So I shall try and get off as I say for a few days. An old friend – once doctor at No. 16 General, is coming across to see me this morning. It's wonderful how those old friendships hold, and crop up again.

I'm rather afraid neither my pen nor my thoughts will run freely this morning; McInnes and the typewriter have spoilt my style. Besides, I'm wondering all the time whether I'm 31, 32, 33? Jerusalem is good news anyhow. I hope Allenby will let the troops realize something of the deeper meaning of it.[213] What a strange Christmas in Bethlehem! I think I know some Portsea boys who will be near there. …

Much love,

Philip

P.S. Write still to T.H. My post reaches me from there via Vokins, but in any case I shall be back there by Monday or so.

---

211 For the Communicants' Roll of Talbot House: see 'The Red Books', p. 284.
212 The Bolsheviks seized power from the Russian provisional government on 6-7 November. This act effectively removed Russia from the Entente.
213 Allenby entered Jerusalem on 9 December, a few days before this letter was composed.

*   *   *

On 12 December 1917, Sgt. H.F. Houlder, M.M., 56th Field Ambulance, RAMC, sent the following letter to his parents:

I wanted to ask you if you and father would send a Xmas subscription, and also get any from any ardent Church people, for the most worthy object for which I could ask their help in all the B.E.F. It is a large, disused house, in a town near the Front Line. It is called Talbot House, as it was started in the first instance as a memorial to Neville Talbot's younger brother Gilbert, who was killed at Hooge during the First Battle of Ypres [sic].

A Church of England Chaplain is in permanent charge of it, a former curate of Portsea, whom I knew at Oxford, – a most excellent creature. I can only describe the place an ideal of what such things should be. Writing rooms, reading rooms, rooms for billiards and games, all properly kept, (so often such places are not), a garden at the back, where regimental bands are invited to play in the summer, a tea-bar, and in the top storey under the rafters a beautifully improvised Chapel. Thousands of men use it in the week, and it is certainly one of the finest places I have ever seen. Of course I can't tell you when I have been there, but I have been there, and have long made a mental note to do anything I could for the place. I thought that Xmas time would be a time when I might get some subscriptions from Church-people. Could you do anything with one or two who could afford something helpful. Address:- Rev. P.B. Clayton, A.P.O., Sec.4, B.E.F.

...

*   *   *

December 1917
64 C.C.S.[214]

My dear old Guv,
Here I am in another hospital, a few hundred yards from the last, but much more of the real thing. My temperature has been normal for days past, so I hope to get back to work next week. That they sent me here for was to try and test my blood for malaria, but as this can only be done when the temperature is up, it's rather locking the stable door etc.

However T.H. is very quiet and I'm having a good rest meanwhile. ... About January 15th will see me home, I hope. They wanted me to go home for Christmas, but I hadn't the heart to leave T.H. and the boys. Christmas love to you all.

*   *   *

214 The CCS was situated at Mendinghem (Proven).

XMAS 1917.

Long months have passed, and still the cry
   Is as it was in olden days
   May happiness in all life's ways
   Attend you.

     II

How oft we asked the where and why
   As month on month was lost in time.
   Yet now we can in happy rhyme
   Be joyful.

     III

Here's to mirth, And bonds that tie
   Though many miles and weeks divide,
  — The waves roll high, nor ebbs the tide
   Of pleasure.

     IV

My wish is then, that yours may be
   A really happy CHRISTMAS season
   Wish was never more sincere
   Than this one.

                J.W. Turton. Dec. '917

*   *   *

On 27 December 1917, Barclay Baron,[215] *serving at YMCA Headquarters Poperinge, wrote to his mother:*

I made my Christmas Communion in the little chapel of which I enclose a picture. It is the 'grenier'[216] at the top of a Belgian house, now used as a soldiers' club. You climb by a ladder out of the billiard room to it – and find one of the most beautiful chapels I know. 'Tubby' Clayton (one of the old crowd from Oxford) is in charge. B.K. Cunningham of Farnham, for some years past one of my special saints, celebrated. The altar hangings came from Southwark. So strangely do the old friends meet – both seen and unseen – at the altar on Christmas Day.

*   *   *

From the Visitors' Book, Little Hatchett
24 December – 9 January 1918
PBC home again, like a bad penny. This time sick leave, after touching 105 in the shade. My first whole Christmas at home since Oxford days, and as B.K. Cunningham is at T.H. for Christmas, no anxiety about its welfare.

Lonely winter weather here, beautiful vegetables, multitudinous letters & telegrams. Neville gets engaged,[217] L. Browne gets quinsy; & the puppies learn to bark.

Midsummer next time, & the war nearer its end.

(P.B.C.)

*   *   *

Talbot House
Sunday night, 13 January 1918

Dearest Mater,
I crossed early on Saturday, and a lot of luck in lifts, so got here before 10 p.m. just in time for Compline. My understudy Chaplain was still here, and took early Services for me this morning, so I had a good night in bed. Everything, including the Boche, very quiet, but the Chapel

---

215 Barclay Baron (1884-1964) became a key figure in the early Toc H movement. From 1923 on, over a period of four decades, he edited the Toc H Journal, designed the distinctive Toc H 'Lamp of Maintenance', chronicled the movement's history and served as its vice-president and travelling secretary. His artistic talents found expression in the composition of a number of Toc H masques, some of which were performed in the Albert Hall, and in the illustration of his articles and books. Baron also played a key role in the reinstatement of Talbot House both after its purchase in 1929 and following liberation in 1944. From 1951 to 1957 he served as president of the Talbot House Association.
216 French for attic.
217 Neville married his cousin, Cecil Mary Eastwood, in April 1918. Cecil Mary died giving birth to a son. Neville named the boy Gilbert after his late brother. The son was killed in Normandy on 20 June 1944, one family's tragic loss in two world wars.

Sitting room at Little Hatchett.

well filled tonight, and a royal welcome all round. It's good to be back at work, though I never enjoyed a holiday more.

All is well here. They have papered my room, and generally done everything to delight me. I'm badly at sea over letters which are simply overwhelming. More than a hundred waiting for me, and most must be answered sooner or later.

Much love,

Philip

* * *

The Rev. P.B. Clayton's war honour

In January 1918, Rev. P.B. Clayton was awarded the Military Cross. The recommendation read:
"For most valuable services in "The Salient" and at Talbot House, Poperinghe, for past two years. In addition to daily Church services at Talbot House he has held services at Ypres every week for Artillery units during period when Ypres was heavily shelled. His zeal and devotion to duty [are] beyond all praise".

(GOC XVIII Corps 6/10/17)[218]

Following Rev. A. Ll. Jones and Rev. E.F. Edge-Partington, Clayton was the third chaplain from St. Mary's, Portsea, to receive this gallantry award. On 14 January, Jones's mother wrote Tubby's mother:

---

218 Lt. Gen. Ivor Maxse (1862-1958).

Dear Mrs Clayton

We heard the good news from my son Llewelyn the other day that your Chaplain Son had been awarded the M.C.

We are all so glad & send you our best congratulations. I know well the joy it gives to Mothers & all at home – when our sons at the Front are decorated – a token that their devotion to duty & bravery in danger has been recognized & approved by those in authority – I think I must copy a sentence for you from Llewelyn's letter: "Tubby has done wonders at Talbot House in furnishing the Western Front with its most Christian Institution & in his work with the Batteries in advanced positions has done splendid work and long deserved a decoration – I should have liked to see him get the D.S.O." Well I too hope that he will get it & that soon.

We are hoping to see both my Chaplain Sons who are in France (for a third son is Military Chaplain at Bradford) early next month, & perhaps they may meet at home for part of the time – How long this terrible war is going on! & the end is not in sight yet. When the Americans can help us more perhaps it will come suddenly. Some people think it will –

With much sympathy & good wishes

Yours very sincerely

Fr. S. Jones

*   *   *

Saturday night, 19 January 1918

Dearest Mater,

I don't think I've often written on Saturday nights, but I have a very easy day tomorrow, as I have a Brigade Chaplain, and another close at hand, who are both keen on helping. So I'm only preaching once here, and have two services out. An idle but happy Sunday. The House is going very strong again, and pretty full too I'm glad to say. And my Committee is very helpful, and we're rolling in money! So all is well. I go to D.C.Gs for a Conference on Tuesday-Wednesday, where I hope, among others, to meet Neville again at last.[219] A delightful letter from him today. I also have a second typist, a help distinctly.

Much love,

Philip

*   *   *

From the minutes of the Talbot House Committee meeting, 26 January 1918

Approved.

Purchases made at St. Omer, and for Christmas cards.

Sanction was given of £ 25 for billiard table, not exceeding £ 10 for gramophone & records, and £ 20 for books for library.

219 The conference discussed the general conditions that would face British society in the future, taking place under the theme of 'Reconstruction'.

*   *   *

Breakfast with Bishop Brent – My father eats a lot, my mother eats slowly. I inherit both habits.
(P.B. Clayton, diary 26 January 1918)

*   *   *

Monday morning, 28 January 1918

Dearest Mater,
No letter last night, as a variety of officers stopped after Evensong, and we went out to supper together.

i)   The Senior Interpreter of the Corps, Col. Andre, of the French Army.
ii)   Major Rees-Mogg of the Life Guards.
iii)   Captain Michelmore, R.F.A., a most remarkable fellow, whom I like enormously, but who is unfortunately moving away.
iv)   Two nice Subalterns.

We had a very happy Sunday together, and I have a busy week ahead; including a visit from Bishop Brent of West New York, the C.G. of the American Army. All well here, and no war on apparently. … The weather here is unnaturally beautiful and springlike. Belgium can have early springs when it wants to, but I fear this spring will be a grim one. …
All these spaces represent interruptions, more or less prolonged this time. A lieutenant wanting the cinema and operator for to-night; two N.Z. Padres to be shown round; on one way we met a staff sergeant about a concert party, and the problem of its transport for Saturday night. So the world wags! Now I must go and find someone to scrounge lunch off, as I told the General I should be out. Who was the villain who sent my photograph to the Mirror on Friday last?
Much love,
Philip

*   *   *

NOTICE
Victory – and After.[220]
For three and a half years Britain (and the world in general) has been trying to turn citizens into good soldiers. The time is coming when we must start turning soldiers into good citizens. The task is going to be a tremendous one, and must begin, at the latest, now.
Here, in Talbot House, we mean to do one bit of study & self-education.

---

220   *Victory and after…?* was the title of a pamphlet written by senior chaplains of the First Army and published by the YMCA in 1918. As part of Bishop Gwynne's 'Scheme of Reconstruction', the Association was enlisted to help ensure that the soldiers' desire for far-reaching social change after the war was properly instructed, and channelled towards victory rather than revolution, through the concerted action of army chaplains and the YMCA's special lectures. M. Snape, *The Back Parts of War*, p.62.

On Tuesday mornings at 11 a.m. papers will be read by experts on e.g.
Town Planning
The Municipality as Landlord
Public Health etc.
& popular discussions on the same lines will be held on Wednesay evenings.

On Thursdays 4.30 – 6.15 p.m. similar discussions e.g. on "Education" will be held in the Chaplain's Room, to which all are welcome.
The Library now has a special section dealing with Social Problems.

P.B.C. 2/2/18

*   *   *

18 February 1918

Dearest Mater,
All well here. I had a day off Friday to Saturday which was most interesting. I went up on Friday night, and slept with some jolly trench-tramway folk. A splendid voluntary service, followed by the notorious lecture on Andorra. Then we started in a lorry at 5 a.m. on Saturday (a lovely morning though very cold) and went up as far as the road goes. After this, I walked all round their tramway track across the ground the Australians paid for, and got really in touch with the war again. An amazing sight, unbelievable in its grim desolation. Nothing for miles but shell holes touching one another and broken pillboxes, dead horses, crosses, and barbed wire. How everyone ever won it I can't conceive. We got shelled a bit, but the Boche can't see what he's shooting at, and we were quite immune 500 yds away from this. Very different to the old days.
  I could write pages on all this, but mustn't try now.
  Today a confirmation of 60 candidates here, and the Bishop and every one at the top of their form.
  I'm really blessed with good friends all round, who take all the strain off me, and leave me free to be happy, and not altogether useless.
  Much love,
  Your son,
  Philip

*   *   *

On Monday we had a Confirmation in the chapel of Talbot House to which I took four men from my Labour Company. The Bishop of Khartoum confirmed about seventy officers and men. These active service Confirmations are always very impressive. There is something so real about them, no taint of cant or humbug. Among the candidates was a black man – a true-blooded Jamaican, who I believe is hoping eventually to take Orders.

(The Revd. Pat Leonard, 20 February 1918)[221]

---

221 J. Leonard & P. Leonard-Johnson, *The Fighting Padre, Letters from the Trenches 1915-1918 of Pat Leonard DSO*, pp. 189-190.

* * *

Monday, 11 a.m., 25th February, 1918

Dearest Mater,

I have told old Jimmy that he must hold back from going with and for the post this morning till midday, so that I can write at least a few words of a birthday (or unbirthday) letter to you. It's long since I've written more than a scrawl, but there has been simply no spare time. Now however things are quieting down, and I foresee a period of something like slackness perhaps, when I can get my letters straight to some degree. I shall probably come home at once after Easter, if I can get a reliable substitute here. The man I want is Money, a N.Z. Mirfield Padre, who has helped me here a lot, and who is coming to take over during the week March 6th – 13th, when I go to the Chaplains' School. I have never been able to do this before, and look forward to it greatly. Hitherto I have only been for 24 hours to conduct Quiet Days. Now I hope to go for a whole week, and a very special week it will be. Neville is taking the Retreat three days, and the rest of the time is devoted to Reconstruction in Church and Society.

Capt. E. Van Cutsem, Town Major of Poperinge.

Unfortunately, much to my perturbation, though I'm not a nervous person as a rule, they have laid on me the Presidency of the Social Reconstruction Day, which means that I have to take the Chair and conduct off my own bat a whole day's Conference among all the leaders of the Chaplains' Dept. out here. This is a great honour, but not one that I covet, especially as it is so difficult to find time for preparation. However I can but do my best with God's help.

T.H. has a much more assured position and more influential friends than ever before; so that the House and the Daughter House are in smoother waters than they have ever been. Rawlinson[222] has been most awfully kind; and as a result all his Staff folk have had orders to help the House in every way, and I can really get what I want without the old difficulty. Besides this, the Staff Officer who is locally responsible[223] is a really delightful man, and a devout Communicant here, so that I have indeed much to be thankful for.

I have now a regular 24 hours off a week, Friday-Saturday, as in the old days, when I go up to those nice trench tramway folk and go all round on a little Ford petrol engine, disembarking at various places with service books and our dear little Pathescope.[224] Next Friday, all being well,

222 General Sir Henry Rawlinson (GOC Fourth Army) replaced Plumer as commander of Second Army in early November 1917. Second Army became Fourth Army in late December.

223 Capt. E.C.L. Van Cutsem (1st King's Shropshire Light Infantry) became Poperinge Town Major in July 1916, holding that position until the end of the war. After the war he was made a Freeman of the town of Poperinge.

224 Film projector manufactured by Pathé, the product associated with the Pathé brothers from 1896.

we are going to have a cinema show in an old Boche pill-box, nearer the Line, I fancy, than a cinema has ever been before.

Much love,

Philip

*   *   *

Tuesday night, 5 March 1918

Dearest Mater,

11.30 already, so I shan't try a literary flight of fancy, and indeed I have nothing in particular to write about. All goes well both here and at Little T.H. Life here is humdrum and very quiet so far as the war is concerned. I haven't got any outside work at present, and so spend my time out in parochial visiting, e.g. this afternoon railway staffs, and on to tea with a celebrated khaki pierrot troupe; then back to a second tea here with various excellent folk, among others the R.A.M.C. Sergeant Major who first taught me The Hellgate of Soissons.[225] Bowes is home on leave, so there is a good deal in the domestic line which he generally relieves me of. But I rather enjoy it. A lot of officers have been dropping in lately, one way and another, which is also good. This morning a big steam lorry loaded with yellow sand made shipwreck in the street, so I scrounged stacks of sand in sandbags for the garden, which is beginning to brighten up in this gorgeous spring weather. The box of books etc. arrived at last yesterday, and is a great addition to our beautiful library, the joy of the whole Salient.[226] Also your two charming pictures. I must write to R.J.B.C.[227] soon. A gorgeous packet of 600 cigars arrived from him a fortnight back, and I gave a box to Lee, the great Town Major of Ypres.[228] …

Much love,

Philip

Lt.-Col. James Lee, Town Major of Ieper.

*   *   *

---

225 A wartime poem by American writer Herbert Kaufman (1878-1947). He regularly contributed articles, editorials and more than 50 poems to the *Evening Standard*, *The Times*, and other leading British periodicals during the First World War.

226 For the Talbot House library, see p. 265.

227 Reginald John Byard Clayton, Tubby's elder brother.

228 Lt.-Col. James Lee, D.S.O., acted as Town Major from April 1916 to April 1918. He resided in a galleried series of dugouts beneath Ieper Prison where Tubby paid frequent visits.

The following "testimonial", left for Tubby by an Argyll and Sutherland Highlander, was laboriously written backwards. Translated with the aid of a mirror, it read (with most excusable misspellings) as follows:

Flanders. Twelveth March Eighteen. To the Officer in charge of Talbot House.

Sir,
On my first visit to "Talbot House" to-day I was almost amazed at the splendid arrangements made to provide what I honestly think it is, a "Home from Home," and I congratulate you and your staff on the completeness of the comforts provided for the Soldiers. I may add that during the years Sixteen and Seventeen I visited very many so-called Soldiers Homes or Huts both in France and Flanders but this splendidly equipted House stands unequalled. May God give you strength and grace to "Carry-on."
    I am yours Respectfelly, Pte. McNaught, A and S. Hrs.,
    Attd. Ninty Seventh Bde. H.Q., "Cinema," B.E.F., Flanders.

*   *   *

15 March 1918 – purchase of theatre costumes from Lester & co. – £ 5.0.0.

(P.B. Clayton)

*   *   *

19 March 1918

Dearest Mater,
All well here, and a Quiet Day with about 40 Chaplains here going splendidly under Archdeacon Southwell.[229] Not exactly a Quiet Day for any of us, I fear, and the Bosche has been at his old game. But T.H. still stands, thank God. I was out district visiting when the nearest couple came along. However the Chaplains are proceeding gamely with the Conference. It would have an interesting and stimulating effect on Convocation to meet under such circumstances, and several good resolutions would be passed without waste of time.

10 p.m.
I have just returned from taking our Dramatic party up to the neighbourhood of L.T.H. in a lorry to perform "The Critic" with myself as Tilburina, the Beefeater and the Earl of Leicester.[230] Rather quick changing required, and gas masks handy meanwhile. But it went splendidly. An

---

229 Fourth Army assistant chaplain-general.
230 *The Critic* is a satire by R.B. Sheridan (1751-1816). It is set at Tilbury Fort, a stronghold at the mouth of the Thames where Queen Elizabeth I has mustered her troops, commanded by the Earl of Leicester, against the Spanish Armada. The plot involves Tilburina, the Governor of the fort's daughter, falling in love with Don Ferolo Whiskerandos, the son of the Spanish admiral who has been taken prisoner and is guarded by the Beefeater at the fort.

up-country audience is always a joy. Now I must to bed, after Compline full of thanksgiving. Truly God is loving unto Talbot House.

Your loving son,

Philip

*   *   *

One of the Chaplains present that day was Rev. Pat Leonard serving with the R.F.C. He subsequently observed:

The Quiet Day, which Irwin had arranged for all the Padres of his Corps, was somewhat of a misnomer for our meditations were sadly interrupted by the arrival of 15 inch shells in the same quarter of the town in which we were congregated. I don't know if all the Padres were as windy as I was, but personally I found the spasmodic arrival of a ton of potential death with appropriate noises highly detrimental to my powers of concentration and to my peace of mind. The nearest one fell in the house across the road killing a woman and tattling down on the roof of Talbot House a perfect storm of half bricks and debris.[231]

Rev. Pat Leonard.

*   *   *

Saturday night, 23 March 1918

Dearest Mater,

We are having rather a stormy time, but coming through safe and sound, and in the best of spirits and true brotherhood. Pettifer distinguished himself greatly last night, and I am trying to get recognition for his gallantry. Today we have been building a real dugout, and I have sent the bulk of the staff to sleep away, as they are rather a responsibility. All goes well, and work is not altogether at a standstill. But as I didn't get much sleep to-night, I shall turn in now, and leave Palm Sunday sermons to themselves.

This may postpone my leave, but I know you will understand.

Your loving son,

Philip

*   *   *

---

231 Leonard, J. & Leonard-Johnson, P., *The Fighting Padre, Letters from the Trenches 1915-1918 of Pat Leonard DSO*, pp. 196-197.

Cyril's Crashed

On March 23, 1918, just after midnight, a great crash woke me. Before we had turned in several heavy shells had landed somewhere in the town, but none really near the House. This one was, however, obviously fairly close, and I lay unpleasantly half awake, waiting for the next one to decide me on my course of action. As yet we had no dug-out worth going to, and I was trying to summon up courage to go to sleep again when Pettifer entered, candle in hand, *à la* Lady Macbeth.[232] On a previous occasion, when I had dared to leave my bed and suggest to Pettifer some precautionary move downstairs, I had been soothed with the reply, "You just stay where you are, sir. What I say is, if it's got yer, it's got yer." But this time the old man was more moved than I had ever seen him. "There's a woman screaming somewhere, and I can't-a-bear it," he said. With that he turned, and I heard him go downstairs and undo the front door. I got the staff into the dug-out, such as it was (bad policy this), while another landed – farther away this time. Then I went out and found the street twenty yards away blocked with débris. It was Cyril's restaurant, which had been blown bodily into the street. Up among the wreckage, which was momentarily threatening to subside still further, Pettifer, assisted by Jimmy, another "old sweat," our cook, was busy. A child, a man, and a woman came out by some miracle alive and uninjured. These were the only survivors from among the eleven inmates, though at the time we had hopes for more, as there were still groans to be heard. The man came down in his shirt only, and besought me in a dazed way for leg covering. I had a greatcoat over my pyjamas, so he had my pyjama trousers then and there. Recouped with a pair of drawers, and sending across, as Pettifer required, the carpenter[233] with a saw to work up the staircase from below if possible, I went to the Club and telephoned for the fire-escape ladder, to reach the parts of the house still standing; and thence to the A.P.M.,[234] our good friend Captain Strachan, who dressed and came on the scene with his men. Meanwhile the shelling had apparently ceased for the night, but our increased resources and the early morning light only revealed the completeness of the catastrophe. Madame Cyril was alive when reached, but died shortly afterwards. Her husband's head could nowhere be found until the following day, when it was discovered in the house opposite –blown by a grim jest of death across the narrow street and through a broken window.

(P.B. Clayton, *Tales of Talbot House*)

Under the headline 'Shelling of Town', the local newspaper 'De Poperingsche Keikop' covered the tragedy as follows:

In the evening a devastating accident happened. Eight people were buried under ruins. Cyriel Vermeulen, hotelkeeper, and his wife Leonie Tanghe, both from Ypres, were killed instantly. Moreover the dead bodies of four maids were discovered: Maria Leclercq and her sister Madeleine from Ypres, Maria Vanhove and her sister Germaine, daughters of Theophiel, locals from our town. H. Seys and a servant woman escaped miraculously unscathed. The unfortunate victims were buried on Sunday 24 March.

---

232 A reference to the sleepwalking scene from Shakespeare's *Macbeth*, during which Lady Macbeth wanders through castle halls whilst recollecting horrific images and impressions from her past.

233 Talbot House staff member, Pte. A. Rose.

234 The Assistant Provost Marshal was a senior military police officer.

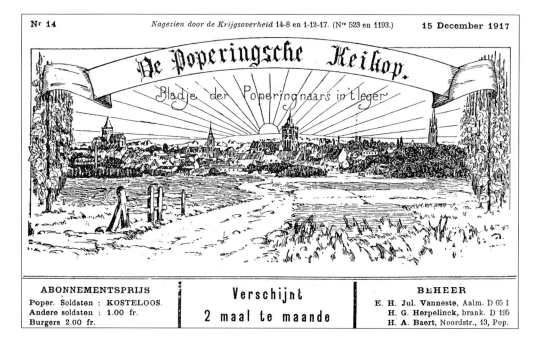

ABONNEMENTSPRIJS	Verschijnt	BEHEER
Poper. Soldaten : KOSTELOOS.		E. H. Jul. Vanneste, Aalm. D 65 I
Andere soldaten : 1.00 fr.	2 maal te maande	H. G. Herpelinck, brank. D 195
Burgers 2.00 fr.		H. A. Baert, Noordstr., 13, Pop.

A few days later Pte. Pettifer received the following note from Tubby:
At the Committee Meeting held on 23rd inst., the following resolution was passed unanimously.

"This Committee expresses their admiration of the gallant conduct displayed by Pte. Moorhouse, 376819 and Pte. A. Pettifer, 378581 who, in the midst of danger, went to the work of rescue from a shelled building, and were the means of saving life." It was also resolved that a copy of this resolution be made in the minute book.

* * *

From Archdeacon H.K. Southwell to Tubby
26 March 1918

My dear Clayton,
The D.C.G. has rung me up this morning and says that he feels obliged to order Cunningham not to go to Pop. The Army Commander stated that he did not wish any concentration of troops at certain places, and instructed me to let those concerned know this. With regard to yourself, I am naturally anxious, but I must leave things to your own discretion and judgment. If you should get many gathered in your "Upper Chamber", there may be trouble. You know best about the situation.

I fully agree that it would be disastrous to close down when other places are running, and I have not sent any order nor do I mean to do so – I would far rather join you myself, if I were free, than ask you to come out, and shut down. I should have said nothing at all but for the Army Commanders words, and all I think you need to do is to watch the situation, and prevent too big a concentration at the wrong times. Your suggestions seem to me excellent, and to provide all that is needed. By all means look after the G.H.Q. Railway Troops if you can manage it. I am sorry to have bothered you so much, it was not in my mind to do so – some people 'got talking' about the Chaplains Quiet Day, and that started them on to me, but I have every confidence in your judgment, and should like to carry on as you think best.

God speed to you & all Easter Blessings

Yours sincerely

H.K. Southwell

*   *   *

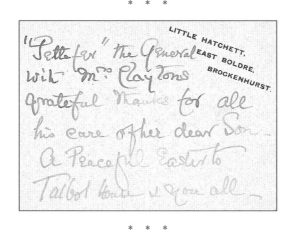

*   *   *

T.H.
Wednesday, 27 March 1918

Dearest Mater,

This will probably be my Easter letter, as I'm likely to be single-handed this Easter, and consequently busy, though the place is not so populous as it was. The Bishop has had to prohibit B.K.C. coming, as he only has a pass for Lines of Communications, and everyone would get court-martialled if he got killed. I quite expected this prohibition in view of great liveliness in these parts, and the Bishop has undoubtedly done the right thing. It will leave me with rather a heavy Easter, but a happy one none the less. I shall try to take the Three Hours myself, and have (thank God!) plenty of reserve energy for extra work, as I've had a slack time lately. But it may mean only scraps to you for the next few days. All goes well here. Our dugout grows more massive daily, keen Churchmen providing freewill offerings of sandbags, timber etc. As soon as it is completed the little garrison will sleep in it at night to avoid sudden excursions and alarms.

… My leave is of course cancelled until leave again opens, perhaps a month hence. It's disappointing, but a tiny thing in comparison with the issues at present. The spirit of the Army is simply wonderful. The men who came back after three hours on the leave boat, and having waited in some cases a year for their leave, came back singing in the train. Yesterday I saw a delightful fellow, a young M.G.C. officer, who said quite simply that the first day of the push had been the jolliest day he had ever had in his life. Our air supremacy which is almost complete will be a tremendous factor that will tell ultimately, and the Bosche cannot stand the strain of his gigantic losses indefinitely. All the usually latent patriotism in us comes out strong at such

Talbot House Chapel, Poperinghe.

HOLY WEEK & EASTER, 1918.

PALM SUNDAY, March 24th.

Holy Communion, 6.30, 7.30 a.m.		Bible Class	-	3.15 p.m.
Morning Service	- 10.30 a.m.	C.E.M.S. Meeting, 4.45 ,,		
Holy Eucharist	- 11.30 a.m.	Evensong	-	6.0 p.m.
		Story of the Cross, 6.45 ,,		

MONDAY TUESDAY WEDNESDAY THURSDAY	Holy Communion	- 7.30 a.m.
	Evensong, with Address and Story of the Cross.	- 6.0 p.m.

Also on MAUNDY THURSDAY : Celebration of
Holy Communion, 6.45 p.m.
(For those on morning duty)

GOOD FRIDAY.

Litany and Ante-Communion	-	-	-	7.30 a.m.
Morning Prayer	-	-	-	10.30 a.m.
Three Hours' Devotion	-	-	-	12-3 p.m.
Conducted by CANON B. K. CUNNINGHAM.				
Mission Service and Selections from " The				
Crucifixion " (Stainer)	-	-	-	6.30 p.m.

HOLY SATURDAY.

Holy Communion	-	-	-	7.30 a.m.
Evensong and Preparation	-	-	-	6.0 p.m.

EASTER DAY, March 31st.

Celebrations of Holy Communion, 5.30, 6, 6.30, 7, 7.30, 8.15, 10.30			
Choral Eucharist	-	-	11.30 a.m.
Festal Evensong	-	-	6.0 p.m.
Administration of the Sacrament	-	-	6.45 p.m.

P. B. CLAYTON,
Chaplain.

S. George's Chapel,

Little Talbot House, Ypres.

HOLY WEEK SERVICES.

MONDAY, TUESDAY, WEDNESDAY & THURSDAY.

Holy Communion	-	-	-	8.0 a.m.
Evensong	-	-	-	5.30 p.m.
Short Service and Address	-	-	7.0 p.m.

GOOD FRIDAY.

Ante-Communion and Meditation	-	-	8.0 a.m.
Morning Service	-	-	-	11.15 a.m.
Evening Service	-	-	-	5.30 p.m.

HOLY SATURDAY.

Ante-Communion	-	-	-	8.0 a.m.
Evensong	-	-	-	5.30 p.m.

EASTER DAY.

HOLY COMMUNION,	6.30, 7.15, 8.0, 9.0, and 11.15 a.m.	
Evensong and Address	-	5.30 p.m.
Administration of Holy Communion	-	6.30 p.m.

Monday and Tuesday in Easter Week.

Holy Communion	-	-	-	8.0 a.m.
Evensong	-	-	-	5.30 p.m.

R. J. GOODWIN,
Chaplain.

times, and the Army as a whole is unshaken and altogether undismayed. Yesterday the only Army Order that came in was a long treatise on pig-keeping, which doesn't look like panic!

We agreed yesterday that the only real danger is that the folk at home (not at my home) may get the wind up, instead of sticking it as the Army mean to do. What a Holy Week! But it is the Living and not the dead Christ who looks down upon it.

… I went for a lovely spring walk yesterday with old Pettifer. We had lunch with old Lord Saye and Sele, who is coming in the Three Hours; and lay on our backs and slept peacefully in a little copse bursting with spring life.

Much love,
Philip

*   *   *

Easter night, 31 March 1918

Dearest Mater,
Just a word before bed, after a long but very happy and peaceful day. Not a shell over during any service time! So there was nothing to mar our happiness. About 150 Communicants during the day, not bad at all, considering the town is practically closed to troops. Old friends and new. One officer (R.T.O.) has been every Easter, i.e. all three. Much help and encouragement all round.

I am fortunate indeed in having as my immediate superior on Corps, Major Gurney,[235] once of the Norfolk Yeomanry, one of the Gurneys. Didn't you know some of the family in the old

235 Major Quintin E. Gurney ('Q' VIII Corps), was elected to the Talbot House Committee on 23 March. A Norwich banker in peacetime, he assisted Tubby with the Talbot House accounts.

days? I wore Mr Powles' beautiful white and gold stole for Celebrating, and have been happy all day long, and not over-tired.

My connection with the Railways is working out very well, and lots of opportunity among them; so I have (thank God) plenty of work ahead, and health and strength to tackle it. *Laus Deo.* All going well down South.

Your loving son,
Philip

* * *

Easter Monday, 1 April 1918

Dearest Mater,
… To-day's Gospel is the one which I always fondly think of as the Gospel which inspires the "Emmaus Inn" of Talbot House.[236] You will be delighted to hear that Pettifer has got the Military Medal for his gallant rescue of civilians from a house blown down about ten days ago. All much quieter now, thank you. Easter seems to have done good over yonder.

Much love,
Philip

* * *

From Pte. Pettifer to Mrs Clayton

3 April 1918

Dear Mrs Clayton
As for taking great care of your son, I think the boot fits the other foot – he takes great care of me. I simply sent *(sic)* him to bed early – that is when he will go, which is not very often – and let him lie there until he wakes up. Then he gets up and comes out as if there wasn't a war on! … If there is any danger about I have always got my eye on him, and will stick to him to the last…

Yours sincerely,
General

* * *

Sunday night, 7 April 1918

Dearest Mater,
I'm going to take a day off tomorrow, and going up to see some old friends roundabout with Pettifer, a good old walk. I do hope it's a fine day, as I've had no exercise for a week. It begins rather early, as an officer going south is coming in to make his Confession at 7 a.m. and then

---

236 Gospel of St. Luke 24: 13-35.

The 'Wunny Wuns' troupe (11th Division Concert Party). Bandsman Erskine Williams, who had played in several concerts at Talbot House, is the soldier standing centre. He was recruited as their scene painter while they were at 'Pop'.

receive the Sacrament. Then at 8.30 one lorry arrives, loads up with timber etc., and four men from my staff I am lending for a week's sandbagging etc. at L.T.H. Then we go to the canteen and buy biscuits etc., £ 30 of them if we can get them, then to Captain Finch R.E.,[237] who adds some more timber and comes himself, then to L.T.H. about 11 a.m. where we disembark stores and men; then finally Pettifer and I go for a walk, getting back here I hope at 6 p.m. for Evensong. Then an hour's accounts with Major Gurney who grows more and more faithful and helpful, then a performance to a crowded house of "Detective Keen".[238] What a mixture life is!

…

With much love.

P.S. I find I am very rich again – is £20 any help at home?

P.B.C.

*   *   *

237 Capt. Finch (OC 33rd Road Construction Company) acted as Chairman of the Talbot House Committee at this time.

238 Percival Knight, *Detective Keen; A Play in One Act*, Commission on training camp activities, Dept. of dramatic activities among the soldiers, Washington DC, 1918.

From Mrs Bowes to Tubby
2 Shaftesbury Road,
Cambridge
7 April 1918

Dear Mr Clayton,
My husband (Major Bowes) asked me to spend a little gift, which was given to him for Talbot House. I think he told me that he had mentioned the matter to you. I now write to say that I have had a Medici copy of a Madonna sent off to you, and I shall shortly be sending a small parcel of books for the Library at Talbot House, which I hope you will accept.

I hope that you are quite "fit" again, and that Talbot House flourishes. George told me so much about it, that I feel naturally a great interest in the Club. I get very little news of my husband just now, but I gather that he is "somewhere in the line". These are anxious days, are they not, for us all?

Believe me,
Yours sincerely
Christine R. Bowes

* * *

On 7 April Tubby received the following signal from Rev. Ronald Irwin, D.A.C.G. 2nd Corps:

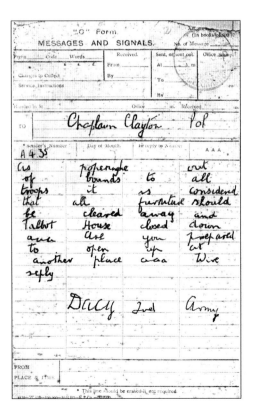

This suggestion was not complied with. Meanwhile Padre Goodwin of Little Talbot House, and Charles Magrath, of Y.M.C.A., departed from Ypres, as the line fell back, to join Tubby at Talbot House.

10.4.1918

Dear Tubbie,

… If we do have to make a sudden exit à la Shakespeare (alarms without, shouting, they hurry off), what are we to do? Can you raise a promise of a 3-ton lorry from an outer area which could sail in to receive the more valuable things? If so, we will hold on to the last gasp and save all we can. If not, shall I burn and smash piano, chairs and all, rather than let the Hun have them? Stores we must give away or destroy. …

    Yours as Ever
    Goodie
    R.J. Goodwin. C.F.

[11.4.1918]
4.30 pm, Thursday

Tout le monde ayant le vent au dessus!! [sic][239] and Magrath hoping to have a lorry tomorrow. I am sending my surplus kit and the more valuable articles from the chapel for a change of air to Poperinghe. They can easily return later, if all goes well.

    Goodie.

*   *   *

T.H.
Saturday, 13 April 1918

Dearest Mater,

Another scrap – it can't be more – to say all is well. Very momentous issues,[240] but by the grace of God we shall not fail. Fortunately, thank God, I am in splendid health and good spirits, and everyone is open-hearted and good. T.H. stands up till now, and its doors are open. I am naturally anxious, but it is good to hold fast by God. The time is historic, and another Waterloo may come, in God's providence.

    Your letter very cheering. Other letters tell me of the death of many friends. But all things work together for good.

    Your loving son

---

239 The meaning here may have been "everyone has got the wind up".
240 On 9 April 1918, the Germans attacked (Operation Georgette) between Armentières and Messines. Their aim was to capture Calais and Boulogne. The British withdrew east of Ypres, thus abandoning most territory captured during Third Ypres. On 11 April, Sir Douglas Haig issued his famous 'Backs to the Wall' communiqué, in which he urged the BEF to "fight it out" to the end, and stated that the victor would be "the side which holds out the longest". On the night of 12 April, "some enormous shells dug craters the size of cottages" in the vicinity of Talbot House.

P.S. Letters will probably be delayed a fortnight; but no news is good news.

P.P.S. I'm sending various papers home, Communicants' Roll etc. They can be sent out again, as packed, if need be.

*   *   *

Wednesday night, 17 April 1918

My dearest Mater,

The end of an eventful day; but I can't explain all the events – no near shaves, though a certain amount of shelling round about.[241] Yesterday the House was closed by order, to-day the A.P.M. intervened and lodged a purple protest against my being moved away to other work, my transfer having come through. He was splendid, and I hope has saved me from being shifted, for I should be very sorry to leave yet awhile at least. We have two vans of furniture on the railway, so I can flit it at a moment's notice if necessary. But I don't think the time has come yet, as the house is quite useful still, and more brotherly than ever. We can't safely use the upstairs floors at all, but one ground floor room makes a beautiful little chapel, and for the rest we can easily cater for our children, who are keener than ever and more thankful – Laus Deo!

Don't worry about me. If I do move, I'll write as soon as I can but "in nothing be anxious".[242] How often Our Lord said "be of good cheer". A habitual and characteristic greeting with Him. Your two letters came to-day, and were a great joy to me.

Now I must to bed!

God bless and keep you all.

Always your loving son,

Philip

*   *   *

T.H.

Friday, 19 April 1918

Dearest Mater,

All well here, and I don't think now I shall be moved unless the Boche moves us all. This is *tres bon*, and I am very thankful to God, and to His true servant the Bishop. The A.P.M. wired to the Provost Marshal of the Army saying it was absolutely necessary that I should be left here, which has saved the situation I trust, from my pastoral point of view.

A tremendous downpour to-day – snow and rain, which is unpleasant, but very good for our side. Yesterday, I went up on the hills with Edge-Partington,[243] and had a wonderful view of the battle, burning towns and villages etc. It was a sight never to be forgotten.

Last night I slept quietly with a Signal School away out of the town, and was much refreshed in body and spirit.

Much love,

Philip

---

241   On this day the Belgians were attacked near to Merkem. They succeeded in holding their positions. Meanwhile, the British attempted to halt the ongoing German advance near Kemmel.

242   Philippians 4:6.

243   One of Tubby's fellow curates at St. Mary's, Portsea.

*   *   *

Saturday, 20 April 1918

Dearest Mater,

All going well and happily. It's rather living on the edge of volcano, but that seems to make everyone happier. All the formality has gone, and we are just brothers one of another. I have more time to spare than of old, as I can't quite settle down to a regular routine of work under the circumstances. But I have a good and useful Sunday ahead to-morrow, please God. It is certainly good to be here.

The Boche we believe, is held up this way, which will annoy him extremely, if it is so. But it's early days to say yet. Meanwhile one simply lives to put one's whole trust in God.

Now I must close down and have lunch.

Much love,

Philip

*   *   *

T.H.

Saturday, 20 April 1918

My dear H.B.C.

Very many thanks for your cheery letter. Life here is a little too exciting at present, but on the other hand everyone is at their best, and one is much more in the centre of things than of old. Our dugout accommodation grows apace; thank goodness we started on it long ago. Our concert hall got hit yesterday, but no real damage was done, and within a quarter of an hour some imperturbable spirits were playing billiards again. I know I should have miscued a good deal.

Little T.H. is evacuated for the time at least, and this has really taken on its place; it's on a war footing, with most of our valuables on a train in safety. I had an amazing view of the battle on Thursday, and from today's news the Boche is held up pretty thoroughly round here. Please God it is me. Forsan et hace olim meminisse juvabit![244]

Your brother,

Philip

*   *   *

Monday, 22 April 1918

Dearest Mater,

All very well and fit here, and the Boche quieter. The House is more useful than ever, – God bless the old place! – and I have just enough staff to carry on with after a fashion. I am now officially appointed at last Garrison Chaplain to P. so my flag is nailed to the mast, and *j'y suis, j'y reste*,[245] which is just what I've been longing for all along.

---

244 "A joy it will be one day, perhaps, to remember even these things" (from Vergil's *Aeneid*, I, 203).
245 French for: here I am, here I remain.

I enclose a postcard with the address of the wife of one of my men, my carpenter, a nice lad (of 25!) who was Confirmed here a few months back.[246] The child (no. 5, I think) was born a few weeks ago and as he can't get home, he is anxious that the missus should not delay the Baptism indefinitely. The question is, can you find a Godfather and Godmother? The Rose family doesn't seem very Churchy, I am sure you can fix this up wisely and well.

Now the post must go. I'll write scraps when I can. Tension much relieved here, thank God.
Love to all you dear folk,
Philip

*   *   *

NOTICE
T.H. and the recent gale of wind
When the history of the House is written, the last fortnight will have a paragraph to itself. Until a fortnight ago, the grand old House was apparently resigned to a placid old age in the suburbs of war, where the rumours germinate. Suddenly at 11.30 p.m. on Sat. week, came a bolt from the blue, a pink order saying "Shut up." To this we replied sleepily: "shut up yourself." Sunday brought the same refrain: "shut up," to which we replied "shut up?" Monday put the lid on it. Our Staff was withdrawn, and we reported broken-heartedly "shut up!" Meanwhile on Sunday night the Staff of Little Toc H in Wipers was given sudden notice to quit. On Monday Mr. Goodwin led a sortie and got away the piano, etc. (we had only put the last nail in our new concert hall there twenty four hours previously!). On Tuesday, enters the hero of the piece in the person of A.P.M. Pop. He championed our cause to such effect, that my movement order is cancelled, and the House is left, denuded, it is true, of staff and creature comforts, but "semper eadem"[247] (I forgot the Latin dictionary is at present in pawn with our noble friends of R.O.D.). We hope soon to have the House in apple-pie order again; meanwhile you will only drive us to misanthropy if you persist in strewing nutshells on the floor.

22.4.18 P.B.C.

*   *   *

Wednesday night, 24 April 1918

Dearest Mater,
Some nice little paper for a nice little note, to report all's well.[248] The place is still going strong, and the Boche still rages furiously. It all gradually becomes more uncivilized – shops shut; civilians flee; the Officers' Club closes down.[249] This last is a considerable loss to me, both gastronomically and otherwise, but I've lots of kind friends who give me meals, so with them and old Jimmy's cooking I shan't starve by any means. And it's all tremendously worthwhile. Folk are thankful T.H. is still an open door, and my opportunities for spiritual work are great

---

246 Pte. A. Rose (763 Area Employment Company) a pianoforte maker in civilian life.
247 Ever the same.
248 This letter was written on notepaper of the New Zealand Y.M.C.A.
249 Kemmel Hill fell to the enemy on the following day.

Civilians fleeing their homes.

e.g. this morning, a young 2nd Lt. I knew and loved last year came in (with his new D.S.O.) to make his Confession and receive the Sacrament, this afternoon some of my old F.A., and tonight I went to two Railway Coys from whom I've just got back, to find that (again during my absence) the Boche has knocked down a piece of garden wall. Only a pipsqueak and no damage even to the rosetrees.

But of course it's very uncertain how long my garrison chaplaincy will last!

Much love to all.

Philip

*   *   *

Saturday, 27 April 1918

Dearest Mater,

A quiet and comfortable night with a delightful Signal School, who pressed me to live with them, of which I may take advantage soon if T.H. becomes untenable. They also housed my men, so I could come with a clear conscience, and am much refreshed. T.H. may close any time, but it has done its share, and can sing its Nunc Dimittis.[250] I have all valuables safely away; meanwhile it is still a haven of refuge to the last.

Very well and happy myself, thank God, and not the least depressed.

Yours always most lovingly,

Philip

---

250 *Nunc dimittis* is a canticle in Christian liturgy, especially at compline and evensong, meaning '(Lord) now you let (your servant) depart' (St. Luke 2: 29–32).

*   *   *

Breakfast for the Kaiser

On 28 April, Barclay Baron (YMCA) was passing through Poperinge in his old Ford:

It was dusk running quickly into dark – we were passing through the silent, deserted streets of Poperinghe; all civilians had been evacuated some weeks ago, the town was strictly forbidden to troops. Talbot House, like everything else, had received peremptory orders to close, but, knowing Tubby's unmilitary manners, I guessed he might still be there. As we drove across the big, blank Grand Place, I felt suddenly near the end of my tether. Dickie and I had been out all day without a bite save a packet of biscuits and a bar or two of chocolate: tea in such a pass, as every housewife knows, is the grand restorative – we *must* have tea, for there would be none otherwise nearer than Mont des Cats.[251] We drew up at the tall white *portes cocher*[252] of Talbot House, nearly hidden now under a wall of sandbags to ward off blast.There was a faint bar of light up the crack of the double doors: Tubby was at home. We forced our way in and found him standing at the foot of the stairs, improperly dressed in breeches and puttees, a faded blue blazer and no collar. We murmured 'Tea!' almost melodramatically, and his old batman, Pettifer of the Buffs, went off to make it. Then

Barclay Baron, who served the YMCA from its Headquarters at Poperinge.

Tubby, looking graver than I have often seen him, began – 'You've heard the news?'

'Lots of it all day, Tubby, but it's not all true.' 'Then you know where our front line is now? In Reninghelst churchyard.' 'We can believe that. We were there early this afternoon.' 'Nothing can stop them now – they'll be in Poperinghe by the morning.' 'What are *you* going to do, Tubby?' The old familiar spark returned to him: 'O me? I'm stopping here to give the Kaiser his breakfast.' 'And me, Tubby', I said '– is there anything I can do for you?' He pondered a moment: 'Yes, there is. You can save some of the stuff. It would be a pity if it all went west.' I knew at once what 'the stuff' would be – some of the precious furniture from the Upper Room at the top of the House. I knew also that it was ready to hand, for they had moved it down some weeks ago to the shelter of a small room on the ground floor. We drank our tea, – or was it the authentic elixir of life? – talked for a time, maybe for the last time our hearts tacitly said, and set to work to pack an incongruous cargo into our open 'Tin Lizzie' at the door. Only the smaller furniture and fitments, of course, could be taken: on the top of them, to hold the load down over the

251 A 150 m high hill, situated 7 miles southwest of Poperinge; a Trappist Monastery is on the summit.
252 Sic: une porte cochère: a carriage entrance.

shell-cratered roads we laid 'the big black and gold carpet', which had covered the chapel floor before the altar since the beginning. As an afterthought someone added, to crown the load, the peal of tubular bells, suspended in a six-foot oak frame, which had so often summoned the household to evening prayers. The time had come for good-night. Tubby and I shook hands, which we had not had occasion to do when we met every day, for we felt this was likely to be 'Good-bye', 'God be with 'ee' indeed. Then he told me to hold on a moment, dashed upstairs and returned with a small green-covered book in which he wrote a few words before he put it into my hand. It was Weymouth's *New Testament in Modern Speech*.[253] Upon the fly-leaf I read: *Barkis from Tubby. T.H. 28 April 1918*. We drove away in pitch darkness. On the camouflaged, cratered road to the frontier and beyond; the car, low on its springs, lurched and rolled; we could not, of course, allow ourselves lights of any kind. And in this rough sea I could fancy that the tubular bells, which incessantly jangled, were playing *Rule, Britannia* and *God save the king*.[254]

* * *

Signal School

My dearest Mater,

It seems best that I should try and write you a wee bit letter this morning, before I go out on a raw May day to start coping with manifold problems, pastoral and structural. I slept here last night owing to the continued kindness of the officers i/c School who not only keep a prophet's chamber always at my disposal, but also take in nightly in the Camp, half a dozen of my staff, for a quiet rest. The place is about three miles from T.H., so has not yet lost its peaceful rural atmosphere. The best news since I wrote last is that Dr Magrath of Wipers Y.M.C.A., one of my very oldest and best friends, has come down and joined forces with me, so that my horizon is ever so much more cheery. It makes all the difference to have as a colleague, a friend as war-wise as any in the B.E.F., and takes a lot of responsibility for others off my shoulders. We are putting the house into sandbags roughly, and expecting dirty weather. Meanwhile we have also salved a derelict hut, which it is my job to-day to get transported in this direction, and then to get erected as a branch establishment, equipped and staffed as a joint concern between Magrath and myself. So long as he is with me "we fear no foe in shining armour",[255] and N.S.T. will probably have suggestions soon – he returns to-day I believe to the B.E.F.[256] – about a new start elsewhere, if necessary. Don't let anyone feel despondent about the war news, the Boche is only buying ground that doesn't matter at an exorbitant price, and we can hold him when and where we want to; there is something – I don't know what – behind our present manoeuvres, which means a decision, please God, in our favour, before the year is out; and the occasional withdrawal is

---

253 Richard Francis Weymouth's *The New Testament in Modern Speech: an Idiomatic Translation into Everyday English from the Text of 'The Resultant Greek Testament'*, first published 1903.
254 Michael Snape, *The Back Parts of War*, pp.184-186.
255 Words by Edward Oxenford and music by Ciro Pinsuti, "I fear no Foe in Shining Armour", was a popular Victorian parlour song.
256 Neville had trouble with his arm and was sent home on sick leave in March 1918. On 13 April he married his cousin Cecil Mary Eastwood. By June he was back in France.

being beautifully carried out. It's hard on the civilians and on public housekeepers like myself, but that is only a minor detail. The great thing is that the Boche is getting no change out of it.

Now I must get busy about the hut erection problem, which means scrounging a lorry off someone, and then sailing down the road to pick it up. All rather good fun. Life is far from being stale and stagnant at present.

Much love to all.

Philip

*   *   *

5th Sunday after Easter
5 May 1918
6 p.m.

Dearest Mater,

I am sitting in a Boche railway truck, now the mess of one of my Railway units, and writing home on a borrowed pad for a moment or two, before a Confirmation class: while the O.C.'s clerk, one of the candidates, finishes off some work with him. All goes well, both at T.H. and with the outlying parish. It's more eventful than it used to be, and harder to do settled work. All the same, one is of some use to a variety of folk, so I have every cause to be thankful. Your dear letter and the guv's arrived yesterday. Please thank him for his and say that I wouldn't dream of accepting help from his generosity at present, I have heaps of money, and no liabilities. The nearer one is to the war, the cheaper it is to live. I have now no shop within 5 miles or so, so am in no danger of spending money. Dr Magrath is a tremendous help in every way, and we live like fighting cocks. The Boche is licking his wounds, and is neither hopeful nor despairing as far as I can see. But I fancy his hopes are on the down grade now, though he can yet give considerable trouble.

It has turned wet to-night, but the guns still rumble on. My thoughts take me to T.H. where a friendly Padre is responsible for Evensong and home to you.

Much love

Philip

*   *   *

"One lives as it were in the passage under Niagara Falls, dry and safe oneself but deafened by the noise."

(P.B.C., 7 May 1918)

*   *   *

Sunday night, 12 May 1918
About 10.30 p.m.

My dearest Mater,

A word or two before I turn in. Magrath (who is a veritable godsend to me in every way, Christian, cheery, brave and wise) is reading the Times and warming his toes before doing ditto. He serves at our Celebrations, and plays the organ at our other services; and puts up wonderful huts and tents for recreation wherever I ask him. If the Army were as well run as the Y.M. we should be home by now. Poor old Army – how one grouses about it – it does its best under many difficulties.

We got back an hour ago from a happy Evening Service in a tent he has erected for some Railwaymen of mine, which has helped me enormously with them. Get a copy or two of his book on Ypres just out, published by Y.M.C.A., price about 1/-, with preface by the grand old Town Major.[257]

Please God, I am now to be allowed to stop here and keep the House open till whatever happens, happens. I wish nothing better than this. I have practically nothing left now that matters – all valuable furniture, etc., being on the train in safety. Even of my own clothes, I am only keeping what I stand up in. In point of fact my wardrobe is badly depleted by a bad business a fortnight back, when a shell hit one washerwoman's house and killed her and all her family. All our washing went at the same time[258] – it seems trivial to mention it, but it leaves me short of socks, etc. But Mrs Fry is sending some. One of Cecil's beautiful surplices and one of Belle's splendid Altar Cloths also went west at the same time. Curiously enough last summer when our washing was done over the road, a small shell spoilt it all, and it had to be redone! But enough of war and its curious ways. Magrath says "What about it?" Which means Good Night to you…

Much love
Philip

*   *   *

On 12 May Tubby received the following note from Rev. Ronald Irwin, D.A.C.G. 2nd Corps:

1.   If 2nd Corps orders Talbot House to be closed down as an Institute to which Troops visit, you must comply.
2.   There is no intention of withdrawing you from your present work.

*   *   *

257   C.J. Magrath, *Ypres – Yper. A Few Notes on its History before the War – With a Plan of the Town* (The Red Triangle Press, London).
258   For Pte. Pettifer's account of this incident: see p. 307.

A white 'signal' bearing the stamp of Town Major, Poperinghe, 15.5.18 provided peremptory orders for closing:

(1086) Wt.W16552/M1615 250,000 Pads. 21/3/17. J.R.&C. E 685 Forms/C2122/6.

Army Form C2122
(in pads of 150)

"B" Form.

MESSAGES AND SIGNALS.

No. of Message........

Prefix............Code..........m. | Received | Sent | Office Stamp

Office of Origin and Service Instructions | Words | At..........m. | From.......... | By..........

TOWN MAJOR POPERINGHE — 15.5.18

TO Chap Clayton
Talbot House
Poperinghe

Sender's Number.	Day of Month.	In reply to Number.	AAA
R 593	14		

Q Orders Talbot House
to be Closed at Once
please acknowledge
and report that this
Order has been Complied
with aaa

From Daly 2 Corps
Place
Time

* This line should be erased if not required.

* * *

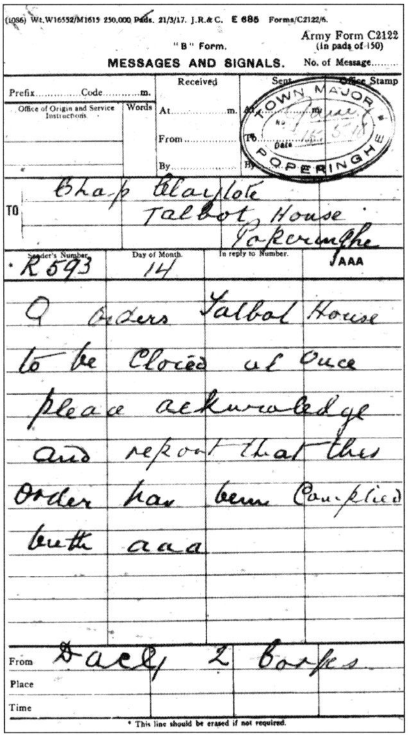

Wednesday, 15 May 1918

Dearest Mater,
More letters still for safe-keeping, etc. Corps has just ordered the House to be closed temporarily to troops from to-day and we can't resist. Probably, indeed it is wise, but it's hard luck on the wayfarers. I shall live here with Magrath and the staff for the time being, and do my outside work from here until sunnier days. It is very hard to close the door, but it's better to avoid a concentration at present, not that the town is bad, but it might suddenly take a turn for the worse, in which case I should go and live with the Railway folk. Anyhow we've kept the door open longer than anyone else, and it is not the Boche that closes it now.

Resurget Domus Talbotensis![259]

With much love to all,

Philip

259 Talbot House will resurrect!

*   *   *

NOTICE

Although, in obedience to the order of 2nd Corps, the House as a canteen etc., must remain temporarily closed, it also remains the billet of the Garrison Chaplain and of Dr. Magrath, who will always be glad to be of any service to any visitors. If the door is shut, the bell on the left is still in the best of working order.

Father Stanton[260] used to tell a story of a small and ragged boy who appeared on his doorstep, and asked to see him "spiritual." On being admitted to the Library, the boy looked doubtfully at Father Stanton's cassock, and opened the spiritual conversation with the remark, "Have yer got such a thing as an old pair of trousers about yer?"

*   *   *

"This House," said the old Bishop in Les Miserables to Jean Valjean, "is not my house, but God's; and is open not to him that hath a name, but to him that hath a need."[261]

P.B.C.

*   *   *

At this very critical period, with the Germans having captured Kemmel Hill, and threatening Poperinge "no place for boys", the landlord, Mr Coevoet, wrote the following note:[262]

Saint-Désir, 20 May 1918
Coevoet Camerlynck
"Chalet Lutherean,"
La Pommeraye
St. Desir par Lisieux
(Calvados)

Monsieur le R.P. Clayton
Talbot House
Poperinghe
I have received your valued letter of April 28, from which I took the sum of 300 francs in bank notes for the rent of my house, Rue de l'Hôpital at Poperinghe, for two periods from March 7 to May 7, 1918. For this I thank you. As I have left the country to put my family in safety in France, your letter has been forwarded to me at our new address in France. If you are able to continue to occupy the house, you will oblige me by sending the rent for the ensuing periods to the above address. Receive, Mr. Captain, the assurance of my perfect consideration.

M. Coevoet

260 Arthur Henry Stanton (1839-1913) was one of the devoted parochial clergy who, during the latter half of the Victorian era, translated the Catholic movement into a language that could be understood by common people. He was curate of the parish of St. Alban's, Holborn for a half-century.
261 Victor Hugo, *Les Misérables* (1862).
262 Translated from the French.

Alida Camerlynck (wife of Maurice Coevoet) and her sister Marcelline seated, with their children and nanny (standing at the back), in the garden of 'Chalet Lutherean' (Lisieux) where they had fled to escape the war in the spring of 1918.

*   *   *

A wire, dated May 20, gave the final and irrevocable order to close down:
To Padre Clayton, Talbot House. Q insist that you shall vacate Talbot House and seek billet elsewhere. Please wire acknowledgement and what steps you are taking. D.A.C.G., II. Corps.

*   *   *

Whit-Monday, 20 May 1918, 2 p.m.

Dearest Mater,
It feels rather like a Bank holiday too! Mac and I got up at 9 a.m. and breakfasted at 9.30, and he is now doing my T.H. accounts (good man) while I am writing letters.
    Then we journey hand in hand to Dingley Dell,[263] a delightful orchard a mile from here, where we have pitched four Armstrong huts,[264] and propose to live for the time, and run a Talbot Park.

263   The following day Tubby, Magrath, "The Gen", and remaining orderlies retired to a temporary camp, which Tubby had christened *Dingley Dell* after the manor of the agreeable old Mr Wardle of Dickens' *The Pickwick Papers*. The camp was situated in a field behind the deserted aerodrome near La Lovie Château, north-west of Poperinge. According to Tubby they dumped a larger hut with the Talbot House signboard on a main traffic route and, in alliance with the YMCA, erected the other huts nearby, all of "which try to carry on the Talbot House traditions of love and joy and peace".
264   Small, collapsible huts made of canvas and wood.

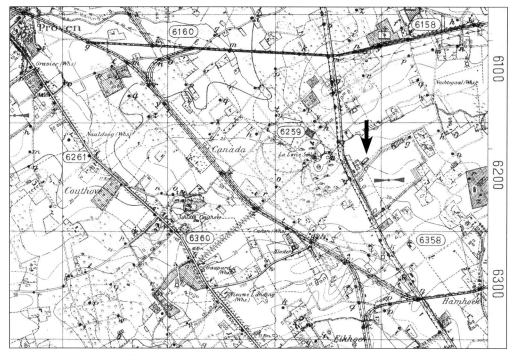

German army map of Proven, March 1918, showing La Lovie Château (map square 6259) and the aerodrome (6258 & 6259). The supposed location of Dingley Dell is marked with an arrow.

The authorities are determined (quite kindly) that the House should be evacuated now. For a fortnight it has been the only House open in the town; and as the town is now altogether out of bounds, it seems only folly to remain.

We have cleared everything worth having even the electric light fittings; and all the valuables, Chapel Furniture, etc., are safely on the train in a truck all to themselves. T.H. will probably reopen here or elsewhere in a month or two. Meanwhile I shall live happily with Magrath in Dingley Dell, and work round my outside parish more easily than from here. It is in one way of course heartrending to leave the House. On the other hand, there is nothing for it now to do; and we can sing our Nunc Dimittis with a quiet and thankful heart. We have been wonderfully guarded, guided and blessed; and though many of our children are now at peace, there are many still in this world who have here found Him and been found of Him. Laus Deo.

Much love, dearest Mater.

Yours always,

Philip

*   *   *

22 May 1918

Dearest Mater,

This is in pencil because it's easiest and slackest. We are camped in a meadow about a mile on the safe side of T.H., very happy. I have been building a cook house all the morning, and should not be ashamed for the Guv. to see it. You never know what you can do, etc.

The weather is perfectly ideal and it's a country holiday to be here; the only things we left behind of value are the Duchess (alias our stately Tabby) and the Golden Butterfly[265] which I was reading yesterday (these the General has now gone down to salve), when Tom Le Mesurier[266] came in. He is a great lad, entirely and certainly a relation to be proud of in every way, modest, humble, and unassuming, with a record such as comes to few men indeed under 21, and not to many over it. He was the ideal visitor for my last day at T.H. He lent me his side-car and American driver to go and scrounge a lost lorry and made no bones of bully and biscuit food, which was all we could offer him. He is going to fly over on the next day off bringing with him Popham of Southwark, his Padre, a very dear friend of mine. I am thankful they are together for both their sakes. I shall be very happy here, please God, and the change from living in a dug-out did me good last night. We are such a microscopic speck with our four Armstrong huts that I don't think the Hun will bother about us. In any case we are mobile now and nearly all my furniture is in a train truck in safety.

Much love,

Philip

*   *   *

Monday, 3 June 1918

Dearest Mater,

Five letters came from you yesterday, all by one post; which is a real feast. I read them at lunch in the interval of a strenuous day.

At 8 a.m. I had a Celebration in one of our tents half a mile from here; then I leapt into a sidecar and went to some nice balloonatics,[267] then back into Pop. where a short service with aid post and police. Meanwhile my next car arrived, and Pettifer took it to draw rations. When

---

265 A popular novel in three volumes by Sir Walter Besant and James Rice, first published in 1876.

266 Tubby's second cousin – for his story, see p. 322.

267 RFC balloon units observed enemy movements and directed artillery by telephone.

they returned full up with Maconochies[268] etc. we went off for a long journey up northwards to an Archies section[269] very isolated, where another service, then home to Dingley Dell to lunch and letters. In the afternoon into Pop. again, but no service possible, so thence with a heroic old Colonel[270] (who alone had turned up as congregation) via his unpleasant home, where he insisted on showing me all the latest shell holes to some old friends returned to the neighbourhood; where tea, and a delightful service to follow. Thence in another sidecar to a railway Coy., after which on a whizzbang along the broad gauge behind a train down to my R.O.D. friends for service at 8 p.m. followed by Celebration. Supper with Phillips, an old Pauline,[271] and Magrath then at 9.30 p.m. and home on a special train (engine and tender) at 11 p.m. to the nearest point on the line. Breakfast in bed this morning!

I can't get my leave as I had hoped this week, but I hope to come on Saturday or Monday next, and so to see something of Hugh.

On Saturday I went across to see Tom Le Mesurier, only to find he had been killed three days before flying over the Boche lines. Everyone heartbroken over his loss. I had no idea from his own modest self what a distinguished record he bore.[272] God rest his soul. He was a splendid boy, a born pilot, and a most noble Christian gentleman.

Your son,
Philip

R.I.P.
Thomas F. Le Mesurier
Captain, 211th Sqdn. 65th Wing, Royal Air Force
26 May 1918 – Age 21 – Dunkirk Town Cemetery, IV.A.24

* * *

From the Visitors' Book, Little Hatchett
11-24 June 1918
P.B.C. on midsummer leave from an Armstrong hut in front of Château Louvie. A very happy holiday: everyone & everything at its best, especially the strawberries. The godchild Nancy blows bubbles[273] without recourse to a pipe & soapsuds. Why didn't I bring more cheeses? Mem. for next time. A secondhand Triumph hired from Bournemouth takes me to Farnham, & brings me back again with many adventures: finally to be ridden back by Lindsay DCM MM etc.

---

268 A tinned ration of stewed beef, carrots, onions, beans and potatoes named after the Aberdeen Maconochie Company that produced it.
269 Anti-aircraft.
270 Lord Saye and Sele.
271 Former pupil of St Paul's School (London).
272 Le Mesurier was an ace, having shot down seven enemy aircraft between June and October 1917. He took part in numerous bombing raids and fighter patrols, and also made valuable observations. He held the D.S.C. & 2 Bars, the D.S.M. and was Mentioned in Dispatches.
273 Hence her nickname 'Bubbles'. She was the daughter of Tubby's brother, Hugh, born on 14 February 1918.

Tubby, his sister-in-law Annie Blanch (née Nepean) and little Nancy ('Bubbles') at Little Hatchett, 1918.

who will need all his bravery to accomplish this task.[274] So back to Louvie, with the hope of reopening T.H. in Proven, if Foch[275] doesn't feint with his left.

(P.B.C.)

*   *   *

R.F.C.
Officers rest house and mess
Wednesday evening, 26 June 1918

Dearest Mater,

I'm just waiting for a promised lift to A.C.G.s, where I propose stopping till Friday. Had a quick and sunny crossing, and discovered one old Guardee friend Lieut. Pigott on the boat, being myself discovered by another old M.O. from 1915 on his way back. So no loneliness, which was good, as the certainty about Cecil[276] had given me acute heartache. But the first "hallo padre" on the boat recalled me to my better self, i.e. the sense of work still to be done, of many mercies at home and out here, and the thanks living which can rise above personal loss. So I go forward to the task whatever it is with hope, and the enrichment of a sorrow which please God will teach truer sympathy.

I had a delightful night at Lambeth,[277] and much talk with the Arch. whose innate goodness is clearer the closer one gets. York was also there, and that doyen of overseas Bishops, Brent, whom I knew in Pop. before now, on his way to the Grand Fleet. What I want now is a week's quiet to write letters and things.

Much love,
Philip

---

274 Pte. John Homer Lindsay, 5th Canadian Infantry Battalion.

275 Marshal Ferdinand Foch had become the Allied commander-in-chief in April 1918. In July he would launch the Allied counter-offensive that brought about the negotiation of an armistice to end the war.

276 Tubby's closest friend since preparatory school, Capt. Cecil Rushton, 214th Squadron R.A.F., was killed on 16 May 1918 when his plane crashed whilst bombing Brugge dockyard. In 'A Man Greatly Beloved' Tubby wrote a moving tribute to him in his *Plain Tales from Flanders* (London, 1929).

277 The Archbishop of Canterbury's official London residence.

R.I.P.
Cecil G. Rushton
Captain, 214th Sqdn., Royal Air Force
16 May 1918 – Age 35 – Larch Wood (Railway Cutting Cemetery), Zillebeke, IV.F.21

*   *   *

D.C.G.s
Friday, 28 June 1918

Dearest Mater,
I'm still here, having a real rest, and writing long overdue letters, and trying to decide about the future. I hope to get a lift up the line this afternoon. I have had some splendid talks with Cunningham and the Bishop, about things in general and what I am to do in particular.

The upshot for myself is that I shall spend the summer working among the railway Troops in our Army area, broad gauge and narrow; a most interesting parish, of which I have already touched more than the fringe. But there is all the difference between being an outsider, and becoming one of them. I shall keep on also some of my kite balloon folk, etc. and so the change will only be gradual as the work develops. I may shift my quarters as soon as I can find "a better 'ole",[278] more central for my work. Probably I shall try and arrange a weekly tour of the various people concerned, sleeping a night here and there. This will be a new interest, and in fallow ground.

My address can remain the same, for the time at least. This scheme stands until the autumn by which time it may be possible to re-open the House, there or elsewhere.

This is a lovely seaside place, though the front is mostly sand-dunes. B.K.C. wanted to take me to the woods behind yesterday, but I said "No thanks, I know what a real forest is."

Much love to you all,
Your son,
Philip

*   *   *

A.P.O. S/63
Saturday, 29 June 1918

Dearest Mater,
I reached here successfully after lunch today, and found Dingley Dell smiling, and real welcome. My stay at D.C.G.'s was a real refreshment in every way. I only left there at 8 this morning, being lucky in a lift. My formal attachment to Railway Troops is going through all right, I think, as folk up here are quite keen on it. This will mean a very scattered parish, and a good deal of toothbrush and razor in the pocket stunt; but that will be quite enjoyable and I love virgin soil.

---

278 Reference to Bruce Bairnsfather's most iconic cartoon depicting "Old Bill" and another Tommy under cover in a shell hole, shells whizzing about everywhere. The latter is grumbling when Bill advises: "Well, if you knows of a better 'ole, go to it." The acclaimed cartoon was first published in *The Bystander* magazine's Christmas number on 24 November 1915.

Monday morning

I hope pencil won't try your eyes, but it means I can write on my knees in comfort. I had a jolly day yesterday, not so many services as usual, which is perhaps as well. In the evening I went down in a sidecar 8 miles each way to my new Railway H.Q., and had small but select congregation.

This morning at 8 a.m. I said a Requiem for Cecil and Tom, and Arthur Cole[279] and Bernard Stenning. I chose today because Stenning's mother asked for it (being his birthday). You will see what manner of man he was if you care to look under S. in the letter file.[280]

Now Paddy[281] is busy building me a study out of six sheets of tin and a scrap or two of wood. The architec-

Two simple wooden prayer-desks in the Upper Room, one bearing a plate in memory of 2nd Lt. Bernard Stenning.

ture is distinctly neolithic, but if it serves its purpose, well and good. I haven't seen the great Higgon yet, but hope to spend next Thursday night there.

Much love,

Your son,

Philip

R.I.P.

Arthur R. Cole

Lance Corporal, 2/1 (Wessex) Field Ambulance, R.A.M.C.

10 April 1918 – Age 23 – Chocques Military Cemetery (Fr.), I.M.38

Bernard C. Stenning

2nd Lieutenant, 5 East Surrey Regiment

26 July 1917 – Age 35 – Godewaersvelde British Cemetery, I.A.10

* * *

279 Tubby's most faithful Upper Room server.

280 Lt. Bernard Stenning (5th East Surreys; attached 228th Field Company RE) received the Sacrament in the Upper Room shortly before his death on 26 July 1917. A simple wooden prayer-desk bears a plate in his memory.

281 Forty-eight-year-old Pte. P. Flynn (763rd Area Employment Company), a gardener from Ireland.

Saturday, 6 July 1918

Dearest Mater,

I'm beginning to tackle the railway job in earnest now. It's a terrific size, and full of odd corners. I went down to the H.Q. on Wednesday, and opened the Ball there. Every week I'm going down there on Wednesday for the night, and fortunately have several old friends to stay with, Higgon himself (who is nearby and in fine form) and Phillips an old Pauline in command of one Railway detachment. The Colonel of the whole concern is a most interesting man, not the least of an army type, but simply a big young capable business manager from a home railway company, and the men are so hard at work that I scarcely know how to begin with them – it's simply a question of visiting on the spot for the present. Anyhow, I have enough to keep me out of mischief – work simply pours in, one way and another.

    With much love,

    Your son,

    Philip

*   *   *

Wigwam Dwellers at Dingley Dell

Toc H built up a cosy little practice in the backwoods, among those whose souls the Army declined to recognize.

It was healthy life in our little refugee camp. A few earthworks of the palaeolithic '14 – '15 period stood in our small field; but on July 10 some Staff Officer riding by remarked our hedge as admirable cover for a section of 18-pounders. Within a day or so, a gunner subaltern arrived,

Tubby was so attached to the hut in which he had lived at 'Dingley Dell' that after the war he had it transported to Little Hatchett, where it was put in the garden. It was returned to Poperinge in 1999 and now forms part of the Talbot House collection.

with a White Knight assortment of compasses and ranging instruments. Dismounting, he busied himself with recording hypothetical zones of fire, picked some unripe blackberries, and finally got inside our hut and outside our lunch. The next day a gun-team complete manoeuvred through the gateway, deposited its *retrousse* tail,[282] did some blackberrying and disappeared. A few gunners were marooned with a sandbag or so of biscuits and bully. They lost no time in vain regrets, but solaced themselves with blackberries, and built against the evening dews and damps a wattle wigwam; and then left a ration card on Pettifer. A load of rabbit wire, gay with some tatters of green canvas, was the next consignment, and the wigwam dwellers involved themselves in the delicate task of erecting camouflage over their snub-nosed deities, taking a hand at stump cricket and the black-berries, as occasion served. Their task accomplished, a series of whole-day matches were played; at the conclusion of which the gun-teams reappeared, the guns limbered up, and the marooned party went off, remembered and forgiven, and the field was left to the cows and ourselves; the wattle hut, the camouflage, and some rounds of ammunition being our sole mementoes.

I was rarely in camp by day, but at night the thickness of the hedge alone separated me from the gunners' wigwam, wherein they croaked and quarrelled, like a leafy city of rooks at sunset. Their conversation was emancipated, but painfully uninteresting. I remember only one episode. "Ginger" had, it seemed received a letter from home, recording a notice to quit. His indignation took the form of a vigorous asseveration that "when he got home he would keep a Lewis gun ready for the landlord. Twelve years' rent he had paid, on the nail, and fair bought the place twice over." I am ashamed to say that I applauded; and conscious of the impropriety, blew out my candle.

(P.B. Clayton)

*　*　*

Tuesday, 16 July 1918

Dearest Mater,
Rose (the Enfield carpenter) has built me a new bedsitting room, a delightful little tin shack, and most serviceable last night, when we had a terrible storm. Thunder and lightning ad lib., as if to say "what a funny thing a human war is after all." Then the rains descended, but fortunately my new house is raised off the ground and so apart from one or two small leaks, all was merry and bright inside. But the Boche must have got very wet, and if any of their night bombers who disturbed the earlier hours didn't get home in time, they didn't get home at all. I hope that the Guv's garden got it all right, and that the crops are not all laid low. Today it's very hot again, though there's a fine wind, and "visibility being good", the war is going on quite actively, with proper inter-vals for meals. It's not very far away, but our field is so out of the way that no trouble comes near us here.

282 Docked-tail horses.

I'm taking a day off today, and have spent the morning reading Rackham's Acts[283] and other good things. I must try and do this more regularly, if I am not to grow shallow and illiterate. The Railway business is going well, and tomorrow night Pettifer and I hope to get down and see Higgon at the Army Artillery School. What a long letter from Charlton – quite in the best vein however. I re-enclose it in case you like to read it. Have you the whiskey all right – it must be difficult to get, even for such a legitimate use. Even out here it is not quite so plentiful (thank goodness) as it was.

  Much love, dearest Mater,
  Your son,
  Philip

*   *   *

Thursday, 18 July 1918

My dear Stuart,
I read your letter yesterday, or rather this morning, in bed at 2.30 a.m. I came in with Magrath at about 1 a.m. after a terrific day, finishing up with a concert to some railway troops 20 miles away. We returned in the pouring rain in the concert party lorry and when we got in found my bedroom flooded, as it was built in a dry ditch. The water was nearly up to the trench boards that make its floor. So we had to turn the staff out and dig drains in the dark to let the water off, and not till then did we get to bed; so I had breakfast in bed this morning to make up, and this afternoon am going to try and scrounge a hut more weatherproof from some kind friend. What a life! I'll write more soon.

  Yours with much love,
  Philip B.C.

*   *   *

Talbot Camp
A.P.O. 3/63
20 July 1918

Dearest Mater,
A wet Saturday, full of intervals of thunder; which I'm afraid may make the glorious victory of the French on the Marne and the contribution of the Australians nearer us less decisive than they might be.[284] But we are at least rewarded for much past suffering. "Let there be sung non nobis and Te Deum."

---

283 See note 120.
284 The Battle of Hamel (4 July 1918) was a highly successful operation launched by the Australian
      Corps and attached American units. The battle was planned and commanded by Lieutenant General
      Sir John Monash. The Second Battle of the Marne (15 July-6 August 1918) was the last major
      German offensive on the Western Front. The attack failed when an Allied counterattack led by
      French forces including several hundred tanks, overwhelmed the enemy right flank.

Myself, I am rather Nelsonic,[285] having been stung in the eye by a mosquito or something, with the result that it looks as if I had been in a street fight. But I hope to be alright for a busy day tomorrow. I went down to Higgons on Wednesday, and it was there that I was stung. So that on Thursday when I saw Neville, I could only look at him with one eye. Next Thursday night, I hope to spend with him also. Life is really rather exciting just now, not that there is much danger here, but one feels that the Boche must be getting desperate, and all his hopes vanishing. It would be wonderful if peace really came upon us unawares, through a victory of real decisiveness.

Shiner and his merry Southamptonians are not far away again now, and I hope to see them too. "Gathering up the fragments that remain"[286] seems my text for this summer, and the band of friendship certainly grows stronger and stronger after many vicissitudes. Meanwhile our canteen is full of splendid fellows who look blank at "1 franc 25", but fork out gladly when told "a silver, two big pennies and a haf." I should love to have T.H. running for them in the old style. How they would revel in it.

Much love,

Your son,

Philip

* * *

5 August 1918

My dear old Guv,

A very wet dismal evening, on which I'm grateful to be sitting in a nice tin hut at Dingley Dell, and not popping off the large guns that are booming dully in the distance.

I foresee an extra busy week ahead, so it's good to have a quiet night. To-morrow I start in a side-car at 9.30 and go round to some Balloonatics, and then go on to another lot at 11 a.m. They will I hope give me lunch, after which I go down to the little town where the new Talbot House is in embryo for the autumn.[287] There I have some boys in to tea and biscuits (no bread purchaseable – far less cakes!) and after supper with the signallers who live below, sleep on the floor of the Church that is to be, in my old Andorra fleabag – Vokins and Pettifer to keep me company, and start the following morning on my travels round again. I'm very lucky at present over motor help, the railway authorities not only lending

Going home, 1999.

285 Napoleonic Wars naval hero Admiral Horatio Nelson (1758-1805) suffered many wounds during active service, including an arm and eye.

286 St. John 6:12.

287 The village of Proven, north-west of Poperinge.

me a car all Sunday and on weekdays when I want it, but also installing a telephone for me, so that I can really keep in touch with my terrifically scattered units. Thus yesterday I finished one service at 5 p.m. within 2,000 yards of the Boche, and at 6 p.m. began another in my Church ten miles back. I travel forty miles most Sundays with upwards of ten services at various stopping places; and now can carry harmonium, and all sorts of Church fittings to rig Church with at each place in turn. This is a real luxury, and what with this and a lot of open-air life and hard walking, I am fitter than I have ever been in Belgium before.

The war is going all the right way just now, and I really think that this is the beginning of the end at last; the Vaterland is sinking slowly and while we must not be sucked down in the eddies, we must be prepared to rescue the women and children. Those on the bridge certainly don't deserve to be picked up, but will probably make a dash for the captain's gig. America has definitely turned the scales,[288] and there is a wonderful unanimity among our own boys as to the shy, apologetic, but clear-headed and stout-hearted men who represent her in such overwhelming numbers. They are full of freshness, enthusiasm, and best of all, idealism, in which we are growing rather bankrupt. Their modesty disarms criticism, and I don't think the earlier labourers will grumble at their reward being equal to ours. Now I must to bed. God bless and keep you all.

Your loving son,
Philip

*   *   *

Monday night, 12 August 1918

Dearest Mater,
Supper in Dingley Dell again to-night which I haven't seen since Saturday. I had better give one more account of my week-end doings, though I fear they are rather boring.

I went down to the new little Talbot House, now established in the Town Hall,[289] on Saturday after lunch. There I spent the afternoon tidying up, seeing folk, and fixing up my Sunday arrangements. The Railway have given me a telephone which is perfectly invaluable and saves me endless journeys and letters. I found one visitor had been three times that morning, so rang up his C.O. and got leave for him to come again. He turned out to be a Cpl. with M.M., whom I knew something of last year, when his great friend Archie Forrest was baptized, confirmed and killed up here.[290] Archie's great longing was that his friend should be confirmed with him. But the Cpl. (a great tough Durham miner) wasn't ripe for it. A third, of the same Company, Percy Herbert by name, was wounded two days before the Confirmation. He came back to the Company a few weeks ago, and we at once started our classes again with a view to the Confirmation yesterday. Well, on Saturday, Cpl. Hilker surrendered as wholeheartedly as he had previously held out, and knowing the situation as I did, I accepted him and presented him for Confirmation alongside Percy Herbert yesterday. I'm sure Archie Forrest's soul rejoiced over the fulfilment of his wish.

288 By July 1918 more than a million U.S. troops had landed in France, commanded by General John J. Pershing.
289 Talbot House at Proven was never officially opened.
290 For the story of Archie Forrest: see p. 311.

On Saturday evening, then, these things accomplished, I went off at 6 p.m. in a box-car (thanks again to the Railway), cigar, books, etc. all aboard, and after various calls, arrived at Railway H.Q. There I had a delicious dinner, and found the Colonel greatly occupied with a portable altar he is designing for me out of oak from Wipers and Elverdinghe Churches; his one stipulation being that he should have it *après la guerre*. I'll give it back to him that he may take it back to China with him and give it to the Mission priests there. It makes an incalculable difference to have a man such as this at the head of affairs. Then to bed in Browne's old 1st class compartment, and Celebration at 8.30 a.m. with the Colonel, Adjutant, Doctor, another H.O. Officer and four of the office clerks.

Town Hall in Proven.

Rapid breakfast and the box-car for my own all day. First to one Railway Construction Camp miles away, service here in the open at 10. They are keen, if not very instructed, and have a choir led by two fiddles and the organ. Then across country to more of the same ilk. Here a lot of Talbot House furniture is stored and with part of it we have fitted up a big recreation hut, with an ex-Church Army Captain in charge. Feeling the time was ripe for it, I had asked as a special favour, that the service here should be entirely voluntary – it had been a parade before. Terrible results were prophesied, but the result was happily convincing in the opposite direction, as the hut was full and the service greatly improved in spirit by the absence of "militarism". I do loathe parades. There I stopped to lunch, also my Scotch driver, and started on at 1.45 to find a Light Railway Repair Train on a Broad Gauge siding. Picking up a derelict Major on the way who wanted a lift, we found our folk at 2.15, and had a short service, leaving at 3 p.m. to pick up my Confirmation candidates. Then on to the Church, where the Confirmation was, and a short wait for the Bishop. An excellent address, though he looked more tired than I liked to see; and a word or two of laughter with him at my simple costume – shorts and a shirt, and a linen tunic – and then back to the Company from which the candidates came. Here rapid tea and a voluntary evensong in their Talbot House hut, and on to the Town Hall; a few minutes late for 6 p.m. Evensong. A good service here, followed by a Celebration with some twenty communicants. Then on once more in the box-car to an Ambulance, half English, half U.S.A., where Evensong again at 8 p.m. and administration of the Reserved Sacrament following. So back at 9.30 p.m. to the Town Hall, where supper and talk to two old friends in H.B.C.'s side of things till midnight, to the accompaniment of air-raid alarms; then to bed in my alternative billet there and doggo till 8.30 a.m. this morning. Now I must to bed – my writing is getting indecipherable and my style more hopelessly egotistical than ever. The news is splendid, thank God.

Much love,
Philip

R.I.P.
Archie Forrest
Confirmed at Talbot House, 9 July 1917
2nd Corporal, "P" Special (Gas) Company, Royal Engineers
26 August 1917 – Age 20 – Wieltje Farm Cemetery (St. Jan – Ieper), B.12

*   *   *

The
PADRE
(non-stop)

Friday night, 16 August 1918

Dearest Mater,

I'm just back from a very jolly visit to Neville. We got a shell or two not far from my new office on Wednesday night, so I put the shutters up quicker than Fezziwig's apprentices on Christmas Eve[291] and came up with Vokins to Dingley Dell to sleep – much closer to the line, but much safer. This is one of the curious things about war that is perplexing to hear of, but always true. Safety isn't simply something which augments and decreases in automatic ratio to distance or proximity. Even right forward, there is generally a belt of comparative quiescence between the guns and the infantry. However, this is getting Philip Gibbsey[292] and must cease forthwith.

291 Mr. Fezziwig is a character in Dickens' novella *A Christmas Carol* (1843).
292 Philip Gibbs (1877-1962) was the officially accredited *Daily Telegraph* and *Daily Chronicle* war correspondent.

Suffice it to say; on Thursday morning Vokins and I sallied forth after breakfast, went over to a railway line and telephoned for a "whizzbang". Meanwhile I discussed a new book of Benjamin Kidd's and the democratic idealism of China with a Lieutenant who fortunately only wanted a listener on both subjects. Then the rail-coach or whizzbang hove in sight – a lovely thing like a family pew on a motor chassis, highly painted and gorgeously upholstered; this is the Colonel's very own, kept chiefly for such as the Rajah of Seringapatam and his suite when they come to view the prospect o'er. How Stuart would love a ride on it and how the driver would love to have her aboard, let alone my own inclinations. On this we travelled at 35 miles an hour stopping only to see the shutters were still up at the Office and to pick up my razor and toothbrush in my town billet. (You see I lead a double life!) Then on to the H.Q. of the Railway Construction Coy., where I got my trousers out of my refugee store they keep for me; had some lemonade, passed the time of day, delivered some Altar linen for Sunday Church and some magazines for weekday refreshment, and collared a lorry, being pledged to redeem one of my pianos which had gone down the line with some other railway folk. We then proceeded for a four hours' long drive I always enjoy, stopping for an early tea *en route*, as rations on Lines of Communication are not plentiful, and it's not fair to arrive with 3 hungry men at a small camp, however hospitable. Where we stopped for tea, I met Baggallay (who used to be on my staircase at Exeter) and as I was talking to him, my eye lit on Neville in a big Army car of his own. Philip got in with the great Æthiopian and we left the lorry to follow at a respectful distance. Our preliminary conversations were interrupted by Neville's distressing habit of knowing everybody everywhere, so that he leaps from his chariot to greet old friends and blocks the traffic both ways without compunction. However, we had not far to go and his chauffeur was an old Brooklands driver, so we reached our objective without much delay. That was Captain Noel Phillips, M.C., R.O.D.,[293] the trustee of the piano, a dear Old Pauline, who used to run the Addison Gardens meetings to which I went when in a good mood on Sunday afternoons. The car went back with a staff-sergeant to find and bring hither the lorry, which came loaded up and (after Vokins had seen Neville) returned. Meanwhile, N.S.T., Phillips, and I had tea, and much talk about the great railway world out here, and what could be done to padre them.

At 6.30 p.m. we set sail in the car for Neville's home, with a lovely glimpse of France at its best upon the way – alas! I've never seen anything much of France during this old war – great noble fertile uplands in green and gold, and all the fields deserted for once, in honour of the Feast Day,[294] though the harvest could not wisely wait – wonderful faith, isn't it? or if not faith, discipline. Arrived at our destination, which Neville calls the cow-house, not because of its nature, but because the mess is rather weak in manly men, we said Evensong side by side, had dinner, and talked far into the night; with the result that we both breakfasted at 9.30 this morning. Then he did some office work in his inimitable way and at midday the car again appeared and we went off to lunch with Higgon. So we three met again, for the first time, I think, since we slept together in a dug-out, the night Higgon was gassed.

<hr />

293   In 1917 Phillips, an old school chum of Tubby's, was railway officer in charge of Ouderdom Dump (Reningelst) when it being heavily shelled a nearby ammunition train caught fire. Leaping into the engine cab, he drove the burning train a mile down the line. For this feat he was awarded the MC. Phillips salvaged a large quantity of precious Talbot House items as well as Tubby's personal belongings immediately after the armistice.
294   The Assumption is celebrated on 15 August.

This afternoon Neville brought me part of my road home until we overhauled a lorry belonging to one of my Kite-Balloon Sections on which I came the rest of the way. I went through the old town to the balloon, which unfortunately went up to look at things just before we got there; so after some talk with the groundsmen, I came home in a tender and had a quiet dinner and letters and such-like, Magrath being out, as company ….

Your loving son,

Philip

*   *   *

19 August 1918

Dearest Mater,

Excuse pencil, but I've lent my dear Waterman to Mac for official, as his has gone west. A quiet day after the Sunday rush. Tomorrow a kite balloon in the morning, and a long rail lorry journey in the afternoon. Tonight many letters. All preternaturally quiet at present. I fancy the Boche either has some last card up his sleeve, or is genuinely in the soup.[295] The coming of the Americans is the most manifest token of God's good providence that our generation has seen – and right is now going to win, thank God. It may take some time still, but I am hopeful of the Boche despairing. "Doubtless there is a God who judgeth the earth".

Thank you for two Treasuries received today, also Church Times and Punch and Challenge. Please keep one of Heffy's puppies for me this time. There's a shell to open the evening performance, but not near here. What a rotten letter! But I've rather written myself out.

Much love,

Philip

To the left: Hephzibah ('my delight is in her') or 'Heffy', the first of a long succession of distinguished pets kept by Tubby. In April 1918 she gave birth to 'Kemmel', named after the village that fell to the Germans in the same month. *To the right:* Bango, a friend's dog.

295   There was a relative lull between the first and second phases of the Battle of Amiens, i.e. between 11 and 21 August. The Allied counter-offensive triggered the eventual German collapse.

*   *   *

22 August 1918 – Begin History of T.H.[296]

(P.B. Clayton, diary)

*   *   *

Monday, 2 September 1918

My dearest Mater,
You will have seen that the Boche has thoughtfully retired in this area, so that T.H. may be a winter resort once again. Laus Deo! But I don't, in point of fact, yet know which place to move to. If he's going a long way back, Little T.H. will be more important than the Mother House. So we'll wait and see. Anyhow it's good to think that the recapture of the Hill cost nothing, whereas it might have been terrifically costly. But I think the Boche is shamming a bit dead just at present – he can't be quite as sick as he seems.

When I got back from my long round yesterday, very cheerful and childish as I always am on Sunday night, sustained by the record of a hard day's work and the prospect of an omelette for supper, the sky was glowing over Bailleul way like it used to looking towards Southampton, only more so. I drank my tea to Stuart's very good health and proceeded bedward with Pearson's magazine and listened to the (not very) distant random gun that the foe was sullenly firing.

I'm trying to write a Treasury article on T.H. and will send it to you in advance, please.
Much love to all,
Your son,
Philip

*   *   *

6 September 1918

Dearest Mater,
I can't tolerate an envelope going enclosing a Purificator for washing and no note with it; so I'm sending this along, though I ought to be hard at work on Sunday sermons, etc. I have no particular news; all goes well at the war and I went up to have a look at it early this morning. The atmosphere of desolation and the autumn mist made this very eerie, but very safe. The old places up beyond are badly knocked about, even worse than they were, but that's not surprising. I distributed Woodbines to all and sundry and fixed up various arrangements with my kite balloonatics, who gave me lunch, for services next Tuesday (I can't get them on a Sunday) and then returned with Pettifer and two Americans on a convenient Signals lorry. The area somewhere (?) is quite a back area again now and too suburban for my liking. However, it can't be helped and is a very minor tribulation.

Old friends still drop in, e.g. Colonel Farmer (one of the founders of the Cavendish Club[297]) a man I'm all out for of the best Cavan type and Thom M.C. & 2 bars. The latter is an amazing

---

296 This resulted in Tubby's *Tales of Talbot House*, first published on 15 September 1919.
297 A London based Club (founded 1911) that was made up of ex-public school boys who were engaged in social-services work.

Irishman, an Anglo Catholic Chaplain, who simply doesn't know what fear is. E.g. during the Retreat, he stood on a railway embankment between his men and the Boche and dared the Boche to come on. Farmer told me this.

I enclose a delightful screed from Mrs Talbot which I haven't yet answered. You will get in due course via Base Censor part at least of my article on T.H. which I want Cecil to get typed and report to me for correction. I contemplate it going (if not too long) into the Christmas Treasury.

Now I must get on with it.

Much love to you, dearest Mater,

Philip B.

*   *   *

10 September 1918

Dearest Mater,

These counterfoils from Army books will serve to show that stationery is also an economy known to me! I'm so sorry I didn't write yesterday as usual. But I only reached home in the pouring rain, groping my way across the mud with Hugh's invaluable torch at 11.30 p.m., and left this morning at 7.45 a.m. So letter writing went by the board. I so often give you accounts of Sunday that Monday will make a change.

Yesterday morning I went across to interview a delightful Division, on the subject of reopening T.H. in their area, failing the old place. But when I left there, I went on to lunch with Major – who told me that the old place may very likely open soon, which altered my outlook. Thence I went down to my "office", spent a busy half-hour on my invaluable telephone, and had a variety of excellent folk in to tea. I had to break away from them at 5.30 and scrounge a lift back. A General's car passed, but the dear old man mistook my intention to cadging a lift for a salute and passed by. As I was getting late, I suborned a despatch rider to overshoot his mark a little and deliver a message to the waiting R.A.F., a long 2 miles away, to hang on till I came. Shortly after, an ambulance gave me the lift I wanted, and I arrived punctually to find the D.R. delivering the message faithfully to the wrong lorry! I then collected the Concert Party – 6 in all – and we started off. We went up to one of my balloon sections, now a long way forward, and found the balloon about to ascend on an emergency matter. The Observer was going up alone, so I offered to accompany him; but just then, the neighbouring balloon began to descend, announcing no view, so this was washed out; and the concert began to an audience of R.A.F. and some jolly infantry. Having made an inaugural speech, I was taken off to dinner in the mess – these Belgian farmhouses are all alike, admirably adapted for habitation in a war area; the Officers live in what is left of the farm, the men in the adjoining buildings, and the barn makes an excellent theatre and billet combined, as the White Company[298] knew. After dinner, we adjourned across the morass that always disfigures the courtyard of these farms, to the concert, which was going strong. At the conclusion, the infantry trooped off to their camp to bed, and concert party got rid of some of their grease paints, and had supper in N.C.O.'s mess, a bakehouse of peace time.

---

298 A reference to "The White Company" Bible class – named after Arthur Conan Doyle's novel – of Portsea parish where Tubby was a curate. It lost many of its most prominent members during the war.

A large audience of soldiers and a number of children watch 'The Balmorals', the 51st Division Entertainment Party. (IWM)

Finally at 10.30 p.m. we made off in a big lorry along a road which a few weeks ago was shelly in the extreme, and returned in the driving rain to our rendezvous. So to bed, the lorry drivers being fortified for their return journey with two of Jack's invaluable cigars.

This morning the General gave me breakfast in bed at 7.15 a.m. – I often have breakfast in bed, and I hope you do too! – and we boarded a cable lorry at 8 a.m. making in the same direction. I had happy services with both Kite Balloon Coys.; and then a long drive towards the old place. Leaving the lorry, I boarded a rail-car full of my dear Construction Coy. men, which took me more or less in the right direction, after which we walked a mile and found some old friends who gave us dinner and gramophone. Then back past the old place, and tea and supper here. I was too lazy to go out again with the Concert party to-night, so Mac has gone instead. I hope shortly to be able to report our return to the old house, which awaits us, dusty but uninjured, save that some tiles are loose and the windows are napoo.[299] Also I look forward immensely to the possible visit from H.B.C.

Life is therefore much more cheery than it has been, though goodness knows I have had nothing to grouse about.

My French is still shamefully bad, though quite unblushingly fluent. If I had only taken trouble to learn it properly, I should have found it not only useful, but of real value in helping me to understand and sympathize with much of the native life round here.

Much love,
Philip

299 Gone, finished; from French *il n'y en a plus*, 'there's no more'.

* * *

Monday, 16 September 1918

Dearest Mater,
The usual fortnightly beginning to my Sunday; a lovely car at 4 p.m. on Saturday, and a ten miles drive to my Railway H.Q. where I played cricket till dinnertime, and afterwards went and chatted to the men (mostly old infantry men) who form the H.Q. Office Staff. We played Yeoman of the Guard on a groggy gramophone ... If Talbot House isn't alive again, I shall put in for the month I am entitled to after 2 years in France – it is now more than 3. ... I'm busy in the intervals, writing a brochure on the history of Talbot House, which will probably find its way eventually into the Treasury, or some such paper; and will so save me the labour of Christmas cards.
    ... I hope the Guv isn't suffering from shortage of tobacco. It's getting a real problem out here. Glad the puppies are well-behaved and possess the old chair that is the historic cradle of their race.
    We are really getting on with the war at last.
    Much love, dearest Mater,
    From Philip

* * *

18 September 1918

Dearest Mater,
Just a line to accompany some Communicants' Rolls that had better come home before they are lost. All serene here and the war going well; though I don't expect to be home – except on leave! – this winter. Leave I shall either put in for in November or in January D.V. It's not fair to take too much, with men still intolerably overdue. I have two without leave for 16 months and 1 for 15! But I think I've got their leave through now at last.
    We hope to get back to the old house in a few weeks and are already busy cleaning, painting, etc. Meanwhile, an open-air summer has done us all good. I hope the fuel question will not be so bad for you as for town dwellers, since wood is easier to come by. If only you also had turf rights! I hope Kemmel is behaving himself, and won't have lost his childhood before I see him; or merge the rampage of youth in the sobriety of middle age! Teach him some tricks if possible, and when he is old, he will not depart from the same. He should learn to fetch what is worth fetching (bunnies apart) and to carry the paper from the lady cyclist to the play-room; to come to heel, and to steer clear of traffic and above all to be a good son to his wonderful old mother. If outside at prayer-time, he must remember that "without are dogs" and not be impatient to demand admittance. I shall expect a Headmistress' Report from Stuart on his terminal conduct and progress.
    Now I must really stop writing nonsense.
    Much love, dearest Mater,
    Philip

* * *

Sunday night – 10 p.m., 22 September 1918

Dearest Mater,

I only write to-night because otherwise nothing will get written till Wednesday. Strictly speaking, I'm ready for bed, as I started out 7 a.m. this morning and only got home to my omelette at 8.30 p.m. But roses, roses all the way; and a most delicious Sunday dinner with some delightful railway folk after service; tea in due course with Archies. But a long day none the less and even the strafe going on somewhere and the Boche overhead wouldn't keep me from slumber.

But I really must tell you about Friday last. I went down to T.H. in the morning at 11 a.m. intending to go through and up to some kite balloonatics, but they rang up to say they were shifting again, so no service possible. When in doubt, I talk to M.F.P.s and I was just exchanging a little badinage with an old friend in the square, when a lovely Sunbeam rolled up with chauffeur in front and a distinguished Naval Officer[300] behind. They were obviously in doubt, so I went across, and found that D.N.O. was returning from an inspection North to a Southern port, and was dying to see something of the front *en route*. He probably would have died outright in doing so, had it not been for this encounter; as his simple idea was to drive on till he got to the front line and then get out and forage round! He at once adopted me as cicerone and I fell at once. Modesty apart, I gave him the day of his life! I can't describe precisely where we went, but on my own area, he saw as much as was safe and a little more; picking up nosecaps, etc., like the veriest tripper. We then went South into the area of the Boche retreat (according to plan) round these parts. We picked up on the way a young balloonatic officer, who gave us lunch and

Poperinghe Police Force 1918.

300 Commander Berkeley Holme-Sumner, Divisional Naval Transport Officer, Rouen.

we then proceeded after the retreating Boche, as far as a car can go and a little further. The first place we went to was the famous hill,[301] which is indescribable; grimmer I think than what I saw of the 1917 Ridges,[302] because then all was mud and most of the slaughter had soaked in. Here Boche were lying everywhere, whole or in bits, shell holes full of them; some glorious French as well and many of those international victims, the transport mules. The tidal wave had come so suddenly and gone with such precipitancy that furniture jutted out from the ruined cottages, and tables still stood laid for meals that were never eaten. I never saw war on this wise before. Trench warfare did not leave things thus. Grim humour everywhere – German notices and British notices previous and posthumous; a rocking-horse without a head on one side of the road and a mule without a head in the opposite ditch, and so on. We climbed up on foot and looked across the valley at the Boche biting his nails; and then proceeded through the ruined villages and the great Town itself, and so home to T.H. when, the House front-door not being open – still blocked with sandbags – we climbed in through the window, and Pettifer who was down putting things straight, made us tea. Curiously enough, my last visitor before the evacuation was also in Navy Blue – dear Tom Le Mesurier. This was my first visitor in the House again, a good omen for the re-opening which will not now, I hope, be very long delayed.

Your letter to-night, so glad about the puppy. Will Kemmel do for its name? though "kennel, Kemmel!" is going to lead to complications.

Now I must to bed.

Much love,

Philip

* * *

Talbot House,
Poperinghe,
27 September 1918

Dearest Mater,

I may not be able for censorious reasons to send this letter for a day or so, though I expect to-morrow will see the beginning of the doings that unloose our lips round here.[303]

I had breakfast in bed at 7.30 a.m. to-day, and then went off to Major Reid (one of my Railway Construction Coys.) arriving at their train at 8.30 as arranged. We then got into their Ford car and went up the line to the ancient city,[304] looking in on the way at their men working fervently on the repair of the track this side. Our job was to reconnoitre the whole Broad Gauge, so as to be ready for the advance. This meant getting up somehow to the front line in such a way as to keep an eye on the railway track throughout. Leaving the car in comparative safety,

---

301 Kemmel Hill.
302 Wijtschate-Messines Ridge.
303 A reference to the battle also known as the *Advance in Flanders*. On 28 September, the Allied Flanders Army Group attacked and broke through the German Front to the north, east and south of of Ieper. Comprising Belgian, French, British and American formations under the command of King Albert I of Belgium, its initial progress was significant, Kemmel Hill and territory lost to the German advance in April earlier that year passing into Allied hands.
304 Ieper.

Charcoal preliminary sketch for oil painting *The Conquerors* (Canadian War Museum), presented to Talbot House by war artist Eric Kennington in 1931.

we walked through the old station which is desolate beyond description and torn to ribbons by shelling; we walked up the track until the presence of some very new shell-holes disturbed us. It didn't look wise to go further that way, so we nipped round and by making a long detour under cover of the town – not that that is very much cover – we arrived at the Lille Gate, heavily camouflaged, which to-night the Boche can see easily, but to-morrow, please God, no. Here the sentry told us that only two at a time might go out, so Reid and his Captain had to go (both being technical experts) and I waited a bit conversing with the sentry and then followed on my own. Though in full view of the Boche and about half a mile from the front line, I had a most peaceful walk, and by and by came up with the other two, when they had reached a less exposed spot. We followed up the track, which was in wonderful condition, all things considered, in spite of communication trenches and barricades, until at last we reached a barricade across it, which linked the front line on each side.[305] Here were eight Welshmen (at least their badges said so), and fortunately I was possessed of exactly 8 of Jack's cigars, which were the very things they needed and deserved. After a little halt, we returned again, this time venturing on following the line right down. Curiously enough, just after we had passed the much shelled spot, another shell landed there. This was the solitary shell that came near us, though a good many landed in the distance where one could see the earth fly and hear the pieces whizz. Oddest of all, there was no machine gun fire, though we must have been as visible as a man on the aerodrome would be from our roof. All of which shows that the Boche is not what he was. So back to lunch with Reid and into Talbot House in the afternoon, and a case of 500 packets of biscuits as a thankoffering to a gallant Scotch battalion moving up into the battle that begins early in the morning.

Much love,

Philip

*   *   *

305 Gordon House, situated along the former Ieper – Roeselare railway, 450 m south-west of Hellfire Corner.

Talbot House
Monday night, 30 September 1918

Dearest Mater,

Things are booming – not shells, but business – and I'm enjoying the prospect immensely. For one thing, the Boche is plainly and palpably hard hit down South, and up here we aren't so nervy as we were. I always like the emphasis on we being delivered from the fear of our enemies – and I think we are so now. Not that things are over by any means, but we have the measure of his strength and know we can stand the strain, if repeated. Rather like that moment in 'Rupert of Hentzau',[306] when Rudolph begins to bend back Rupert's hand holding the revolver!

I am now officially Garrison Chaplain of Proven and while I'm not moving my billet in there completely yet, I start an office there to-morrow and shall be there daily, travelling up and down by friendly trains with a free pass for myself and Vokins, who will be my office boy. I have a large room, a 'salon', large enough to divide into a Church and an office and tomorrow have planned a great entry, with the aid of railway folk and Archies. The Talbot House truck goes down to be partially unloaded of its previous contents – furniture, Chapel fittings, etc. 10 male housemaids remove the lumber at present occupying my room, school forms, etc. Various R.E.s hang curtains and make partitions, etc. and an Archie lorry carries the stuff to and fro from the truck. What a hectic afternoon ahead! Great fun.

How lovely Hatchett now after the rain.

Much love,

Your son, Philip

* * *

NOTICE

October 1st

Pheasant shooting begins, and Charles Letts' Diaries for 1919 are published. Hitherto the world has apparently no memorable event to which the day is sacred. Future generations will however remember it as the day on which Poperinghe reopened,[307] and Talbot House was found, like Macbeth's Scotland, standing where it stood.[308]

Since you saw it last, the mice have broken the windows, aerated the concert hall – which was always stuffy – and punctured the roof and the garden wall in several places. But good fairies have been busy since then, and the paint and whitewash are scarcely dry.

You will find some alterations, which we hope you will approve, but the Dramatis Personae remain much the same –

Chief of Staff – Eddie Evans, the Welsh Comedian.
George, the Librarian – L.-Cpl. G. Trower.

306 A sequel to Anthony Hope's celebrated novel *The Prisoner of Zenda* (1898).
307 Tubby, having received orders to "close the House at once, and to shut myself within it for ten days", had no sanction from II Corps, in whose jurisdiction the House was then situated. He was granted permission to re-open on 9 October 1918.
308 Macbeth, IV.iii.164: "Stands Scotland where it did?"

The library in the front room.

Decorative painting on the door of the front room.

The Man that knocks the hammer with the nails – A. Rose.
First Aid – C. Vokins.
The Strong Man from Ireland – P. Flynn.
The General – A. Pettifer.
Actor-Manager – C. Willmott.
and so forth.[309]

The first floor is ready for you, with a larger Library and a bigger billiard table. Old friends of the House will find the old arrangements rudely disturbed for the time being. The old Chapel is temporarily dismantled, and the temporary Chapel, always open as ever, is in the room on the ground floor behind the tubular bells. Evensong daily at 6.30 p.m.

The Library has also shifted downstairs, and is in the front room, quite cosy, though depleted of many books: this is a hint your generosity will not fail to act upon. The Chaplain is ensconced in the room opposite the staff room at the back, with a tesselated pavement, a stove with a poor digestive system, and a series of vivid mural paintings of antlered stags and swans with necks like giraffes.

On the first floor there is an excruciating piano, a bad billiard-table, an excellent bagatelle board, a complete set (up to the time of going to press) of chess-men, and the usual mouldy collection of pens, ink, and blotting pads.

The concert hall received the side blast of an obus, and is closed for a week or so. But the garden will soon make up for it all. Keep an eye on our mustard and cress. We certainly shall, if you go to look for it.

P.B.C.

*   *   *

5 October 1918

Dearest Mater,
… It's difficult to foresee what the advance will mean to T.H. Probably we shall move up before Christmas, but the old House will I hope remain in Chaplains' hands to the end, which I think is really nearer than we know. I long to see H.B.C. when he comes, probably next month I gather. Meanwhile I must not think of leave until we know better how we stand. I have been looking round the shops here to try and get a late birthday present for Stuart, but can find nothing worth having. So she must take the will for the deed. This office is really a wonderful insight into the vitality of the Church, hampered though it still is. But when we are free – !

Shop in Casselstraat, Poperinge.

309 See Appendix IX for a list of Talbot House staff.

I hope next week to write properly about T.H.'s reopening and much else. But now it is impossible, as every day brings its advance, and I don't exactly know till I get back tonight what has happened during the last three in our area.

Last Sunday (have I written since then?) I had lunch on the old railway cutting that had been in Boche hands for years, and watched the Belges attack the slope opposite.[310] I think I did write after all.

Enter now Chase, also ex-Portsea. Keymer[311] last night, and Chase today! Floreat Portsea!

Much love,

Philip

* * *

Tuesday, 8 October 1918

Dearest Mater,

The post now goes out before the post comes in, so one is always a day later with answering, even at the best! The dear old House is still shut, waiting for leave to open, which is slow to come through. But patience is a virtue, and meanwhile there is plenty to do. Magrath goes off today to his old haunts, leaving me solitary after 6 months of rough and smooth together. I expect I shall go back to the Bishop's for my month's work there shortly, leaving (I hope) Victor of Mirfield in charge here. The job before me is, as I think I told you, to get the Ordinand's question really moving at last, please God. There are now 1,435 candidates on the Roll, but we want to recruit at least 4,000. And beyond this, those now on the Roll are quite out of touch with one another and with the progress of the scheme. So that there is much to be done.[312] Ultimately, before Christmas, I hope, we are getting E.S. Woods out from Sandhurst, to whom I shall hand over, and return to T.H. rejoicing.

Of course, it's possible the war may end suddenly! But the period of demobilization will then give the chance of doing much please God, if the reaction in spirit is not too great. Four of my staff are going on leave on Thursday, so we shall be painfully shorthanded for the time being, but it's good they should get their chance, after so long – 18 months in one case! It is a most ghastly inequality.

We are in a very bad area now, comparatively, and shall feel I fear rather high and dry. I half wish the Boche wouldn't go back so far and so fast. A few shells have a wonderfully brotherly influence on a community.

The Forest must look lovely now; there is little of the autumn glory round here. I long to see Kemmel while he is yet a puppy, but I don't expect now to get home much before Christmas.

From your son

Philip

* * *

310 The Zonnebeke railway cutting from where he watched the taking of Moorslede.
311 Rev. Bernard William Keymer, R.A.F.
312 For Tubby's role in this scheme, see p. 290.

NOTICE

The dear old House is now open again, like the flowers in May. Like them, its first attempt at opening met with a cold snap, so it went to sleep again. Now the lawful time for awakening has come, and it proceeds with prudence to unfold itself. The ground floor is pretty well advanced. The first floor is partially ready. The second floor is totally bare still. The Chapel in the attic (the oldest Chapel in the B.E.F.) is practically complete again; and Services will be held on Sunday at the old times, D.V.

On the day of our opening, four of the Staff have gone on leave, long overdue.[313] So the blue blazer will be dirtier than ever during the next fortnight.

Owing to the canteen shortage, the Church Army are helping us by running a tea-room in the Nissen hut dans le jardin, but you will have to wait for your grocery queue till the C.A. canteen opens in the Square, etc. Mr Legge, a fellow-citizen of "Pompey" with myself, is the Church Army worker who is kindly taking the tea and biscuit problem off my rheumatic old shoulders,[314] so that all epicures, who do (or don't) like Serjeant-Major's tea, will find themselves up against him, while I hold the sponge and the prize money.

P.S. – The absence of a canteen will mean to the House the loss of its only certain source of income. So presents of books, etc., for the Library will not only win you a smile from George, but will provide what we can no longer afford to buy. My wrist watch was in pawn long ago; and even the House is in POP.[315]

9.10.18. P.B.C.

*   *   *

A.C.G. informed the Committee that Little Talbot House, Ypres, should retain its name, and that the Chapel would be served by various Army Chaplains, with a Church Army Chaplain resident.

(P.B. Clayton, Minutes of Talbot House Committee meeting, 11 October 1918).

*   *   *

Talbot House,
14 October 1918

Dearest Mater,

We are fully established again, and in full swing for the time. But of course we're in danger of being left high and dry. However there is also apparently quite a danger of the war finishing altogether, which will save a lot of trouble! French plus some American ambulance men are now on our visiting list, so that bar the Portuguese and Italians, we have experienced all representatives in the Old House.

---

313 Tubby's diary entry for 10 October reads: "Flynn, Ray, Moore, Evans proceeded on leave yesterday for today – 19, 18, 15, & 13 months' men – so heaven forbid that it should be again postponed."
314 Douglas Legg found his vocation in the Upper Room and placed his name on the roll kept by Tubby. He went on to be ordained in the Anglican ministry. For his account, see p. 291.
315 Play on words: in Poperinghe and in the pop shop (pawnshop).

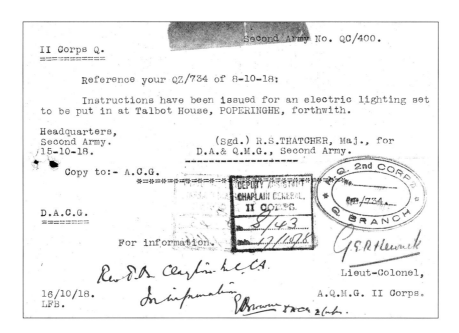

As soon as things quiet down, I shall probably go to the Bishop's for a bit. Meanwhile I'm desperately shorthanded, with half of my staff on leave, and the House full to overflowing. The Chapel is more beautiful than ever, and it is good to be here. A lovely day to-day for the boys, and I hope they have taken full advantage of it. The French are perfectly charming, and I am so glad to have them. As soon as I can, I'll go and look for George Robbins' grave – Olivia has written to me – but I doubt anything being traceable.[316] The country is altogether unrecognizable, even since last year. The shell holes overlap for miles on end. …

Much love,
Philip

*   *   *

Talbot House
17 October 1918

Dearest Mater,
A quiet day, so far as the House is concerned. I'm not sorry as I've a bit of a cold, and am able to slack and write letters. The streets are full of overwrought civilians, thousands of whom have been redeemed out of Egypt, after a week which none of them will ever forget. The Boche is going back far and fast, and we hear that the Navy have found Ostend empty. This means Toc H in Brussels, I expect, before long! Meanwhile one simply sits tight, as there's nothing to be done until one gets orders etc. The Boche is evidently retreating fairly cheaply for him, and still

316 See footnote 78. George is Olivia's brother.

more cheaply for us. So that it postpones the decision again, perhaps, if his Army don't crumple up under the strain….

Your son,
Philip

* * *

19 October 1918 – 115 refugees to breakfast. It's a long day that has no ending.

(P.B. Clayton, diary)

* * *

NOTICE
"To move, or not to move, that is the question"
Owing to the inconsiderate retirement of our old neighbours, the Boche, Toc H is in a pretty fix. If we move – e.g. to Courtrai, we may be high and dry by the time we have reached it with all our lorry-loads of belongings. Also, if the period of demobilization is really at hand, this may be an important salvage centre. And once we vacate the House, we shall never get it again.

Briefly, therefore, T.H. will remain here for the present.

For if the Boche goes to Brussels, we shan't cut any ice in Courtrai.

Or if the Boche goes to Blazes, we shall be wanted here.

Q.E.D.[317]

But we expect you to get down here somehow, and see us sometimes. You really must try.

October 20th 1918, P.B.C.

* * *

Friday, 25 October 1918

My dear old Guv,
Very many thanks for your sweet letter.

Yes, the House is desperately safe now, & I don't like it being in a backwater. But it can afford to rest on its laurels awhile; & by Christmas we shall know whether to move forwards or not. I expect to go to the Bishop on about Nov. 10, so hope H.B.C. will be able to come this way ere then. Has the pipe-lighter reached you safely, & has the mater got a cheque from me? The post is slow slow at present, & I haven't heard. I have another pipe lighter up my sleeve, if needed. I wish I had taken the opportunity & bought them all off the poilu[318] – they were amazingly cheap, & are rather good souvenirs.

Lt. Roberts, the Corps Amusement Officer, who was at Exeter with me, is a great ally, is living with me here at present; with his troupe shewing in the town. There's still a good deal to be done one way & another, & in the interim I'm really grappling with some of my many arrears of letters. Pettifer is pawing the ground for a day "with a little bit of sport" (IE shelling!) so I shall probably make a long journey on Monday & go & see if I can get as far as the war & look

---

317 *Quod erat demonstrandum* ("which had to be demonstrated"); the phrase is traditionally rendered in an abbreviated form at the close of a philosophical argument, thus signalling the completion of the proof.

318 French slang for a soldier, especially an infantryman; orig. meaning 'hairy one'.

The 'Eighty Eights' Concert Party (88th Battery, R.G.A.) in the Talbot House garden.

up some old friends alas en route, if possible, George Robbins' grave, though it must almost inevitably have disappeared completely.

Much love, dear old Dad

Your son,

Philip

Talk of coincidences! I met a Cpl. with a Hants badge in the House last night. I said "I'll bet you're not a real Hampshire man!" He said, "Yes I am, I come from a little place called Boldre!"[319] His name is Butt: such a nice chap.

* * *

Talbot House
27 October 1918

Dearest Mater,

A good Sunday, though only a little work to do. T.H. full to-night after a very quiet week. Men came from afar, but will mostly be across the mud by Sunday next, after which we shall be high and dry indeed. I spent a long day yesterday, crossing the wilderness, and searching on the way for George's grave and two others. But I failed to find any of them. I have written

319 Six miles from the village where Tubby lived, i.e. East Boldre.

details to Olivia, and will have another try this week, if possible. M. Coevoet-Camerlynck, the owner, wants to come back into the House on November 15th. If so, I think T.H. will have to be suspended for a month, until we know where we are a bit: while I go to D.C.G.'s. The Army will decide what is to happen, and at all events we shall hand the House back in splendid condition, if we do so.

I'll send my Philip Gibbs despatch on the impressions of the old battlefield later on. Meanwhile this must suffice as bed calls. ...

Much love,
Philip

*   *   *

Searching for George's Grave
On the Saturday, All Souls' Day, I set out on a grim and rather curious task. I borrowed, as my helpers, some good friends from P. Special Company, together with Lieut. Roberts. We went to Ypres, now finally deserted; passed through the Square, no longer hurriedly, emerged by the Lille Gate, no longer crouching. Our object was to find, if it were possible, the grave of my first cousin, Captain George Upton-Robins of the Duke of Wellington's, who had been killed in April [sic] 1915. All that we had to guide us was the fragment of a map drawn on an envelope by a brother officer at the time, who had himself been killed a little later on. The feature noted was a sniper's tree; a tree which no doubt in that early period still held aloft in its ill-omened branches the body of a man. Needless to say, the tree had disappeared. We knew the grave lay somewhere between Gordon House, which had been our front line a few weeks previously, and the railway embankment, honey-combed with dugouts and pitted with the shells which searched for them. Working our way in a wide fan formation, and carrying tools in case we had to dig, we spent the short and shivering afternoon attempting to recover the position. Just before dark, incredible

good fortune came to our aid. There, in between the shell holes linked and re-linked like a long chain of lakes, one of the searchers came upon a splintered wooden cross plainly belonging to the early period. The horizontal batten which should bear the name itself was nowhere to be found, until one member of our party discovered that the upright was composed not of one beam but two, thrust in together. Withdrawing one from the retentive soil, we found that this itself was the old cross-piece and that the pencilled writing could be read. The name upon it was my cousin's name. No one who knew the ground as it then was can fail to understand the sheer amazement with which this strange coincidence was greeted; for the ground had been most bitterly contested, and had been German soil on two occasions. Graves had been wrecked, burials disinterred, reburied and then disinterred again. The obscene malevolence of shelling had repeated these appalling resurrections under conditions which cannot be described: yet in the very heart of this

George Upton-Robins.

Shelter, watercolour by Eric Kennington.

affliction the upright of the cross stood sentinel. Experienced minds may question whether the cross had not been moved, and afterwards found lying anywhere and re-erected, by a reverent instinct, where it was found and not upon the spot. Actually, as I heard some two years later from those who cleared the ground and transferred the bodies found into their present peaceful resting place, the body of my cousin was identified.

(P.B. Clayton, diary)

R.I.P.

George Upton-Robins
Captain, 3rd Bn. East Yorkshire Regiment
attd. 2nd Bn. Duke of Wellington's (West Riding Regiment)
5 May 1915 – Age 36 – Railway Dugouts Burial Ground, Transport Farm (Zillebeke) Annexe
Mem. A.1

*   *   *

7 November 1918 – Armistice in the air, & push as alternative.

(P.B. Clayton, diary)

*   *   *

From Lt. Roberts to Tubby:
11.11.18

Dear Father Clayton,
We have cleared off rather suddenly to Courtrai, where I hope to see you in the near future. The addresses are all entered. I have left some odd letters in the letter pad, not knowing if you want them kept or not.

Will you please let me have my mess bill for these three weeks? Please do this. I owe you a great deal and shall not be satisfied until it is paid.

There are many other debts I can never repay. It is impossible to tell you adequately what a happy privilege it has been to live with you and to see your magnificent and blest work. God bless and keep you forever,

Ever yours very sincerely,
Lt. Roberts
O.C. Corps. Concert Party

*   *   *

Talbot House,
Poperinghe
13 November 1918

My dear old Guv,
I told the mater I would try and write you the account of my last week-end of war, so here goes. Earlier in last week Colonel Lomas, the head of the Railway Construction in this area, had come in on his way through to ask me to go across into Macedonia (i.e. the other side of old No Man's Land) and give them some more Sunday services. (In point of fact, he wants me to go and live with them, but this would mean the end of T.H.)

So on Saturday afternoon I sallied forth on my 30 miles journey, intending to catch the French return leave train passing through. But as it happened, I was picked up by a lorry running to Wipers, and no sooner did it drop me there, than a French flying tender offered me a lift all the rest of the way. They were carrying some stores, and also a goat, a grandmother, her daughter, and two babies. So I climbed in with these, and was nearly suffocated. Charitably, we will put it down to the goat; though I have my doubts. However, I fraternized with the five words of Flemish I know (one word ahead) fed them (except the goat) with some scraps of chocolate, let out four anchors at the stern (i.e. clung on as tight as possible, for the road is still terrible) and wished for Roulers. Every time one goes across the devastated area, it is more impressive, though already the shell-holes are clothed with green, and the industrious Flemish folk are dwelling in pill-boxes, and have even brought some cows with them. A company of Chinks[320] hold Zonnebeke, and enjoy rushing about in sham affrays, with Boche helmets and rifles. But the peace of God

---

320 Pejorative slang for Chinese, the above reference relating to members of the Chinese Labour Corps. From April 1917 onwards the British Army employed, amongst other foreign workers, Chinese labourers on a three-year contract. Their number on the Western Front would eventually rise to some 95,000. Primarily used for construction and demolition work, road and railway building, trains and

swallows them all up. On each side there is a crescendo of desolation. Trees first scarred, then blasted, then stumps, then non-existent. Houses first roofless, then barely recognizable, then pieces of walls with dugouts against or under them, then brickheaps; then vanished utterly. If you dug you might find bricks, even floors and cellars; but it is wiser not to. For the rest, wire all rusted and tangled, rotting sandbags, broken wheels, piles of unused shells, boxes of ammunition, timber for the roads, duckboard tracks, grotesque direction posts in two tongues, dead mules flung into inadequate shell holes go on in one huge nightmare across the rise and fall of the ground. Here and there rough crosses still stand, but most in the vortex have been blotted out.

The clearance of this ground is already proceeding in various ways, but it will be years before it resembles anything normal. If allowed to right itself, it would become in time a type of moorland like the open Forest. But the pillboxes and the tanks will always stay, unless blown up, which would be sacrilege. The tanks – there must be quite a hundred altogether – are the most eerie things of all; riddled with explosives, they yet retain not only their outline with its peculiar menace, but the exact position in which they met their death. They seem like monsters of the iron age, frozen in the act of springing. A child could read in their shattered contour what each one purposed, and how each failed. You can almost see their brown driving bands wrenching in vain to lift free of the fatal pool, or their noses peering desperately over the insuperable bank. However, I mustn't loiter in no man's land any longer.

Behold us then emerging in looking-glass land, even the goat slightly impressed, the fields grow recognizable, the houses uninhabitable, and the road merely vile. This ground was rushed in the advance, so it has suffered only slightly by comparison, and the graves are scattered and isolated. The great defence line here still stands – it was never held, or it could have been held for ever; but cannon fodder was too strictly rationed by then.

We turn into the broad highway from Menin to Roulers (how jolly it is to be able to mention names at last!) and are stopped for the civilian's passes by a garrison guard boy I know well. During this stoppage, I climb out and perch myself on the step in front – rather this than more goat. After 3 or 4 kilos along here, I reach my nearest point and drop off, complete with thermos flask, biscuits, etc. (food is scarce up there), and my Church essentials including Uncle Ernest's Communion set. I walk to the train which is Construction H.Q., and have a riotous late tea in the old Boche van which is their mess, and hear all the news. They are all in their element, heaps of real big engineering at last, miles of destroyed track, broken bridges, etc. and *carte blanche* to get it done quickly. Shop, as they talk of it, is full of fascination. Five out of the seven officers are keen communicants, as I know of old; but to-morrow it can't be. Late evening service after the day's work is the most that may be this Sunday. All the Companies are racing against time too with their particular parts of the line. So I decide to join one of the reconnaissance parties on the morrow, and am accepted. Then more talk after dinner and a spare bed in the medical hut.

Breakfast at 7.30 and start in box car at 8, with survey party on the southern line. Renaix is one objective, but fighting is still going on, and yesterday the Boche still held the Scheldt, where he had another unassailable position, with a broad stream in front, and a hill[321] 5 times Kemmel for observation. Now, who knows? He is said to be in full retreat. The infantry have crossed and found no trace of him. As we approach the Scheldt, signs of desperate fighting and whirlwind shelling are painfully

ship stevedores, they helped clearing battlefields and constructing cemeteries from the Armistice to early 1920.

321 Kluisberg (Mont de l'Enclus).

recent. Our village is almost Wiperesque; and Avelgem lying on the side of the stream is as though a tornado has struck it. Here we can go no further by road, for the bridges are down. Here also our survey begins. Leaving the wreckage of the station, we pick our way along the line which is on a steep embankment. This has been mined and blown already every 100 feet or so, and there may be more still beneath. Only too obviously, the infantry came this way yesterday. Suddenly the line stops in nothingness. Bridge No. 1 has gone, but 100 yards up stream there is a gang plank bridge resting on the invaluable petrol tin floats. By this we cross and find ourselves in the Boche front line, still warm with him as it were. We are now really on a kind of island, for the river proper is beyond. Again we splash our way – for he has partially flooded the ground – to the railway embankment, and come along (more craters) to the great gulf where the big girders lie banking up the driftwood against them. Clearly there is no alternative, but I like it not. So I go first, taking my time, sliding down one broken girder on to a floating timber baulk – then along this to a friendly packing case, and then the girder again. Thanks to my playmate at Bruges,[322] I'm not such a fool at this as I might be. Only the officer comes after me. The rest stay to take measurements. We go on together, the two of us.

It looks as if something else would soon happen inside the buttress on the further bank. Anyhow there's a chamber there in the side of it, with some sticks of chocolate stuff that we leave severely alone. Up yonder is a sugar-beet factory, with half the machinery looted, and the rest looking highly suspicious – no thank you. We leave it and get back on the track. I wander on ahead, and find some Belgians wringing their hands at the door of a cottage beside the line. The Boche have taken everything, and smashed the rest; there was much rifle fire here yesterday, and their garden is full of hand grenades. Will Monsieur move them? I select a Mills bomb, which looks homely, and rid them of that at least. How it got there I don't know. The rest is Boche stuff with wooden handles, and I suggest the digging of a large "trou" in the field, which they approve. I give them 2d. of bicuits and pass on, as the O.C. has overtaken me. So along for half a mile – no signs of anyone, Boche or British; except for one plane, equally lost apparently, overhead. Every level crossing has been blown up with buried Minenwerfers, and at one a big pile of them remains apparently unused. But we don't investigate. Now comes a boy of 12 or so, back from Mass: very excited at our advent, he walks down the line with us, and tells us more than we can understand in queer French. Yesterday the Boche went along here for the last time. Their windows are broken by an explosion on the railway, but the mine nearest their home burnt and did not explode; but their cowhouse is blown down. The school has holidays this week, and he will rebuild it with his father. The Boche took their money and gave them notes in exchange.

At the remains of the next station we sit down and picnic. It is a heavenly day. Resuming our march, we come to a railwayman's cottage. Outside are two small girls. I offer them chocolate, but they run indoors shyly. I pursue them. The door is opened by their father, who welcomes me in with rejoicing. Their mother is making a savoury dish of horsemeat from a horse killed near-by. It is the first meat meal, they assure me, they have had for two years! I leave them to their Sunday dinner. We don't get to our objective – there is not time, so we turn off two miles on and come back by road. It is longer, but it's worth it: for now we meet our own folk in all their glory. Infantry pouring through, with their bands playing them along. Not a gorgeous military spec- tacle, for they are all tired. But all along the road the villages are out to welcome and to wonder. The bands play everything and anything to keep them going. The men, weary though they are,

322 See footnote 276.

put their thumbs in their packstraps, and step out well. Those that have no bands, whistle or sing snatches. They do not look proud, but infinitely patient, and kindly, and domestic, and withal there's a little twinkle in their eyes. I see some old friends among them, but they are mostly the younger brothers. Most of my generation lie quietly asleep with the tanks keeping guard over their slumbers. Plainly I must keep Monday's doings to another session.

Much love,
Philip

*   *   *

Tuesday, 19 November 1918

Dearest Mater,
I have now, thanks to Neville, a chance of moving T.H. to Courtrai and getting to work almost at once. So I shan't, as I was planning, come on leave this week. Whether I come before Christmas depends on how the new job opens up. M. Coevoet the owner will be back to-morrow, I expect, and I shall be glad to leave the House free for him. We had our final Thanksgiving Services on Sunday.

…

Much love,
Philip

*   *   *

19 November 1918 – Last service in this Chapel. Oldest shrine in BEF. Crowd in my memory. Emmaus Inn.

(P.B. Clayton, diary)

The Upper Room, pen drawing by Cyril Worsley, 1917.

Epilogue

With the Armistice, Talbot House should have lost all relevance and purpose. Its disbandment became a matter of weeks only. However, Tubby was convinced that it had a mission and that its spirit of comradeship and service could be perpetuated in the post-war world. The soldiers had departed, but Toc H's impact remained in their hearts. Laying the foundations for a better world had to be communicated to the next generation.

At Christmastide, Tubby posted a special holiday greeting card to some 2,000 men whose names were on the Communicants' roll. It foreshadowed the publication of *Tales of Talbot House* and the establishment of a new Toc H in London. Before the close of the year, Tubby took a lorry-load of 'relics', including the furniture of the Upper Room, to the Ordination Test School at Le Touquet, where he was assigned to work as a tutor. And on 6 February 1919, he lunched with Neville in Poperinge for the last time, afterwards calling on Maurice Coevoet in the old house, which was his home once more. After paying the outstanding rent and damages, he wrote: "So the end, like all else, is only a new beginning". But that, indeed, is another story...

Tubby bids farewell to the Coevoet family, February 1919.

ANYTHING may be written on this side, the other, by the law of Ancient Lights, is the private playground of the long-suffering A.P.S.

I vote the forthcoming booklet on Talbot House a $\begin{Bmatrix} \text{sound} \\ \text{rotten} \end{Bmatrix}$ scheme

I will $\begin{Bmatrix} \text{pay} \\ \text{borrow} \\ \text{scrounge} \end{Bmatrix}$ 2/6 to $\begin{Bmatrix} \text{get} \\ \text{get rid of} \end{Bmatrix}$ it.

$\begin{Bmatrix} \text{By all means} \\ \text{On no account} \end{Bmatrix}$ T.H. should be set up in Town.

I won't $\begin{Bmatrix} \text{stir a finger} \\ \text{leave a stone unturned} \end{Bmatrix}$ to help.

You've got my RANK $\begin{Bmatrix} \text{exactly right.} \\ \text{unutterably wrong.} \end{Bmatrix}$

I am now a $\begin{Bmatrix} \text{Lance Corporal} \\ \text{Field Marshal} \end{Bmatrix}$ and hope to be discharged soon.

This address will find me $\begin{Bmatrix} \text{till} \\ \text{after} \end{Bmatrix}$ the $\begin{Bmatrix} \text{cows} \\ \text{boys} \end{Bmatrix}$ come home.

Road————————————

Town————— —————

County————— —— Sig.———————

Yours $\begin{Bmatrix} \text{ever} \\ \text{never} \end{Bmatrix}$

Tubby's 'whizz-bang', a parody of the Army Field Postcard.

Part 2

A Home from Home

NOTICE
Unwelcome Visitors

Welcome yourself to T.H. We don't put 'salve' mats on the doorstep, but have a Salvage Dump[1] next door to make up for it. But we want you to feel it's true of your arrival just the same. For you are surely not one of those who

1. Imagines the House has an off-licence for magazines, stationery, etc., e.g., I put a current number of Nash's magazine in a cover, heavily stamped, on the first floor last week. In twenty-four hours the cover was empty. This is how misanthropes are made.
2. Imagines we have the Y.M.C.A. or some unlimited funds at our back. At present we are trying hard (like my Sam Browne does) to make two ends meet. Three noble Divisions (55, 39, 38) help us from their funds. But otherwise, we are in a bad way. My tie-pin was in pawn long ago: and even the House is in Pop. Writing materials for use in the House cost some £6 a month, so that he who departs with his pockets full of envelopes is guilty of what Mr Punch calls "Teuton conduck."[2]
3. Woe worth the imbecile who begins three letters one after another on three sheets of paper, with a fourth to try nibs and fancy spelling on; and, with one large boot on a fifth sheet, and the other on a pad of blotting-paper, splashes ink about like a cuttle-fish (is it?), and draws a picture (libellous, we hope) of "my darling Aggie" on a sixth sheet, and then remembers that he really came in to play billiards!

A good Talbothousian will take his share in the diverse activities of the House; and whatever talents he has will be willingly used in the common interests. Singers will sing (so will the Chaplain, with the best intentions, poor fellow), reciters wil raise their arms and lower their

---

1   Lat. *salve* means welcome. With "salvage dump", Tubby was referring to the ruins of the house next door.
2   *Mr Punch* is one of the main characters in the *Punch and Judy show*, a traditional, popular puppet show in which Mr Punch fights humorously with his wife Judy. *Conduck*: Cockney pronunciaton of *conduct*. *Teuton*: German.

TALBOT HOUSE, POPERINGHE.

EVERYMAN'S   CLUB.

35, Rue de l'Hôpital
(FOUNDED BY 6th DIVISION IN 1915).

CHURCH SERVICES

(IN THE CHAPEL on 3rd Floor).

DAILY :

Holy Communion	-	7.30 a.m.
Short Evensong	-	6.15 p.m.

SUNDAY :

Holy Communion	-	6.30 a.m.
,, ,,	-	7.30 a.m.
Morning Prayer	-	10.45 a.m.
Choral Eucharist	-	11.30 a.m.
Prayer Meeting	-	5.15 p.m.
Evensong	-	6.0 p.m.
Litany and Address	-	6.45 p.m.
Holy Communion	-	7.15 p.m.

THE CHAPEL IS ALWAYS OPEN FOR PRAYER AND QUIET.

SOCIAL SIDE

(Open 10.30 a.m. to 8 p.m.).

Ground Floor :
  DRY CANTEEN, MUSIC ROOM, Etc.

First Floor :
  WRITING ROOM, GAMES ROOM,   -   -
  LIBRARY (containing nearly 2,000 Vols.),
  CHAPLAIN'S ROOM, BALCONY   -   -
  LOUNGE.   -   -   -   -   -   -

Second Floor :
  BILLIARD ROOM (2 TABLES)   :   -
  WRITING ROOM, READING AND   -   -
  CLASS ROOM   -   -   -   -   -

The TEA HALL (in the Garden):
  EDUCATIONAL CLASSES OF A VARIED
  CHARACTER. WHIST DRIVES, SING-
  SONGS, CINEMA, LECTURES (with or
  without Lantern), Etc.   -   -   -   -

G. B. BOWES, Major
(Chairman of Committee)

TALBOT HOUSE was opened on December 15th, 1915, to provide a Parish Church and Institute for Troops in the Town. The Chapel was first made by "The Queen's" Westminster Rifles. The hangings came from the Bishop's Chapel at Southwark. The 14th M.M.G. presented the stained-glass windows, and various other gifts came from the Guards, etc., besides many personal memorials.

Field Survey Co., R.E. 9852—250—14-11-17.

P. B. CLAYTON, Chaplain.

voices, conjurers will borrow (and return) coins of realm (if any), chess-players will try to convert draughtsmen to a nobler calling, letter-writers will drown their spelling in a common ink-pot, readers will deal gently with the printed page, all bets (none are allowed) will go to the Harmonium Fund, Sidesmen will sidle, and Churchwardens will churchward (and no one will come back a week later to pick up their gas helmets),[3] everyone will drop in on the poor old Chaplain, especially at tea-time, and all (except conscientious objectors) will climb up to the Chapel for family Evensong at 6.15 p.m.

The House aims at reminding you a little tiny bit of "your ain folk." Hence pictures, flowers, and freedom. Help to strengthen the illusion of being of a Club-able spirit.

This is not a G.R.O., but just a G.R.O.use by the Chaplain.

*   *   *

From the middle of the 18th century till 1911, the house was lived in by the Lebbe family, hop merchants by trade and tradition in Poperinge. The glass panel of the door separating the front from the back hall bears the engraved initials 'LV'. The 'L' stands for Lebbe. The 'V' is uncertain. The wives of three generations of the Lebbe family had a surname beginning with 'V': Van Isacker, Vantours and Vuylsteke.

Come along in and have a look round.

Don't dally with the doormat; it is accustomed to neglect.

Here is the entrance hall. On the left hand its walls are covered with maps, not of the war, but of Blighty. See how the London we love, without knowing it, is worn away by the faithful fingers of your fellow-citizens. Here is another, of Canada this time, and another of Australia, with a knot of students in slouch hats. Here, beyond, is a Madonna, painted on latrine canvas by a gunner artist. Beyond, a rendezvous board, where you put your envelope which serves as a visiting-card, and hope some other hero from Prangley-on-the-Marsh will find it there and make an assignation accordingly. On the right there is a notice-board, which is different in its outlook on life to the one outside your orderly-room. Beyond, a staircase, and beyond that a gorgeous, framed artist's proof of Wyllie's "Salient".[4] Looking straight through the hall you catch a glimpse of a well-kept garden, where men bask, as in St. James's Park, and a snug concert hall in a hop-store lies out beyond. But the hall has other doors. Here is a shop, which has a "merry Christmas" atmosphere all the year round, and a music-room beyond it, with an irresistible old piano, not likely to be come by honestly!

Now upstairs! Quite homey this! Carpets, flowers, and pictures – not patriotic prints, either. Lord! what a library! These people, obviously, think we've got minds worth feeding, as well

3   Rev. R.J. Goodwin, the chaplain in charge of Little Talbot House, had forgotten his gas helmet following a visit to Talbot House.
4   1915 watercolour 'Air combat over Ypres Salient' by William Lionel Wyllie (1851-1931).

as bodies and souls. Four thousand books, and most of them presented by old Talbotousians. Who were they? Look at the photographs round the walls. Writing-rooms, games-rooms, and, upstairs again, billiards! English billiards, too – not that foreign cannon-ball game. Who expected to find English tables so near the line as this? Over there lie two lecture-rooms, with a large class on housing reform and a smaller one on French – one taken by an R.E. captain, the other by an intelligence sergeant.

Excelsior![5] once again! A companion-ladder this time, leading to a loft. Not likely to be furnished? Isn't it, though? Here's a chapel, full not only of exquisite simple majesty, but of an atmosphere like nothing else we have ever experienced in France.

(P.B. Clayton, Tales of Talbot House)

I REALM OF THE BODY

The ground floor of Talbot House ministered simply to a man's first needs. The garden brought him rest; the canteen, tea; the piano and hall just introduced him to the fellowship.

(P.B. Clayton)

*   *   *

'Tommy in Wonderland'

Through an elaborate, iron-grilled doorway I could hear the sound of laughter and music, and pushing through the door I found myself at once in a different World. It was amazing, I felt like Alice when she stepped through the looking-glass. There were soldiers all around me, of course, and Army slang in the air, but, in stepping across that threshold, I seemed to have left behind me all the depression and weariness of the street. There were walls with paper on them – clean paper, too! – carpeted stairs, pictures on the walls and vases with flowers in them.

(N.N., 58th Division, September 1917)

5   Latin for "higher".

Detail from the iron-grilled door.

1 From the Notice Board

The discipline of the House was not enforced by Army orders, but by light-hearted little notions, that arrested the reader's attention and won his willingness on the right side.

(P.B. Clayton)

> **IF YOU ARE IN THE HABIT OF SPITTING ON THE CARPET AT HOME**
>
> **PLEASE SPIT HERE**

1.1 Matters Domestic

NOTICE
How Not to Win the War
Scene 1: Half-way down the garden. Two chairs and garden table; with tin board and draughtsmen thereon; also a rubbish-box in foreground.

Enter two gunners with two mugs of tea and a paper bag of fruit. One gunner upsets draughtsmen on to the grass, and deposits mug on table. The other amends this procedure by seating himself on the ground, turning the half-full rubbish box upside down, and placing his mug thereon.

Finally, enter Padre: *tableau vivant.*

Scene 2: The first floor writing-room. Both windows tightly closed. Various literary gentlemen busily engaged in calligraphy.

Enter two R.A.M.C. representatives, afraid of too generous a supply of fresh air on the balcony. Each carries three magazines, and two books from the library. These they deposit among the inkpots, pens, and blotting-paper, and proceed to absorb in a slow but expansive manner.

Enter more persons desiring to write letters. *(Curtain.)*

*   *   *

NOTICE
My Cold
No one else seems anxious to issue a bulletin about my cold, so I do it myself, unasked. There are three kinds of cold known to medical science: viz.

A cold.
A bad cold.
A Clayton Cold.

It is the last that I have.
Temperature (or is it pulse?) '101' fuse.
Articulation: foggy.
Laundry bill: 50 % increase.

At present, I am engaged with my 15th specific cold-cure: a series of large globules, coated in sham sugar, to be taken one every fifteen minutes till health or death supervenes. Another certain remedy recommended is: 1 pt. of hot salt water taken hourly. But I prefer even a cold.

P.B.C.

* * *

NOTICE
Exchange and Mart
A handsome, kindly, and middle-aged individual, who prefers to remain anonymous, finds that his neck is growing thicker during long years of warfare, with the result that seventeen-inch shirts and seventeen and a half collars produce a perpetual strangulation. If this should catch the eye of any gentleman upon whose neck the yoke of the Army life is producing the contrary effect, an exchange of wardrobe would be to the welfare of both. Address, P.B., C.F., The Office, T.H.

* * *

NOTICE
RATS!
On the literary principle by which Mrs Beeton[6] is said to begin her chapter on the cooking of apples with a brief reference to the Fall of Man, this notice should open with some reference to the anti-episcopal tendencies displayed by rats in the lamentable food-hoarding case of the late Bishop Hatto.[7]

But our need is too urgent for literary allusions.

What the House has to face is a plague of rats, all of them heavy or welter-weight, against Don Whiskerandos, our cat, who is featherweight only, so can't be expected to make good.

---

6   Isabella Mary Beeton (1836-1865), universally known as Mrs Beeton was the English author of *Mrs Beeton's Book of Household Management*, one of the first popular household cookery books in English.
7   From the old folk tale "The Mouse Tower" that relates the story of Hatto II, the Archbishop of Mainz, a cruel potentate who during a famine imprisoned and burned alive a large number of hungry peasants. Legend has it that he was instantly besieged by an army of mice who, crawling up to the top floor of a tower, devoured him alive.

Wanted therefore; *the loan of a good ratting terrier, ferrets,* or other rat-strafing rodent. A rat seen last night measured about four feet from stem to stern.

* * *

NOTICE
How the Wheels Go Round
By "I" o "U" Corps.
For the next few days, the total staff of the House is five, including Jimmy, the presiding magician of the maconachie. A reasonable complement for the House, hall, and garden is eleven, including the canteen. So, if the antimacassars aren't watered, or the asphidistras dusted, or the pot-pourri jars distributed for a few days, don't think "there's something rotten in the state of Denmark".[8]

* * *

NOTICE
STOP PRESS
A tidy draft of reinforcements in woollies – i.e., socks, etc. – has reached T.H. from the ever-generous Mrs Fry of Bristol. Applications for the same should be made to the Chaplain. All queues prohibited by Sir A. Yapp.[9] Allotment, one sock per battalion.

January 14, 1918.

* * *

NOTICE
A year and more ago a gunner Officer, of an eminently mathematical family, ran a series of competitions for Talbotousians versed in such strange studies. Now his brother, himself a high Wrangler,[10] has volunteered to restart these competitions, & to act as judge & critic.

A prize will be awarded for the best solution ie showing working etc. Each problem will be a separate competition. A new problem will be set each fortnight.

No. I.
In how many ways is it possible to give change in England for £ 1.

Answers, in envelopes marked "Problem I" should be addressed to "Lieut. W.R. Angler RGA", & left in the office.

Ap. 4th P.B.C.

---

8   A reference to Shakespeare's *Hamlet* (Act I, Scene 4) where Marcellus, having just seen the ghost of Hamlet's father, says "Something is rotten in the state of Denmark".
9   Sir Arthur Yapp, a YMCA pioneer, had been called upon by the Prime Minister, Lloyd George, to assist with the running of the government's Food Economy Campaign.
10   A mathematics scholar at Cambridge University.

*   *   *

NOTICE
S.O.S.
Please can you help directly or indirectly concerning any of the following?

1.   Put me in touch with Donald Cox, unit unknown, of 58th Division, the author of a delightful poem on Talbot House in the Divisional Magazine.[11]
2.   Discover local artists in neighbouring units prepared to play various parts in our production shortly of Sheridan's Critics.[12]
3.   Someone who can make a tidy job of some simple engraving on silver in the Chapel.
4.   An organist for Sunday Services.
5.   An expert typist close at hand, who would help me in spare time. Sergt. McInnes, the oldest British inhabitant of Poperinghe, left during December, leaving me the village veteranship. But no one to replace him in his voluntary Secretaryship has yet appeared on the horizon.

                                                                1/9/18 P.B.C.

*   *   *

NOTICE

Don't leave cycles outside, they will be scrounged by passersby.
Don't leave cycles in the hall, they will be borrowed by the chaplain.
You *may* leave cycles in the garden where it is hoped they will be safe.[13]

*   *   *

1.2 Anecdotage

NOTICE
How to find your bearings on a dark night without a compass
This is an old scout's tip.
Take a watch, not your own, tie a string on to it, swing it round your head three times, and then let go, saying to the owner: "That's gone west".
     The points of the compass being thus established, you proceed rapidly in the safest direction.

                                                                       P.B.C.

*   *   *

11   For the poems by Donald Cox, see p. 337.
12   See Part 1, note 230.
13   Town Major's diary states on 13 September 1916: "Many bicycles are being stolen: about 3 a day being reported to this office. Ordered police to leave bicycles about and watch them." And the Register of the A.P.M. mentions: "Bicycle with accessories stolen from Talbot House at 4.30 p.m., 19 Dec. 1917. Owned by Rev. H.C. Cox, C.F."

NOTICE
Scene: *The Wipers' Road: any time after dark.*
Enter Wayfarers (1st) and (2nd).
1st W.: "Bill, 'ere's a riddle for you. What is a lorry?"
2nd W.: "Give it up."
1st W.: "A lorry's a thing what goes the other way."

The Pess-Optimist.
Wot a life! No rest, no beer, no nothing. It's only us keeping so cheerful as pulls us through.

*   *   *

NOTICE
National Symptoms on Sick Parade
1.   The Irishman:
       "Och, docther dear, I'm kilt intoirely."
2.   The Scotcman:
       "Ah'm no varra weel the s'mornin'."
3.   The Englishman:
       "I don't know what can be wrong with me. I can't eat."

P.B.C.

*   *   *

NOTICE

In honour of the return of Paddy (Pte. Flynn) from leave to his post on the staff of the House, the following chestnut is issued to all concerned:

Scene: *Irish parade-ground.*
Drill Sergeant   "Now then, Rafferty, get those big feet of yours in line, can't you!"
Pte. Rafferty   "Arrah! Sergeant, they're no my feet at all, at all. They're Pte. Murphy's in the back row."

P.B.C.

*   *   *

NOTICE
How to Check Bad Language
This is a splendid story, really requiring a Scotch accent.

Once upon a time, Doctor Geikie, of Edinburgh, was crossing the Atlantic on the same ship as a loud-voiced, foul-mouthed American. One rough day, when everyone was confined to the smoking room, the American told a series of filthy stories, and then turned insolently to the old Doctor and said: "I just reckon you haven't added much to our fun, Doctor." "A'weel," said Doctor Geikie, "I'll tell you a story the noo. Once upon a time, there was a puir wee birrd that had his nest in a tree by the roadside; and one fine day, after a horse passit by, he came to feed on the droppings. An' when he had his fu', he just skippit back to the tree and began to sing. But a boy came by wi' a wee bit gun, and shot him i' the lug as he sang." Dead silence, broken by the American. "Waal, Doctor, if that is the best you can do, I guess we don't think much of it. None of the boys see any d-d point in your tale at all." "A'weel," said Doctor Geikie, "the moral, sir, is surely plain enough to you. If you're full of dirt, dinna brag about it."

A.C. per P.B.C.

2. Friendship's Corner

NOTICE
This Space is Reserved for Friendship

This Board is intended for the use of men who wish to get into touch with friends, who may possibly see a message left for them. Please use cards provided or put communications in an envelope before placing in the rack.

P.B. Clayton.

FRIENDSHIP'S CORNER : A SURVIVING LIST

ROYAL ARTILLERY.
Gunner S.MORRISON. 'D' Howitzer Battery. 2.1a Brigade.R.F.A.
B.E.F. would like to hear from Private G.MORRISON.

Bomdr J.ELLIS. 1158 R.G.A. 204 Siege Battery. B.E.F.

Sgt S.LONGMAN. 120 (S) Bty. R.G.A. would like to hear from,
or meet,his brother Fred. 90 Heavys.

Gunner H.BUCKWORTH. No.362.610. 350 Siege Battery. R.G.A.

Gunner J.CLARKE. No. 61365. 123 Siege Battery. R.B.A. B.E.F.

Can No. 312508 Driver James PIKE. R.G.A. meet his brother,
No 38699 Private F.PIKE. 22nd Cheshire Regiment.

Gunner A.J.EDWARDS. late 28th Siege Battery. R.G.A. Attached
29th Light Railway Operating Coy. R.E. would like
to meet old pals.

No. 137460 Bdr W.R.EVANS. 279 Siege Battery. R.G.A. B.E.F.

CVERBURY. R.F.A. (Covent Gardens) 1st Section. 48th D.A.C.
would like to meet Bob HAYNES.

Gunner A.W.GASSER. R.G.A. 129 Siege Battery. B.E.F.

Gunner J.C.MEE. No. 74636 R.G.A. would like to meet his
cousin on the guards C.G.

Corporal ROWSON. No. 19767. "D" Battery. 155th Bde R.F.A.

Bdr F.R.HAYWARD. No. 74632. R.G.A. would like to meet his
brother George.

F.GIBSON. R.F.A. Headquarters. would like to meet his
brother Sergeant D.GIBSON. A & S.H. at WINNEPEG CAMP.

Gunner R.COX. No. 147582. 118th Siege Battery. R.G.A.

Gunner T.C.ALDERSEY. 279 Siege Battery. R.G.A. would like
to meet :-
Rfl'mn W.E.LEACH. (4548) 6th King's Liverpool Rgt.
Pte Wm. GREGORY. 18th Service Liverpool Rgt.

Bdr A.W. HARRIS. No. 126621. 54th AAA Section. "F" Battery.
(Sidmouth . Devon.) would like to meet any Devonian.

Gunner Geo. GILCHRINT. No. 347441 118 Siege Battery. R.G.A.
"D" Sub-section. B.E.F.

Gunner J.LAW. No. 84160. 278 Siege Battery. R.G.A.would like
to trace Ernest or Herbert his brothers.

Bdr R.YEOMAN. D/150 Howitzer Battery. R.F.A. would like to
meet any old friends.

Bdr G.S.CHILVERS. 228 Siege Battery. R.G.A. would like to
hear, or meet, any of the old 2/1 E.A.ESSEX men.

Bdr G.E.MORRIS. R.F.A. 70th Battery. would like to hear
from any friend .

Fathers and sons here met, brothers and neighbours. Could this wall speak, it would be eloquent.

*   *   *

And they met…

One day Talbot House received a stray lance-corporal, discovered scanning most excitedly the Rendez-vous lists in the hall opposite the kitchen door. These lists were a device wherby men could acquaint their friends in other units with their prospective presence, and thus hope to achieve a meeting. Lance-Corporal Quin found to his tense amazement that his own brother had been in the House the previous day. He had not known till now. They had not met since 1914. Could he now be found and summoned? I took fire at this, and went to the Town Major. There I learnt that the brother's battalion had just moved to Abeele, on their way south. I took a Signal form and (with an element of connivance) drafted a most official wire to the Adjutant of the brother's battalion, demanding that Pte. Quin should be sent back immediately to the Town Major's Office. No reason was vouchsafed. I wonder what the Adjutant conjectured. But, sure enough, it worked; and the two brothers met in Talbot House that very afternoon. It was well they did, for one was killed soon afterwards. This was the sole occasion when I deliberately deceived the British Army, making no bones about it.[14]

(P.B. Clayton)

Pte. Ralph Morris, 763 Area Employment Coy. (left) and Gnr. Cyril Mumford, 25 Siege Battery, R.G.A. Picture taken near Talbot House, December 1917.

3. 'Wander into the Canteen…'

Here you will find a tea-room to your liking, together with a piano repaired, the keys of which are almost automatic to the old tunes. These were not, as the sentimentalist stationed at home believed, the songs of the Retreat, like *Tipperary*; still less were they the songs which make for war. Jests took their place; and *Major–General Worthington*, the number favoured in the Guards Division, competed with the sentimental ballads which went on rhyming "Roaming" with "Gloaming." Then there were other veins of melody brought to the house from Yorkshire and Tyneside, like *Ilkla Moor* and *Blaydon Races*.

The airless room, hard by the canteen, was never wholly certain of its functions. One month it was the shop,[15] and then the card-room, and finally a narrow shrine for billiards; where cues for the small table had a way of pushing their butt ends through open doors into the crowded traffic – never mind!

(P.B. Clayton)

14   For another example of Tubby's 'deceptions' or 'conspiracies', see p. 330.
15   See Appendix X for a survey of all products.

*   *   *

Just as you came in the door, on the right hand side, was a table with two buckets, one full of tea, one full of cocoa, and a set of mugs.

(N.N.)[16]

*   *   *

Julian and I had our meal with Clayton and three private soldiers – the first time I had ever sat down to eat out here in uniform with soldiers.

  (Capt. Burgon Bickersteth, Royal Dragoon Guards, August 1917)[17]

*   *   *

16 Unknown veteran to Albert Hill, Talbot House warden (interview 23 June 1995).
17 Bickersteth, J., *The Bickersteth Diaries 1914-1918* (Barnsley: Pen & Sword, 1995), p.207.

NOTICE
NO SWARING ALOUD HEAR

*   *   *

From Donald and Herbert with Love
In the autumn of 1917, in prospect of the Third Battle of Ypres, my division, the 18th, was to be found in the neighbourhood of the notorious Salient. One day I noticed a horse-drawn limber which bore the logo of my brother's division, the 14th. He was a driver in the Field Artillery, and his horselines would be the place to find him. By devious means I discovered the lines and made my way to see him. Having met, we made arrangements, when duty allowed, to meet on a certain date in Poperinge, where I had heard one could have a cup of tea, as, both being total abstainers, an estaminet was out of the question. So, in the dark of night we made our rendez-vous, met with joy and enjoyed our cuppa, in what could be no other than Talbot House.

We were so interested in each other (only two years divided us) and our news that I have no memory of anything else, save that I said to him that, being met, we should send something home to Mother. "Have you got any money?" I asked. "No," was the reply, haven't you?" We found we were both in the same position, but between us we found three francs, which was just enough for a silk postcard to send home to the best of mothers, with our love.

(Pte. Donald Hodge, 7th Queen's Own Royal West Kent Regiment)

Donald Hodge.

Herbert Hodge.

4. 'Come into the garden and forget about the war'

In April 1916 I spent two happy days at Talbot House, and in that Garden, where all was Peace in the midst of war.

(Sgt. Jacob Bennett, 2nd Bn Scots Guards)

Talbot House from the garden, 24 April 1916. On the foreground, three Welsh Guards; Pte. Pettifer sitting against the wall of the bath-house. The hole in the back of the house caused by a German 5.9 inch shell has been boarded up.

* * *

I was sad and lonely as I re-entered "Everyman's Club." During the preceding three weeks I had lived in a land of mud and death. Many of my best friends had passed over, others I had seen mangled, wounded and in agony. The noise of the bombardment still dinned in my ears and I could not rid myself of the sights and smells of battle.

I passed through the house, into the garden, and sat down awhile to rest. From a neighbouring house the voices of women, busy in the ordinary duties of the day could be heard. The grass was almost unbelievably green. The leaves had scarcely begun to fall, the branches moved gently in a passing wind and a bird was singing in the tree-top…

(N.N., 58th Division, September 1917)

* * *

Memories of the Garden
I can recall innumerable scenes in the old hallowed garden of Talbot House. Not that the garden was a solemn place; it was indeed most cheerful. When a man meets an unexpected friend, the English instinct is for perambulation. The Englishman obeys an inner law whereby he talks most easily when pacing to and fro. The garden, therefore, narrow in its shape, and tortuous in its pathways was day by day throughout three springs and summers, used as an ambulatory annexed to this great temple of true friendship.

A man would blunder rather suspiciously into the entrance hall of the Old House, wonder why he had come, drift from the notice board to put a finger on the map of "Blighty" or of Canada. As he was doing this, out of the little cluster waiting their turn behind him someone would say "Hello," and they had met.

Then for the open door into the garden, every small path of which would be explored, retraced, explored again, by two men talking hard. "What was the news from home? How was young Jim? How was the old girl getting on without him? Did he remember Bill? Why, poor old Bill, he finished up at Wipers." And what of Ted, their mutual enemy, who had shown such ingenuity in proving himself indispensable at home! And then to deeper things, not often spoken. Then back to a joke, and then some tea, and then a game of draughts, a letter home signed by them both, and then perhaps into the Upper Room when the bell went for evensong.

At other times the garden was too crowded for any quiet walking, and men were like lizards everywhere, basking and half-asleep; or else, in 1917 especially, a regimental band controlled the grass plot, and no one nearer than the kitchen garden could hear their own minds working. But the great scene of all was the only sermon ever preached in the garden. The preacher was Cosmo Gordon Lang, the then Archbishop of York, and the date must have been late in July, 1917. The Archbishop had come up that morning from general headquarters; and to welcome him, and hear his message, the garden was more crowded than it had ever been in all its history.

There was no room for any sitting-down, except that the whole high wall was lined with seated figures of successful climbers. The grass, the paths, even the borders too, were thronged with troops. The archbishop took his stand upon the little platform at the summit of the steps to the old concert hall, and gave out as his text the greatest words of Maundy Thursday night: "Father, the hour is come; glorify Thy Son, that Thy Son also may glorify Thee."

A Corps band in the garden, 1917. Many regiments, including
the British West Indies, are represented – one by its mascot goat.

He said that he had seen that very morning the plans for the
forthcoming battle, whereby, as all men knew, the breaking of
the Salient at last was to be the supreme objective. He did not
flinch from saying that the cost of this huge enterprise must
necessarily be paid by many to whom his words were addressed,
in life and limb and suffering. Let this then be their one great
prayer: "Father, the hour is come; glorify Thy sons, that Thy
sons may also glorify Thee." None of the few who have survived
since that sad summer day are likely to forget the deep solemnity which fell upon us all. It was not that the announcement
told us anything we did not already know; yet here was fatal
truth imparted with authority. And when the archbishop's hand
was lifted for the final benediction, we knew that we had in
immediate prospect losses we scarce dared to dwell on.

The Hour indeed was come. The sons were glorified. They
died all through the months that were called summer, as much
by drowning in the mud as by enemy action.

This is indeed the Garden of the Resurrection.

(P.B. Clayton)

*   *   *

Cosmo Gordon Lang,
Archbishop of York.

'Funk-hole'

The garden was, so to speak, the largest 'room' in Talbot House. And it had other uses than a pleasure park. Under the patch of lawn nearest to the house there exists a solidly-built and roomy cellar. It was approached through a hole in the garden wall. This was an admirable 'funk-hole' when shelling or bombing began. Women and children, more than soldiers, were its natural guests then, and though its protection against a direct hit would have been very little, it did at least create an illusion of safety.

(Barclay Baron, YMCA Headquarters, Poperinghe)

5. The Concert Hall

With the coming of the spring, 1917, the 8th Corps built us a concert-hall, ingeniously contrived out of an adjoining hop-store.[18]

(P.B. Clayton)

* * *

A doorway was knocked through the end wall of the neighbour's premises into a long workshop, which became the 'concert hall'. The opening was more than a man's height from the ground and a wooden staircase was built up to it. The grass round its foot was trampled away by the heavy boots of nightly audiences. Perhaps some will hear those great nights of song and laughter echoing in the garden still.

(Barclay Baron, YMCA Headquarters, Poperinghe)

18   The attic chapel proving too small, the hopstore was utilized as a church hall, especially during 1917.

5.1 Music and Drama

I can still see the room, its beams and cosiness, the varie-
gated soldiery, with "Tubby" radiating benevolence around.

(Owen Dowding)

*   *   *

Talbot House. Crowded. Played piccolo solo with a lot for
me in it with oboe.

(Bandsman Erskine Williams, 11th Divisional Band, 12
September 1917)

*   *   *

Still, there's Toc H to go to!
To-morrow I sing for the Padre at Toc H. 'Would I mind
singing *Nazareth*, please?' So it shall be that, and Theresa
del Riego's *Noel*. What is it to be versatile. The juvenile lead
of *Winter Nights*, and *I miss you so, Honey* fame becomes the
serious tenor. War does queer things!

Bandsman Erskine Williams.

  … The concert at Talbot House was remarkably good. One turn was by a man who had
been a professional conjuror in civilian life. He caught the men's hats as they threw them at
him, made them disappear in a trice and then reappear out of his back; an awfully clever trick.
An R.A.M.C. private with a well-trained voice recited in a nice sort of talking-way – not a bit
ranting or melodramatic. He made our hairs stand on end, and then lumps come to our throats.
I got on all right. But I prefer *Winter Nights* and *Florrie was a Flapper*. Let me make the men
laugh; that's what I want to do. Laughter; always laughter.

  After the concert all sorts of people came and begged me to sing for them. Some had heard
me at the cinema; others at Toc H. I haven't the vaguest idea how it is to be done, but I've promised to sing for the lot.

  And a couple of miles away men are being killed as I write this. It is so insensate. Why should
I be 'carrying on' like this and the other chaps going west? What is the meaning? Who, or what,
decides, and why?

  I don't want a cushy job like this. I'm ashamed of it. Still, if I can only manage to make the
men laugh a bit with my songs, help the Padre by singing serious ones, tie a bit of string round
some mysterious part of that brute of a harmonium whilst Fatty gives anguished directions[19] –
well perhaps it'll count as excuse. A pawn in the game hasn't much importance, anyway. War!
Will people ever realize what it means if one lets oneself think?

  Still, there's Toc H to go to!

(2nd Lt. G. Ll.-W., aka Corps Cyclist Wallah, late December 1916)

*   *   *

---

19 'Fatty' was a corps signals officer, based at La Lovie Château, who on several occasions popped into
    Talbot House to get the harmonium in order. See p. 64.

'Old Plum'

Lord Plumer visited the Concert Hall occasionally. On one such unexpected visit, a regimental humorist had the ordeal of singing *Major-General Worthington* – a favourite number with the Guards Division – with the Army Commander in the front row. The unfortunate comedian had espoused a breast of ribbons, a red face, and a monocle. But the original was imperturbably appreciative of the parody, which cannot have escaped him. Such was his charity.

(P.B. Clayton)

*   *   *

Those Were the Days!

The small number of children who had not been evacu-ated to France or Switzerland were also invited to some of the Concert Parties. Among these were Jeanne Battheu and her sisters. Their father was a photographer, who also worked for the Intelligence Service. His shop was only a few houses away from Talbot House and he got to know Tubby well. Here is Jeanne's account.

The Padre gave us a great welcome. We had to get up the stairs and through a hole in the wall we entered the barn. It smelled like hops, and the walls were nicely decorated with English flags and regimental flags. We always sat on the first row, on benches. The concerts were ever so beautiful. Once the men were dressed up, they descended on the stage. One guy was naked to the belly button. And you know what? He put his finger in his belly button and pushed until it reached his spine! And our eyes went wide open! We had never seen anything like that, a belly button… and of a man! That sticks in the memory! We were only kids, you know. And they did all kinds of other tricks to make us laugh, tricks with their hands and with playing cards. We laughed our socks off! And there were variety shows with music. Wonderful, magical they were. There was always a pianist and we learned the songs. I still know them by heart. I have got a nice picture of a concert party, taken by my dad, and another one of Arthur Burgess, a handsome boy of 17. He always played the female roles here. They called him 'Titch'. He often came to our home

Lord Plumer, 1918.

L/Cpl. Arthur Burgess, 1/21 Bn London Regt., aka 'Titch'. Picture taken by Camille Battheu.

and got a good meal. And he loved my mother. "Mammy," he called her. He was just like a brother to me. We often played together. I never saw him again after the war. And his superior was Lt. Merrifield. He was a great artist and played the violin. After the war, my sister saw his name on a poster in London. Merrifield performed in a big theatre there. Those were the days! Those were the days!

*   *   *

This picture of 'The Duds', the Concert Party of the 19th King's Liverpool Regiment, like many pictures of artists who performed at Talbot House, was taken by Camille Battheu, Jeanne's father. Soldiers would send these home as postcards. Camille kept this print as a souvenir. Nine members of the group signed on the back.

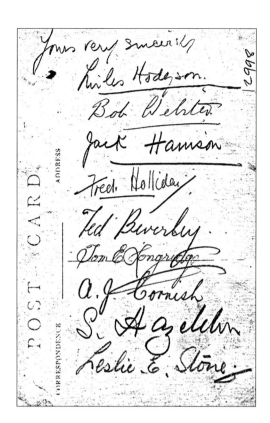

R.I.P.
Alfred J. Cornish
Corporal, 19th Bn The King's (Liverpool Regiment)
28 March 1918 – Age 29 – Pozières Memorial, Panel 21 to 23

Leslie E. Stone
Private, 19th Bn The King's (Liverpool Regiment)
6 May 1918 – Age 25 – La Clytte Military Cemetery, V.B.1

R. Webster
Corporal, 19th Bn The King's (Liverpool Regiment)
22 March 1918 – Age 26 – Savy British Cemetery, I.G.12

*   *   *

A Late Concert

Talbot House has shut for the night, the last straggler has been ejected, the last penny has been taken at the canteen for a hurried cup of tea, but as yet no move has been made to turn out the lights on the ground floor. Visitors are expected. By special permission two Companies of Infantry billeted near by are coming in for a late concert. In the hop-loft across the garden the Sunday furnishings have been carefully stored away and the stage has been set with old sheets of canvas to form wings and back cloth. The tramp of marching men is heard and the stirring marching song *O Rogerum* reverberates through silent Pop; our guests have arrived. Crowding in with cheery *badinage* to all and sundry they file through the House and take their seats in the hop-loft as keenly interested as if they were in the pit of their own local theatre at home. The concert begins, but not before a dark and secret conference between Tubby and the musical director has taken place to decide how some half a dozen scratch turns collected in the course of the day by the former are to be sandwiched into an already complete programme. Now all is arranged and Tubby steps on to the platform to open the proceedings with a cheery word to the troops. He meets with a certain amount of good-natured heckling but gives as good as he gets. To-night we are very fortunate. Some of the 55th Divisional Concert Party are with us and some of the Divisional band, not to mention two dear old souls from a labour Battalion who are going to do their best. The pianist is now heard at work playing popular songs and the full-throated response from the audience sets the keynote for the whole evening's proceedings. Who is the comedian, just taking his applause? Why, Du Calion,[20] the well-known music hall artist who does and says such clever and alarming things whilst balanced at the top of a long ladder. True, the height of the hop-loft forbids the use of this ladder, but what of that? – the troops don't expect to find a music hall artist of his eminence playing for their pleasure in a spot like this. A quartet of brass instruments has just played some popular opera airs, which please all mightily; an aged Permanent Base man (who earns his living in peace time making and selling woollen flowers at fairs and on race-courses) has obliged with *She's the pride of Liscarrell, is Sweet*

---

20   Du Calion took part in the 1919 Royal Variety Performance held at the London Coliseum in the presence of King George V and Queen Mary. The orchestra was conducted by Sir Edward Elgar.

Extract from Canteen Stock Book, February 1918.

Katie O'Farrell and has made the whole room sing the chorus with him in true sentimental fashion; a tenor and an elocutionist have charmed us; whilst last but not least Tubby has sung *The Midshipmite* and has had everybody singing a beat behind him in the lugubrious lines which refer to the 'Lowland Sea'. The concert is over, the Commanding Officer has made a speech of thanks, the troops have given three cheers for the artists and away they march to their billets with *Rogerum* helping them along. The Staff lock up and retire to rest hoping the concert will, however slightly, have helped their comrades to face still cheerfully the horrors and rigours of the Ypres Salient.

(Rfm. Ronald Brewster, 1st Bn Queen's Westminster Rifles)

* * *

The Talbot House Dramatic Party
Early 1918 we had a dramatic party of our own,[21] which acted, with amazing éclat, "Detective Keen" and similar dramas, complete to the last revolver and the dumbest telephone. As a spring pantomime, we rose to "The Critic", in which I regret to recall that I doubled the parts of the Beefeater and Tilburina, an arrangement at which Sheridan would have shuddered.[22]

On March 19 we even gave a performance in the Y.M.C.A. just inside the Lille Gate at Ypres, being (I think) the only theatrical party that accomplished this. The New Zealanders there paid courteous attention for a while; but the noble work of the master wit might have found no purchase on their Caledonian souls,[23] had not the whispering whine of several gas-shells without caused the heroine suddenly to dart into the wings, reappearing thence with a "boxspirator"[24] at the ready. This quite broke the ice, and all went merrily henceforth.

(P.B. Clayton)

21   The moving spirit was Charles Willmott, who after the war became manager of the Empress Theatre of Varieties at Brixton, London.
22   See Tubby's letter of 19 March 1918.
23   Caledonia is the Latin name for Scotland. Many early New Zealand settlers originally hailed from Scotland.
24   The small box respirator (SBR), developed in late 1916, was the most effective gas mask issued to Allied troops during the war. Uncomfortable to wear and a severe impediment to breathing, it nevertheless protected against most forms of gas except for extremely high concentrations.

*   *   *

NOTICE

Anyone who thinks that their unit would enjoy a visit from our Concert Party, or a perfor-mance of our Pantomime or of 'Box & Cox'[25] or 'Detective Keen'should get in touch either with Q.M.S. Johnson (8th Corps Sigs.) or Serjeant Evans (Delousing Station) or Pte. Wilmot[26] or myself here in the House.

If transport can be arranged, we can gladly bring any of these shows to you, but cannot for the present use our Concert Hall here, as closely packed audiences in the town are for the time taboo.

30.03.18 P.B. Clayton

5.2 *Cinema*

We watched a new film of Charlie Chaplin's exploits, featuring his single-handed capture of the Kaiser.

(P.B. Clayton, spring 1916)

*   *   *

Cpl. Charles Gethin.

As an electrical engineering student, I was invited to install and operate cinematograph equipment at Talbot House. The low powered projectors however could not penetrate the tobacco smog created by the smoking assembly, so I installed powerful extractor fans -- capable of removing their headgear! During the cold winter months, the Tommies nicknamed this discomfort "the agony" and constantly cried out for it to be turned off. And I responded by projecting a slide on to the screen stating: "You cut out the fags and I'll cut out the agony". And it worked.

(Cpl Charles Gethin, The Cameronian Scottish Rifles, 1916-1917)

5.3 *Lectures, Debates and Discussion…*

NOTICE

Fixtures for this week

Tuesday
11.30 a.m. in the Chaplain's room.
An officers meeting to discuss a paper by Lieut. Redfern on:-
"Town Planning and Housing."

---

25   See Tubby's letter of 6 December 1915.
26   The three had been appointed to the Social Sub-Committee (see Appendix IV) a week earlier.

Wednesday
7.00. p.m. The same lecture in the Hall at a general meeting, followed by questions.

Thursday
4.30 p.m. in the Chaplain's room.
A Conference on Moral Education.
6.45 p.m. A Chess Tournament in the Hall at which the challenger will play 12 games simultaneously.[27]

Saturday
7.00 p.m. A Dramatic Performance by the Talbot House Party.

17.03.18 P.B.C.

*   *   *

The evening was spent at Talbot House debating the respective virtues of Luxury & Economy.
(L/Cpl. William Stone, R.E., 19 September 1917)

*   *   *

I have met Mr. Clayton, and had tea with him. He still has debates – on Friday the subject was "this House is convinced the war will finish this year": but I'm sorry to say that the house was not convinced at all.
(Driver Arch Thomas, R.F.A., 51st D.A.C., autumn 1917)

*   *   *

NOTICE

On Wednesday next, Jan. 30th, at 6.45 pm
a Public Debate will be held in the Hall.
The motion before the House will be
that this House is profoundly convinced that the War will be over this year. (1918)

Prime Mover: Opposer:
   Lieut. Gray.   Spr Jenkins A.R.O.D.
Seconded by   Seconded by
   A Pte. I. Dunno W.H.O.[28]   Spr Birkett, RE Sigs.
   also
      Rfm. Barrs, N.Z.R.

---

27   For anecdote related to chess tournament, see p. 268.
28   Word play: I don't know who.

It is of touching historical interest to note that, when debated in 1915, the motion was carried by about 100 to 10: the wording being "convinced".

In 1916 by 150 to 8: the wording being "decidedly convinced."

In 1917 by 200 to 15: the wording being "firmly convinced."

Which may lead the philosopher to the thought that
Resolution (not resolutions) will bring about the desired result.

Final score: 1918   48-48
Carried by casting vote of the Chairman

PBC

*   *   *

Burning questions… all of them hotly debated

More serious debates were concerned with the Economic Position of Women, whereat there was no trace of sex hostility, the Nationalisation of Railways, the Drink Problem, the Ethics of "Scrounging,"[29] Ireland,[30] Federation, etc. A debate most interesting, both in its matter and its spirit, was on the Colour Problem in the Empire, at which two British West Indian sergeants made excellent speeches in English to an audience largely composed of Aussies and Canadians. Beyond the formal debates, the House ran in 1916 and 1917 a series of lectures on Town Planning, the Housing Problem, Back to the Land, etc., when officers with professional knowledge of the questions received the keenest and closest appreciation. Such enterprises, again, have their pitfalls, and I remember my qualms at one of these meetings when a man I knew to be bitter got up in question-time. He said, however: "I like the Army even less than most of you here" (awkward pause), "but I can't go away tonight without telling the officer that it has made all the difference in my outlook from henceforth to see he is

The House staff entertain the British West Indies Regiment after a debate on 'The Colour Problem in the Empire'.

29   A word of unknown origin, commonly in use among regular divisions, for which Territorials employ "winning" or "making" as a synonym. See Tubby's letter of 1 December 1915 for the scrounging talent of Pte. Pettifer.

30   The independence of Ireland was a very contentious issue, particularly after the 1916 Easter Rising.

ready to come here at the end of his day's work and put in an hour or so helping us to understand rightly things we have so much at heart."

(P.B. Clayton, Tales of Talbot House)

*   *   *

'Grousing Circles'

The winter of 1917-18 was supremely wretched. The defeat of our summer hopes, and the full extent of our autumn losses, were common, though whispered, knowledge. Rancour and ill-feeling between officers and men first then forced themselves upon my attention; and, with a sufficient audacity, we instituted, to counteract some of these poisons, a series of informal meetings called "grousing circles", to which a nucleus of trustworthy friends brought men with grievances, while a few splendidly helpful officers dropped in to listen and occasionally to advise. These meetings were so manifestly good that, when reported to the Army Staff, they were not only sanctioned, but several local troubles were quietly adjusted. The chief causes of complaint were simple in the extreme- the admitted injustice of the distribution of leave, the inequitable distribution of the bread and biscuit ration, in which the infantry (as usual) came out the losers, the absence of restaurant accommodation for men, the grotesque inequalities of pay, and so forth.

(P.B. Clayton, Tales of Talbot House)

The Grouser "Just our rotten luck to arrive 'ere on early closing day!"

5.4 'A little Treat for the Belgian Kiddies'

Proposed by Major Bowes seconded by Sapper Laycock that two parties be given to Belgian children on 6th December and 1st January at approved cost of 250 francs. Details to be left to Social Sub-Committee.

(Committee meeting held at Talbot House 10 November 1917)

Announcement and invitation

NOTICE
A CHILDREN'S PARTY

There are in Pop. a pathetically large number of civilian youngsters, and last Christmas Talbot House gave them a great party, of which they still talk. We want to do this in style this year, and so propose having two parties, the first on St. Nicholas Day (Dec. 6th) the great children's day in Flanders, when they put carrots up the chimney for his donkey and find gifts in return; but these last three years there has been little fun for them. The second party after Christmas: if neither Peace nor an H.V. (High Velocity) has descended upon the House before that.

Meanwhile, please get busy writing home, and asking for small cheap toys, dolls and boys toys; we shall need about 500 such in all, and can easily collect them, if your ain folk lend a hand.

Parcels should be asked for from home in good time, so that they can arrive by Dec. 1st.

They should be addressed to:

The Chaplain,
Talbot House,
A.P.O. Section 4,
B.E.F.

Please let me know if you can send anything, so that I know what we can count on.

P.B.C.

* * *

NOTICE
Our Party For Belgian Children

The first party is due on Thursday next (6th), S. Nicholas Day. The children come at 1.30 and perambulators call for them at 4.30 p.m. Hundreds of delightful toys have arrived from home, thanks to the families of loyal Talbotousians. If in any case these have not been written to, please strafe me, and the letter of thanks shall go forthwith. Appended is the form of invitation.

P.B.C.

The Chairman and Committee of Talbot House, consisting of officers and men of the British garrison, desiring that their young Belgian friends according to old custom should spend the Feast of St. Nicholas happily, have the honour to invite M……………... to the Children's Party, which will be given on December 6 at 1.30 p.m. in Talbot House, 35, Rue de l'Hôpital.

The party will consist of all sorts of games, refreshments, a distribution of toys and a Cinema show. For the little ones who are not thus invited a second party will be held on January 1.

Marcel Leroy, who attended the party on St. Nicholas Day 1916.

We regret that the lack of space at our disposal does not permit us to invite the parents. Those who wish to conduct their children home after the party can come and fetch them at 4.30 p.m.

(Translated from Dutch)

Party time

On three occasions we fêted the Belgian children with incredible energy. Their great day was always December 6, the Feast of Saint Nicholas, on the eve whereof the carrot is well and truly laid at the foot of the chimney to win the favour of his donkey at the conclusion of its precipitate downward career. Our parties took a prodigious amount of organising, and for weeks beforehand both the A.M.F.O. and the post corporal had their endurance greatly strained. Our first fête nearly broke down at the outset, for on the arrival of the school I approached a dismal little boy, and asked him in French what he would like to play, to which he responded with a sad philosophy: "Belgian children have forgotten their games." Sure enough, an attempt at "hunt the slipper" was a miserable failure; but the happy inspiration of an apple, smeared with ration jam, and dependent on a string, between our pensive philosopher and a rival, both blindfold, quickly attained international celebrity. Five hundred cups of tea, after they were made, proved a novelty not so palatable; but the memory of this false step was drowned in Fry's Cocoa, brewed in supplementary buckets. After this, a Pathé film of a real Belgian pre-war fête (happily, yet honestly, come by) brought the schoolmaster to his feet with a speech more eloquent than intelligible. How is it that all our Allies are born orators, and we so slow at the uptake?

The last children's party almost ended in tragedy, for before its completion bombing began. No harm was done, and the children were imperturbable – far more so than their parents and their hosts. A rumour, however, reached Blighty, with the result that some melancholy Jaques[31] in the House of Commons starred a question as to the number of Belgian children who had been massacred at a party in Poperinghe by bombs dropped from an English aeroplane!

(P.B. Clayton, Tales of Talbot House)

*   *   *

---

31   A character in Shakespeare's *As You Like It* that always sees the worst side of things.

Among the children attending the parties were the Battheu sisters and Margareta Santy.

And at those parties they tied pieces of string to the branches of the trees with apples hanging from them. They had covered these with jam, but we didn't know. We were blind-folded. And then they set us off, and we had to bite into these apples and our faces were full of jam. And the soldiers loved it, how they laughed. We didn't feel the cold. And then they filled our arms with big chunks of cheese, bags of toffees, choco-late and toys, and all sorts of other things. We didn't know what toffees were, but we soon found out when we tasted them. We were very happy, that's for sure. The soldiers loved the children. A lot of them had children

Jeanne and Rachel Battheu. Rachel died in 1917.

of their own of course, and some spoke of their little sisters and wept. And then we had to go inside for tea, and the padre took so much joy out of it. And that took all afternoon. I attended at least two parties, the first time on St. Nicholas Day in 1916, and my two elder sisters, Simonne and Yvonne went as well. Even little Rachel was taken there once, sitting in a dog-cart. She couldn't walk anymore after our house had been hit by a bomb. It was like paradise for us children.

(Jeanne Battheu)

*   *   *

One day I was invited to a party at Talbot House. I got a doll as a present. All the children were offered cocoa and cakes. At the back of a hall we played games. One of the soldiers also played the piano. There were chairs and when he stopped playing, we had to quickly go and sit on one, but there was always one chair short. The kid who managed to sit on the last chair was the winner. Oh! how we roared with laughter![32]

(Margareta Santy)

*   *   *

Margareta Santy, wearing a dress made out of a kilt that a Scottish soldier had left behind in his billet.

32   Dumoulin, K., Vansteenkiste, S. & Verdoodt, J., *Getuigen van de Grote Oorlog*, De Klaproos, 2001, p.20.

Extract from Canteen Stock
Book, December 1917

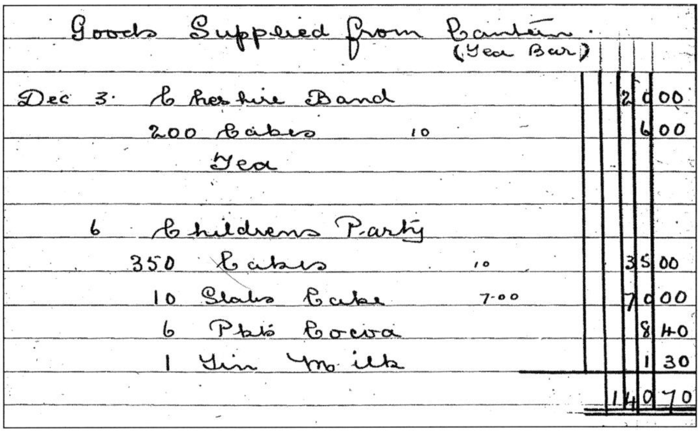

Goods Supplied from Canteen. (Sea Bar)				
Dec 3.	16 fer hire Band			2 0 00
	200 Babes	10	—	6 00
	Sea			
6	Childrens Party			
	350 Babes	10		35 00
	10 Slabs Cake	7·00		70 00
	6 Pkts Cocoa			8 40
	1 Tin Milk			1 30
				140 70

Letters of Thanks

Poperinghe, 22 January 1918

Honoured Gentlemen,
Yesterday our children had a wonderful day which they will long remember. For them it was a handing out of presents or a sort of St. Nicholas. I praise myself lucky that I can speak on behalf of all the little boys to thank the worthy benefactors for all those generous gifts. Also a word of thanks to the numerous English children who have so nobly parted with their toys to give them to their little Belgian brothers in unoccupied territory. They will always remember this generosity.

Thank you again, honourable gentlemen, and may this war soon end in a peaceful victory for our Allies.

Please accept, honourable gentlemen, the expression of my respectful and grateful feelings.

Em. De Keirsgieter,
Governor of the Municipal School

(Translated from Dutch)

*   *   *

And another...

Poperinghe, 8 February 1918

Honoured Sirs,
In the name of our 232 pupils we have the honour to thank you with all our hearts for all the toys which they have received through your generosity. With real satisfaction they remember the pleasant day they spent and the kindness of their worthy benefactors. Very willingly they pray that the good God may protect the worthy officers from all disasters and may grant them all the desires of their kind hearts.

Permit us to send you, honoured Sirs, the expression of our feelings of high esteem.

The Sisters of Boesinghe
Girls' school at "Hooge"
Poperinghe

(Translated from Dutch)

St. Nicholas Day Party, 6 December 1916. At the far right of the picture, Tubby Clayton with child on his shoulder.

5.5 *Hannah: Protégée of Talbot House*

For three years the House collected more than the yearly maintenance of an adopted child for the Waifs and Strays Society.[33] This little girl, whom none of us had ever seen, was the object of the most affectionate solicitude among small and great. The Military Police in the Prison at Ypres collected eagerly on her behalf even during the exceedingly rough period of April, 1917. Major Harry Jago, D.S.O., M.C., of 2nd Devons, asks anxiously for her in the last letter before his death.[34] One Lancashire lad, than whom no more loyal friend could be met with, told me for three Sundays in succession how his officer was giving a prize for the best-kept mules. And it was not until one night, when he came in triumph and laid the prize-money in my hand for the little girl, that I knew the secret of his ambition. Yet another, having lost his sole chance of leave, through its closing down for the fighting time ahead, paid in the hundred francs which he had saved to spend at home. If any endowment ever carried blessings with it, Hannah Mitchell was blessed indeed.

(P.B. Clayton, Tales of Talbot House)

Hannah Mitchell.

*   *   *

33   See part 1, note 84.
34   Capt. Henry Harris Jago (2nd Devonshire Regt), killed in action 24 April 1918; commemorated on the Pozières Memorial to the Missing (France), Panels 24 and 25.

Hannah Elizabeth Mitchell was born on 10 October 1914 at 163 Charles Street, Stepney, London. She was baptized on 1 November at St. Faith's Church. Her mother was Hannah Rosina Mitchell, aged 32 in 1917, living at 46 Wilson Street, Stepney. Her father, William Mitchell had died of consumption, aged 37 on 29 January 1917.

Application was made to take Hannah into care because her mother had obtained employment. This meant there would not be anyone at home to look after her. Her relatives were unable to help, having families of their own to support and in most cases, husbands serving at the front. Hannah's father had always experienced weak health. Enlisting in the King's Own Scottish Borderers, he served in the Anglo-Boer War, aged 16. Called up as a reservist in 1914, he went to France. Invalided in 1915, he returned to the front and was wounded and gassed at Ieper the following summer. Discharged as unfit for further service in October 1915, he found employment as a gardener with hopes that this would improve his fragile health, but he contracted consumption and died.

Hannah was described as being a 'particularly strong, healthy, well developed child … a very affectionate, happy, little girl.' She was accepted into the care of the Society on 22 February 1917, admitted into St. Elizabeth's Receiving Home on 7 March and boarded out on 4 April.

Talbot House offered to contribute £15 per annum towards her support.[35]

* * *

Tubby wrote to the Society on 9 April 1917:
I hereby forward a cheque for £22 for Hannah. You would greatly oblige me by letting me have a letter from you, suitable to hang on a notice board, with a few words of thanks to the men who have so willingly subscribed. I shall always be glad to hear from time to time of Hannah's welfare, and will communicate your remarks to the soldiers who take quite a personal interest in her.

* * *

On 16 April, Prebendary C. Rudolf replied as follows:
The very excellent amount of £22.12 which you and the soldiers have been good enough to raise will more than pay for the support of the above girl for one year and I should like to take this opportunity of thanking those who in any way assisted, all the more because I can quite understand that their help was given at no little self-sacrifice.

* * *

The following year, on 8 April, Tubby received another letter from Prebendary Rudolf:
Hannah Mitchell, who was supported by Talbot House, last year, is still in the care of this Society, and I must leave it to you as to whether you think the men would prefer to assist again with her support, or whether you think they would prefer to help George and Reginald Barker,

---

35   Information obtained from a letter by Ms E. Webb, Project Supervisor, The Children's Society, 11 October 1999.

to whose case you refer, and particulars of whom I enclose. For both these cases we shall need a great deal of help in these days, when the cost of living has so greatly increased.

It is exceedingly good of you to take so much interest in the Society, and I remember very well the handsome sum which you were able to send last year, as a result of your efforts. You will readily realize that the charitable public have so many claims upon them, that it is difficult for the Society to obtain fresh subscribers, and when you come to remember the greatly increased cost of keeping children under our care, I feel sure you will realize that the future is a source of much anxiety. I think you may be interested to know that the Society has now provided for more than 1800 children whose fathers have either been killed at the Front, or are now serving with His Majesty's Forces, and it will be our privilege to look after these little ones, until they are old enough to earn their own living, or until their fathers are able to claim them.

Will you please convey to the men my most grateful thanks for their generous help, which is all the more acceptable as I can fully realize that it is rendered at no small self-sacrifice.

Just at the moment, I cannot recall exactly what collecting boxes were sent to you last year, but I am sending you a few, together with some pamphlets, but if they are not what you require, please do not hesitate to let me know.

With grateful thanks to you personally.

*   *   *

Subsequently Tubby put up the following two notices:

NOTICE

Every Lent Talbot House has collected a considerable sum for the Waifs & Strays Society. Last year, we set ourselves the ambitious task of adopting a child – H. by name (aged 3) – and paying for her maintenance under the excellent care of the Society. The result was splendid. More than £20 was raised here, and another £2 in the Prison at Ypres. This Lent, the Society have asked us to undertake her maintenance for another twelve months. This will mean a big effort and widespread sympathy and self-denial; the vein of copper is more difficult to work than it was last year, and that of silver almost beyond reach. But if everyone helps who can, we shall do it. Collecting boxes will be placed in various parts of the House; and may gladly be had on application for the various messes in the neighbourhood. All Church Collections will go to the same object, until Easter. Already donations of 20 frs. (H.A.C.) and 1 fr. (Sigs.) have come in, before this notice is posted. Remember: "What I spent, I lost; what I gave, I have."

14/2/18 P.B.C.

The case paper about H. may be seen in the Chaplain's room. Her father was a Mons man, invalided out of K.O.S.B's in '16, who died of consumption.

P.B.C.

*   *   *

NOTICE

Hannah Mitchell Fund

I am getting rather windy as to the £18, which is our minimum endowment required for our Waifs and Strays Society contribution, in order that the House may not fail this year for the first time to support our adopted child. We have about £10 so far, with only another fortnight to go. Of course, there are several boxes out which will help greatly if they come back in the same plethoric condition in which they returned recently from the Wheeler-Sergeant of the Essex Battery.

But there will have to be real generosity during the next fortnight, if we are to make good.

Meanwhile, may I thank Pte. Wallace, who does not give his address, for the gift of 10 frs., which is going to the Fund. All Sunday offertories, etc., also go to it, until Easter Day.

18.3.18 P.B. Clayton, Chaplain

*   *   *

In a third notice he announced the result of the collection that had been made:

NOTICE

Hannah Mitchell is safely provided for during another year. The old House has raised in all £16 1s. 8d., to which Little Toc H is adding another £6, raised in Wipers, also during Lent. For the information of the casual visitor it must be explained that the child is the adopted daughter of Talbot House, which guarantees to pay £ 22 per annum for her maintenance to the Waifs and Strays Society.

This year, owing to local conditions of change and depletion, the task looked well-nigh beyond our reasonable hopes, but thanks to the real sacrifice of several true Talbotousians, it is faithfully accomplished. Laus Deo!

April 2, 1918 P.B. Clayton, Chaplain.

*   *   *

In 1932 Tubby sent the Waifs and Strays a notice board relic inquiring for the latest news of the girl as "her name meant much to us in the old days within the Salient". The Society found Hannah's story so interesting that they felt it was worth reproducing in their journal:

Soon after she was received by the Society she was boarded-out in a country village with a couple who had recently lost their own daughter. The friend who was instrumental in placing H- under the Society's care visited her from time to time, and one day, when H- had been in her new home for about two years, wrote as follows: --

"The foster-parents love this little girl like their own child, and she is really helping to fill the sad blank in their lives caused by the death of their only daughter just five months before this little one was sent to them. Very curiously this child is extraordinarily like their daughter, both in face and ways, and they seem quite to have put her into the vacant place in the family, and indeed I think she is a God-sent little messenger to comfort them and bring sunshine into the home again."

Church of England Incorporated Society for Providing Homes for Waifs and Strays,

otherwise known as "WAIFS & STRAYS."

Patrons   -   -   THEIR MAJESTIES THE KING AND QUEEN.

No. 7087   Patron of the "Children's Union"   -   HER MAJESTY QUEEN ALEXANDRA.

Printed at the Society's (St. Aldhelm's) Home for Boys, Frome.

EIGHTEEN POUNDS WILL SUPPORT
A CHILD FOR ONE YEAR

*Head Offices: Old Town Hall, Kennington Road,
London, S.E., 11.*   ▭ 8 APR 1918

Received *from Jacbot House, Poperinghe. B.E.F. per Rev. P.P. Clayton*

the sum of ————————— *Sixteen* *Pounds,*

Twelve *Shillings, and* *Two* *Pence being a*

Contribution *in aid of the War Emergency Fund*

towards the support of Hannah Mitchell.

£   16 : 12 : 2.   *E. de M. Rudolf*

Secretary.

Cheques and Postal Orders should be crossed "LONDON & SOUTH WESTERN BANK, LIMITED" Kennington Road Branch, and made payable to "Waifs and Strays Society."

When H- was about twelve years old she was legally adopted by these same foster-parents, and the following letter was received just over a month ago from the friend to whom we have already referred: -

"H- is now grown up, is very tall and of an affectionate nature, bright, quick, most intelligent and a great lover of all things beautiful. She is also much interested in her Church and foreign missions and belongs to an association for corresponding with children in the Colonies and has sent me wonderful letters to read from girls in New Zealand – 'pen friends,' she calls them. She is a thoroughly happy girl and very charming, and her adopted parents are as devoted as ever; they have even made arrangements for her future in the event of their death. Of course, H- has not the *slightest* idea that she is not their own child. Her confirmation two years ago was a very happy day; I went down for it and was much pleased to see her so sweetly serious, as if she quite realised what she was taking upon herself. *I always think if the Waifs and Strays Society had never given a happy home to any child but H- (instead of doing the same for thousands) they could feel that their work had not been in vain.*"

The same friend, then a nurse, was with H-'s father at the time of his death, and his last conscious words were an entreaty on behalf of his children: "Above everything, make them good, and especially the baby (H-)." The Society humbly and gratefully acknowledges that it has been privileged to do its share in carrying out the father's dying wishes.[36]

36   N.N., 'A scrap of cardboard', in *Our Waifs and Strays*, July 1932, p.121.

II REALM OF THE HEART & MIND

Notice.

EXCELSIOR!

The number of otherwise intelligent human beings who hang about the hall, reading silly notices, & catching well-deserved colds, is most distressing.

An occasional straggler drags himself up the staircase, generally in futile search for the canteen, which confronts him in the garden.

Otherwise oil - fuel upstairs waste their sweetness, & the rooms & pictures their welcome.

COME UPSTAIRS

AND

RISK MEETING THE CHAPLAIN.

As Kipling so finely says:
" What shall They Know of Talbot House
Who only the grand Floor know "

A Relic of Talbot House in 1917.   P.B.C..

*   *   *

Across the Hall came the sound of voices and a piano but I wanted to investigate the stairway – so miraculously reminding me of home.

(N.N., 58th Division, September 1917)

1 The Library

To imagine Talbot House library you must conceive of a very large cupboard, or a very small room, literally so crammed with books that the librarian himself could sometimes scarcely enter. To borrow one of these books you left your army cap in pawn, and took the volume to any part of the house or garden where you spied a comfortable chair or a corner unappropriated.[37]

(P.B. Clayton)

TALBOT HOUSE.

This is a library -

not a dormitory !

P.B.C.

* * *

An Australian private reportedly returned to his unit wearing a British field officer's cap due to two similar books being on loan at the same time!

(M. Curtis)

37   Many books were donated by individuals. Also publishers such as J.M. Dent & Sons, The Cambridge University Press, MacMillan & Co, etc. supplied "invaluable reinforcements". Other books were gifts from the YMCA, Church Army and a number of public libraries. A great many were ordered from booksellers in Oxford and Cambridge. The total number of volumes was estimated at 2,000 by the end of 1917. Some 10 percent survive to this day. Most have Talbot House stamps, labels or inscriptions. Lost books still occasionally find their way back to the library.

* * *

Box and Cox
'Monty' Morris and L. Corporal Trower were equally matched and amusingly confused, playing Box and Cox as Hon. Librarians in the smallest room on the first floor back. Indubitably thin, strikingly tall, each with a scholar's stoop – not on parade – they mingled wit and wisdom to all comers; until men asked for books which they well knew could not exist, simply to get ticked off, as they deserved. As cookhouse doors were proverbially 'lousey' with quarter-master sergeants hanging round, so was it with our Academic Entry, when Monty Morris or L/Cpl Trower was there to seize the caps from borrowers' heads. Trower went up the line, not to return; and Monty failed to sparkle the next night. Then the time came when he was sorely wounded, and lost his hearing, ere the war was won.

(P.B. Clayton)

* * *

Upstairs on the first floor I found a tiny room lined with books and even a cursory glance showed me that they were books to read – the sort of book I had been starving for for months. A while later, seated in the lounge with a book on my knee, I was suddenly aware of a friendly voice saying: "Ah – poetry, good man! – Yes, that's fine," and looking up I found myself under the twinkling glance of a rotund and smiling padre.

(N.N., 58th Division, September 1917)

* * *

Took "The Revival of Religious Life" last time I was in Talbot House. It has given me a glow to read it. Thanks.

(L/Sgt. George Stretton, letter to P.B. Clayton, 3rd June 1917)

* * *

NOTICE
We are at present, as Mrs Malaprop says, "Enamelled of the idea"[38] of having an Encyclopedia Britannica in the Library, and you will march lighter to the Rhine without it in your pocket.

(P.B. Clayton, 1916)

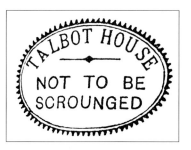

* * *

---

38   For Mrs Malaprop, see Part 1, note 62. What Mrs Malaprop (or Tubby…) meant to say was *enamoured of the idea*.

I am afraid I pinched Masefield's Everlasting Mercy from the library, but I didn't mean to. I took it out and lent it to another fellow, who lost it.

(Pte. Alfred McClelland Burrage, 1/28 London Regiment (Artists Rifles))

* * *

Books are what I want most…

Andrews, C., *The Renaissance in India. Its Missionary Aspect* – Presented to the Talbot House Library by Mrs Guy Dawkins, Teddington – 17 July 1917

Cecil, H., *Conservatism* – Presented by Capt. L. Stemp, R.F.A., VIII Div. – 23 Febr. 1918

Cohran, M., *Sevenfold Might* – Presented by Father H.C. Money – 15 Jan. 1918

Colvin, A., *The Making of Modern Egypt* – Presented by Lieut. Pigott, 4th Bn Coldstream Gds

Eck, H., *Sin* – Presented by Rev. C.B. Prior – 6th Febr. 1918

Eliot, G., *Scenes of Clerical Life* – Presented by Miss Partington, London – 1 Feb. 1918

Fox, S., *A Chain of Prayer Across the Ages* – Presented by F.H. Dunford – May 1916

Keats, J., *The Poetical Works* – Presented by L.Cpl. Chorley J.K., 58 Labour Company – 15 October 1917

Kipling, R., *The Five Nations*, vol. II – Presented by Miss Macfie, V.A.D.

Redesdale, *Lord*, *Memories* – Presented by Lord Cavan, XIV Corps, May 1916

…

R.I.P.
Guy S. Dawkins
2/Lt., 2 Scots Guards
25 September 1916 – Age 27 – La Neuville British
Cemetery (Corbie), II.F.18

2 Church Shop

NOTICE
Church Shop
Cpl. Trower, the Librarian, has also charge of the Church Shop. This was started some time ago for the use of padres. But as a large number of men wish to

Samuel Giles, R.E. Signals Section,
librarian at Talbot House.

purchase Bibles, religious books, etc., they also can gladly have the run of the shop, on application to him.

Dec. 1st, 1917 P.B. Clayton, Chaplain

3 The Canadian Lounge

Let me take you to an ingenious lounge, built outside on the lead roof by a Newfoundland draft in 1917.[39] It is the oddest makeshift, supported mainly by a telegraph pole rammed through the lead and footed very roughly on the tiled floor below. Wire, walls covered with cardboard inside and felt outside, with linen windows here and there. Here chess, draughts, Ping-Pong, and conversation flourish from 8 a.m. to 8 p.m. at least. It can hold some 70 men, inured to spatial propinquity.

(P.B. Clayton)

*　*　*

How we used to lounge in the spacious rooms packed with games of all descriptions, while outside old Jerry was trying to be funny distributing his bits of steel, and our old mansion hardly soiled.

(R. Bilton, Railway Operating Department, R.E., 6 April 1919)

*　*　*

By a Hair's Breadth

One Sunday afternoon, July '17, just before Passchendaele, the house and garden held some seven hundred. One more arrived, being a 9.2 shell which blew the house next door to smithereens. Our grand old house drooped like a tired lily, then righted itself. I scuttled from my room into the lounge, expecting to discover death and wounds in all directions. I won't pretend that there was not confusion, but here is the truth, not one of all my customers had sustained a wound that Sunday afternoon. One man reclining in an easy chair sharpening a pencil with a pocket-knife had cut his finger – that was the sole bloodshed occasioned by that nearest of all shaves.

(P.B. Clayton)

*　*　*

Veni, vidi, vici[40]

My memory goes back to one wet night, late in the Autumn of 1917, when all our 14 Chess Boards were set out in the Canadian Lounge. The semi-finalists played at 6 p.m. and at 7 p.m. the finalists were bloodily engaged, when I was summoned to the old front door by Pettifer to see an unknown gunner who was a middle-aged man, muddy and tired.

He said to me, "I hear you've got some Chessmen." And I said, "Yes, no less than fourteen boards, though all of them are in use for the time being, but if you come and wait you will get a game."

---

39   This temporary room was alternatively known as the Newfoundland Lounge.
40   Latin for "I came, I saw, I conquered" (Julius Caesar).

He paused to have a single cup of tea while I explained to him what was occurring. All neighbouring Units had sent in their Champions and fourteen final rounds were now proceeding. He said to me "Can you arrange this for me?" I should be glad to play the winners." I said, "What do you mean? It is half-past seven and the House closes at nine. Even supposing that they are all winning it would take you all night to play the lot!" Then he replied, "I don't mean that at all. I want to play the fourteen games at once."

I told the Champions, and they were amused, but once more set the boards. Then he came in, and as an unknown gunner in the Salient walked up and down the lines, played fourteen games, and within half an hour won twelve and drew with two. He then said "Goodnight." and vanished in the darkness of the Salient. I never knew his name!

(P.B. Clayton)

4 The Chaplain's Room

The Chaplain's Room was the pivot round which the kaleidoscope of the House revolved.
(Barclay Baron, YMCA Headquarters, Poperinghe)

* * *

Here conversations of a deeper kind could run their course immune from interruption.
(P.B. Clayton)

* * *

The Padre has his special sanctum at Toc H where you go to talk with him. Outside the door hangs up the sign: 'Abandon rank all ye who enter here.' One does. So you find Generals and recently-arrived privates meeting there on equal terms and discussing 'the heavens and the earth and the water under the earth.'

(2nd Lt. G. Ll.-W., Corps Cyclist, autumn 1916)

The innkeeper's first parlour was on the ground-floor, now the steward's private room. When this became the tea bar in 1916, he moved his room upstairs using the Generals bed room for his kip. . . . In 1917 this room became a little room for tea and quiet writing: while the innkeeper moved next door so as to keep an eye on the Canadian Lounge. All the team-workers helping with the house knew this room best of all, next to the Chapel: and strangers ceased their shyness, once inside.

Ask Alan Colthurst, then Staff Officer, now Padre TOC H, Leeds!

26.8.31.   T.

CHAPLAINS ROOM.

* * *

Which of us will ever forget those cheery tea parties, when, no matter how full the room, there was always space for new-comers; when we ate and talked and smoked and chaffed, for was it not written over the portal, "All rank abandon, ye who enter here"?

(Major G. Brimley Bowes, Chairman Talbot House Committee, 1917-18)

* * *

I arrived booted and spurred with red tabs on my uniform, a staff officer, and stood hesitant in the open doorway. I faced a room packed with laughing soldiers of every rank with Tubby dressed in blue blazer and shorts, who laughed loudest of all. At sight of me there was a hush, – Tubby stopped talking – with his mouth wide open – then – Good Lord. Come in Sir. I found my cap with its red band seized and then thrown unceremoniously under his bed, a place made for me beside a corporal of signallers and a chuckling voice in my ear saying "Now then sir, talk". I sat tongue tied, but was soon chatting with the corporal as if he was my best friend. Such was the magic of Tubby.

(Staff Officer Alan St. George Colthurst, 235 Brigade R.F.A., December 1916)

* * *

There was no rank at Talbot House. You never knew whether you were rubbing shoulders with a General or a 'Tommy'. There was no stickiness about it all. That was largely due to Tubby's influence over the whole thing.

(The Rev. Harold Lovell, chaplain British West Indies Regiment)

5 Writing-rooms

Here men found their hearts. Their hearts were in their homes. So here the spirit of the house provided pens, ink and paper, and strong envelopes.

(P.B. Clayton)

*   *   *

Opposite the library, across an insecure landing, was the first-floor writing-room, a pleasant place apart from its linen windows, which had long ago replaced the shattered glass. Here, round the trestle-tables, bedecked as well as they might be with a bowl or two of flowers, men sat and wrote illimitably, or stood and waited their turn. To watch the twenty lucky ones at work was a first-hand insight into the varieties of educational standards which still exist in England. Here was the accomplished penman lolling at his ease and flingering fireworks of phrases into every paragraph. Here also was the great dumb son of the soil squaring his elbows to a task more exacting and unusual than any which the war called upon him to perform. One common failing of the British race when engaged in the agonies of composition is to lean all too sternly upon the comparatively frail instrument which conveys their thoughts to paper. The result is pitiful and disastrous, and the ink flies everywhere.

(P.B. Clayton, Plain Tales from Flanders)

*   *   *

One of the writing-rooms. Through the window one can see the entrance to the Concert Hall.

NOTICE
Go easy with the stationery.

*   *   *

One of the earliest letters posted from Talbot House was by Lt. Col. Archibald Buchanan-Dunlop, C.O. 1st Bn Leicester Regt., "who had organised the carol-singing to the Boche on the first Christmas Day".[41]

---

41   P.B. Clayton, *Tales*, p. 22. The news of Buchanan-Dunlop's exploits made headlines at home, where he would become briefly famous as the 'Major Who Sang Carols Between the Trenches' *(Daily Sketch,* 5 January 1915) – a circumstance that caused some difficulty with the military authorities in the New Year. B.-D. became one of the first staunch supporters of Talbot House and wrote an account published as an appendix to *Tales*.

Talbot House
P-
17 Dec. 1915
7.30 pm

My Own Darling Wife
I'm writing to you in the reading room of the chaplains house here. I had a very busy morning indeed and then went to the final of the Regimental Football, in the rain. For half time it was an excellent game, and then our side soon away from the others. The ground was very wet and difficult. Then we went on to the Picture House, where I had obtained leave to have the "Royal Box" (the only one) so eight of us went. Had tea there, and saw the pictures right round. Then I came straight on here where I dine. When I get back to billets I hope I may find a letter from you waiting for me darling. It's rather a miserable day; very wet and gloomy, just the day for the cinema. I sent a Christmas card last night to the Colonel of the 17 Regt of French Infantry and wrote on it – "Avec les meilleurs voeux de vos frères d'armes du dix-septième Régiment d'Infanterie Britannique" – I hope it will fetch up all right. The French appreciate such things very much. Tomorrow I expect I shall

Lt.-Col. Archibald Buchanan-Dunlop.

spend with my officers visiting the trenches, a long, fatiguing and muddy day. Then on Sunday night we shall probably go in.

Ever your own devoted & adoring lover and husband.
Archibald

*   *   *

Novelists and poets like Ralph Hale Mottram, Gilbert Frankau and Alfred McClelland Burrage cherished the tranquility of the place:

I didn't return to camp but got some writing materials and polished off half a short story in Toc H. It was a great relief to me to write when it was at all possible – to sit down and lose myself in the pleasant old world I used to know and pretend to myself that there never had been a war.
(Pte. Alfred McClelland Burrage, 1/28th London Regiment (Artists Rifles))[42]

*   *   *

42 From *War is War* (London, Victor Gollancz, 1930) , p.155, a memoir of his experiences which appeared under the pseudonym "Ex-Private X".

TALBOT HOUSE.

The Wastepaper Baskets

are   purely   ornamental.

By   Order.

P.B.C.

6 The General's Bedroom

The Robin Hood Principle

Between 14 December 1915 and 7 April 1916 a small green copy-book was utilised as a Visitors' Book. It contains the signatures, primarily in pencil, of 1,083 officers going on or coming back from leave that had spent the night in Talbot House. Almost every formation/unit serving in the Salient is represented. Some 245 of the signatories died in the war.[43]

Charcoal sketch by Eric Kennington.

On the first night (December 15) I find by the visitors' book that one officer – curiously enough a namesake, viz. Lieutenant Clayton of the West Yorks – going on leave, stayed with us[44] and from then onwards the doors were open day and night. Men swarmed about the place from ten a.m. to eight p.m., and officers flowed in from seven p.m. till the leave trains came and went. From each officer we demanded five francs for board and lodging, on the Robin Hood principle of taking from the rich to give to the poor. For this sum the officers secured on arrival from the leave train at one a.m. cocoa and Oliver biscuits, or before departure at five a.m. a cold meat breakfast. The bedrooms were communal, save for the dressing-room, which we turned

---

43   The Visitors'Book can be consulted on the Talbot House website.
44   The first guest, Lt. Clayton, had breakfast on 14 December, returning from leave.

ambitiously into the "General's bedroom," on account of a bed with real sheets. For the rest, stretcher beds and blankets provided more facilities for sleep than a leave-goer required, or than a returning officer expected. Those were the days of simplicity.

(P.B. Clayton, Tales of Talbot House)

* * *

Allow me to submit to your attention the middle room with a wonky door-handle, which faces on the Rue de l'Hôpital. This room intended as a dressing-room is far the smallest. It just held one bed. The bed, however, was beyond compare; a genuine, downright, honest and upstanding affair with four legs and an iron frame, even a mattress – what could any man ask more?

We had one pair of sheets throughout the War in Talbot House. This pair belonged by right to this impressive instrument for rendering an upright human being pleasantly horizontal now and then. No one below the rank of a field officer slept in that bed. Majors competed for it, colonels cut cards, and brigadiers, recalling Philip Sidney,[45] insisted that another's need was greater. The competition lessened later on when in the month of May, 1916, an Officers' Club was opened in Guards' divisional headquarters, thanks to the energy of Neville Talbot.[46]

One final point about the general's bedroom was that the blissful winner was quite free to make up his mind whether he preferred, seeing that one sheet must be at the wash, to sleep above or below the one sheet which thus remained for him.

(P.B. Clayton)

* * *

One day in April 1916 Brigadier General Sweney arrived. While entitled to a General's bedroom, he won all hearts by his preference for a stretcher.

(P.B. Clayton, diary 1916)

* * *

45   The English poet, courtier, diplomat and soldier Sir Philip Sidney (1554-1586) was widely considered the ideal gentleman of his day. Mortally wounded during the Battle of Zutphen, he is said to have offered his cup of water to a wounded soldier stating "Here, my comrade, take this. Thy need is greater than mine."
46   For Officers' Club, see p. 71.

Major Henry Duncan Bentinck, Coldstream Guards, frequently came down to spend a night in the General's Bedroom.

(P.B. Clayton)

R.I.P.

Henry D. Bentinck
Major, 2nd Bn Coldstream Guards
2 October 1916 – Age 35 – St. Sever Cemetery
(Rouen), Officers, A.11.4

*   *   *

Major Henry Duncan Bentinck.

III REALM OF THE SOUL

Here you are on holier ground perhaps than any, even in the Salient… Perhaps 100,000 during the three years have climbed the stairs before you. Certainly some 20,000 in all have received the Sacrament. Some 800 have been confirmed; some 50 grown men were here baptized. The idlest mind would reverence the place; and you, I know, will kneel.

(P.B. Clayton, *Plain Tales from Flanders*)

Painting of the Upper Room by Kenneth Barfield, 1917, from which coloured postcards were made that were freely distributed after services. Many 'Talbotousians' treasured these as souvenirs for the rest of their lives.

1 The Chapel – "the Shrine of the whole Salient"

No sooner was the House established than it became customary for one company of the Queen's Westminsters to be billeted in rotation next door. They really adopted the House as their own. Their machine-gunners were the prime movers in the transformation of the big hop-loft into the Chapel, being quick to grasp its artistic possibilities.

In the garden shed we found a carpenter's bench, which was set aside at once as our altar for the worship of the Carpenter, and carried up to the first chapel, which was the big landing on the second floor. This was our altar always, whence tens of thousands have received the Sacrament, many taking their first Communion, and not a few their last.

Around our altar gradually gathered many memorial gifts, and many still more sacred associations. The Bishop of Winchester sent us out some splendid old hangings, dark red and dark green, which had once been in use in the private Chapel at Southwark. These were hung so as to form a baldachino, beneath which was set the carpenter's bench, raised on a rough dais. Perugino's "Crucifixion," cunningly framed by L/Cpl. Bert Stagg of the Queen's Westminsters in the broken top of a wicker table, with a lick of gold paint round the bamboo edging, formed the altar-piece. Subsequently this was replaced by a splendid Crucifix. The iron Figure itself was found in the mud of the Canal Bank, near the dead end at Ypres in 1917. It was covered with rust and mud. After a careful cleaning it was given to the 120th Railway Construction Company to be placed upon a Cross. The only difficulty was that a Sergeant in charge had scruples about the actual process of nailing, which I remember trying to allay. An exquisite silver-gilt chalice, also a memorial, with a veil of perfect Flemish lace came later. It was the work of some Belgian nuns in one of the Poperinghe convents and purchased from them by the 6th London Field Ambulance as a memorial to many of their members who communicated here. A white burse was sent out, I think, from home in 1916. The most sacred memories attach to the silver-gilt Chalice and Paten left to me by an Oxford uncle who died early in the war. I had these sent out to Poperinghe in 1916, and they were used henceforth. The Chalice bears an inscription round its base to the following effect: "He was seen of above 5,000 brethren: some are fallen asleep." The number here stated is far less than the full figure. It is probably true that some 25,000 men in all have made their Communion amid these surroundings, many of them going hence to an almost immediate death in action. The first Chalice of the House was an Army Chalice, used for the Christmas Communion of 1915, when over 500 of the London Rifle Brigade and a great number of the Queen's Westminster Rifles made their Communion in the Upper Room, led thither by their Chaplains, Crisford and Reed, two men to whom my debt is incalculable. In 1916 a fine altar-frontal of green and gold, the noble work of the Sisters of Hayward's Heath, was given to the Chapel by Lt. Stokes of the Welsh Guards in memory of the officers and men of the Guards Division. The weakness of the central space was so pronounced that we left it carpeted, but open; thus bringing the sanctuary down into the midst of the congregation, who were benched on either side. From the king-beam of the loft there hung a great gilt candelabrum, which bathed the whole Chapel in a warm glow of light, with sconces from the side walls to complete the illumination. A strip of carpet, flanked by two black candlesticks, emphasised the unity between ministrant and recipients. All through the three years gifts to the Chapel came in. A Confirmation chair was given in memory of a wonderful boy, Lance-corporal Archie Forrest, P. Special (i.e. Gas) Company, R.E., who was baptised and confirmed

Crucifix presented by the 120th Railway
Construction Company.

The silver-gilt Chalice and Paten that were in
constant use in the Chapel.

Silver wafer-box commemorating Rfm.
Newton Gammon, Q.W.R.

Oak carving of a kneeling monk, given by 18th
Siege Battery in memory of Fitter Charles Payne.

and received his Communion in the little Chapel all in six short weeks, before he and many of his comrades passed from war to peace in the terrible summer of 1917.[47] The great standard candlesticks made out of old carved bedposts were the gift of Driver Ketchem of the Canadian Royal Garrison Artillery, in memory of the Australians and Canadians who worshipped with us. A tiny Font (a replica of the old black Font at Winchester Cathedral) stands upon a further pillar of the old bedstead from which the candlesticks were constructed. This pillar was in memory of Lt. G.W. Morris, and was made under the direction of a brother officer. The Font was used for a great number of baptisms – Britons, Canadians, Australians, New Zealanders and British West Indian natives. A Cherub's head from the famous series of carvings which ran under the organ loft in Ypres Cathedral was secured by Major-General Fielding, G.O.C. of the Guards Division,[48] in the midst of the general ruin in 1916. It was given to Bishop Gwynne, who handed it on to Talbot House. The Alms Box was made for us in February 1918 by the 334 Road Construction Company R.E., whose memorial it is. Their O.C., an ever-helpful friend, died in the influenza epidemic in February 1919, immediately on his return. The motto on the box is "What I kept I lost; what I gave I gained." An oval silver wafer-box, commemorating Rifleman Newton Gammon, Q.W.R., supplied the bread of blessing for those who knelt where he had knelt before them. A beautiful old *prie-dieu* bore the names of Kenneth Mayhew (6th London) and William Wellings Locke (133 Field Ambulance). The white prayer-desk came immediately after the opening of the Chapel from the Refugees' Stall, then situated in a barn off the Rue d'Ypres in Poperinghe. It was previously the property of M. Flamand of Ypres, and was purchased from his *avocat*, who would also sell me the great oaken carving of the "Last Supper".[49] The simpler wooden prayer-desks came out from England, having been bought for us by Miss Rose Innes and Colonel Talbot, who between them sent out a great deal for the furnishing of the old House during its first year. One of them bears an especial plate in memory of Lt. Bernard Stenning of the East Surreys, who was Scout Commissioner for Surrey (and was killed after a few weeks' fighting). This desk was used by him and many hundreds of others for their Confession. Many other dedications on pictures and on candlesticks, Bible and Missal,[50] spoke of the saints that had been of Caesar's household, and lifted the hearts of those that came after out of the loneliness of their discipleship into a fellowship with many witnesses. Certain other relics there were in the Chapel that had a pathos all their own – a figure of the Virgin brought down triumphantly by a tired man from a German dug-out beyond Pilkem, early in August, 1917; an old faded blue and white linen streamer bearing the monogram "M" brought for us by the Queen's Westminsters from Ypres Cathedral in December 1915; a wooden carving of a monk, found in the ruins of Vélu on the Somme, and brought as a gift to the Chapel by Charlie Payne, a delightful gunner, who was killed before he would deposit it in the place whither he had brought it with such loving care. Even the small semicircular windows were transformed by the ingenuity of Charles Pugh and his comrades of the 14th Motor Machine Gunners into

---

47   For Archie Forrest's story, see p. 311.
48   Fielding signed the Communicants' Roll on Easter 1916.
49   For the story of the Last Supper, see p. 80.
50   The Missal, bound in dark leather with gold tooling, was presented to the Upper Room by Lt. H. Stokes (Welsh Guards) in May 1916. On 26 October 1916 Mr & Mrs Albert Sheffield posted a Bible with the inscription "Friends in West Ham pray God's Blessing on the Services in Talbot House Chapel Poperinghe."

a passable semblance of stained glass, and when the rest of the windows of the house were blown in these remained intact. Church music was an early problem of pressing urgency; and in January, 1916, Major Edmund Street of the Sherwoods, one of the most gallant Christian gentlemen a man could meet, arrived back from leave with a portable harmonium somehow blended with his kit. This groan-box, though much given to weakness at the knees, served us faithfully for six months. In Holy Week, 1916, I managed to borrow Godfrey Gardner, organist of the Royal Philharmonic Society and then lieutenant in the Suffolk Regiment, for a week's duty at Talbot House, and his skill on this tiny instrument was a miracle of adaptation. When Major Street died on the Somme his sister in Canada sent Ten Guineas to be used in what way we thought best. With the 10/- a small French picture in a faded gilt frame, called "Venez à Moi", was purchased, I think, in St. Omer in 1916 as a Memorial to one of the earliest lovers and helpers of the House.; the £10 was used for the foundation of the Service Candidates' Fund.

This inventory of Chapel ornaments is, perhaps, a tale of little worth in the judgement of one who is accustomed to the lavish elegancies of a home parish. Yet, you will bear with me, when you remember how far a little beauty went amid such surroundings as ours. To live day after day not only in danger but in squalor; to be gipsies in season and out, in a nightmare fit for Cain; to be homeless amid all that is hideous and disheartening, habituated only to a foreground of filth and to a horizon of apparently invincible menace; to move always among the wreckage of men's lives and hopes, haunted not only by a sense of being yourself doomed to die, but by an agony of mind which cried out at every step against the futile folly of the waste of time and of treasure, of skill and of life itself – this is what war meant to a soul sensitive to such impressions. Thus it was that the homely beauty of the Chapel, with its inward gift of hope and fellowship, drew many who learnt their hunger in the grimmest school which the spirit of man has yet experienced; and eyes, hardened by indomitable will to withstand the brutalising obscenities of war, softened to appraise our simple seeking after sweetness and light.

(P.B. Clayton, Tales of Talbot House)

RAMOURS & OF WARS

SEE THAT YE BE NOT TROUBLED.

AND YOU SHALL HEAR OF WARS &

OF YOUR CHARITY

PRAY FOR THE SOULS
OF THE GALLANT DEAD

R.I.P.
Archie Forrest
Confirmed at Talbot House, 9 July 1917
2nd Corporal, "P" Special (Gas) Company, Royal Engineers
26 August 1917 – Age 20 – Wieltje Farm Cemetery (St. Jan – Ieper), B.12

Newton E. Gammon
Corporal, 1/16 London Regiment (Queen's Westminster Rifles)
1 July 1916 – Age 32 – Thiepval Memorial, Pier and Face 13 C

Godfrey D. Gardner
2nd Lt., 9 Suffolk Regiment
13 September 1916 – Age 34 – Thiepval Memorial, Pier and Face 1 C and 2 A

William W. Locke
Private, 133 Field Ambulance, R.A.M.C.
25 July 1917 – Age 23 – Gwalia Cemetery (Poperinge), I.E.8

Kenneth S. Mayhew
Private, 6 (London) Field Ambulance, R.A.M.C.
3 December 1917 – Age 24 – Anneux British Cemetery, I.D.12

Gilbert W. Morris
Lieutenant, 8 King's Own Yorkshire Light Infantry
1 July 1916 – Age 25 – Blighty Valley Cemetery (Authuille, Fr.), IV.E.5

Charles M. Payne
Fitter, 18th Siege Battery, Royal Garrison Artillery
9 September 1917 – Age 22 – Duhallow A.D.S. Cemetery (Ieper), VI.C.6

Bernard C. Stenning
2nd Lt., 5th Bn Royal Engineers East Surrey Regiment
26 July 1917 – Age 35 – Godewaersvelde British Cemetery (France) I.A.10

Edmund R. Street
Major, 2 Sherwood Foresters (Notts and Derby Regiment)
15 October 1916 – Age 40 – Grove Town Cemetery (Méaulte, Fr.), I.B.7

Joseph F. Wardle
Lt., 334th Road Construction Company, R.E.
14 February 1919 – Age 32 – Rangemore (All Saints) Churchyard (Staffordshire, UK.)

2 A Place of Worship

2.1 Communion

A Crowded Congregation

A first impression of a crowded communion service during which "the Chapel rocked like a huge cradle", comes from a letter home, written on 15 October 1918, from Busseboom by Leonard (sadly, his full name is not recorded), a gunner of the 99th Brigade, R.G.A. The censor appears to have overlooked the fourth sentence!

Just a few lines to let you know I am still 'in the pink,' and trust you and Dad are quite well. I am expecting your Sunday letter to-morrow and hope I shall not be disappointed, but thought I must write and tell you about my splendid Sunday evening. We had a very wet morning – it had been raining all night, too – so I decided not to go to the Church Parade at the battery billets. The weather cleared after dinner, and the evening was glorious, so Brewer and I obtained permission to *pop* into the old town for evening service. We had no idea at what time it commenced, but it so happened that we arrived just in time, and were shown into our seats by a Captain who

The Westminster chimes struck on the gongs summoned worshippers to the Chapel. The order in which the four brass plates have to be struck is marked on the framework.

was wearing the Military Cross ribbon. The Padre commenced the service by announcing the hymn, 'We love the place, O God' – specially appropriate, as it was the first service after renovation. We sang the hymn most lustily, led by a somewhat wheezy harmonium, and the usual evenong service then began. The Magnificat and Nunc Dimittis were sung to the well-known chants: -s | m:s | f: -||m | r:f | m:r | d; and m | m:m | m: - || m | f:l | s:-f | m, respectively. You will remember that there is some very fine tenor in both, and the way that crowded congregation sang them was good to listen to. The service was 'choral,' and the ferial responses were used. The M.C. Captain read the lesson from Dr. Weymouth's translation – a small portion describing the houses founded upon the rock and upon the sand respectively. The other hymns during the service were: 'The day Thou gavest, Lord, is ended', 'Holy Father, in Thy mercy,' and 'Peace, perfect Peace.' Holy Communion followed, to which quite a large number remained, including several Americans. While some were communicating, the remainder sang softly, kneeling, 'And now, O Father.' To close, we sang two verses of 'Abide with me.' The Chaplain then invited to us into his room, and asked all new friends to sign the Communicants' Roll, after which he presented us with a postcard view of the room in which the service was held, and also a little cross made by some of his former Sunday school children in London. I am sending you the card, and shall carefully keep the cross to bring home with me next time. I cannot tell you how greatly I enjoyed the service; it seemed to put new life into me. ...

* * *

A Tiny Crucifix
A series of gifts of very great simplicity came until the end of 1917 from the children of the Portsea Sunday Schools. These children set to work to provide Talbot House with a great number of tiny metal Crucifixes, moulded with great simplicity and costing only a few pence each. They furnished these with serviceable thread, and sent them out a hundred at a time. These were then given to the Communicants of Talbot House (if they were desirous to have them) as from the children. They received as well a little printed slip which recorded not only their Army unit, but also their home address. In the end of 1917 Miss Kidd, the Superintendent of the Infants' Sunday School at Portsea, was compelled to write to Talbot House and to break

TALBOT HOUSE CHAPEL (C. of E.)

Communicants' Roll.

Communicants are asked to fill in this paper and leave it for entry on the Register, which has now been kept practically complete for two years.

No. *7616*   Name *Roberts L.P.*
(In full)

Rank................   Regt. *1/5 Loyal N. Lancs*

Home Address *Clwydian Cottage   Vale St*
            Denbigh, N. Wales   P. B. CLAYTON,
                                  Chaplain.

to me news typical of much that was then happening. The Ministry of Munitions having by now been greatly speeded up, and having taken over for the time being the entire metal supply of Great Britain, insisted, we were told, that ornamental work of every kind must cease. As a result it now became impossible to get these tiny Crosses made at all. The metal was too precious! The metal in a single shell would have made all, or nearly all, these little symbols of salvation, which ceased to be bestowable! Men to whom Talbot House was very dear indeed grew bitter when they heard that these tiny Crosses could no longer be obtained because the dies and stamps which issued them were laid aside in order to augment the awful processes of war.

(P.B. Clayton)

An unidentified ex-soldier wrote to Tubby on 6 January 1919:

Although I was near Ypres for a long period, I only once had the privilege of visiting Talbot House, but the memory of that visit will never be effaced. I still have in my possession a wee Crucifix which you gave to all those who attended service on the particular day when I was present. It has been through heaps of attacks and I treasure it very much.

*   *   *

Philip Hancock, 58th (London) Division, provides us with another peep into the Upper Room:

How well I remember when our Division came to Poperinghe in September 1917 to be in readiness for the Passchendaele offensive. On the Sunday evening about six of us (all pals) were looking for a service somewhere and happened on Talbot House: what a wonderful home-like atmosphere the place had. We were told by some other Tommies on entering that the little room upstairs was crowded out and we should not be able to attend service. We were just on the point of returning away disappointed when we saw you making your way down the staircase packed with fellows. I can see you now and hear you singing the hymn which was being sung at the time in the Upper Room, 'Praise my Soul the King of Heaven' – and you did. 'Don't go away, boys, we are having a second house, there will be a second service.' So we waited and thank God we did. The memory of that quiet Sunday evening service helped us over many dreadful and difficult days which followed in that awful month of St. Julien and Langemarck. Some of the boys went under, but their last days were cheered and their hearts made glad by the message of Toc H, and we talked of these things in our dug-out afterwards.[51]

*   *   *

Services were not always attended by large congregations, as Sapper Will Leonard, 4 Siege Company, R.E., tells us:

One summer day in 1917 returning to my unit after suffering a slight dose of gas, I entered Talbot House shortly after 5 o'clock in the morning. The padre was up and surprised to see me. 'My dear Leonard, where have you come from?' 'Short hospital spell; I'm just rejoining my Company,' I replied. 'Have you been able to receive Communion lately'? 'No.' 'Would you like to?' 'Yes.' 'Reserved Communion or would you like the full service?' 'If possible, the full service, please.' We climbed to the Chapel and he did his priestly job, from the first prayer to the Blessing, for one lone soldier. It sticks in my memory over the forty-three years since.[52]

*   *   *

Another soldier left a pencilled intercession on a tiny scrap of paper for use in the Upper Room after he himself had gone up to the line. The date is 29 March 1917.

Will you pray very earnestly for me that I may have strength given me to do that which is right and to make an effort to help others; not so much by what I say, but by my whole life. I have wandered away very far, but I want to put things right and your prayers will mean so much to me.

*   *   *

The Red Books

It would be hard to say when it exactly was that we began to think that documents concerning Talbot House were really worth retention. The general influence of Active Service was hostile to careful record-making. We lived from day to day most literally.

Yet in a way I cannot now define, there was from the first opening of Talbot House an under-current of conviction that something was beginning which deserved a system of record. It was no afterthought that Talbot House would need its Register; and, while most Padres kept their lists of men so far as they were able, it was especially true of Talbot House that signatures were constantly requested. In the two Red Books are the names, and in many cases the signatures of some three thousand officers and men who made their Communion in the Upper Room. Men signed their names in silence for the most part, realising as they did so that this might be

---

51   Lever, T., *Clayton of Toc H*, pp.54-55.
52   Lever, T., *Clayton of Toc H*, p.51-52.

the last occasion when they would attest the great solemnity which they had just experienced. The Red Book, or (on days of a great multitude) separate sheets of paper, lay on the table on the second landing below the Chapel staircase. Officers and men gathered round this table and subscribed their signatures, as they came down from the Upper Room. While they were doing this after the Celebration, I would often follow them down the companion ladder and stand there talking to this man or that, or shake hands at the top of the staircase leading to the first floor, with old friends and new. One may wonder how it has come to be that only some three thousand signatures or names survive. We must indeed recognise that many men, some of the very best, were far too shy to sign their names. They were unused to doing so in any Church, or they were in a hurry; or they just felt, without a definite reason, that they would leave it where it stood and let the others sign who fancied it. The only way of getting Englishmen to accept an innovation is to assure them that it is an old custom now to be revived. Meanwhile, what happened to the little slips which bore the signatures and home addresses? When they were signed, they were ensconced in two unworthy sand-bags in my cupboard. Sand-bags were used for almost anything and when Lord Northcliffe's department of Allied publicity[53] tried to flood Talbot House with their literature, this was also ensconced in sand-bags, and some of these were also piled into my cupboard. A few weeks later, after Kemmel fell, and life became still

---

53   Alfred Harmsworth (1865-1922), Lord Northcliffe, was the founder of the populist *Daily Mail* and *Daily Mirror* newspapers and was the owner of *The Times*. Advocating an all-out struggle against Germany, his press empire held enormous sway over public opinion. Made a viscount in 1917 for his service as head of the British war mission to the United States, he accepted an appointment as the Lloyd George government's director of propaganda against Germany and other enemy countries.

more precarious, we were compelled to build a rampart of sandbags across the marble step in the front part of the House. This rampart was constructed rapidly with sandbags taken from my cupboard, as if they contained something more solid than mere propaganda pamphlets. One sandbag full of our Communicants' Roll paper was, by a desperate oversight, built into this rampart and never recovered. Perhaps two thousand signatures were lost therein. At the Armistice the other sandbag was brought home and its contents extracted. It provided the only list of Foundation Members' names and addresses, from which the nucleus of post-war Toc H was formed.

(P.B. Clayton)

From scores of Communicants' slips, a leather-bound and illuminated volume was made in calendar form for open display in the Chapel of All Hallows at special Toc H services. From it, a red-bound Liber Vitae – "Roll of Honour of Talbot House, Poperinghe and Ypres, & others of the Elder Brethren commemorated in Toc H"- was produced in 1928. A daily calendar of remembrance, those commemorated within are representative of Great Britain, Ireland, the Dominions, India, and the U.S.A.; of every front and all three services – the Navy, the Air Force, and nearly every regiment of the British Army. A copy of this book was put in the chapel of every Toc H House worldwide.[54]

August		
1 Herbert E. Lomas Bridger	Gdsm., 1/Coldstream Guards	w. 1917
Frederick George Burrow, M.M.	A/Sergt., 15/Hampshire Regt.	a. 1917
Martin Duff Ormond	Pte., R.A.M.C.	w. 1917
3 Harry Smith	Sergt., Border Regt.	a. 1917
4 Noel Godfrey Chavasse, V.C. and Bar, D.S.O., M.C.	Capt., R.A.M.C.	w. 1917
8 Percy Valentine Cooper	A/Captain, 7/The Queen's Regt.	a. 1918
Maurice Gray	A/Captain, The Bays	a. 1918
Ernest Hoar	Pte., 19/Canadians	a. 1918
Cyril Arthur Victor Russell	Corp., 7/The Queen's Regt.	a. 1918
9 Geoffrey Morgan Hoyle	Lieut., 2/Foresters	a. 1915
10 Sydney Henman	Lieut., Royal Engineers	a. 1917
Vincent Sladen Wing	2/Lieut., R.F.A.	a. 1917
11 John Lister	Pte., 6/West York Regt.	w. 1917
Ronald Campbell Maclachlan, D.S.O.	Brig.-Gen., Rifle Bde.	a. 1917
12 Alfred Green	Rfn., 8/Rifle Brigade	w. 1915
Hugh Arthur Rees	Corp., 1/Canadian Scottish	w. 1916
13 Herbert Frederick Smith	L/Cpl., 16/Manchester Regt.	a. 1917
15 Ronald Harold Beckh	2/Lieut., 12/East York Regt.	w. 1916
16 John Willie Bottomley	Pte., 9/East Surrey Regt.	a. 1917
John Fowler	Pte., 1/7 Worcester Regt.	a. 1917
John Griffith	Lieut., Royal Engineers	w. 1922
George Valentine Jordan	Pte., 1/7 Worcester Regt.	a. 1917
18 Guy Baron Reed	Lieut., 8/Bedford Regt.	w. 1917
George E. Watson	Rfn., 20/K.R.R.C.	a. 1916
20 Percy Edward Evans	Pte., 1/8 Worcester Regt.	w. 1917
21 Arthur Lewis Kennaway	Lieut., 1/Dorset Yeomanry	a. 1915
22 David F. M. Hackett, M.M.	Lieut., 7/Leicester Regt.	a. 1918
Robert Wynne Stanley Walker	Lieut., R.A.M.C.	s. 1922
23 Bernard Henry James Freeman	Rfn., London Rifle Bde.	w. 1918
Wilfred Lawrence Lamaison	Lieut., 16/London Regt.*	w. 1918
Timothy Whiteside Rossall	Pte., 4/Loyal Regt.	1921

Queen's Westminster Rifles

2.2 Baptism

We had a wonderful baptism of a Bombardier tonight in Evensong, which was packed.

(P.B. Clayton to his mother, 8 July 1917)

*   *   *

Some 50 grown men were baptised in the Upper Room. The tiny biscuit china Font used therefore has a curious history. It was sent out from England to Australia about the year 1880 to my Mother, and was used for my own Christening many miles up country in Queensland in December 1885. It was rescued after the great Queensland Floods in 1894, when most of my father's property there was destroyed. It came home to the family, and when I went to France in 1915 it naturally did not occur to me that a Font, however small, could conceivably be required. Soon after, however, it became clear that quite a number of those with whom I had to deal had never been baptized, and my Mother, therefore, sent me out the Font, which

---

54   The *Liber Vitae* can be consulted on the Talbot House website.

was first used at No. 16 General Hospital in France on the 19th September 1915 for the baptism of Sergt. W.H. Berry, who was like to die as the result of severe wounds received at the opening of the Battle of Loos a few days previously. I can well remember the scene of its first use thus, with a drummer boy, Webberley, kneeling by the side of Sergt. Berry's stretcher at the entrance to a Hospital tent. The Font came with me to Poperinghe, and was used there during the next three years for a great number of baptisms. The last one conducted with it was that of three B.W.I. Ammunition Carriers, sponsored by three of their own Sergeants who were already Christians. This Baptism was held at Evensong on a week-night in the Autumn of 1917, and was attended by a large number, both of Canadians and Australians, as well as home countrymen. At the actual moment of baptism five Chinamen, who had somehow made their way in to the House

and up to the top of it, climbed the steep staircase to the Chapel, and stood quietly witnessing the Ceremony, the significance of which it is possible they were able in some measure to grasp without interpretation.

(P.B. Clayton)

Walter H. Berry
Baptised at No. 16 General Hospital
Serjeant, Rifle Brigade
4 April 1920 – Deal Cemetery (Kent, UK), 2 474

Allan Bostock
2nd Air Mechanic, Royal Air Force
Baptised at Talbot House

Robert C. Talbot
Bombardier, 131st Heavy Battery
Baptised at Talbot House, 13 September 1917

John W. Davis
16th S.B.A.C.
Baptised at Talbot House, 21 February 1918

2.3 Confirmation

Hundreds of soldiers were prepared and presented for confirmation by Tubby. When Randall Davidson, Archbishop of Canterbury, visited the Western Front in May 1916 he took Confirmation in the Upper Room. His personal Chaplain recorded the event as as follows:

In an exceedingly upper room, a long garret transformed into a chapel, the Archbishop took a Service for the Chaplains, and then confirmed about 36 or 40 men presented by P.B. Clayton. That place is a place of many memories, and among them both here on earth, and beyond, there must surely remain that of the old Archbishop sitting in his chair, with the lighted candles behind him as the darkness came on, and the candidates kneeling before him, whilst outside in the street there was the ceaseless rumble of troops moving up to the Salient and the intermittent sound of firing.

(The Revd. J.V. Macmillan, 17 May 1916)

R.I.P.

Frederick Ostick
Private, 2 Sherwood Foresters
(Notts and Derby Regiment)
16 September 1916 – Thiepval
Memorial, Pier and Face 10 C,
10 D and 11 A

James Wyard[55]
Private, 2 York and Lancaster
Regiment
20 May 1918 – Age 27 –
Ipswich Old Cemetery,
BA. IA. 21

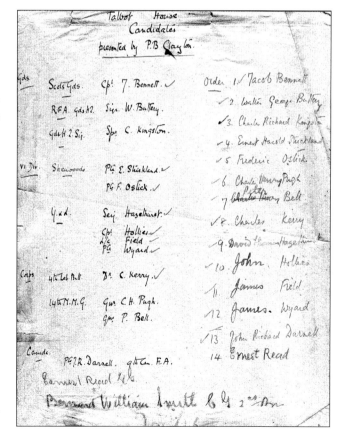

55   For the story behind the confirmation of the 4 'Yorks & Lancs', see p. 325.

* * *

On 14 August 1917, Rev. Julian Bickersteth MC, Senior Chaplain 56th (London) Division, accompanied "a party of his lads" to Talbot House to be confirmed.

The Confirmation service took place in a well-known church club, the only one of its kind at the Front, I believe, and called after the Talbots, Talbot House or Toc H. It is a large house in the centre of the town and fitted up splendidly. There are reading rooms, writing rooms, a library, quiet rooms, card rooms, canteen, café, open-air lounge, garden, concert room, and every possible device for making the soldier comfortable. Delightful pictures cover the walls, and facetious remarks are pinned up at various places by the altogether admirable chaplain-in-charge, imploring those who use the club not to remove all the writing paper from the writing room or otherwise pillage the club.[56] But the great thing which gives character to the Club is its chapel. It is right at the top of the house under the old oak rafters. A beautiful altar decked with rich hangings and canopy at once catches the eye. A Sanctuary lamp burns before it. A fine carpet is laid on the steps leading to it. A beautiful Crucifix and other altar ornaments adorn it. Some really good pictures are on the walls. A small side

Rev. Julian Bickersteth.

altar is provided for daily Celebrations, all in perfect proportion and taste. The whole is a veritable 'House of God'. I have never been at a more impressive Confirmation Service. Perhaps 120 men from thirty or forty different units brought in by fifteen or twenty chaplains were confirmed. The Bishop (the DCG) spoke well. The singing was all in unison and most uplifting. The men who were confirmed were many of them mere lads, but here and there an older man was amongst them.

The whole service, with its beautiful setting and with the knowledge that many of those confirmed had come straight from the battle and were to return again that night, could not fail to move the least impressionable. One of our candidates had been killed that very morning and two others wounded. When I mentioned the death of this boy to Neville Talbot, he was most sympathetic… but full of Christian hope: 'He will be confirmed in Heaven. I do feel we must get a right view of the passing of our Christian lads. What a splendid Confirmation Day he will have, and yet I know how you feel, old chap'.[57]

56 For the light-hearted notice he refers to, see p. 228.
57 Bickersteth, J., *The Bickersteth Diaries 1914-1918*, pp. 204-205.

Confirmed at Talbot House, 14 August 1917

Pte. Gwynne F. Jenkins, 33rd Field Ambulance
L/Cpl. Ernest Greenwood, 5th Field Survey Company, R.E.
Frank A. Thomas, "P" Special (Gas) Company, R.E.

* * *

Horace Manton Brown, Lieut. 4th Bn Suffolks, received his Confirmation from Bishop Gwynne (D.C.G.) in Talbot House Chapel on December 18th 1917 on his 21st birthday. Known to his intimates as 'Baby' Brown, my memory of him is, without sentiment, most properly described in terms of light. His single-eyed sincerity of purpose, coupled with a keen humour, revealed a man of men, bound to go far. But God had other plans than ours for him.

(P.B. Clayton)

R.I.P.

Horace M. Brown
Lieutenant, 4 Suffolk Regiment
14 April 1918 – Mendinghem Military Cemetery,
IX.E.33

Horace Manton Brown

2.4 A call to Holy Orders

Chief among other objects for which Talbot House appealed was the Service Candidates Fund, which indeed was opened by large offertories from Talbot House, the first donation being from Major Street's family.

(P.B. Clayton)

* * *

NOTICE
Ordination Candidates
It is not known widely enough among Churchmen in the Army that the Church at home has adopted a great plan whereby to add to her Ministry after the war a great body of the best men from the Army and Navy, irrespective of their financial ability to meet the cost of their training. Already, under this scheme, over 1,400 candidates for Ordination have come forward from all

ranks and all Fronts: 150 of these have been enrolled in Talbot House.[58] I shall be glad to get in touch with any further candidates, and to explain the scheme to any inquirers.

P.B. Clayton

The candidate's pledge stated:

"If God decides to bring me through this war, I vow to take it as a hint from Him that I shall help and serve the Church in future throughout the life that He gives back to me."

* * *

The Room of Decision

To Douglas Legg, a young Church Army worker, one particular Upper Room service meant the end of doubt as to what his vocation should be:

For me the Upper Room had more than a mystical meaning; it was to be the Room of Decision. Tubby had spoken to so many of us about Ordination. For months the problem had been worrying me. Ways and means made any decision a very grave matter, while personal unworthiness made it appear an impossible one.

It was Easter Day 1917 and the House was crowded. A celebration of the Holy Communion was announced at an early hour. We crowded into that Upper Room to greet the Risen Christ. Many more were waiting below to kneel at the Altar before the Lord Himself. Reverently, and most lovingly, the little bent figure of Tubby administered the Bread of Life and the Cup of Salvation. "This is My Body – this is My Blood". For several hours that celebration went on – that Easter meeting with the Lord. We knew Him in the Breaking of the Bread.

When I think back to that Easter Day I have often wondered at the supernatural strength that must have been given to Tubby on that occasion, for he showed no sign of fatigue.

I like to believe that many men felt a call to Holy Orders on that wonderful Easter Morning. My decision had been made.

3. A Place of Spiritual Refreshment, Strength and Guidance

Many war weary officers and men found spiritual refreshment and peace in the Chapel.

On one occasion I found General Plumer sitting alone and thoughtfully in the Upper Room. "A good place for rest and quiet after a particularly heavy day," came the reply to my anxious query.

(Rev. F.I. Anderson, A.C.G. Second Army)

---

58   During the latter stage of the war, the list, having grown beyond the scope of Tubby's private responsibility, was transferred to Bishop Gwynne's headquarters at St. Omer. Lists from other parts were then added to it and, by the time of the Armistice, some 2,000 names had been collected. By December 1918, a men's school, under the Rev. F.R. Barry was established in the old Machine Gun School at Le Touquet and an officers' school under the Rev. E. Talbot (elder brother of Gilbert and Neville) at Radinghem. Tubby was detailed to the former. In January 1919, he returned to Great Britain in search of a building for the Service Candidates' Ordination Test School. Obtaining the derelict Knutsford Prison (Cheshire), F.R. Barry became the first principal and Tubby an instructor.

* * *

The Earl of Cavan.

From time to time also, Tubby's 2nd cousin, Frederick Lambart, 10th Earl of Cavan (GOC XIV Corps) came by to "spend a few wonderful minutes of calm" at Talbot House. On one occasion he described how, in the quietness of the Chapel, the anxieties of a critical moment of the war dropped away:

In the early spring of 1916, I came away from the trenches after having spent the whole of a grim day witnessing destruction descending upon my men. As I left the line, the torrential rain, the bitter cold, and the evening Hate began to break my spirit. I had long been a stranger to despair; but as I made my way down the shell-torn road, I felt that the Salient was doomed, its fate certain. My car came to the outskirts of Poperinghe. There a switch road, avoiding the shelled town, would take me straight back to my Corps Headquarters in Château De Lovie. Instead, I left the car, instructing the driver to take it back to Lovie and explaining that I myself would follow in due course. Buttoning my trench coat round me, I walked directly to the doors of Talbot House and entered. I was greeted by Clayton's batman, Private Pettifer, who asked me whether I wished to see his master. 'No,' I replied, 'I have come just to try to say my prayers'; and without more ado I climbed the first stairs and then the ladder that led to the Upper Room. Here I saw one officer and three men kneeling at benches. I knelt down myself and prayed, as I had never prayed before, that Almighty God would give me comfort, self-reliance, courage, and would take away despair. I never knew how long it was before the answer came; but come it did, and I found myself being then upheld. At first came quiet, a sense of peace, confidence revived.

I felt as if an overwhelming burden had been lifted from me and that I was free and strong once more. I rose from prayer, refreshed, renewed; knelt again to render parting thanks, descended the stairs, went out into the darkness and walked alone back to my Corps Headquarters.

*   *   *

Another, Staff Officer Alan St. George Colthurst, 235 Brigade R.F.A., recorded his chapel visits and what they meant during the gloomy winter of 1916:

I felt myself being drawn to the Upper Room again and again and my parched soul received much comfort. There was a unity of mutual understanding such as I had not experienced until that time. All were "on the level" in Christ for all might meet him face to face at any moment.

*   *   *

On 19 June 1917, Rifleman Basil Lawrence (1/21st London Regiment) posted a letter to his fiancée, Lily Rydon, that was to become a highly treasured correspondence. Like many others at that time, the writer suffered from acute fear and anxiety:

This week I have been privileged with a view of the reality of the help of Christ at all times; on Whit Monday I was at Talbot House (a place I have often mentioned) and was telling the Padre there I had been unable to communicate the previous day, so after a talk he asked whether I

Rfm. Basil Lawrence.

TALBOT HOUSE CHAPEL

WHITSUNTIDE SERVICES

26th, SATURDAY.   6 p.m.

> Evensong and Preparation Class.

27th, WHITSUNDAY.

> Holy Communion 5.30, 6, 6.30, 7, 7.30, and 8.15 a.m.
> Morning Prayer 10.30 a.m.
> Choral Eucharist 11.30 a.m.
> Social Meeting, 4.30 p.m.
> Prayer Meeting 5.15 p.m.
> Festal Evensong 6.30 p.m.
> *Holy Communion 7.30 p.m.
> > * For those on Morning Duty.

CANON B. K. CUNNINGHAM will preach at Morning and Evening Services.

Intercessions will be offered throughout the Army on Whitsunday for Missionary Work, and collections will go to the Army Missionary Association.

P. B. CLAYTON, *Chaplain.*

would like a service in the Chapel. I was able to go up and have a good long quiet time for prep. and self-examination, and then made use of the privilege of Confession. I mean in the presence of a Priest. I shall never forget it in all my life. It was the most wonderful experience I had ever had because it was the most humiliating. The Service that followed was naturally made the more real. I have had to mention this because it affects what followed – you see we were going into serious action about which you have read this week. Before the action I spent a couple of days on trench garrison duty and still had that same nervous feeling which of course was noticed as usually. However a couple of days out of the line and then again for action. We were in the assembly trenches, and then zero moment arrived announced by two deafening explosions followed by all the guns opening. Fritz was dropping his heavies near by and we dreaded the walk across the open to get to the other trenches, but during the intervening time I got one of those wonderful visions of Christ – of His Passion and Crucifixion – of His great Love, and by just fixing my eyes on that vision of the Cross I was calmer than ever before, so much so that as I happened to be the leading man in the team I went calmly across the open and into our old frontline trench. Then – from my old critic – "Basil, you are getting better." What a difference it made! Of course we proceeded on 'over the bags' and on to our objective and the business went on. The night was fair considering the position we were in; but early during the following evening we were subjected to the worst bombardment I had ever been in, during which I was able to pass humorous remarks with the others. Why? Because I had had a vision of Christ with extended arms in front of us all and instead of bearing all our sins, He was bearing all the harm from the shells, and I knew they would be diverted from us – I even said to the others, "Lads, if any drop near us they will be duds." Sure enough, and to me it was only because of faith, two dropped on the parapet and were duds, otherwise we should have been 'goners'. When it got quiet one of the team said, "Basil, did you say the usual?" I said, "Yes of course" – while the critic came up and shook hands and I knew God had given me the victory over fear and nervousness... I shall never forget it in all my life.[59]

Basil B. Lawrence
Rifleman, 21 London Regiment (First Surrey Rifles)
4 November 1917 – Age 26 – Naval Trench Cemetery (Gavrelle, Fr.), A.7

* * *

After the carnage of Passchendaele, Signaller Henry Whiteman, Royal Artillery, found himself in the Upper Room with Tubby, the former full of hatred and loathing for the misery and horror he had experienced:

I knew fire, gas and water, at Ypres, Somme, Messines, Cambrai and St. Quentin; once wounded and twice gassed. I had memories of battles, bombardments, blood and hate when our regiment was ordered to muddy Flanders opposite Passchendaele to face more. After months of bombardment and little progress, I had my second dose of gas from shells accurately lobbed around our observation post, and I was sent away to the rear of the line to rest awhile. During this short

---

59   Lever, T., *Clayton of Toc H*, p.55-56.

stay at Regimental H.Q. I visited Toc H Poperinghe, and sat glum and filled with hate for the Germans and the whole set up. I was alone and just bottled up all this something within which was nothing short of murderous! Up came a Padre, who turned out to be the Rev. P.B. Clayton. "Come soldier", he said, "nothing is too sour but it can be sweetened." He sat with me awhile, and then invited me to the Upper Room and there he said a simple prayer… All that he said changed a hateful heart to a grateful one and I returned to my unit that evening thinking deeply on those things revealed to me by this cheerful, spiritual, understanding Priest of Christ's Church.

*   *   *

It was not only individuals who found strength and guidance in the Upper Room, as Rev. A. Llewellyn Jones, chaplain to the Welsh Guards, noted in a letter (23 July 1916) to his Vicar at Portsea.

You will be interested to hear that our weekly Chaplains' Meeting – the devotional part of it – is held in the little Chapel which P.B.C. made so very dignified and beautiful. Last Thursday, we met there for a Corporate Celebration, and one of our number addressed the rest on the text "It is good for us to be here." It is a really refreshing thing to get back there on cycles, or by some other method, and meet for devotions and mutual counsel and our plan of having a corporate Celebration from time to time, when it is possible, with an address, is very good.

Rev. A. Llewellyn Jones.

*   *   *

Let us leave the final word about the Upper Room to Tubby.

I cannot leave the old Chapel thus. I must climb once more the steep and narrow stairs, and find the lamp glowing above the altar in that Upper Room. It is empty else, but indeed I can people it at will. Here are many dear friends and brave hearts. Arthur Cole will be my Server, and Charlie Williams will lead the singing. Bernard Stenning, Alfred Atkinson, Fred Burrow, Bertie Hoptrough, Cyril Russell, Basil Lawrence, Arthur Aked, Landels Folkard, Percy Cooper, Bill Ogden, Harry Bacon, and a hundred more, will draw near to kneel where He, who is invisible as they, may minister to them the medicine of immortality. Here, in the times of prayer, hearts have been open. Here the blind have received their

sight, the lame have walked, and the lepers been cleansed indeed. O ye spirits and souls of the righteous; O ye holy and humble men of heart; O ye of the furnace seven times heated; bless ye the Lord. For it was with Him that ye walked unharmed in the midmost of the fire.

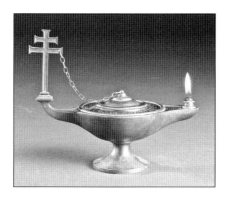

R.I.P.
Arthur Aked
Private, 17 Northumberland Fusiliers
29 November 1917 – Age 25 – Buffs Road Cemetery (Ieper), E.52

Alfred Atkinson
Private, 1/8 The King's (Liverpool Regiment)
20 September 1917 – Tyne Cot Memorial (Passendale), Pnl 31-34 and 162, 162A and 163A

Harry Bacon
Private, 1/8 Worcestershire Regiment
10 November 1918 – Age 21 – St.-Sever Cemetery Extension (Rouen, Fr.), S.II.GG.19

Frederick G. Burrow
Corporal, 15 Hampshire Regiment
1 August 1917 – Wytschaete Military Cemetery, VI.D.8

Arthur R. Cole
Lance Corporal, 2/1 (Wessex) Field Ambulance, R.A.M.C.
10 April 1918 – Age 23 – Chocques Military Cemetery (Fr.), I.M.38

Percy V. Cooper
Captain, 7 The Queen's (Royal West Surrey Regiment)
8 August 1918 – Age 26 – Beacon Cemetery (Sailly-Laurette, Fr.), II.H.10

William L. Folkard
Confirmed at Talbot House, 14 August 1917
2nd Lieutenant, Royal Air Force
15 November 1918 – Stowmarket Cemetery (UK), F.63

Herbert C. Hoptrough
Corporal, 15 Hampshire Regiment
20 September 1917 – Age 2 – Tyne Cot Memorial (Passendale), Pnl. 88 to 90 and 162

Basil B. Lawrence
Rifleman, 21 London Regiment (First Surrey Rifles)
4 November 1917 – Age 26 – Naval Trench Cemetery (Gavrelle, Fr.), A.7

William Ogden
Lance Corporal, 26 Field Ambulance, R.A.M.C.
20 April 1918 – St.-Sever Cemetery Extension (Rouen, Fr.), P. VI.N.1B

Cyril A.V. Russell
Corporal, 7 The Queen's (Royal West Surrey Regiment)
8 August 1918 – Age 21 – Vis-en-Artois Memorial (Fr.), Pnl. 3

Bernard C. Stenning
2nd Lieutenant, 5 East Surrey Regiment
26 July 1917 – Age 35 – Godewaersvelde British Cemetery, I.A.10

L/Cpl. Charles Williams
Lance Corporal, 213 Army Troops Coy, R.E.
30 March 1918 – Age 32 – Pozières Memorial, Pnl. 10 to13.

*   *   *

TALBOT HOUSE.

Down these stairs
in signal phial.

By Order.

P.B.C.

Part 3

A House of People

I THE INNKEEPER – CAPT. LEONARD BROWNE

TALBOT HOUSE.

Genius is constutionally untidy.

But—!

P.B.C.

But what of Boniface[1] himself?

My only qualification for the task is that for almost a year I was in daily contact with the subject of this narrative. Having a practice of a very suburban character among R.E.'s who were building broad gauge railways, I had a certain amount of spare time which was devoted to various forms of labour in connection with the House.

My first sight of Boniface was early in September 1916, when a little bowed old figure celebrated the Eucharist in the Upper Room. It was new to me to find one so absorbed in his great task that he was obviously oblivious of his congregation.

He had just returned from a few months' convalescence at the Base, during which Talbot House passed through many vicissitudes.

I had visited the House in August and found it practically empty. Then Neville Talbot appeared one Sunday and announced that a most wonderful padre was soon to return to the House which he had helped to create.

At that Communion service Boniface appealed for helpers. So I went and routed him out in the Officers' Club next morning. There I found that the little bowed old figure was really a juvenile like myself. We sat in the garden behind the Club and talked for hours. I discovered

---

1   A reference to the character Boniface, a jovial innkeeper, in the comic play *The Beaux' Stratagem* by
    George Farquhar (1678-1707).

298

very soon that the situation was rather serious, for a fiat had gone forth that Talbot House was to be closed unless audited accounts were produced within a fortnight. Apparently Army Headquarters had different ideas about finance from those which held sway in Talbot House. But who was to do this auditing of accounts? It seemed a simple undertaking at first sight, so I offered my services. Investigation showed how rash I had been; I had rushed in where any sensible angel would very carefully have refrained from treading. The account book was exhibited to me with pride, not unjustifiable so far as its size and material went. Within, it was ruled after the approved fashion of the modern account book. But there the resemblance ceased. Genius had ignored the fettering lines and columns which bind and hamper ordinary mortals. There were five or six headings written across the page – "Furniture", "Garden", "House Expenses", "Entertainments", and one or two other items which I have now forgotten. Then there was a column for receipts. In this column there continually occurred the item "Found in officers' box", 20 frs. or 100 frs., and so on. At first sight it appeared that a dishonest innkeeper was brazenly entering the results of his midnight researches in the baggage of his guests. Enquiry, however, showed that this really referred to the money placed in a box by the officers who used to stay the night at Talbot House in early days. This formed a considerable source of revenue.

A glance at this amazing book was followed by the enquiry, "I suppose you have got receipts corresponding to these entries? Oh yes," replied Boniface, "there is a whole cupboard full of them," and he flung open a cupboard in the wall as he spoke. Truly the cupboard was full – full of scraps of dirty paper with inscriptions in French and Flemish and English. Old receipts from Hazebrouck, St. Omer, Dunkirk, Bailleul, and Boulogne showed how far the range of purchase had spread. But there was no order or system in the whole.

Drawing of Tubby, 1916.

Anyhow, Army Headquarters was informed that the accounts were being audited, and that was the main thing.

A fortnight's work showed that the receipts produced did not approach the expenditure by some thousands of francs. A good many transactions had evidently taken place by cash alone. Audited accounts could not, alas, be produced, but fortunately the financial conscience at Army Headquarters had gone to sleep again, so all was well. Audited accounts were *not* produced and the House was *not* closed. Most satisfactory.

But, strangely enough, further probing after several months revealed the fact that the House had been the gainer to a large extent by the "defalcations" of the innkeeper. While I am on the subject of finance I must mention that bogey which constantly haunted us when a full blown Committee came into being, presided over by a Quartermaster-General.[2] Large purchases were constantly being made from Gamages,[3] and their bills were frequently coming in. I would question P.B.C. very sternly, "Are you sure this is all we owe to Gamages?" An affirmative reply

2   For the Talbot House Committee, see appendix III.
3   Gamages, founded by Mr A. Gammage, was a well-known department store at Holborn in Central London It also had a large mail-order business and issued a wide range of catalogues. These were dispatched postage free to any part of the globe.

would send me to the Committee with the assurance that £30 would clear us entirely of debt so far as Gamages was concerned. The Olympians would agree to this payment, with the severe proviso that no more purchases should be made without official sanction. I was so reduced in morale that I was willing to promise anything. P.B.C. was always kept out of the way of this Committee as his life was not considered safe at the hands of such dangerous men. A week or ten days would elapse, when a plaintive voice would greet me with: "Here's another bill from Gamages, but it's only a small one, £20. But I thought the last bill brought us up to date? Yes, but this is for things which I ordered just before the Committee meeting."

The old account book frequently contained the entry, "Taken from cash box, 400 frs." This meant that P.B.C. had managed to get a lift to Boulogne one fine day. The correct procedure on these occasions was to empty the cash box, and sally forth to make purchases for the House – the joy of acquisition was always worth experiencing. The results of these expeditions were always exciting, both from the point of view of the wrecked accounts and from the point of view of the wonderful things produced.

Talbot House presented a most perfect illustration of "a round peg in a round hole." Those who know our innkeeper in the flesh have realised how round the peg was. But rotundity was no bar to activity: while activity was no bar to rotundity. A pair of spectacles with large black rimmed glasses; a short substantial figure; a rather innocent expression on the kindly face – all these combined to make a living embodiment of Mr. Chesterton's famous Father Brown.[4]

Clothing was always a trial – buttons *would* persist in coming off, breeches *would* grape at the knees, shirt cuffs *would* wear out – but after all an innkeeper of the highest order has no time to dally with such details of artificial civilisation, so my efforts to secure some sort of average tidiness were in vain.

The House was generally a scene of great hilarity, for Boniface was always full of fun. At our tea parties in his room he would offer some nervous youth a box of matches, in which all the matches were stuck to the bottom of the box. Another man would strike a match which was only intended to smoulder. Concerts and debates showed the innkeeper at his best, when his deep voice sang rollicking song, or his quaint repartee rendered the House weak with mirth. Always ready for a rag, he found kindred spirits in many men who felt the need of letting off steam in practical jokes. I remember going with him on May-day 1917 to Bergues, where he ran riot in the quiet old town, and might have been seen walking through the streets carrying a wooden horse which he was taking back to Poperinghe.

Some of the notices of the House have been mentioned, but I must add one which is well worth recording. A sapper had been helping him with some job in his room one day, and by mistake had left his own penknife behind and had taken that belonging to Boniface. Next day a notice appeared:

If the Sapper who helped me yesterday, and left his penknife in my room, will apply to me he will receive two apologies:-
1)   An apology for the trouble I am giving him.
2)   The apology for a knife which he left behind.

---

4   G.K. Chesterton (1874-1936) and Tubby were old school friends. It has been said that the former based his famous detective, Father Brown, on Tubby.

His energies and activities were so great that he never rested. Whether he was making his weekly pilgrimage to the "slums" to visit his beloved batteries, or whether he was actually in the House, his work never ceased. Occasionally disaster overtook him in the shape of "a temperature", and then my turn came. There would be a battle from which I emerged triumphant, while Boniface retired to bed. Our great dread was "evacuation to the Base", so every endeavour was made to prevent his being sent to a Medical unit. On two or three occasions I looked after him myself, but once the kindly C.O. of a Field Ambulance, which was billeted close by, lent us a nursing orderly twice a day. But Boniface could never understand why the stream of visitors should not continue even though he was in bed. "Gunner Smith is coming down from Ypres and I shall be very disappointed if I do not see him; and there is that splendid Sergeant Jones of the R.E.'s who is coming in to tea." In the end I had to put a notice on his door forbidding anyone to enter. Then Boniface turned his face to the wall in anguish of spirit, and I, feeling that it had been better if I had never been born, sat in the next room and read Macbeth.

To make quite sure that no one could disturb him when his temperature was about 105, I put the old "General" on duty at his door to keep out anyone who might ignore the notice. On returning in the evening I was touched to find the General "asleep at his post" in a chair. He had probably been up all the night before, but he wakened up covered with confusion, rather feeling that he had let down the tradition of The Buffs. However, when I came back at the same time next evening I was seized by the arm in the dim light, while a hoarse voice whispered: "You can't go in, Sir; it's Doctor's orders." It was flattering to feel that my instructions were being so faithfully carried out after the lapse of the previous day.

During one of these spells in bed the Corps Commander of the period arrived on a surprise inspection. He was an officer of sanitary instincts, and I had the pleasure of taking him round. He made scathing remarks on the insanitary condition of the House, as evidenced by an empty matchbox lying in the garden. I sympathised with him most heartily, and experienced all the delights of being "Army" and not "Corps", so that my connection with Talbot House was entirely unofficial and irresponsible. Then I suggested that he might visit the patient, and the thrilling spectacle was witnessed of a very self-possessed publican being visited by a rather bashful Corps Commander whose bedside manner was a trifle stiff.

Only one who had no idea of time or space or money could possibly have carried on at Talbot House. P.B.C. regarded time as an arbitrary division of the day; space was better ignored. One of his favourite dicta, on which he acted with great fidelity, was "the only way to arrive in time is to start out late: if you start punctually you will probably never arrive." Occasionally he actually proved this by experience.

But it was this spirit which enabled him to cope with hundreds of men without ever making anyone feel that he was *de trop*. Many a time I have sat in that room of his at Talbot House and watched a succession of men coming in, many of them tired and jaded after a tramp from "Wipers". "My dear old man, how ripping to see you."

Boniface had the true spirit of hospitality which put the most awkward man at his ease, and made him feel that there was one who really cared nothing for a man's stripes but would be the same to all. Many a man sore from some injustice, or homesick and weary, has received the cup of cold water in "His Name" in the lower room, just as thousands received the "Cup of Blessing" from the same hands in the Upper Room. How much this welcome was appreciated by those who received it is well shown by the thousands of men who flocked to the House every week. Shy lads from Devon and Somerset, men from Northumberland and Durham, awkward, but keen and intelligent, self-possessed Londoners, men from Australia, Canada, and New Zealand, all fell under the same spell. Truly love is all powerful, and it was the power of an unselfish love for them which brought these men back to the House over and over again. I remember one hot Sunday afternoon in June while a lot of us were sitting at tea in the House, a great burly, red-haired Australian gunner arrived on a push bike from Armentières. He had only come to see the padre for a few minutes. As a matter of fact he had exactly half-an-hour, which he had to share with other people, but he went away with a light in his eyes which mirrored the feelings within.

It is wonderful how the childlike spirit appeals to men – or at any rate to the best men. It seems to have the power of drawing out the very best that every man possesses. An infinite belief in human nature, especially in the men of the B.E.F., enabled P.B.C. to get into the real "back-shop" of most men's minds. He was able to lift them up out of the sordidness of their surroundings and set them on their feet again.

The B.E.F. rightly inculcated in men the idea of caution, but at Talbot House we transliterated the familiar French warning and wrote up: "Plaisez-vous, confiez-vous, les oreilles de l'Ami vous écoutent."[5]

And Boniface followed his men about and visited them whenever he could. He felt that his work at Talbot House was too safe, so he did what he could to share the hardships and dangers of his customers.

The spirit of laughter and prayer filled the House, and the innkeeper showed to his guests the qualities of the Friend and Lord of the House.[6]

II 'THE GENERAL', MY BRAVE OLD BATMAN – REV. P.B. CLAYTON

Permit me to introduce you to a real old soldier – "the General," as he was universally known to three generations of Talbot House clientèle, and to all the children of the neighbourhood. On and off the Army has known him for thirty-one years as No.239, Pte. Pettifer, A., 1st The Buffs; and though now attached on grounds of debility to what is vulgarly known as an Area Enjoyment Company,[7] the peak of his cap retains the dragon that no right-thinking man would desire to see replaced. He has refused to put up his proper array of good-conduct badges, as they would interfere with the set of his sleeve over his elbow. For chest protection he wears a Military Medal, an Indian Frontier ribbon, the South African, and the so-called Mons. He is sagacious past belief in the ways and byways of the Army, which he entered as a band-boy in the year of my birth.[8] Long ago he might have put up sergeant's stripes; yea, and have been by now Q.M.S., or even R.S.M.; but he would not. Uneasy lies the arm that wears a crown, and to be "the General" is honour enough in his honest old eyes.

---

5   A parody on the well-known French wartime poster *Taisez-vous! Méfiez-vous! Les Oreilles ennemies vous écoutent*, i.e. "Keep quiet! Be on your guard! Enemy ears are listening".
6   P.B. Clayton, *Tales of Talbot House*, pp.112-125.
7   Labour Corps Area Employment Companies were formed in 1917. They were used for rudimentary tasks i.e., road repair, supply transport, salvage work, etc. Manned by officers and other ranks medically rated below the "A1" condition, they were often deployed within range of the enemy guns, on many occasions for lengthy periods. In times of crisis, spring 1918 in particular, they were deployed as emergency infantry.
8   Pettifer, born in 1874, was aged 11 then.

When this particular war broke out, Pettifer got down from his cart in Hackney, left the missus with one less dinner to see to, and the nibs[9] without their Sunday escort, and rejoined the Buffs. In November they arrived in France, and wintered in the bracing locality of "Armonteeres", coming to the salient in May, 1915. A year after his landing he was told to report as batman to a new and unknown chaplain; but even this was better than the listening-post job[10] that he had "clicked for" (and volunteered for) again and again. By that time there were only some twenty-eight of *the* Buffs still with the regiment.

Pettifer, having at the first interview characteristically announced his inability to meet any domestic requirements, soon, developed unique capacities in that direction. Shortly after we fetched up at Talbot House, his powers of acquisition made themselves only too visibly felt. I became afraid to mention a need lest its fulfilment should bring disaster and disgrace. I was, for instance, overheard to say that a carpet for the Chapel was most desirable. Within an hour a carpet had arrived. Enquiry revealed the painful fact that it had come from next door. "They won't be wanting it, sir; they *do* say the family are in the sou' of France." It is incumbent upon the

The old General in war paint.

clergy to take their stand at such moments upon bed-rock principle. "General, I can't say my prayers kneeling on a stolen carpet." Silence hereafter for a space: then a bright idea. "Well, sir, if yer won't 'ave it in the church, it'll do lovely for yer sitting-room." When even this brilliant alternative is dismissed as Jesuitical, and the carpet restored to the place it came from, a few days elapse tranquilly. Then "the General" scores heavily one morning: "Yer remember that carpet, sir?" I admit it. "Well, the A.S.C. 'ave scrounged it now."

But God fobid that "the General" should be thought anti-social or unneighbourly. Nothing could be further from the truth. He is withal the most adaptable of companions, and will find, in the most unlikely places, neighbours from Hackney who deal with the very same tradesmen. He is never at a loss in any British atmosphere, and in an incredibly short space of time will effectively "smarten up the parade." In foreign society he is equally at his ease, largely because he has eschewed all attempts at their methods of speech, and continues, like so many of the best

9   His two sons, Arthur and William.
10   An advanced post, usually in no man's land, occupied at night by sentries.

Englishmen, to regard their inability to understand him as a species of chronic deafness, to be overcome by slower articulation, sedulous repetition, and a raising of the voice in utterance. It is certainly amazing what excellent results may be thus obtained.

There is, moreover, not a child in Poperinghe whose face does not light up at his approach. It is they who have conferred upon him the title of "le Général", by which he is greeted in every narrow street. And to many of the old folk as well he has been a benefactor in dark days; wheeling their "sticks" away to safety, or greatly concerned for the still more difficult removal of the bed-ridden. Fancy bed-ridden old in such a town as this has been![11]

Robin Hood

Pettifer's views of property are rigidly conservative, if so be that the thing really belongs to anyone about; but when it comes to common stores, provided by the home Government, he is a Robin Hood, concerned to place the booty where it will be most useful in relieving urgent need. On one desperate day, when Talbot House was burning wads of paper, Pettifer sallied forth. Here is his narrative:

It was the time when they were short o' coal, y' see; so Dr. Browne and Tubby had bin talkin' about where to get coal, and they sent for me and asked me could I get some? I told them I'd try, but I might have to buy from the Belgians at 150 francs a ton – if you could get it. Any road, I said I'd see what I could do. I went up to the station, and there 'appened to be a large corporal of the Engineers there wi' a lorry load. I asked him where 'e was goin' with the load, and 'e said 'e 'adn't any instructions; anywhere, but it was for the army. So I ses to 'im, "What about runnin'

it up to Talbot 'Ouse?" 'E ses, "I don't care, so long as the army get it." So I said, "The army'll get it orlright if you run it down to Talbot 'Ouse." He got it there, and backed it up the back road to the gate into the garden. I told 'im to shoot it down there and "my men" would shift it. "My men!" I said to 'im. I wish you'd 'eard me! 'I asked him, "Suppose you'd like a drink for this?" an' 'e said, "It's worth it, with a double lorry load like this – well worth twenty francs! Will you be satisfied with eighty francs?" I said. So I went to Dr. Browne and told 'im I'd got a double lorry load, three tons, and I wanted eighty francs for it. He said, "That's all

11   Clayton, *Tales of Talbot House*, pp.54-62.

right, Gen," and give me eighty francs. And then 'e says, "I want a receipt for it!" Well, as the coal was pinched I 'ad to tell him I'd got if from the Belgians. "Get it in Belgian," ses 'e. I didn't know what to do. I went out and give the corporal 'is money and said, "I dunno what to do, they want a receipt in Belgian. Orl right," ses he, "I can write Belgian." So he wrote the receipt out, and I was satisfied and didn't know what was on it, and gave it to Dr. Browne, and *he* seemed quite satisfied, and the lorry driver went away quite pleased with *him*self … [12]

Gaiety

Now when the War began, Neville Talbot was Chaplain and Fellow of Balliol, and Pettifer was driving a cart in Hackney. But both men had seen active service, before we others knew the fashion of a Brigade. This was a bond of mutual confidence, expressed in elementary jocundities between them. The old Gen had all sorts of devilments up his sleeve. Here follow two of his narrations.

When Neville came once he 'ad a tiny little flask, so I looked at it with longin' eyes and thought to myself, "it's no good to him." I left it there for a couple of days, and he didn't seem to want it, so I drank it and filled his flask up with water. Then he suddenly got a bit of a cold and did want it, but I 'ad the first cold and he didn't get it. Of course when 'e looked for 'is rum, it was only water. So 'e sent for me, an' I ses, "Yessir, you want me? Ah, yes, you dear old Buff. Good old Corps, the Rifle Brigade," I said – not meaning it, of course. 'E looks at me with such a face and ses, "You know, Gen, I'd a little flask of rum 'ere." I said, "I know you did." 'E said, "What happened to it?" I said, "I drank it." 'E said, "What for? Because I 'ad a cold. That's what I wanted it for, but you need not 'ave filled it up with water." So I ses to 'im, "Parsons mustn't 'ave rum for colds." And 'e ses then, "What must parsons 'ave?" I looked at 'im nearly burstin' with laughin', and ses to 'im – "Gruel and boiled onions." And 'e ses to me, "*Get* out of it, the Buffs are no good!" And as I went out of the door I ses to 'im, "Rotten lot, the Rifle Brigade."

* * *

Another time, 'e came before they had the Officers' Club – an' we used to 'ave felt slippers. An' 'e came unexpectedly. I put 'im upstairs and give 'im a bed, put 'im comfortable and went downstairs. I 'adn't been down long when 'e rang a bell. I guessed what 'e wanted, a pair of slippers. "Yessir?" 'E said, "You dear old Buff," and I said, "Good old corps, the Rifle Brigade. Ave you a pair of slippers for me? I 'ave, sir." An' the only pair I 'ad left was fives, and 'e took about twenty-fives. I took them up and put them down at the side of 'is bed – 'e was finishing 'is prayers. "There you are, sir. Thank you, ole man." So I went downstairs an' 'ung about, cos I knew any minute I'd 'ave to go over the top. I didn't 'ave to wait long. The bell rang. Up I went, my sides burstin' with laughin'. There 'e was at the side of the bed, kickin' out like a two-year-old, like this, 'ands on the bed and kickin' out for all 'e's worth, sayin', "The slippers are no good, the Buffs are no good." An' I ses, "No more is the Rifle Brigade!" and out I bolted![13]

12   P.B. Clayton, *Gen in Four Fyttes*, p.10.
13   P.B. Clayton, *Gen in Four Fyttes*, p.12-13.

Pathos

A strong sense of the ridiculous never need harden hearts; and Pettifer, caught in a serious mood, is not to be forgotten.

'After we were comin' out from Hooge about the twelfth of May 1915, comin' along they 'appened to be shelling the town with a large gun, just seventeen minutes between each explosion. An' we were comin' out and found a little girl on the roadway. She'd been buried and blown out again – buried quick I should say, in 'er clothes, about six years old. 'It was a bit of a cemetery just there, an' I took this youngster an' rolled 'er in my overcoat an' buried 'er. 'An' I think it would be some time in '16 I told Tubby about this, an' we thought we'd look for 'er. We looked about, but we never could find it again. The place was blown to bits.'

* * *

'One day they were shellin' Pop an' I run down to the old lady – the old lady who done 'is washing – out of the back gate of the garden an' down the lane an' the 'ouses just facin'. I went down to see if the washin' was finished, an' the old lady sed it would be about another half hour if I'd call back for it, an' I said I would. There was a long report, quarter of an hour after I came away, an' I went out of the back gate, an' it 'ad been a shell; it 'ad gone clean in the old girl's 'ouse an' 'er an' 'er daughter were blown to pieces. So we never got no washin'.'

The agony of composition

The time had come for Pettifer to communicate with his wife and family.[14] The day had been staved off when he must write; but staving off has never solved a problem. Behold him, therefore, canning his part nobly, preparing the utensils of the profession of letters, drilling the ink-pot to remain alert, and seeing that the nib remains uncrossed. It was decided by public vote that a picture post card would be inadequate; it must be a letter at least – a good long letter.

After an hour, the following is composed:

Dear Sue,
I shall be home Friday or Sat.
With love to the boys,
    Gen.

14   Pettifer was not a regular correspondent. In this respect Tubby said of him: "Apart from sundry letters to my mother, composed and re-composed for weeks on end, I scarcely know his hand." Three of Pettifer's letters have survived: two to Tubby (1 June and 12 August 1916) and one to Tubby's mother (3 April 1918).

Watercolour of 'Pettifer's Den' on the 2nd floor of Talbot House.

A protest is then lodged upon the touch line that this lacks fire and verve and poignancy and eloquent descriptions of the Spring. Gen admits that there is something lacking. Again he is left alone: again an hour. The following letter is then found before him, complete without a blot and spelt correctly:

Dear Sue,
I shall be home Friday or Saturday. Give my love to the boys. Don't forget to water the sweet peas.
    Gen

Postscript

Pettifer resumed his former role upon the rebirth of Talbot House in London. When Tubby became vicar of All Hallows in 1922, 'the Gen' became jack-of-all-trades in the church and round about Tower Hill until 1951. After his death, on 16 June 1954, his ashes were placed in the crypt of the church he had served for so long.

Of his faithful companion, Tubby once said: "No man knows me so well, nor have I leant on any man so much throughout my life."

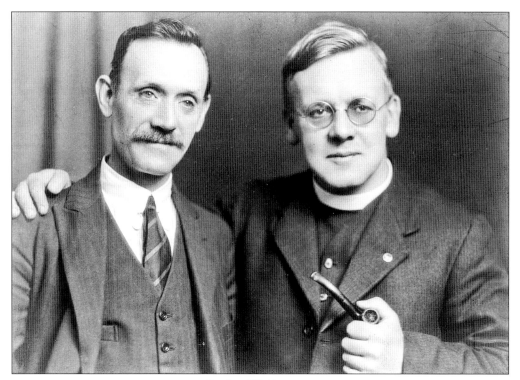

'Gen' and Tubby, 1928.

III THE CUSTOMERS

1 A Scrap of Memories by the Innkeeper

I kept a rest-house back in Poperinghe, and my customers from time to time invited me to repay their calls. In the rest-house they rested – that is, they turned to other things than war. There was less said about the war in Talbot House than probably anywhere else in Europe at the time. As a topic it had its limitations, like the weather. As a conversational opening its vagaries were of value, but no more than that; the real thing was to get relief from it, relief comic, serio-comic, educational, spiritual. Outside there were sharp words of command, feet moving together, the

TALBOT HOUSE, POPERINGHE

rumble of congested traffic, the narrow crowded pavements, the slatternly shop-windows. Inside was comfort and warmth, and light and music, and a touch of home and of the love that came out to them thence. It was only second-best, of course, but it was not make-believe; and during the three years of Talbot House in Poperinghe, let alone the six months' life of the daughter house in Ypres more than half-a-million men in tunics came in and out of the large white house that stands next to the chemist's in the Rue de l'Hôpital.[15]

* * *

NOTICE
To all members of the human race, and others who are unwise enough to enter this House.[16]

You are "for it" now. Once inside Talbot House, and there's no saying what you will have to do to get out again. You may of course be in luck's way, and out of mine.

Hundreds of men have come in and out several times, and lived to tell the tale of a peaceful hour in an armchair, with a neighbour's snores as lullaby. On the other hand, if a middle aged person in a very old tennis blazer sights you, it's all up. You will find yourself mending electric

---

15   P.B. Clayton, *Plain Tales from Flanders*, p.7-8.
16   A reference to the opening line of Chesterton's novel *The Napoleon of Notting Hill*: *"The human race, to which so many of my readers belong. ..."*

bells, tipping cues, mending lamps, or licking envelopes, before you know where your support line is. Can you sing; recite; act; conjure; debate; play chess; paint scenery; run a cinema? Even if you can't, it won't make any difference. He is always doing things he can't do. If you come from Australia, he was born there. From London, he was educated (!) there. From Hampshire, he lives there. He knows seven words of Welsh, and has even been once to Scotland.

The best thing to do is to promise him what he wants, to keep him quiet, and, quickly camouflaging yourself with a red hat band,[17] you will find him flee from you.

P.B.C.

1.1 L/Cpl. Archie Forrest – From baptism to death

Archie stands alone in my experience – no easy thing to do. He came from Blackburn,[18] where no doubt, there are others like him in the raw material, lean, quick and curly haired, with an element of fierceness in doing what they do with all their might.

His time with Talbot House was possibly six weeks of more or less daily visiting, while "P" Gas Company who were working from Poperinghe went up by night to carry their terrible cylinders into position beyond our front line. By 1918 it had been discovered that far simpler and less costly ways could be employed; light tracks for trains were run right out into No Man's Land, and trucks full of "Rogers" – as the gas cylinders were called – could thus be let off together by means of an electric-fuse cable attachment. But in the summer of 1917 these facilities were not available, and men staggered for miles under the load of a great cylinder full of the deadliest poison, with themselves and their burden exposed to every burst of shelling or machine-gun fire. The actual casualties of "P" Gas Company during the six weeks of July and the early part of August 1917 in the neighbourhood of Forward Cottage,[19] where they were working, amounted to 150 men, out of the carrying parties only 100 strong and continually reinforced; of one section, if I remember right, every man except one pioneer was a B.Sc.

After a few testing visits to Talbot House, Archie Forrest had summed up Christianity, and found it greatly to his liking; after a week he had presented himself for baptism; a month later he was confirmed, and made his first Communion; the week following *(sic)* he was killed a little past midnight at Saint-Jean, on his way back to safety.[20] That was all. Yet, as any surviving member of the company would tell you, his life during that six weeks irradiated the whole horizon of his friends, and they were many and various; Pioneers, Sappers, and even Sergeants of other sections, spoke of him with something akin to envy; even among the officers, by no means

---

17   As worn by staff officers.
18   In March 1915, Archie, a weaver by profession, enlisted in the 13th Royal Welsh Fusiliers. He transferred to the Royal Engineers the following January, seeing action at the Somme, Arras, Vimy Ridge, and Messines. It was during the Vimy fighting that Archie briefly met his father, Isaac, who was a driver with the 42nd East Lancashire Royal Horse Artillery. It was a moment of respite destined to become a treasured memory.
19   Forward Cottage, off Admiral's Road (currently Moortelweg, Wieltje) was part of the frontline stabilised following the Second Battle of Ypres.
20   Archie reportedly was hit by a sniper's bullet – the glow of the cigarette which he was smoking as he walked along may have provided the target – on 25 August. Back at home in Lancashire his mother awoke in the middle of the night and went round to her sleeping family to inquire "Which of you called me?". Archie's death is recorded as 26 August by the CWGC.

Oak chair in memory of L/Cpl. Archie Forrest, given by
his comrades of 'P' Special (Gas) Company.

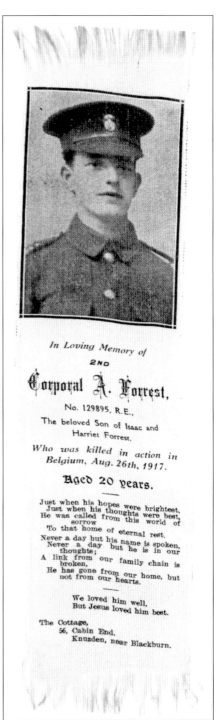

In Loving Memory of
2ND

Corporal A. Forrest,

No. 129895, R.E.,

The beloved Son of Isaac and
Harriet Forrest,

*Who was killed in action in
Belgium, Aug. 26th, 1917.*

Aged 20 years.

———

Just when his hopes were brightest,
    Just when his thoughts were best,
He was called from this world of
    sorrow
To that home of eternal rest.
Never a day but his name is spoken,
    Never a day but he is in our
    thoughts;
A link from our family chain is
    broken,
He has gone from our home, but
    not from our hearts.

———

We loved him well,
    But Jesus loved him best.

The Cottage,
    56, Cabin End.
        Knuzden, near Blackburn.

so accessible, one or two found themselves, to
their private astonishment, following in the
direction in which his whole life led. After his
death nothing would content the company but
that some gift from them in his memory should
stand for ever in the Upper Room, which he had
taught so many of them to frequent. A curious
chair, with a back contrived in such a way as to
act upon emergency as a table, was their gift to
the Chapel on his behalf. It was to serve sometimes as a credence-table, and at confirmations
as a Bishop's chair, and it stands close to the tiny
font at which he was baptized.

Archie indeed had found in Talbot House
the true birthplace of his soul.[21]

———

21   P.B. Clayton, *Plain Tales from Flanders*, p.41-43.

War widows near Lijssenthoek Military Cemetery, Poperinge – Toc H/St. Barnabas Pilgrimage, March 1923.

R.I.P.
Archie Forrest
Confirmed at Talbot House, 9 July 1917
2nd Corporal, "P" Special (Gas) Company, Royal Engineers
26 August 1917 – Age 20 – Wieltje Farm Cemetery (St. Jan – Ieper), B.12

Postscript
In the aftermath of Archie's death the family was desolate: his loss was a shadow which never went away. A portrait of him in oils done from memory by a family friend showing him in army uniform hung in pride of place in the family parlour. When Talbot House, London (Mark I) was opened in 1920, a room was endowed by a wealthy family in memory of Archie.

In March 1923, St. Barnabas Hostel and Toc H arranged a collective pilgrimage to Flanders' battlefields for the benefit of people who did not have the means to visit the graves of their loved ones. Amongst the 850 participants were Archie's mother, Harriet, and his sister Elizabeth ('Lizzie'), for whom Archie had been an inseparable companion and 'best mate' in a poor and difficult childhood. After attending a memorable service in Lijssenthoek Military Cemetery (Poperinge) on Palm Sunday, they were taken to Wieltje Farm Cemetery where they spent a few quiet moments at the graveside of Archie.

Lizzie remained devoted to her brother's memory and the Christian message of Toc H would inspire her to engineer the perfect memorial – not one in stone, but in human involvement and enthusiasm – to the mover and shaker Archie had been: a branch of the Toc H League of Women Helpers in his hometown, Blackburn.[22]

1.2 An unknown gunner – Requiem for a Friend

One summer day, in 1917, a concert of the easiest kind was being held. The sing-song some-what lagged. Volunteers from the audience were numerous; and those who volunteered most frequently were appreciated least of all.

At this stage, when I had almost reached the point of putting myself on, an unknown gunner entered the hall, and I asked him whether he could sing. He gave me an odd look; and, shrugging his shoulders, passed towards the platform. On the platform were a few pieces of scenery, among which he disappeared. A moment later he came back in full view upon the stage, and the universal genius at the piano struck up a lively tune.

The gunner now removed his tunic, and took from the pocket a tooth-brush, rag and polish tin, and sat himself cross-legged on the one stage chair. By this time the piano had died away completely, and the audience was watching and expecting the preliminary patter of a comic song. What happened was far different. A humming began to come from between the man's lips as he polished his buttons. The tune gradually took shape, most exquisitely rendered. When the air had taken hold of our minds, it reappeared clothed in words, and these were the words he sang:

> "Ther was no one like 'im, 'Orse or Foot,
> Nor any o' the Guns I knew;
> An' because it was so, why, o'course 'e went
> an' died,
> Which is just what the best men do."

By the time the first verse was sung we were spellbound. We knew that we were in the presence of a great artist. Many such had at various times found their way to Talbot House, but none so strangely as this unknown man. There were whispers of identification, but the anonymity was not withdrawn. Then he proceeded to the verse:

> "We fought 'bout a dog – last week it were –
> No more than a round or two;
> But I strook 'im cruel 'ard, an' I wish I
> 'adn't now,
> Which is just what a man can't do.

---

22   The postscript draws heavily from an unpublished article "In Memoriam Archie Forrest – Lizzie's Story" by Mrs Bernice Chitnis of London following her 2011 visit to Flanders to honour the memory of "Uncle Archie".

'E was all that I 'ad in the way of a friend,
An' I've 'ad to find one new;
But I'd give my pay an' stripe for to get the
beggar back,
Which it's just too late to do!

So it's knock out your pipes an' follow me!
An' it's finish up your swipes an' follow
Me!
Oh, 'ark to the fifes a-crawlin'!
Follow me – follow me 'ome!"

By this time we had realized something more. This man was a great artist, yes. But this thing was not art in the sense of sudden enrichment of an entertainment by a mere skill. The man was singing his soul. There had been losses in his battery, and he had come down with Kipling's immortal song[23] in his mind and found a concert which he could convert into a congregation with whose aid he might offer that amazing requiem:

"Take 'im away! 'E's gone where the best men go.
Take 'im away! An' the gun-wheels turnin' slow.
Take 'im away! There's more from the place 'e come.
Take 'im away, with the limber an' the drum.

For it's 'Three rounds blank' an' follow me,
An' it's 'Thirteen rank' an' follow me;
Oh, passin' the love o' women,[24]
Follow me – follow me 'ome!"

As he finished there was an absolute silence, the one possible tribute. The gunner rose, slipped on his tunic and came down the hall. Leaving the concert to look after itself, I pursued him. I did not ask him who he was. I do not know to this day. I only tried to thank him, as I would thank him now once more if he yet lives. In all my experience I have never known a man's soul thus shining through his art. He was in no mood for talking, and quickly disappeared into the night.[25]

1.3 Sgt. John Waller – On eternal leave

It must have been in February 1922, when I was seated in a train running from Toronto to Port Hope, reading the *Toronto Globe*, that my eye caught the announcement of a farewell party to a Canadian missionary and his wife returning to duty at Nagano, Japan. The name "Nagano" caught fire in

---

23   Rudyard Kipling's poem "Follow me 'ome", *The Seven Seas* (1896). It reflects a soldier's grief for a fallen comrade.
24   Reference to 2 Samuel, 1, 26, where David mourns Jonathan's death in battle.
25   P.B. Clayton, *Plain Tales from Flanders*, p.49-52.

my mind, and I leaned back to recollect the circumstance under which I had first heard it. In the early days of Talbot House, when the Canadians, together with the Guards, were holding the main battle-line of the Salient, Talbot House was serving a day and night purpose which made bedtime obsolete. The house nominally closed at 8 p.m. for the troops; at that time, onwards until 5 a.m., it was filled with officers going on leave. At 8 a.m. it reopened for the day's work. I slept, therefore, for the most part, in a chair in my sitting-room between 5 a.m. and 8 a.m. on mornings when there was not a Celebration of Holy Communion. On one such morning, in April 1916, I was woken by a delightful Canadian sergeant, whom I had never seen before, amused to find me asleep. His story was soon told. He had come down from the line during the night, happy in the possession of his leave warrant; but he was not, however, due for the train until the night following. When his warrant had reached Battalion Headquarters he had been on duty at Forward Cottage,[26] a listening post in advance of our

Sgt. John Waller.

trenches, where, in the shell-holes behind the fragments of an old wall, it was deadly to move in the daylight. All day long, through the rain or the sun, men on duty there could only crouch in a confined position, with a few sticks of chocolate (if they were lucky) to keep them going. But when, under the cover of dark, he had come in, he had been rewarded with his leave papers. My next inquiry was concerning his home. At that time I had little knowledge of Canada, but I was certain when I heard the name Nagano that it did not sound Canadian. I said: "Nagano? Where?" and he replied: "Japan. My father and mother are missionaries, and my brothers and I were born there." During the day that followed our friendship became firm, as it could under such conditions; though normally the space of time would have been quite inadequate for the formation of ordinary friendships between the British. We clambered up to the old Chapel together, and prayed for his father and mother, and brothers mercifully too young for the war. That night, a few hours before his leave train was due to begin the crawl down to the coast, an orderly arrived from the transport line of his battalion. This man bore a note which the Sergeant opened carelessly, thinking it to be a message of good luck or some minor thing. The brightness left his face as he read it, and was succeeded by a strange tense struggle which I could not but notice. He handed the buff slip to me without a word. It was an order from the Adjutant that his leave was postponed, owing to a court martial upon one of his men, for some minor offence, to be

26   See note 19.

held on the following day. The Sergeant was required in evidence, and his leave must be deferred. We climbed again to the Chapel and prayed in the darkness now; and in the darkness he left me to return to duty. Yet after the first shock the spirit within him set finely to self-conquest, and no violent complaint was heard. For weeks after I awaited his return; until I found that his battalion had been hard pressed in a sudden emergency, and that he himself had been killed.

This was the solemn story which the name Nagano summoned to my mind as I sat in the train approaching Port Hope. In Canada the railway telegraph system is readily available, so I wrote and dispatched a telegram to his mother and father from the next station. It caught them on the train from Toronto to Winnipeg, where the *Globe* said they would be stopping for another farewell meeting. I myself left Trinity College, Port Hope, by the next day's train for Winnipeg, and on Winnipeg station platform I met two grey-haired people. They knew my name from his last letter; but little more than that. Their train was due out for the West within the next half-hour, and we therefore sat in the waiting-room at Winnipeg and I told them the story which I have told you.[27]

R.I.P.
John C. Waller
son of John and Lydia Waller, of Nagano, Japan.
Lt., 4th Bn, Canadian Infantry (1st Central Ontario Regt.)
3 May 1917 – Age 21 – Ecoivres Military Cemetery (Fr.), VI.H.10

Guards and Canadians in the tea-room of Talbot House, 24 April 1916.

27 P.B. Clayton, *Plain Tales from Flanders*, p.55-58.

1.4 Pte. John Henry – C-in-C of Billiards

It all began with the small billiard-table, which came from Messrs. Gamage. Billiards are made for men, not men for billiards; and I had cause to regret that most seductive table before long. There was the furor of its first arrival. Then, for a week or so, the room in which it stood was inaccessible, a solid throng of hopefuls: the butt-end of the cues plying a doubtful passage. Imagine every beast owned by the Zoo given freedom to congregate, and in turn to drink out of a six-foot tank during a water famine, and you are not far from picturing the proceedings in that billiard-room. News spread, and callers multiplied. We did not feel at home with them, for they had come with one intention only. By now, the precious table was moved up for more space to the floor below the Chapel. I was not quite happy about this, since sound (like gas) will rise, and that of cannons is peculiarly penetrating. Billiards, like other games, ceased by the strict traditions of the House during family prayers; but I found that at other times the Chapel stillness suffered.

What did we do on Sundays about billiards? The solemn fact is that I put this issue (like all others) to the men most affected. They weighed the pro and con of Sunday billiards, and voted clean against it. I was amazed at this, but carried out their self-denying ordinance. A few Sunday's later two infantrymen turned up with passes from the other side of Ypres. This was their one day off, after a very rough turn of duty. They had come quite openly for billiards, to the sole English table available in Flanders. What should I say? I wavered. I told them that a general vote of the players had been taken, and that they had decided to leave the table covered every Sunday. I added that they were welcome, if they wished, to say 'this rule does not apply to two men coming, as we have come, out of the line, and for a single afternoon, which happens to be Sunday afternoon.' I left them to decide. Once more, these two men came to the unexpected

Billiard-table in the canteen, 1918.

verdict. They said, unitedly, that as the other players had decided, they would themselves abide by this decision. This humbled me a lot.

The little table prospered mightily, but proved a constant worry. Conceive of the accessories, fetched from their guardian Jimmy Moorhouse in the kitchen, and then too much required to be returned. Ponder the untipped cues, chalked by the simple process of thrusting them aloft against the plaster ceiling. Imagine, not too accurately, the emblematic language!

Now Talbot House was known to be a place free from this style of talk. Action was necessary, and on the board below I advertised for someone strong enough to act as overseer and C.-in-C. of billiards. A lithe Australian corporal, with three wound-stripes, whom I had seen about the House for some days past, came in and volunteered. I asked him for particulars. He told me he was a patient at No. 17 C.C.S.,[28] allowed out in the daytime, and at night occasionally. I answered this would suit me admirably, provided the Commanding Officer gave him a signed sanction. This he produced next day, stamped and correct, and it was duly filed with other Staff attachments in my cupboard. The cupboard was unlocked; keys were almost unknown in Talbot House. Weeks passed, and every day my good friend Corporal Henry presided over billiards. Himself no mean performer, he ruled the roost completely. I heard him do it once, and was horrified to find that his remedy for bad language was so homoeopathic that the green baize turned blue. I felt inclined to creep away and wonder, but read myself a lesson in deportment, and went and 'told him off.' He took it penitently, and checked himself and others. After that incident, he (for the first time) climbed into the Chapel. I did not welcome him. He was too raw and too uncomfortable. He took to coming often. By and by, I had a talk with him there.

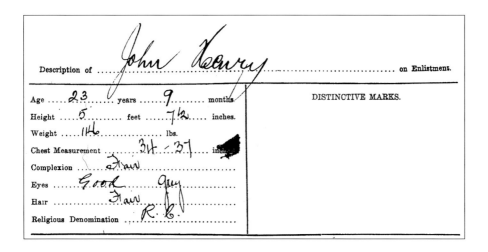

An element of mystery hung round the man. Handsome and devil-may-care, he played his part most faithfully and with a growing understanding. The House and its ideals had been Greek to him; but he was coming on. He was the Esau-type,[29] intolerant of any kind of softness. But when he met a man, he met his fellow, and measured him with promptitude for friend or foe. Australians love or hate. Then the blow fell. One autumn afternoon in '17, two military police came to the Chaplain's room. I knew and liked them both. I told them to get chaired; their answer brought me out of mine. They had come on duty for Corporal Henry, a deserter. First, for my part in this. Where was my authority for harbouring him? How came he on the Staff of Talbot House? I took my Staff file – a metal skewer pricked through a sheaf of papers – from the cupboard. The C.C.S. attachment had been torn away, as a mere scrap of it remaining proved quite clearly. I told them it was stamped and signed by the Commanding Officer. They said the stamp had possibly been 'come by,' but that the signature had been a forgery. I rang my bell for Pettifer; but Henry himself came up. He strode in his shirt-sleeves, with all the grace of movement characteristic of the man.

'You wanted something?' he began to say, and then he saw the trap. I'll not foreget his face. The two men closed with him; but his strength and desperation were such that he almost beat them back. Had he been armed – and he had a pistol in his pack upstairs – he would have killed and died. I cried out to him that I hadn't planned his capture, that I was still his friend. The handcuffs now snapped upon his wrists. He stood a prisoner, silent. Then 'May I get my coat? It's in the kitchen. I promise to come back.' His captors laughed at the idea. I went and fetched it, brokenly. The man meant much to me. I told him so, as best I could. I told him that I knew about the stolen paper. He said sadly, 'I wish I'd told you everything.' The escort took him out.

Extract from the Register of the Assistant Provost Marshal.

I never saw him again. He lies, I fancy, in some French-British cemetery. His grave may be unknown. Unknown, but not dishonoured; for a strange aftermath brought me, not 'everything,' but things I longed to hear.

His trial as a deserter was conducted in the Australian area, then down south. My part in the proceedings was spared me, first by the fact that my own ignorance, in view of his efficient forgery, was admitted; secondly, through my illness at the time.[30] His own unlikely story was found to be correct. Since he had left Australia, he had had cause to know his wife was faithless. She was now living with another man. He had been wounded twice – that also was

---

29   Esau is described as "a cunning hunter, a man of the field" in Genesis 25:27.
30   At this time Tubby was recovering from one of his periodic attacks of fever.

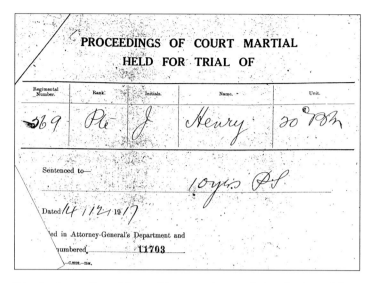

PROCEEDINGS OF COURT MARTIAL
HELD FOR TRIAL OF

Regimental Number.	Rank.	Initials.	Name.	Unit.
369	Pte	J	Henry	20 Bn

Sentenced to— 10 yrs P.S.

Dated 14 / 12 / 1917

'ed in Attorney-General's Department and

'umbered 11703

—C.2225.—25M.

quite accurate. And, in the next attack, after he heard the news, he was reported killed. Actually, he had slipped his identity disc on a dead man, and himself vanished utterly, leaving her free to marry.

They sentenced him to a long imprisonment; but when, in 1918, the Australian Corps faced the carrying of Mt. St. Quentin,[31] they sent some prisoners back to their battalions. Henry was one of these. A few days later, I had a letter from him, telling me this, and that he hoped his conduct in that attack would clear his character. No other letter followed; and some discreet inquiries led me to believe that Corporal Henry fell – a foolish word – soon after it was written.[32]

Postscript

John Henry was a boundary rider in western New South Wales, an independent type of man, strong-willed, capable and not amenable to discipline. On 20 March 1915, aged 21, he enlisted in "B" Coy, 20th Battalion A.I.F., and took part in the Gallipoli campaign prior to deployment on the Western Front. Arriving in France on 29 May 1916, he was reported wounded and missing on 3 August; later reported killed in action. In fact, he had absented himself without leave whilst his battalion was in the trenches at Pozières. Four hundred and five days later, on 12 September 1917, he was arrested by the Military Police at Talbot House. Tried by a Field General Court Martial on 14 December, he was found guilty and sentenced to 10 years penal servitude. On 22 December, he managed to escape, but surrendered himself two days later. On 4 January 1918, he was incarcerated at No. 10 Military Prison, Dunkirk. His sentence was commuted to two years imprisonment with hard labour not long afterwards. Released from prison and sent back to the front, he remained with his unit for the rest of the war. In early 1919, he was sent on an education course before embarkation at Le Havre on 4 April, returning to Australia via Liverpool where he disembarked on 4 July.

* * *

NOTICE

The good player chalks his cue before he plays, the bad player afterwards.

---

31   As part of the Allied counteroffensives in the late summer of 1918, the Australian Corps crossed the Somme river on the night of August 31 and stormed the German lines at Mont St Quentin and Péronne.

32   P.B. Clayton, *Gen in Four Fyttes*, pp.19-24.

1.5 Capt. Cecil Rushton & Capt. Tom Le Mesurier – Chivalrous knights

Comparatively few men of the R.F.C. were enabled to visit Talbot House in Poperinghe. No aerodrome was really near the town; the nearest was in front of Château Lovie,[33] but none the less, some pilots and some men managed to find their way there when off duty on ground level. We all delighted in their coming; because what they stood for seemed to bring back the days of knightly chivalry, and dissipate the dull monotony of the long struggle in the trench-line system. Moreover, many of the subalterns were transferred to the R.F.C. as the need arose, so that old friends came back in a new uniform, and talked about the land behind the enemy's line, which most of us would never live to see.

My young cousin, Tom Le Mesurier – while still in his teens – became an Acting-Major in the R.N.A.S.,[34] gaining (with much amusement to himself) two bars to a D.S.C. On May 21, 1918, he took a day off and came into Poperinghe, steering a side-car through the deserted streets; the only door in all the town which still lay open was that of Talbot House. He came inside and found me desolate indeed; for the final order had arrived early that morning, terminating the respite of three weeks which the Provost Marshal of the 2nd Army secured for Talbot House, and ordering me to close and leave that morning. This was the bitterest moment of my existence. I had petitioned for some lorries, which were, however, held up by shelling. Finally they got through, and were loaded to an accompaniment of shrapnel descending in the Square, and sent off to make their way to "Dingley Dell," our makeshift quarters outside Poperinghe. Young Tom and I were left alone to shut the front door finally. This done, I got into his side-car, and we went off to overtake the lorries. He shared with me that day the final cup of tea in Talbot House, and the first meal in Dingley Dell. Finding me gloomy and discountenanced, he spent his time talking, with even more than his essential cheerfulness, about the R.N.A.S., and of the glowing future which lay beyond the War.

On June 1, I hopped a lorry down to Dunkirk to repay the call. I had two objects: lunch with Cecil Rushton, my oldest and dearest friend in life, followed by tea with Tom. All through the years at Poperinghe, I had promised myself this excursion, but never fulfilled it. Dropping off the lorry opposite the camp of the R.A.F. Night-Flying Squadron, to which Cecil Rushton was attached, I walked into the orderly room and asked for him. The Adjutant looked curiously at me, turned to a telephone, had a short consultation with the Mess, and turned to me again, saying: "I am sorry, there is no news of him. He took the Handley Page over Bruges Dock, and nothing has been heard of them."[35] I turned away, and crossed the Dunkirk road, and blundered down towards the R.N.A.S. Camp. Here I went straight to the Mess and found the officer

33   Situated 2 miles to the NW of Poperinge, this airfield became operational in May 1917 when 21 Squadron arrived as part of the build-up for the Battle of Messines. They were joined by 23 Squadron the following month. Other units based here at various times were 29, 35, 65 and 74 squadrons.

34   Formed in July 1914, the air arm of the Royal Navy performed patrol duties over the North Sea, pioneered the use of aircraft carriers and strategic bombing. It was also responsible for the air defence of Britain until 1916. On 1 April 1918 the RNAS merged with the RFC to form the RAF.

35   During May 1918, 214 Sqn, based at Coudekerque, concentrated offensive efforts against docks, mainly Brugge, but with Oostende and Zeebrugge as alternate targets. On the night of 15/16 May four HPs were dispatched to attack the Brugge submarine bases. One failed to return. Its crew members, Major J.I. Harrison, Capt. C.G. Rushton and Lt. W.J. King were buried at Steenbrugge. Exhumed after the war, the remains were buried at Larch Wood Cemetery (Zillebeke).

Capt. Thomas Le Mesurier.

Grave of Capt. Cecil Rushton at
Steenbrugge. After the war it was
moved to Larch Wood, Zillebeke.

commanding. I introduced myself, told him of Cecil Rushton, whom we knew, and said that I had come to see young Tom Le Mesurier. We were standing on the verandah at the time; he said: "Come down the steps," and walked across in front of me to the taking-off ground. Here he found an old rigger, a real old hardened sailor with a square grizzled head, a man as toughened as a man can be. This man was sobbing unashamedly. The senior officer turned round to me and said: "This was his rigger. Le Mesurier went out on early duty, and was shot down in flames over the Nieuport line."[36]

I found another lorry back towards Dingley Dell.

R.I.P.

Cecil G. Rushton
Captain, 214th Sqdn., Royal Air Force
16 May 1918 – Age 35 – Larch Wood (Railway Cutting Cemetery), Zillebeke, IV.F.21

Thomas F. Le Mesurier
Captain, 211th Sqdn. 65th Wing, Royal Air Force
26 May 1918 – Age 21 – Dunkirk Town Cemetery, IV.A.24

1.6 General Sir Herbert Plumer – Sympathy for a footslogger

I remember very well the first time I was privileged to see Lord Plumer, and so does Pettifer. I was doing something I ought perhaps not to have been doing, scrubbing floors or something of that kind, in the upper part of Talbot House when Pettifer came rushing up to me telling me that a tremendously important General was down in the hall with a sergeant. I went downstairs hurriedly trying to find the absent parts of my military regalia. When I reached the staircase I found Lord Plumer, the Army Commander. He said to me, 'Are you Clayton?' I replied, 'Yes, Sir,' He then said, 'I have got this sergeant here and I want you to look after him for the night, and please remember that he is my guest.' When Lord Plumer had gone I turned to the sergeant and said, 'How did this happen?' The sergeant

---

36   Le Mesurier and his observer, 2nd Lt. R. Lardner, left at 10.10 am. Taking a new machine on a test flight, they crossed the enemy lines before encountering difficulties. On their return, the aircraft reportedly broke up 20 feet above Pervijze. Lardner died at the scene, Le Mesurier shortly afterwards. Three days before his death he had been recommended for promotion to Squadron Commander.

said to me, 'Well, it's like this, padre, my leave came through and I had a pretty desperate time of it walking and had gone almost as far as I could when I saw Lord Plumer. He said to me, 'Where are you going, lad?' I said, 'I am going on leave, Sir,' The Army Commander then said, 'You have had enough walking for the time, take a ride in my car; I think I know of a place where I can put you for the night.'

1.7 Major Harold Philby – Thoughtful for his men

Early in 1916, I first met Harold Philby. I did so with interest, as I had often heard of him. "A rising soldier" was the official attitude. "A good friend to padres" was a verdict which caught my mind. A few months later he was second in command, and then, for a while, Commanding. He was a topic with the "Cat and Cabbages" (The York and Lancs.) and their well-being his single motive for work, and thought behind it, and prayer behind that again.

Major Harold Philby, 5 August 1914.

In March, 1916, I heard from him: a terse, half-humorous remonstrance. Four men, one of them his own old platoon sergeant, had been before Christmas half-prepared for their Confirmation. Then the Brigade padre had been transferred, and the men disappointed. Philby had come across this fact, and could not tolerate it. The men must fulfil their aspiration; and therefore, as they knew very little as yet of the ordered Christianity of the Prayer book, he had them sent to the transport lines, whence they were to report to me daily for instruction until their Confirmation could be completed. I was to see to this matter without fail. They could be spared from the Line meanwhile.

So the four came to me daily, led solemnly in by Sergeant Hazelhurst; and I did my best with their difficulties. Ten thousand difficulties don't make one Single Doubt, and in some three weeks they were ready and I proud of my pupils. On May 17 they were, with a hundred more, presented to Bishop Gwynne, and confirmed in the Upper Room.

That evening, when the others had perforce dispersed, I had succeeded (by intrigue with the Transport Officer) in keeping them as my guests. We were to have one last class, in preparation for their first Communion on the morrow; after which they were to go straight back and up the line to their battalion. Supper being ended, and the House otherwise empty, we climbed once more into the Chapel at about 9.15 p.m. We began upon our final class, gathered in a knot of consecrated friendship before the side altar. After a while I stood and turned to talk with them.

Suddenly through the further window, a low semi-circle, I saw the horizon glow with flame and fury, as against the dull monotony of star-shells which marked the sullen curve of the Salient night by night. Something on a narrow sector was happening, and happening hard. We all walked towards the window to watch, and as we stood there, I felt Sergeant Hazelhurst's iron grip upon my arm. "I don't like it, Sir," he said, "I don't like it." It must have been about that moment that Harold Philby died.

We did not know it till the morning. After their first Communion at 6.30, and after breakfast, they were saying good-bye in their bluff Yorkshire way, when a man came down from the transport lines to tell us. It had been a raid, and a costly one. The men were wanted at once; – and Major Philby? – Yes. Then Hazelhurst broke down. Philby had been his subaltern, and a subaltern is his first Sergeant's son in the spirit. So this great dalesman stood there, denouncing and arraigning the God he had just agreed to serve, of whose sacred food he had just partaken, whose love and strength were his. I honoured him for his outcry and for his anger, and I think God did so too. So they left me, three scared men and one outraged great-heart, and I have never seen them again.

R.I.P.

Harold P. Philby

Major, 2nd Bn York and Lancaster Regiment

17 May 1916 – Age 28 – Hop Store Cemetery (Vlamertinge), I.A.16

1.8 Capt. Marshall Webb – A Tormented Spirit

This is the story of Marshall; inaccurate, no doubt, in detail; for my friendship with him, while as deep as with any, was not the kind that asked the name of his school or the comfort of his upbringing. He was, I think, within the first half-dozen officers to discover the true nature of Toc H.[37] He was then a Captain in the Divisional Signals, a Regular, well ahead of his promotion, for I suppose his age was a little more than twenty. He had won the M.C. a few months before I joined the Division. He was still revelling in the war, which was to him little else than a rough amusing football match, exactly suited to displaying his ardent Irish spirits at their highest. He was popular in the best way both above and below, and – what was most difficult of all – with his own subalterns, one of whom I remember especially for his almost absurd fidelity to his leadership.

I did not think at the start of it that Marshall had depth behind. He had learnt the code of the present generation, which regards a "heart upon sleeve" as the supreme indecency. The first I knew of the hinterland of his character was contained in a letter in which he writes at length on the problem as he saw it – the eternal problem – of fortuitous preservation: why one should be taken and another left. His own mind, as expressed in his letter, was clear that, whatever the meaning of death, unsought security must compel very serious thought about the future. He put it to me that it would be right to challenge those who came through more than any other set of men who ever had been through anything, to justify their existence; and that if he was to be

---

37   Capt. Marshall William Treherne Webb of Kilmore, Nenagh, Ireland (6th Divisional Signals Company, RE) signed the Visitors' Book on 18 February 1916 and the Communicants' Roll at Easter 1916.

thus challenged, he himself would be inclined to reply that the bill was a true one, and his life no longer his own. He would therefore be prepared, if he came through, to try to find some work for God, not merely to prevent another war, but in the wider service of His Kingdom.

This letter was passed from hand to hand, in confidence, both among many of my fellow-chaplains and others more highly placed at home. It was the idea here framed which force forward in many minds the Service Candidates' issue which I had sketched, as a theory only, in the *Challenge* of April 1915.[38]

After this letter, others went to and fro, all interspersed with visits and long talks; until, a few months later, his name was definitely entered on the list of Service Candidates. By this time he was on the Somme, and beginning, so I heard, to lose a little of that light-heartedness which, coupled with his fine soldiering, had been so wonderful an attribute. The iron was beginning to enter into his soul, and the sheer tragedy of war was threatening to engulf him.

By Easter 1917 he was, I think, a Major of Signals, attached to a Corps Staff, and working sleeplessly to perfect his signals for the great battle which was immediately to succeed the Feast of the Resurrection.[39] On the second or third day of the highly successful operations he came, unsummoned, to his G.O.C., saluted, and announced with utter seriousness that he had just come down from the line, and that it was his intention to cease to operate the Signal Service from noon that day. The General, who must have well deserved his post, asked him quietly to repeat what he had said; as he was not sure that he had heard correctly. Marshall did so, explaining that everyone who went to see the present state of the action at close quarters, the hell that had already been let loose, and the further hell inevitably to follow if his Signals did their work, must come at once to the conclusion that at all costs the thing must cease. A truce must be arranged; and, a truce once made, he was well assured that neither side would be persuaded by any politicians to renew the war. He added that, before he broke the Signals, he had seen that his duty was to report to the Chief under whom his service for the last three weeks had been performed. He was there for him to do with him what he wished, but obey he could no further.

The General, whose name I have never known – I heard this part of the story from Marshall himself – stands finely in my mind. He told him he was quite plainly overstrained and did not know what he was saying; and no wonder, considering the service he had rendered and the almost entire absence of sleep and food which had been his condition for at least the last few days. He would send for the Medical Officer attached to Corps Headquarters and report Marshall sick, and nothing more, giving him whatever time he needed to recuperate, and return to his senses and his service. Nothing whatever should be said about what had passed between them. Marshall told me that he was thrilled by this generosity; and, to save himself from breaking down under the kindness of it, declined it roughly, swore that he was not ill, that his mind was clear and his purpose firm. The war was wrong, and he would gladly give his life to end it. The General, still master of himself, and knowing that he had seen him early on the Easter Sunday, suggested that the Corps Chaplain should be called in. This was done, and the Chaplain tried, poor fellow, to do his best proving once again the justice of our Cause. Marshall told me, in a lucid moment later, that this was the most appalling agony of it all. At last, he asked the General to send away the Chaplain, and when this was done surrendered to

38   See Part 1, note 122.
39   The Battle of Arras (9 April to 16 May 1917).

the doctor. The doctor, after a cursory examination, decided he was shell-shocked, dispatched him down the line, first in an ambulance to a C.C.S. and thence by train to the Base. In both hospitals Marshall's power of self-control gave way utterly. The sight of the suffering, which he felt was due in one respect at least to his late branch of the service, well-nigh maddened him. He cried, "My God, my God, my work!" until he had to be separated altogether, and placed so far as might be out of earshot. From the Base he was sent to England, and kindly treated wherever he went. From this stage onwards this part of my story is hazy, for I never received from him a clear account of it.

I gathered, however, that after some three months he was – physically, at least – in some measure restored. He then sent in his papers; and in fear, imaginary or actual, of recruitment under the Compulsory Service Scheme he fled to his home in Ireland. There his mental health again grew serious. He had intervals of clear thinking, during which he sometimes wrote to me, but some of his letters, even then, began to be unmeaning.

In December 1920 his mother told me that he had been moved to London, and that she was seeing him daily at a private mental hospital at Putney Hill. She warned me what to expect, but no warning could have prepared me for what I found: the ghastliest parody imaginable of the man whom I had known and loved, utterly broken in physique, laughing sometimes eerily at nothing, sobbing with a startling suddenness, refusing food and drink.

He knew me at once, and asked with plaintive eagerness for news of Talbot House. His questions were intelligible, but his mind could scarcely hold the simplest answer. Staggering from his chair, at one stage, he drew me to the farthest part of the room, where was a child's desk with a seat attached. On it he threw himself, and feverishly seizing some scraps of scribbling paper and some stumps of coloured chalk proceeded to draw – that is, to scratch – a series of coloured lines; explaining all the while the trees and houses he thought he drew, and giving me, in a few minutes, four or five of these terrible scribblings, to be, as he said, pictures for the new House,[40] as he had no money to give.

Then, having been prompted beforehand to do so, if I could, I tried to fall in with his now happier mood, and urged him slyly to drink to the health of Toc H in the egg-flip which lay untasted and rejected by him. With care and cozening, by drinking myself alternately, I succeeded in inducing him to swallow some of it. Indeed, so successful was I, in this matter only, that a few days later an old member of the House, then seeking work, was set to be his guardian and companion for these last few weeks. Again and again this pathetic toasting of Toc H worked as a momentary talisman, and to the end the very name of the House was the only one to which his mind would respond. Broken, self-starved, and mad beyond dispute, he died on 9th January 1922.[41]

2 Some Reminiscences by Talbotousians

2.1 "HIM"

I was not very well acquainted with Poperinghe at the time, and I just dropped in to enjoy the hospitality of Talbot House. I went upstairs to the writing room, and had hardly got as far as

---

40   Talbot House, London.
41   P.B. Clayton, *Plain Tales from Flanders*, pp.27-33.

Tubby, 1915.

"Dear Mother," when the door opened, and a smiling figure in a black garment entered. With one hand on my shoulder and the other rubbing his eye, HE announced the evening service, after which there would be something else in the Lecture Room. I felt the hand being withdrawn from my shoulder, the door opened and closed again, there was a cheery word of recognition to somebody outside – and the other two members of H.M. Army in the room looked at one another and smiled.

"Thats HIM," said West Yorks to me, "HIM all over."

"HIM? Who? I enquired. "I'm a stranger here you know."

"Oh, are you?" said West Yorks, "then you don't know HIM I suppose."

"Well, that's HIM," said West Yorks again, "and I bet before long, he knows you, and you know him. He's got a way with him, he has. I don't know what the proper name for it is, but he makes you like him, if you can compree what I mean. I believe its because he's always got a smiling face. He runs this place, you know, and I never saw a chap put in so much time or work in all my life. He gives us something different every night practically. Last night, for instance, he had got some officer pal of his to give a lecture on 'round the world with a steam roller' or something. I forget the exact title. All I know is that I could not go, and I've heard that the lecture was "it". Then to-night, as he said, there will be a whist drive.

"Did you see that notice in the Hall about the Debate, when you came in?" went on West Yorks. "HE goes and acts as Speaker and generally keeps order. Last Wednesday HE took a box of cigars with him, and everybody who made a speech received a smoke. (Fine way of teaching you to speak in public you know). I remember very well, he asked somebody to get up and try to make a silly speech, as all the others had been so good. Somebody did, and I'm blowed if HE didn't go and give him two cigars for it. Thats HIM all over. I have known him get chaps to speak – chaps who before had hardly realised that they had a tongue in their mouths."

"You don't see much of him on Thursdays he goes up the line somewhere I believe. Proves what I just said about the time and work he puts in."

"On Friday he has some Shakespeare business up in his room. I went once just to see what it was like, but I always go now. He tells you all about the play before you start, you know, and that makes it so much easier. You each take a character, and – well its gone eight o'clock before you know you've started."

"Saturday night he has a discussion, up in his room. Just lately it's been on how Army Chaplains can improve their work. Just as if HE wants any telling how to go about his job as a Chaplain! Why, the other Sunday night I heard him offer to give any chap a lift as far as Wipers. Practical chaplaincy, I call that."

"When you come here to Church on Sunday, it makes you feel like being at home, if you've got any feelings at all. I can't describe this part of the business. I have not got the gift of the gab like some chaps. All I can advise you to do, is to come and see for yourself. Meanwhile, I must get on with my letter."

"Thanks, chummy" I said. "HE must be a wonderful man."

"He is" answered West Yorks briefly.

"And isn't West Yorks right?"[42]

2.2 Capt. Philip Gosse – Conspiracy for Good

In the autumn of 1916 Capt. Philip Gosse, a medical officer with the 69th Field Ambulance, was responsible for the evacuation of the sick and wounded from the front line to White Mill Dressing Station at Vlamertinge.[43] He was billeted in a Poperinge convent when the following incident occurred:

One day while we were at the Pension des Bénédictines at Poperinghe, Clayton came to see me on an urgent and serious matter. We had not met since 1914, although we used to see a good deal of each other before the War, when our homes were only a few miles apart in the New Forest. He had come to tell me about a deserter who had appeared at Toc H, and he wanted to discuss with me what should be done about him. It was nothing extraordinary for a deserter to go to Clayton, for he was the recognized friend and confessor of all soldiers who were down on their luck or in need of help or advice. When he first saw him Clayton failed to recognize the scared-looking young soldier, but on hearing his name remembered a boy who was an orphan

---

42   N.N., printed in a wartime number of *The Nutshell*.

43   Subsequently appointed Second Army "Rat Officer", Gosse carried out research on infectious diseases and rats. He was also a keen naturalist, trapping rare mammals, practising taxidermy and shipping stuffed examples to the Natural History Museum. His wartime recollections, *Memoirs of a Camp-Follower*, were published in 1934 and later reissued as *A Naturalist Goes to War* (1942).

Execution post in the courtyard of Poperinge Town Hall. Eight men are known to have been executed here. Picture taken by Camille Battheu.

and had been brought up by two ladies in very reduced circumstances who lived in the New Forest.

It seemed that at the age of sixteen or under the lad had enlisted, and soon afterwards was sent out to France to the trenches. He had been with his battalion nearly a year, during which time he had been blown up and buried by shells, and seen his friends killed and wounded, until at last, broken in spirit and sick in body, he had bolted. There was no getting away from it, the lad had deserted. Clayton took me to see the boy at Talbot House, where we found a scared, pale, trembling youth, far more fitted for a hospital than a battlefield.

It was clear that if something was not done about it the wretched lad would be court martialled for desertion and stand a very good chance of being shot. Instead the two conspirators arranged a plot.

I admitted the deserter into our dressing-station as a case of marked debility and shell shock, and put him to bed, where he slept twelve solid hours.

The difficulty was what to do next. After much discussion, a medical report was made out stating that we had found Private H- wandering about, that he was not responsible for his actions, and that he had been admitted forthwith to the ambulance, to await despatch to a hospital at the base. The plot was successful, and the lad at last got back to England, from whence he ought never to have been sent.[44]

2.3 Sister Alison Macfie – A memorable visit

The year 1916 found two of us nursing at a big Belgian Red Cross hospital in the one corner of Belgium which remained free. Here at La Panne King Albert and his Queen lived in a villa on the outskirts, and the Hôtel de l'Océan, then standing alone among the sand dunes, became the central building of a large hospital of which the greater part consisted of huts. The hospital was under the direction of Col. Depage, who was "Médecin en Chef" and a well-known surgeon in Brussels, with an English Matron and a large staff of Belgian and British sisters and nurses: and

44   Philip Gosse, *Memoirs of a Camp-Follower*, p.102-103.

here Queen Elisabeth of the Belgians came daily to do the dressings of some of the patients, to the great encouragement and happiness of all.

In the spring of 1917 reliefs were required for another small Belgian hospital near Poperinghe, where the nurses were badly in need of long overdue leave. My cousin and I found ourselves trundling along over the rough roads in a Red Cross car, proud possessors of "laissez-passers" from the Armée Belge which took us into the British section of the line, and of special permits from the Adjutant-General of the British Armies in France, allowing us to proceed to Poperinghe "within the area occupied by the British Army" and to stay there for a specified period. We were tremendously thrilled to be for a time among the British units, and close to the heroic defenders of the Salient of Ypres.

The Hôpital Elisabeth[45] was situated in a field behind Château Couthove, a few kilometres from Poperinghe. The lane leading to the hospital is easily called to mind as on one corner was the Military Laundry and on the other the De-lousing Station. I shall never forget a visit we paid to the laundry and the sight of large heaps of socks in every stage of decay being turned over by two old women, who picked out any which were capable of further use. The hospital had military and civilian wards, and a small maternity ward. Our ward was filled with old men who, with their wives, had refused to leave their homes until they were bombed out of them.

A side-line of the Hôpital Elisabeth was the keeping going of the lace-making industry. The Lace Car used to go out every day, taking the thread to the skilled lace-makers who remained in the area, and collecting their work when finished.

The Easter Festival came while we were at Couthove, and we asked if we could possibly attend an English service. We were therefore taken by ambulance into Poperinghe on Easter morning and there deposited outside the big iron-work doors of Talbot House in the Rue de l'Hôpital. I have a hazy recollection of many people about the place, as we were conducted up the stairs to the upper floors. I do remember very distinctly, however, that on climbing up the steep stair to the Upper Room and on reaching the level of the floor with my head, I looked around and saw nothing but a sea of very muddy boots and khaki puttees, all much the same in colour. There had been services going on continuously since dawn, and still the Chapel was crowded. Room was made for us, and we knelt before that sacred Bench beside men for whom this was a rare and deeply valued opportunity in the dark and dangerous life of the trenches round Ypres. I can still feel that atmosphere of tense attention, as row after row of worshippers went forward in response to the divine invitation. When we came down from the Upper Room we found the Padre, who had taken the service greeting the congregation as it stood about in the hall or vanished into the garden or out into the street. Some, like ourselves, being newcomers, were specially welcomed and filled in the slips of paper which constituted the Talbot House Communicants' Roll. That was my first visit to Talbot House, and my first encounter with the "Innkeeper", Tubby.[46]

*   *   *

45   As the hospital in Château D'Hondt (see Part 1, note 72) in Poperinge was more and more vulnerable to enemy shelling and aerial bombing, new hospital wards were erected in the grounds of Château Couthove from early 1916 onwards. The first patients arrived in July of that year.

46   A.B.S. Macfie, *The Curious History of Toc H Women's Association, The First Phase, 1917-1928*, pp.2-7. In 1919, Alison Macfie joined the first Toc H Executive Committee and in 1922 founded the Toc H League of Women Helpers.

From left to right: Alison Macfie, R.A.S.M., Dorothea Macfie, at Couthove, April 1917.

Talbot House Women

Sister Mary Dorothy Allen	Q.A.I.M.N.S.R.
Sister Ethel Webb-Johnson	Q.A.I.M.N.S.R.
Sister Katherine Evelyn Luard	Q.A.I.M.N.S.R.
Ella J.V. Maclaverty	F.A.N.Y
Staff Nurse Dorothy France	Q.A.I.M.N.S.R.
Sister Eva Rose Stapleton	Q.A.I.M.N.S.R.
Sister Annie Dorothea Macfie	V.A.D.
Sister Alison B.S. Macfie	V.A.D.

T̲.̲ ̲ ̲ ̲oT HOUSE CHAPEL (C of E)

Communicants Roll.

Easter 1917

Communicants are asked to fill in this paper & leave it for entry on the Register, which has now been kept practically complete for two years. The little crosses which those on the Roll have always received, given to them by the Infants' Sunday School of St: Mary's portsea.

Alison B.S. Macfie   No

V A D   Regt :

ss *Rowton Hall Chester*

P. B. CLAYTON,
Chaplain.

TALBOT HOUSE CHAPEL (C of E)

Communicants Roll.

Easter 1917

Communicants are asked to fill in this paper & leave it for entry on the Register, which has now been kept practically complete for two years. The little crosses which those on the Roll have always received, are given to them by the Infants' Sunday School of St: Mary's portsea.

Name *A. Dorothea Macfie* No

Rank *V-A D.*   Regt :

Home Address *Ladies' Army & Navy Club London W.*

P. B. CLAYTON,
Chaplain.

Sisters Mary Dorothy Allen and Ethel Webb-Johnson at Talbot House, April 1916.

Sister K.E. Luard

Sister K.E. Luard, R.R.C. and Bar is one of the few nurses who made their way to Talbot House. When I first went to France, I found her at Le Treport, and had the joy of working with her there. Then she went up the line and specialized in a peculiar post, as dangerous at it was devoted. She had charge of Advanced Casualty Clearing Stations, set up before each Battle area in turn; and for the next three years worked nearer to the line than many men, and saved more lives thereby than any one can reckon. Her hospitals in the Salient were at Brandhoek and at Elverdinghe; and both were shelled and bombed – no doubt by accident; for troops and guns and dumps lay all around them. Yet the risk was worth the running; for the presence of her unit with its marvellous equipment and magnificent team-spirit meant that men who would have died of their wounds on a longer journey, were succoured and saved by immediate operations, conducted on the fringe of the battle itself. Miss Luard is the only woman who came *down* the line to reach Talbot House. Very few surviving men served in more constant danger.[47]

(P.B. Clayton)

47   Luard's *Diary of a Nursing Sister on the Western Front 1914-1915* was published anonymously in 1916. It was followed in 1930 by *Unknown Warriors* (Chatto & Windus, London) which contains extracts of her letters.

2.4 *Lt. John Nicholson – In Spite of Himself*

One of the jolliest feelings I know is to find that you haven't utterly forgotten how to do some-thing you've not done for years. There's a subtle moral value, for instance, in the discovery that you can still play indifferent billiards; your very miss-cue has a precious personal flavour. You remember that, somewhere tucked away under the everlasting khaki and the eternal sameness of badges and numerals, is a thing called "me," which is somehow different from all the other things called "you." One of the best turns you can do for a man is to give him a chance of expe-riencing this feeling. It keeps him alive.

That is what Talbot House was always doing. Books once familiar nodded from their shelves, reminding you, with comforting flattery, that you were still part of their world. A deep chair almost embraced you – and you woke with a start, rubbing the dreams from your eyes. There's a wealth of solace for the *mind* in a real chair, a sense of possession which is almost regal. These things are symbols. They were a real part of the scheme; they helped you to feel that you were not just a cog in the machine of war, but a person with likes and dislikes, a standard of comfort, and, oddest of all, a mind! In their degree they, too, ministered consolation.

There's nothing like a debate for shaking off mental cramp. To an old hand, condemned for years to the silence of the ranks or the boredom of shouting phrases which you mayn't vary by a hair's breadth, it is almost a fierce joy. There's a moment of horrid trembling at the knees when you first rise, and then you plunge headlong. Happy is he who, after a few fumbling sentences, falls unconsciously into his stride, and dear to his heart is the applause with which a generous audience rewards the effort, however "footling." This, too, we owed to Talbot House.

It was not of set purpose that I found myself pledged to stop a gap. I had been gazing absent-mindedly at the announcement of a debate, on which the opposer's name had been newly erased – even debates must yield to the necessities of war. Suddenly I felt a pressure on my arm, kindly, persuasive, but infinitely compelling. Someone suggested – oh! so tactfully – that I was exactly the person he was in search of, and hinted that I might yet save a difficult situation. It's horribly "intriguing" to be wanted as an individual and not just as "one other ranks." There's a subtle flattery about it which scatters objections and modesties, like the paving-stones of the Grande Place before the snub and solid nose of an 8-inch "A.P." Of course, I yielded. Can you show me a man who didn't? Two days later, as I crawled self-consciously through the ever-open door, I'd have given a week's pay to get out of it. My head was spinning like a top; my knees were a striking illustration of the "make-and-break" action of the armature of a Service "buzzer." Thoughts I had none.

It consoled me a little to find that the debate was in the open air. The chairman's "Order! order!" produced a horrid silence. My opponent, calm, confident, persuasive, piled up argument upon argument. My brain reeled. I covered an old envelope with frenzied jottings in a vain attempt at coherence. All too soon he sat down, smothered in applause. I heard my own name. I rose, clutching the arm of my chair.

The imps that had taken possession of me did a war-dance on my brain – a crew of merry rebels. I swallowed vigorously – and plunged. I shall never know what I said. My opponent afterwards compared my effusion to "a séance of Mrs. Besant"![48] I don't know whether that was meant as a compliment or a protest …

---

48   Annie Beasant (1847-1933), a prominent British theosophist, sought to understand the mysteries of the universe and the bonds that unite it with humanity and the divine.

The war-dance stopped, and I sat down. The rest of the evening is indistinct. I have a vision of a hundred men, at a word of command from the chairman, flocking over to my side of the House, whether with intent to mob me, or to give me much-needed support, I could hardly say.

I reached home safely. Next day people came and asked to borrow books about it. I assured them that for years I'd read nothing but *London Opinion* nor at best *John Bull*.[49] They looked a little hurt. I hope I was nice to them. They wouldn't tell me what I had said. That, patient* (impatient) reader, is the most accurate account I can give of an event which will always be a mystery to me. On one point I am clear – in my immeasurable debt to Talbot House, I must include a most remarkable experience.

*   *   *

Perhaps, for the honour of the House, I should add a word of explanation. I had not tasted that evening of the waters of forgetfulness, but the night before I had unexpectedly been treated to a double dose of T.A.B.[50]

*Strike out word inapplicable.

2.5 Rfm. Donald Cox – "The Witness of a Wayfarer to Talbot House"

FIRST GLIMPSE
>   Voices of many soldiers,
>   And plenteous light;
>   Warmth, comfort and a shelter
>   Out of the night.
>   How everyone seems happy,
>   And all their faces bright.

THE STAIRWAY
>   Oh, pretty painted lady
>   That looks out from yon frame,
>   You're more to me than canvas;
>   More than an artist's name.
>
>   There's something in your smile, dear,
>   That calls to me to come;
>   You grace my mother's table
>   At home! At home!

Donald Cox.

---

49   *London Opinion* and *John Bull* were two popular periodicals of the day.
50   Nicholson's account was published as an appendix to Tubby's *Tales* (1919).

THE BALCONY[51]

This is no balcony above the blue
Soft lapping waters of a still lagoon;
Where maidens wonder if their lads be true,
And will come soon.

Nor from the ground does Romeo's loving song
Thrill the night air to tell his Juliet
That though true lovers' paths be hard and long,
He'll not forget.

More beautiful is this. Those few green trees,
Among whose branches vagrant breezes roam,
Tell of grey towns, green fields and sparkling seas,
That men call Home.

THE LIBRARY

Behold! all ye who want companions fair
For half a day, a day, perhaps a week,
Enter and take your choice, for here you find
The very book (or books) your soul doth seek
Love you far shores? here's tales of distant lands;
Or incident? here's history to your hands.
Or do you love the men who nobly live?
Biographies shall satisfaction give;
Fiction, to lose yourself a quiet hour;
Training, to give your body grace and power;
Poetry, with her poppied embrace;
Religion, to give your spirit grace;
Oh! all you men who recreation seek
Come, choose your boon companion for a week.

THE CHAPEL

Here is a quiet room!
Pause for a little space;
And in the deepening gloom
With hands before thy face,
Pray for God's Grace.

Let no unholy thought
Enter thy musing mind;
Things that the world hath wrought –

---

51   A reference to the Canadian Lounge, see p. 268.

Unclean – untrue – unkind –
Leave these behind.
Pray for the Strength of God,
Strength to obey His plan;
Rise from your knees less clod
Than when your prayer began,
More of a man.

FINIS

Refreshment, rest and cheer for all those men
Who hapless roam,
And over all – a touch of sanctity –
A breath of home.[52]

Charcoal preliminary sketch for oil painting *The Conquerors* (Canadian War Museum), presented to Talbot House by war artist Eric Kennington in 1931.

---

52   These poems, composed in 1916 by Rfm. Samuel Donald Cox, 2nd London Rifle Brigade (56th Division), first appeared in *The Direct Hit*, the divisional journal. They were reprinted in *Tales of Talbot House* (1919).

Part 4

Beyond the Walls

***

I SLUMMING

1 An outpost of Talbot House – Major Hugh Higgon

The bounds of Poperinghe were not the bounds of Talbot House.

It would, perhaps, be accurate to say that the T.H. atmosphere was strongest in and around the ancient town, but wherever one might be in the salient a man, if he so desired, could get a whiff of its healthy gas.

Me and my battery were first subjected to an attack of T.H. gas on a certain Sunday in September, 1916.

That well-known figure, the incumbent of Talbot House, in the course of his wanderings, had buttonholed a gunner Q.M.S. in a waggon line near Vlamertinghe. "Would the Q.M.S. get a few men together for service on the following Sunday – just a voluntary service to be held under the lee of a hedge. He knew what was meant, didn't he?"

The Q.M.S., being a man of action, went to the adjutant of the brigade, with the result that at 2.30 p.m. of a hot Sunday afternoon a brigade church parade of "all ranks that could be spared" was held in the waggon lines.

For nearly an hour we waited in the hot sun until, patience exhausted, we became more and more un-Christian in our thoughts, and our attitude, from being at least neutral, became distinctly hostile towards all padres, and to this one in particular.

About 3.25 a perspiring, rotund, and somewhat confused cleric arrived – cheerful in spite of the black looks of the congregation – and the service began.

As it proceeded, most of us felt that there was something about this service that one too often misses in the ordinary church parade – an indefinable homeliness, a sort of genuine friendliness – and we wanted another, but, *not* a compulsory service.

No more parade services were held, but from that Sunday onwards for the better part of a year the batteries of that brigade received the help and felt the influence of Talbot House even to the furthest of limits of the parish, and, if the truth be told, outside the parish altogether.

If you wend your way down the Vlamertinghe-Ypres road for about three-quarters of a mile and then look to your left, you will see in the middle of that dreary wilderness a cluster of farm

This army map of 1916, 'won' from 162nd Heavy Battery, R.G.A., was put up in the hall of Talbot House. Thousands of muddy fingers left ever so many marks and still show the places most frequented by the troops. Ieper is completely worn away. The curved front line is clearly marked off, and also Poperinge, the most popular place of rest and relaxation, disappears under the dirty fingerprints.

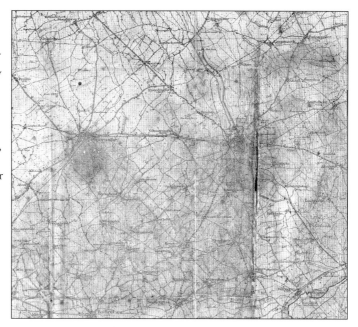

141st Heavy Battery R.G.A., January 1918.

Ypres asylum, picture taken by Camille Battheu.

buildings in tolerably good repair. This is or was "Cat Farm",[1] the then habitat of the H.-Q. of the 141st (East Ham) Heavy Battery.

There, every Thursday night, P.B.C. held a church service in the old barn and afterwards talked to the men, and every Friday morning he held a Communion service in a wonderful little chapel fitted up in the granary; and from thence he went to the Ypres asylum (then tenanted by a detached section of the battery), where another short service took place.

Who can tell the value of those simple and homely services? I am sure few of us will forget them.

From this battery, P.B.C. gradually extended his sphere of activitiy to other units in the brigade, and, though it was seldom that the gunners could get back to Poperinghe, when they did have the opportunity of a visit to Talbot House, they all felt sure of a warm welcome and a kind word from a true friend.

Several of the officers of 141st Battery went off to take command of other batteries, and wherever they went, provided they remained in the salient, there the indefatigable padre was sure to follow them, and their new batteries were gathered in to the ever-increasing flock of Talbot House.

In May, 1917, after thirteen months in the line, 141st Battery went out to rest at Wissant, near Calais – thither we were followed by P.B.C. – back again to the salient at the end of May, in action at Reigersburg Château, thence to Kruisstraat, and finally to Dormy House at Zillebeke for the July 31 "push". Wherever we went we never lost touch with our padre.

Towards the end of September, 1917, the battery, after considerable rough handling by the Boche, left the salient, and, except for a few days at the end of the summer of 1918, did not return; but many of its members have kept up correspondence with our wonderful little chaplain. They still feel his influence, and remember with gratitude his visits – visits made unfailingly,

---

1   The farm owed its name to Charles Decat, who resided there in 1914. Subsequently known as *Leeward Farm*, and so marked on trench maps, it was situated along 'The Sleeper Road,' a planked thoroughfare that ran parallel to the famous Ypres Road.

This Crucifix accompanied Tubby on his journeys to all parts of the front.

sometimes under shell fire, sometimes during a gas bombardment; services held now in a barn, now in a dug-out, once on the sands at Wissant, and occasionally in a gun-pit.[2]

*   *   *

I remember well how you used to come to Cat Farm with your portable cinema on a Wednesday night. And how we enjoyed the pictures (when it worked), and most important, the following morning when four or five of us would receive Holy Communion at your hands in the old loft at the farm. I often realise now what a great help that Service was to me, a lad of 19 …

(N.N., 141st Heavy Battery, R.G.A.)

2 A celestial breakfast – Rev. P.B. Clayton

The scene here set is a farm unpleasantly adjacent to the crossroads at Brielen. The date is something in the spring of 1916; the time of day is breakfast; the actors first discovered are a breakfast-party – reading from left to right – of the redoubtable Major of 141 Heavy Battery, Royal Garrison Artillery, the senior instrumentalist of six emphatic pieces of ordnance – each designed to throw a 60-pounder shell seven miles on any object specified or unspecified. Three junior officers were also present; the adjutant and two subalterns, one a new acquisition, rather ill-at-ease and consequently clumsy. Another man was apparently a chaplain by profession, by no means ill-at-ease, in actual fact enjoying himself hugely with a sausage, bacon and two fried and sizzling eggs, recently wafted hitherward by the magic hand of Bombardier Hammond. They now reposed upon a stout enamel plate, itself secure upon the Mess-table.

    The Mess table in early life was a barn door, or something of the kind, which, during its transformation, has received much soap and elbow-grease – the surface made perfect with a table-cloth composed of the Times newspaper. This reading-matter is sometimes attractive when conversation languishes at meals. The butter-dish, for instance, but half conceals the Births, the marmalade the Marriages; the tea-pot calls attention with a sooty ring, when lifted into

2   Higgon's account was published as an appendix to Tubby's *Tales* (1919).

Charcoal preliminary sketch of a field kitchen by Eric Kennington.

action, to prices in Mincing Lane or news from Madagascar. Meanwhile, the early summer sun is shining very sweetly. A number of small sparrows are singing at their work, attempting to enlarge their vocal register.

At this point I must beg your pardon for mentioning an occurrence which gives the atmosphere too perfectly to be discarded upon grounds of propriety. It will be remembered by students of the Apocrypha that the prophet Tobit was cured of blindness by a drop of lime descending from a bird. When the curtain goes up upon our breakfast scene, the first thing to occur is simply this: the place of Tobit's eye is taken by the fried egg about to be consumed by the shy subaltern next door to the chaplain. The subaltern starts back in horror and amazement. His chair is an empty ammunition box – not adapted to staccato movements. The crisis is accompanied by merriment, in which the bombardier begins to join, then suddenly remembers that even facial freedom is forbidden to good soldiers. By a miracle of self-restraint his countenance again becomes impassive; he whips away the plate, the subaltern confusedly restores the ammunition-box to its place, and the calm voice which the Major keeps in reserve for periods of crisis, says suavely: "I rather think, Lieutenant Hopkinson, that your first duty in the new Battery you have joined must now be to erect a 'sparrow-pluie'!"

I cannot now remember what came next, but the whole atmosphere of that celestial breakfast still remains with me. I had reached the Battery, on my weekly visit, the night before from Talbot House. I had brought up with me the Pathescope, with a new film of Charlie Chaplin's exploits, featuring his single-handed capture of the Kaiser. This finished, we had had our family prayers and then turned in, and in the early morning held Communion.

3 A Pyx in Flanders – Rev. P.B. Clayton

In the early summer of 1917, the 154th Southampton Territorial Heavy Battery, commanded then by "Shi" (Major Herbert Shiner, D.S.O., M.C.), had moved one section forward to the field in front of Transport Farm[3] – a deadly place indeed. It had become my custom to spend at least one day and night each week with the three batteries which were my forward flock. Pettifer and I for three years thus set out together, generally on Thursday morning, returning to Talbot House some time on Friday. It was what we called our slum visiting, and seldom passed without unexpected incidents. All sorts of units in turn lent transport to ferry our spiritual munitions to and fro. These included a baby Pathé Cinema, one or two tins of films; one sandbag holding hymn-books and Communion services; another full of mundane printed matter; my Communion case (always called the Crown Jewel Case), the State Paper Case;[4] sometimes Edmund Street's portable harmonium; and other human frailties, including several tins of Mrs Fry's cocoa, which were secured by influence with her gardener when wounded. Then there was sterner kit selected, according to the state of the military weather; lastly, one heart in mouth and boots alternately – Pettifer's heart was always where it is. From all this stuff we were easily separable. It sometimes went by luggage in advance and lay awaiting our arrival at No. 10 Bridge, Ypres,[5] where the first tin of cocoa might be broached. It travelled by every method and at every speed, from the G.S. wagon or the gun-limber to the breathless luxury of Godfrey Pope's box car,[6] or a Flying Corps tender. If we had calls to pay on the way up, we might travel with it to Vlamertinghe and then kiss it good-bye until to-morrow or some other day. The astounding thing was not that it disappeared, but that it all came home.

One thing, and one thing only, never left my person on these journeys. That was a small and simple Pyx, sent out to me for Talbot House in 1916 as the gift of the poorest street of my district in Portsmouth. It was seldom, if ever, that I carried the Sacrament from Talbot House itself towards the line. This would have been one way, and surely one which few would then have questioned who were in contact with the realities of war. Another thought, however, had possessed me. It was that the unity of each battery should be knit up in the use of the Pyx, hallowed by all for all.

In all three batteries many officers and men had come forward by this time for Confirmation, or had returned to their Communions. In the 154th these privileges were by now accepted by the majority. Each battery had, apart from its wagon lines which lay near Poperinghe, a Battery Headquarters in the neighbourhood of Ypres, a rear section near Headquarters, and two forward sections advanced and in constant danger.

The arrangement which by long experiment was found to meet their need most simply was this. At Battery Headquarters there would be a sort of guest night, with a cinema show, a sing-song, or a debate, or all three put together. This would be followed by an evening service on a week-night, and next morning by a Celebration, at which Communion would not only be given

---

3   Also known as Railway Dugouts Burial Ground, it is located 2 kms south-east of Ieper town centre, on the Komenseweg. Throughout 1916 and 1917 advanced dressing stations were situated in the nearby dugouts.
4   An old despatch case containing personal and Talbot House related papers, communicants' roll, etc.
5   The bridge over the Ieper-Komen canal when entering Ieper from the direction of Poperinge.
6   Pope was the RFC's chief signal officer.

Lt. Herbert Shiner, 1915.

Drawing of Tubby's Pyx by Barclay Baron. It carries the inscription: "A Pyx for the great Gift of Love, from the poor of Beeston Street, Portsmouth, to the B.E.F. In constant use, 1915-1918, in Talbot House, Poperinghe."

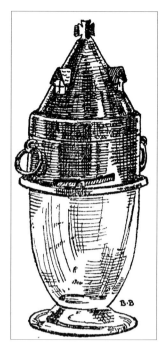

Entrance to dugout, watercolour by Eric Kennington.

to those present, but prepared for communicants in the advanced sections. To these, during the day that followed, it would then be borne.

The Headquarters of the 154th were at the time recently advanced from an old farm near Dickebusch to the gaunt nightmare of St. Eloi. There, opposite Bus House (where the ruins of a London bus had left the name behind them), stood the B.C. post with the rear-section gun in the field and farther ditch. Here, then, we Celebrated on this especial morning, and passed with a full Pyx down the long slope that led towards Ypres. At Transport Farm, a dressing-station, some of the 6th London Field Ambulance were then at work. We met some we knew, but it was not a place for any unnecessary delay. A hundred yards beyond there was a field filled with still smoking shell-holes. Across this field our way lay, to a spot in the embankment where the men of the forward section were sheltered when off duty, in the famous railway dug-outs – a series of crumbling caves dug into the embankment, and walled with great planks. We passed across this field with no shells landing near us. The subaltern in charge of the section was awaiting us, and a considerable body of men gathered within the largest tunnel. As we entered, shelling began again in close proximity, and, as some shells were by their sound gas shells, we dropped the gas curtain behind us. The Communion was then given to the officer and some N.C.O.'s and men, perhaps eighteen in all. I saw that some whom I had hoped to find were missing.

No eyes which have looked upon these things in actuality can ever hope to find their like in any church on earth. The intense reality, the humble eagerness, the unity of aim, the thought of one another, the constancy of friendship thus forever knit, were like great shafts of light streaming upon a dark and narrow way, whereon a Figure all-commanding stood plainly to be seen. The crouching men, outlined in candlelight against the background of the oozing boards upon the yielding carpet of moist clay, made this the Food of Immortality indeed, delivered within the sepulchre itself. Death stood without and knocked, but Christ within forbade his instant entry; for, even as we knelt, such sounds came very near. Some minutes later and the Act was over. The officer and I went towards the entrance and put a hand upon the gas curtain. It seemed something was impeding its movement. When at last it moved, a body, half fallen aginst it, lay prone at our feet. Seldom had War done his work with less disfigurement. It was impossible for either of us to realize for a moment that it was death indeed which we beheld. Then both our minds leapt to the same understanding. This lad was one for whom the officer had taken, so far as it might be, peculiar and special thought. It was due to a hint from the officer that I had been much in touch with him, and that I had a fortnight ago brought him and a few others down to Talbot House for their Confirmation. Evidently what had happened was this. He had been on duty at the farthest gun, and stayed perhaps for some adjustment behind the few that were already spared. Hoping to be in time for the Service he had then followed them, and while his friends received, had died at the entrance without a cry. The truth was evident and too sacred for any words then, or even now.

A few minutes later, when we had lifted the body and carried it to one side, so that the men coming out behind us might not see it as they came, I asked for the other absentees. These were four signallers attached to this section of the battery; one from the Signals Corps and the other three gunners lent to him for duty. The officer told me that they were stationed on the embankment fifty yards away. I made my way towards them, and found them crouching on the slope of the embankment where the shelling was still heavy, though intermittent. As they could not leave their instruments, the only way was to minister to them in the open. And there, upon the side of the embankment, we five men knelt down together. After a few words of the prayers, I opened the upper part of the Pyx to minister therefrom. Having done so, I felt for the tiny lock whereby the lower portion of the Pyx (this part of glass) might be freed for the second ministration.

At this moment the air immediately above our heads was filled with the bursting of a shell. We had all taken off our tin hats, and knelt there entirely unprotected. The shell burst perhaps fifteen feet up, and every bush about us was cut with flying fragments. The whole air was charged, as it seemed, with that unmistakable sound of metal whining and tearing and thudding to the ground. Not one of us was touched: I would almost say that not one of us was frightened. Completely deaf for the moment, I ministered the Cup, replaced its cover, said the Lord's Prayer, and rose from one knee to give the Peace. A few moments later I left them and stumbled down the slope to summon Pettifer and pass upon our way. We did this without, so far as I remember, any further incicent. But what further could there be to equal those which I had witnessed in that last half-hour? Mine eyes had indeed seen His salvation.[7]

R.I.P.
W.H. Hall
Gunner, 189th Brigade, Royal Field Artillery
15 June 1917 – Railway Dugouts Burial Ground (Transport Farm – Zillebeke), VII.B.6/18

II LITTLE TALBOT HOUSE

1 Introduction – Rev. P.B. Clayton

The establishment of this daughter house in Ypres was the tardy fruit of a hope Dr. Magrath and I had long shared; and he, with his unrivalled knowledge of the town, in which he managed to live longer than even Town-Major Scott, did more than any of us to make the dream come true. The old House had always a number of faithful friends in Ypres, and early in 1916 the Military Foot Police on No.10 Bridge ran a kind of cocoa tavern for sundry wayfarers, for which a generous friend of the old House provided the raw materials. Divisional chaplains held services in the Infantry Barracks, in a cellar in the Rue de Dixmude, and in the house which subsequently became

Ypres Reservoir Cemetery with ruins of Ypres Prison in the background.

7   P.B. Clayton, *Plain Tales from Flanders*, pp.127-134.

ours; and in '16 and '17 I held weekly services on Fridays in the Prison, where the Town-Major's headquarters were. But co-ordination was difficult, and concentration in any one spot was plainly inadvisable. In the autumn of '17, however, the town – or what was left of it – became comparatively healthy, and the following notice appeared on Talbot House board:

**LITTLE TALBOT HOUSE
Y P R E S.**

Was born yesterday in Ypres. It stands (more or less) in Rue de Lille, and was once a large lace factory. The red brick frontage on the road is quite imposing, but the back premises are not quite what they were. However, there are six rooms upstairs, and a convenient and capacious cellar. We are sending up some stuff from the old House, and passers-by must look in and see Mr. Goodwin, the chaplain in charge. Church tithe for the present may be paid in kind, the kind being roofing-iron and sandbags. Gas and water already laid on.

14/11/17

The house we secured was one of the only two still standing in the Rue de Lille – the Post Office being the other. The first lorry load of furniture we brought up was blown to bits by a direct hit on the room in which we had dumped it, a few hours after its arrival. We moistened the lips, and brought up a second load. With this the House opened, and from November to April fulfilled its task ideally, under conditions increasingly dangerous. One morning, when I arrived on a visit, the House was literally ringed with new shell-holes; and even as Pettifer and I approached it, part of the outer wall, weakened by continual concussions, fell of its own accord. Yet within, the work went on uninterruptedly. A few days before the evacuation we were still hopefully building and sandbagging the new hall. Then came the withdrawal from Passchendaele, and the front line was drawn closer to Ypres than ever before. With machine guns posted in the streets, the town billets were evacuated by order; and Goodwin and his staff arrived at Poperinghe late on one Sunday night.

(P.B. Clayton)

2 Little Talbot House – Dr. C.J. Magrath, YMCA

It was somewhat cheerless in Ypres in August, 1917, and on one of the most cheerless days at the end of that month I was introduced by the 146th Battery to a padre who had just arrived. He looked cheerful; that was my first impression: he wasn't a non-smoker or a temperance fanatic; those were my second impressions: he seemed to fit in; that was my third impression. I didn't know I was meeting Little Talbot House in embryo; in fact, I had never heard of it, nor had anyone else, though a few people had been interested in getting something of the kind going. But Ypres at the moment was not propitious. Later on the padre – his name was R.J. Goodwin – after migrating to various dug-outs – began to talk about Little Talbot House, and as a preliminary step came to live with me in a vast underground fastness under the Lille Gate Cemetery.[8] Negotiations for a suitable place resulted in getting the Lace-School in the Lille Road allotted, and the business began. Heaven knows – I do not – whence came the furniture. Some was pinched from the parent House: the canvas, the chairs and tables, the paint, the doors, the electric light fittings (oh yes, we were civilised before the war stopped; now we use candles!) *et*

tout ça. I only know that they did come, that they got sorted, erected and fixed. I remember as in a dream, one or two hectic afternoons divided between bumping one's head on the beams in the cellar, and standing perilously on a rickety ladder trying to reach something which one obviously couldn't reach. This consumed most of the month of November; in December R.J.G. "moved in" (i.e. his valise was carried down the road).

Little Talbot House was a going concern, and it did go. The rooms upstairs were canteen and reading rooms; downstairs in the "catacombs" were the chapel – it took one right back to Rome in A.D. 70 – and the sleeping billets and kitchen. (Later on, when things were quieter, the new

---

8   A spacious ancient lock room in which moat water flows into the vaulted Ieperlee stream, the bed of which is approximately 8 feet lower. The cemetery surmounts the top of the old rampart, extending down to the edge of the moat.

chapel got going upstairs, but that was not till March, 1918). At night the chapel was curtained off, and part became a reading room.

Of those who found comfort – spiritual and mental – there, of those who came with troubles, who came to ask questions on every conceivable subject, who fed, read, and even slept there, R.J.G. could tell you himself. Let this only be recorded by one who was a "gadget", that there was not a man who came there who did not go away cheered and brightened, not one who did not love R.J.G., not one who did not return when he could. It was (as time goes) a brief episode; three months almost covered it; Low Sunday, 1918, saw the House empty, Paschendaele evacuated, and the Bosches advancing fast on Ypres. Yes, brief but bright; and only the God in Heaven knows what fruit that three months sowing produced.

R.J.G., here's luck to you now and always. As a helper of lame dogs over stiles, you were one of the best; I and hundreds more shall never forget you and that little oasis in the Lille Road.[9]

S. George's Chapel,

Little Talbot House, Ypres.

HOLY WEEK SERVICES.

MONDAY, TUESDAY, WEDNESDAY & THURSDAY.

Holy Communion	-	8.0 a.m.
Evensong	-	5.30 p.m.
Short Service and Address	-	7.0 p.m.

GOOD FRIDAY.

Ante-Communion and Meditation	-	8.0 a.m.
Morning Service	-	11.15 a.m.
Evening Service	-	5.30 p.m.

HOLY SATURDAY.

Ante-Communion	-	8.0 a.m.
Evensong	-	5.30 p.m.

EASTER DAY.

Holy Communion,	6.30, 7.15, 8.0, 9.0, and 11.15 a.m.
Evensong and Address	-	5.30 p.m.
Administration of Holy Communion	-	6.30 p.m.

Monday and Tuesday in Easter Week.

Holy Communion	-	8.0 a.m.
Evensong	-	5.30 p.m.

R. J. GOODWIN,
Chaplain.

---

3 Memories – P.C.H.

The following extracts from the diary and letters of an anonymous sergeant with the initials P.C.H, Royal Garrison Artillery, contain rare reminiscences of Little Talbot House.

16 December 1917
I have been to a C. of E. service this evening. You remember 'Talbot House' that I told you about? I found out today that there is a 'Little Talbot House' in the town 'close handy'. It has a nice little Chapel, similar to the other one only in a cellar instead of an attic. It was lighted by electric light and had a nice wood fire going. It was a very nice service. The Chapel was quite full. There were several officers in the congregation. It was good to be able to go and I hope to go again. The House is not so pretentious (imposing) as the larger one. I think there is only one room above ground tenantable, which is fitted up as a reading and writing room and has a piano in it.

---

9   Magrath's account was published as an appendix to Tubby's *Tales* (1919).

The Cellar Chapel, Little Talbot House, 1917.

21 December 1917
I spent quite a pleasant hour this evening at 'Little Talbot House'. Three of us had quite a nice little sing-song, practising Christmas Carols with the Chaplain in the cellar behind the Chapel. The Padre played the harmonium… altogether we succeeded in making quite a joyful noise, though some people may not have thought it such!

31 December 1917
I had quite a nice Sunday yesterday to finish up the old year. In the evening (5.30 p.m.) I went to Little T. House and enjoyed the service very much. The little cellar Chapel was well filled: an officer played the little harmonium very nicely; and the singing went splendidly. It was a Christmas service… We have the 'Evening Prayer' with a few omissions and modifications; the Padre wears surplice and cassock; and the service is mostly Choral (on Sunday evenings) but it is robbed of much of the usual Church formality, and I like it very much. Last night we had "Angels from the Realms of Glory", "O come all ye faithful", and two special carols; also the Te Deum to finish up with, as a hymn of special thanksgiving. The address was brief and without text, the thought being Christmas (the Incarnation) being the fulfilment of an ancient vision, gradually becoming more clear throughout Old Testament history, and the starting point of a

new vision – the Kingdom of God on earth. He quoted … (from Blakes Jerusalem) "I will not cease from mental fight, etc. …" Mr. Goodwin is a very good speaker. He never has a note but his delivery is very clear and thoughtful. I shall miss the service when we go away from here.

21 January 1918
To tea at Little Talbot House with Mr. Goodwin. Pleasant time. An East Lancs Chaplain, named Webb, was also there. Mr. G. told me they were having post cards of the Chapel printed for Easter. The house in peace time was called the 'Lace School'. It was run by some nuns. Stayed to service. Afterwards spoke to a Presbyterian from John O'Groats.

7 February 1918
Attended service at Little Talbot House, and afterwards stayed to lecture by Rev. Bury on the Religious and Moral Aspects of the Sex Problem – or something to that effect. It was a fine, manly, outspoken and very helpful and inspiring address on a very difficult subject.

10 February 1918
After tea, went to Little Talbot House. Not quite so crowded as last Sunday. Quinquagesima Sunday. Subject – Blind Bartimeus. After service went to Recreation Room. Picked up a bound volume of some old Church Magazine. Found it contained a number of articles on Thomas Edward – Naturalist. Stayed to read some of them to refresh my memory on the subject. In some general conversation a machine gunner related his experiences at the Battle of Cambrai.

14 February 1918
After tea, went to service at Little Talbot House, and stayed to lecture by Dr. Magrath, on "Wypers, past and present". He was very amusing, as well as instructive.

28 February 1918
Went to Little T. House this evening. On the way saw an attempt on one of our balloons by a Hun plane. Both occupants descended in parachutes and I hope got down safely. The first one did not appear to have opened quite properly. The Hun was driven off by some of our planes and I don't think the balloon was much hurt.

3 March 1918
Went to Little Talbot House morning and evening. The morning was a Communion Service, address by Rev. Goodwin on the Parable of the unclean devil that returned with seven others – the last state worse than the first. In the evening the preacher was Father Money, C.F., C.R., of the Mirfield Monks.[10] The service was conducted by another clergyman who was apparently an artillery officer. I liked Father Money very much… "If any man will come after me, let him deny himself and take up his cross daily and follow me." He preached under difficulties as our cellar Chapel ceiling is very low and he is very tall; so he could not stand upright…

10   Padre Humphrey Money (New Zealand Expeditionary Force) regularly helped out at Talbot House and was left in charge during Tubby's absences.

17 March 1918

This evening I went to Little T. House. Mr. G. is away on duty elsewhere for a fortnight, and another Padre is carrying on for him (Padre Elwood). He is a very nice man. Has been out here for 3 years and wears the Military Cross ribbon. It was crowded as usual tonight with mostly fresh faces. The congregations are continually changing as different lots relieve one another. After the service I went for a walk round the ramparts of the town where we are. Most of these old continental towns are moated and fortified to an extent which we never see in our sea-girt island. These particular ramparts were built nearly 800 years ago. They have undergone many assaults and sieges in times past, and it is wonderful how well they have withstood the worst which modern warfare has been able to do against them. It was a beautiful evening overhead, and I was interested to note the various sounds that greeted the ear. They represented both war and peace – the world as man has made it, and nature. In the distance was the spasmodic rumble of artillery, and occasionally the rattle of a machine gun, with, every now and then, the whistle and thud of an exploding shell. Added to these were the distant sounds of various traffic – the rattle of wheels and the clatter of hoofs on the hard metalled roads; the hum of lorries and motors, and the noisy little motor cycles. But, through all the other sounds came the persistent notes of one or two thrushes who were sweetly singing their evening hymn, on the boughs of half-ruined trees; and in a Y.M.C.A. Hut, not far away they were singing "The Gospel Bells are ringing". Some strange sights also greeted the eye. In the direction where the front line runs were to be seen the flashes of guns, and occasionally a 'Star' shell rose above the horizon, flickered for a moment, and disappeared from view; while overhead far removed from this mad world, the crescent moon, closely attended by Jupiter, shone serenely in a patch of blue, with increasing brilliance as the glow of sunset faded from the western sky.

19 March 1918

Yesterday afternoon I went to Little T. House to lend a hand with the new Chapel. Mr. G. had asked for volunteers. I spent a pleasant hour or two as a plasterer's labourer! They are cementing the floor. It will be very nice when it is finished. We shall be able to stand up without fear of bumping our heads!

24 March 1918

Battery left Ypres.

4 Dr. Charles Magrath, "the YMCA hero of Ypres" – Barclay Baron

At the end of April 1918, a fortnight after Little Talbot House closed down, Dr. Charles Magrath, YMCA, joined forces with Tubby at Talbot House. Having resided in Ieper longer than any man during wartime, he held on to "his quaint little system of dug-outs in the bowels of the earth near the historic Lille Gate". Barclay Baron wrote the following account of this remarkable man:

In the area of Second Army at its fullest extent we worked at nearly eighty points. They extended from Proven in the north to the old town of Bailleul on the south, as far back as Hazebrouck station, a busy junction for troops, and as far forward as the dug-outs at St. Jean and Hussar Farm in front of Ypres. Perhaps the most interesting in point of its situation and the man in charge was at the Lille Gate of Ypres. Vauban's great eighteenth-century ramparts which still

Barclay Baron's billet at YMCA
Headquarters, Poperinge.

defended the city on its eastern boundary – a broad bastion of earth faced with many thick-
nesses of brick which the heaviest artillery of the First War chipped but never breached – were
tunnelled with galleries where a divisional staff, with gas blankets over the entrances, could
carry on office work in perfect safety. This great underground system ended beside the Lille
Gate in a sort of cave, deep down. Here Dr C.J. Magrath, a schoolmaster from Sheffield, ran
an unusual YMCA. It was cool in summer and could be kept cosy even in the hardest days of a
Flemish winter; heavy bombardment could do no more than make its electric lights blink. You
entered, stooping, from the cobbled street at the limit of the town and went down by narrow
steps to the tiny canteen where men chatted and smoked and drank tea elbow to elbow.There
was also a low outlet on the outer side to the moat, where dud shells and rusty coils of barbed
wire fouled the muddy water.

Magrath was apt to welcome a visitor like myself with a 'Wipers Cocktail', his own recipe
which he said consisted one part of canteen lemonade, one of SRD (Service Rum Diluted) and
one – its most potent ingredient – of moat water. On a still, sunny afternoon when I dropped
in he suggested that we should take our tea on top and we carried a teapot, a couple of enamel
mugs, condensed milk and packets of biscuits up to the small cemetery which covered his
dug-out. We lay on the grass among the wooden crosses, surveying on one hand the southern
curve of the Salient and on the other the ruins of the city, much of it by this time no more than
breast-high. Presently a heavy shell exploded at the further end, sending up a spout of brick dust
somewhere beyond the famous ruin of the Cloth Hall. A few minutes later there was another,

Dr. Charles Magrath (centrally seated), Ypres, 1918.

this time nearer, and I looked at Magrath. 'All right', he said, 'this is the afternoon *strafe*. It'll take them at least six to get round here – there's time for another cup.'

Every four minutes the punctual, painstaking German gunners lobbed a shell in a neat line across the city. At the fifth explosion we picked up our tea-things and went down below. We were scarcely settled there when a tremendous 'crump!' made the lights stagger and the glasses rattle on the shelf. 'All over for the day', Magrath commented. This was one of the quiet periods there occasionally fell, a lull between battles.

Magrath was no mere troglodyte. He was out and about in the city or tramping over the torn ground in front of it where St. Jean and other points lay in his 'parish'; loaded with a haversack of cigarettes, a newspaper or two and other small luxuries, he was a welcome visitor among fighting men. In Ypres itself he became one of the most familiar characters, and before our troops left it behind, easily its oldest inhabitant. Army units took their turn and moved out to go up or back, town majors, medical officers and chaplains came and went, wounded, exhausted or transferred: 'Mac' was still there to greet newcomers with his high-pitched laugh. Several times, filling a gap, he was recognized as unofficial acting town major of Ypres, which he now knew like the back of his hand. He was decorated with the Belgian Croix de Guerre before he came home.[11]

---

11   M. Snape, *The Back Parts of War: The YMCA Memoirs and Letters of Barclay Baron, 1915 to 1919*, pp.162-163.

Appendix I

Note on Talbot House – Rev. P.B. Clayton (11 June 1917)

The House was founded, under the authority of Col. May, then AA & QMG of VI Division, in December 1915, & was named by him after Rev. N.S. Talbot, then SCF of the Division. A Chaplain from 16th Brigade (Rev. P.B. Clayton) was appointed to run it as a Church & social centre for officers & men of the Division. It was opened on Dec. 15th 1915, half of the House then being allotted to officers & half to men. During the next six months, its scope gradually extended far beyond the single Division, and it became a rest house for officers of both Corps, & a recreation house for troops by day. In June Rev. N.S. Talbot was appointed to XIV Corps to extend the work of Talbot House in the direction of an Officers' Club, i.e. to leave Talbot House as the men's department only, to be supported as previously in finance by the Officers' department in an adjoining house.

Shortly after both Houses came in the area of VIII Corps, and the Committee of the Officers' Mess decided to substitute a system of subscriptions from the Divisional Canteens in the area for direct financial support from the Mess towards Talbot House. The monthly rent for the House & hall is 220 francs, & the cost of upkeep – games, writing-paper, books, billiards, & gifts to various units up the line – amount on an average to about 600 francs a month in addition. Towards this, each division of VIII Corps agreed to contribute 120 frs a month, & of X Corps 100 frs, leaving a deficit to be met by private donations, & the profits of the small refreshment bar in the House.

The House aims at being a home from home for troops in the area, and is used by 5000 men a week at normal times. Debates, concerts, whist-drives etc. are held weekly. Two small billiard tables are in constant use, and there is a reference and lending library of several hundred books.

The religious work of the House, which is not financed out of public funds, centres in a beautiful Chapel on the top floor, built originally by the Queen's Westminster Rifles, in which many gifts from various units as well as a number of personal memorials are congregated. Regular daily & Sunday services are held, all voluntary & well attended.

Note
Owing to the irregularity of the payment of subscriptions by some Divisions and the difficulty of raising constant subscriptions from private sources, Talbot House is now indebted to Rev. P.B. Clayton for a considerable sum which he has lent out of his private purse in order that the house should be kept going.
12/6/1917
H. Leslie Parker, D.A.C.G. VIII Corps

Appendix II

Further Note on Talbot House – Major G.B. Bowes, Chairman (26 December 1917)

In June 1917 Fifth Army took over the area hitherto occupied by VIII Corps, and Poperinghe came under XVIII Corps for administration. Representations as to the financial deficit and the inadequate staff were made to the D.A. and Q.M.G. XVIII Corps who approved of a committee being formed of officers & other ranks from XVIII & XIX Corps & Fifth Army, & appointed Major Dulcken, Secretary of the Officers' Club, as Chairman. As the latter took very little part in the work, I acted for him, as Vice Chairman, until he resigned in October, when I was appointed Chairman.

The D.A. & Q.M.G. XVIII Corps increased the Staff, and issued an appeal for funds, not only to his own units, but to other Corps and to Army Troops. Through the donations and monthly subscriptions received from these and individual units, the deficit of Frs 2438.25 was wiped off and a reserve fund created, and many things needed for the house were obtained. The library has been much increased mainly by gifts from friends, and now numbers over 2000 books, and is greatly used. Frequent concerts are held, also lectures, debates, whist-drives etc. The house is now self-supporting from the profits of the dry canteen and tea-bar. In November XVIII Corps moved out of the area, and Talbot House as a part of Poperinghe, came under II Corps for administration. Further accommodation is required for concerts & lectures, and this may be provided by the allotment of further portions of the adjoining house in which the tea-bar is situated. A considerable amount of RE work is required to make the house more comfortable, especially as regard light and warmth, and increase its usefulness. It is frequented by hundreds, and often thousands of men daily. Some of its most constant supporters coming from Army Troop units, which are rather more stationary; but it is used by most units, of whatever Corps, which are within reach.

An attempt has been made to start a little Talbot House in Ypres, where a house, formerly a convent (lace school) in the Rue Lille, has been placed at our disposal.

At present, the work is mainly confined to the cellars – with a tiny chapel, & canteen, a Chaplain of Heavy Artillery (VIII Corps) being in residence, with a staff of 4. But a scheme for repairing a portion of the house, to make it habitable, has been submitted to VIII Corps (in whose area it is), and as soon as circumstances permit, it is hoped to proceed with the work.

The moving spirit of Talbot House is of course the Rev P.B. Clayton, C.F. who has been there almost continuously since its opening and is mainly responsible for the religious and social tone and atmosphere of the house. His absence just now for several weks owing to illness is a great loss to the house.

Appendix III

Talbot House Committee (October 1917)

President:	Lt.-Gen. Sir Ivor Maxse, K.C.B, C.V.O., D.S.O., Commanding XVIII Corps
Vice-Presidents:	Lt.-Gen. H.E. Watts, C.B., C.M.G., Commanding XIX Corps Brig.-Gen. P.M. Davies, D.A. & Q.M.G. XVIII Corps Rev. Neville Talbot, A.C.G. Fifth Army
Chairman:	Major G.B. Bowes, T.D., Delousing Station, Poperinghe
Vice-Chairman:	Major L.H. Rugg, R.E., O.C. Fifth Army Tramways
Treasurer:	Capt. W.A.T. Kidd, O.C. 214th Army Troops Coy. R.E.
Secretary:	Pte. E. Evans, Delousing Station, Poperinghe
Members:	Rev. H.G. Marshall, D.A.C.G. XVIII Corps Rev. P.B. Clayton, C.F., Resident Chaplain, Talbot House Capt. Coatbridge Williams, Adj. 43rd Labour Group Capt. R.F. Gunn, "D" Battery Tank Corps 2nd Lt. Lowman, R.E., O.C. P.P. Cable Section 5th Army C.S.M. G.T. Barber, 213th Army Troops, Coy. R.E. Sergt. Millar, Town Major's Office, Poperinghe Sergt. McInnes, Fifth Army Intelligence, Poperinghe L/Cpl. Blackhurst, R.E., R.T.O.'s Office, Poperinghe Sapper Laycock, Fifth Army Signals, Poperinghe

Appendix IV

Report of Social Sub-Committee (28 August 1917)

GAMES.
An inventory has been made of the games in the House. One of the Billiard Tables needs more secure foundations.

LIBRARY.
There have been several additions to the Library of which increasing use is being made. The Vice-Chairman, at the request of the Sub-Committee, has written to several of the leading publishers asking for presents of books. The Sub-Committee have decided to make a card-index catalogue of the Library, and recommend that a member of staff be detailed to look after the issue of books and keep the catalogue up to date.

CINEMA.
The House is in possession of two sets of apparatus. The Sub-Committee recommend that films be hired either from England or elsewhere, at a cost, including minor repairs to apparatus, not exceeding 200.00 Frs. monthly. The Cinema would be used in the House during winter evenings, and might be lent during the afternoons to Rest Stations in the vicinity.

ENTERTAINMENTS.
The Sub-Committee decided to continue the weekly debates (occasionally leaving an evening for impromptu discussions of subjects suggested by those present), and to organize sing-songs daily or as often as required. They also hope to arrange for some dramatic entertainments during the winter, and to enlist the help of various Concert Parties.

LECTURE.
A Lecture was given by the Rev. John Kelman, C.F., on the 15th of August on his recent experiences in America, in putting the case of the Allies before audiences often admittedly hostile. His eloquent and inspiring address made a great impression upon all who heard him.

(Signed) G.B. Bowes, Major
Chairman, Social Sub-Committee
Talbot House

Appendix V

Report of House Sub-Committee (29 August 1917)

PREMISES.
The Committee made an examination of the premises and decided on certain repairs and alterations; the former, involving repairs to gutters and a covering to the roof garden, and minor repairs, are nearly completed. The Canteen has been extended to another room which has been fitted up with shelves, counter and gangway, and new inner doors have been erected for the main entrance. Shelves have been added to the Library, and more are being made.
Women were employed to clean the whole premises, as authorized by the Committee.

STAFF.
Application was made to the 18th Corps for five additional men, to bring the number up to 10. Two have been supplied, but additional ones are urgently needed.

HAMMOCKS.
6 Hammocks to enable men on night duty to sleep in the day-time have been indented for on O.O. 18th C.T. He is unable to supply, but authorizes local purchase, the cost to be refunded by him.

ROUTINE.
Sanction has been given to keep the House open after 9 p.m. to men going on leave, on production of their leave warrant. This is a great boon to men coming from the line who have to report to the R.T.O. for the leave train about mid-night, and have nowhere to go in the meantime.
After the recent fighting, a number of men (6 or 7 daily) from the 154 Heavy Battery R.G.A. were housed and fed (the O.C. paying the cost), for 24 hours, and were provided with dry underclothing and lent khaki suits while their own were dried.

NEW "ADVANCED" TALBOT HOUSE
The Committee have the refusal of a house (formerly a Lace Factory) in the Rue de Lille, Ypres. Only the outer framework of the house survives, and much work would be required to make it habitable: but there is a good cellar dug-out, and three rooms are more or less available. Two H.A. Chaplains, Rev. H.C. Cox and Rev. E. Victor, are anxious to make a start by opening on a small scale here, and can secure the work of R.G.A. fatigue parties to do the necessary

clearance. The project is to open a Games Room, Reading Room and Church Room in the three still standing. Also a small canteen, if staff and transport can be provided. They are relying on the Committee for a small grant of Games, Periodicals, Writing Paper, Pictures, etc. most of which can come from our present stock. The Committee recommends that a start be made on these lines.

(Signed) G.B. Bowes, Major
Chairman, House Sub-Committee
Talbot House

Appendix VI

Report of Finance Sub-Committee (29 August 1917)

When the Committee took over the management as from July 1st 1917, there was a blance in cash of 133.15 Frs., and liabilities 2 571.40 Frs. viz. A.W. GAMAGE Ltd., 723.50 Frs. Rev. P.B. Clayton. Balance of loan, as shown by the accounts 874.00 Frs. and due to him for bills paid on A/C of the House 973.90 Frs. totaling 1 847.90 Frs. Rev. Neville Talbot, A.C.G. 5th Army, kindly undertook to raise the greater part of this sum and other donations were promised. Since that date, donations from this and other sources have been received amounting to 3 750.50 Frs. including 700.00 Frs. from the 19th Corps and 1000.00 Frs from the 48th Division. All the above liabilities have now been cleared off.

As the result of an appeal from 18th Corps H.Q., 10 Divisions have promised a monthly subscription in most cases of 120.00 Frs. while they are in the neighbourhood, and several units of Army Troops and the various Corps Troops have also subscribed, so that we may look to an income from subscriptions of about 1 230.00 Frs. monthly. The turnover of the Canteen has greatly increased, and the profits from this source will probably amount to 1 500.00 Frs. monthly.

The House, therefore, may look to a monthly income of about 2 700.00 Frs. The expenses estimated at 800.00 Frs. a month are also increasing owing to the larger number of troops using the House; and a further increase will take place when the new scheme for an advanced Talbot House is in operation.

The balance of the donations and surplus of income over expenditure is being kept as a reserve for future capital and other expenditure.

The Sub-Committee recommends that an A/C be opened with Messrs. Cox & Co. France Ltd., Boulogne Branch.

(Signed) G.B. Bowes, Major
Chairman, Finance Sub-Committee
Talbot House

Appendix VII

Constitution of Committee of Management and Financial Instructions (26 January 1918)

---

1. Management

The management of the House is vested in a Committee consisting of the Chairman, Vice Chairman, Resident Chaplain, Treasurer and Secretary, and not less than two nor more than four other members. The Officers and Committee represent as far as possible the Army, and the one or more Corps which are in and near Poperinghe at any time, including the D.A.C.G. of the Corps administering the Talbot House and some members who are likely to become permanent. Not more than one third may be "other ranks". All automatically vacate office on leaving the Area. Vacancies are filled by election.

The Chairman is responsible for the pay and discipline of the Staff and general military administration, and may delegate any of his powers to the Resident Chaplain or other Officer or member of the Committee. One member of the Committee has supervision of the Canteen, and one is specially concerned with Little Talbot House. The Committee meet monthly, or oftener on the requisition of three members, four forming a quorum. There shall be a President and there may be two or more V.-P.'s, who will be elected by the Committee. Resolution (2) of 26/7/17 appointing four Sub-Committees – House, Canteen, Social and Finance – is rescinded, except as regards Social Sub-Committee to arrange lectures, debates and entertainments, supervise library etc.

This Committee may contain members (Officers or Other Ranks) who are not on the General Committee, the Resident Chaplain being Chairman.

2. Financial
1. The banking a/c. of T.H. is with Messrs. Cox & Co. (France) Ltd., Boulogne Branch, in the names of the Chairman and Treasurer who sign cheques jointly, and any monies not banked are held by the Treasurer subject to paras. (2) & (3).
2. The Sgt. i/c. T.H. is allowed a sum for Petty Cash, accounting for the same to the Treasurer with Vouchers.
3. The N.C.O. i/c. Canteen hands over at stated intervals to the Treasurer; the takings of the Tea Bar and Grocery Bar, retaining Frs. 1500 for further purchases, and accounting with signed vouchers for all monies spent.

4. The Resident Chaplain may authorize expenditure not exceeding Frs. 1000, if funds permit, reporting same to the next meeting of the General Committee.
5. All bills for payment by the Treasurer, or Sgt., must be initialled by the Officer who authorizes the purchase, and vouched for as correct.

Appendix VIII

Talbot House Constitution (30 January 1918)

TALBOT HOUSE, POPERINGHE

I. Introductory
    The House is a centre of Church, educational and social work for the Troops in and near Poperinghe.

II. Administration
    1. The administration of the House will be under the A.C.G. of the Army in whose area the House is.
    2. The Resident Chaplain is appointed by the D.C.G.
    3. The other personnel of the House will be provided and administered by the Corps in whose area the House is.
    4. The Chairman of the Committee (see III.1 below) will be responsible for the pay and discipline of the staff of the House and for the general military administration.

III. Management
    1. The President of the House shall be the A.C.G. of the Army in whose area the House is.
    2. There may be two or more Vice-Presidents who will be elected by the Committee.
    3. The management of the House is vested in the Committee.
    4. The Committee shall consist of:
        The Chairman, appointed by the A.C.G.
        The Vice Chairman.
        The Resident Chaplain, appointed by the D.C.G.
        The Treasurer.
        The Secretary.
        The D.A.C.G. of the Corps administering the personnel of the House.
        One, two or three other Members.
    5. As far as possible the Committee shall be representative of the Army and of the Corps which are in and near Poperinghe at any time. It shall include some members who are likely to be fairly permanent.

6. Not more than one-third of the Committee may be other ranks.
7. Committee members automatically vacate office on leaving the area.
8. The Committee fills vacancies by electing new members.
9. One member of the Committee supervises the Canteen.
10. One member of the Committee is specially concerned with Little TALBOT HOUSE, Ypres.
11. The General Committee Meeting shall be held monthly.
12. Special Committee Meetings, if found necessary, may be called by the Chairman and Resident Chaplain jointly.
13. Four members shall constitute a quorum.
14. A Sub-Committee shall be appointed by the Committee to arrange lectures, debates and entertainments and to supervise the Library etc.
15. This Sub-Committee may contain members who are not on the Committee.
16. The Chairman of the Sub-Committee shall be the Resident Chaplain.

IV. Financial Arrangements
1. The Banking account of Talbot House is with Messrs Cox & Co. (France) Boulogne Branch, in the names of the Chairman and Treasurer jointly.
2. Any monies not banked are held by the Treasurer except as shown in paras. 3, 4 and 5 below.
3. The Resident Chaplain is allowed a sum not exceeding Fs. 1000 per month, if funds permit accounting to the Treasurer for the same with Vouchers and reporting expenditure to the next monthly Committee Meeting.
4. The Sergeant i/c of the House is allowed a sum for Petty Cash, accounting for the same to the Treasurer with Vouchers.
5. The N.C.O. i/c the Canteen hands over the takings of the Tea Bar and the Grocery Bar to the Treasurer at stated intervals, retaining Fs. 1500 for further purchases and accounting with Vouchers for all monies spent.
6. All bills for payment by the Treasurer or the Sergeant i/c the House must be initialled by the officer who authorizes the purchase and vouched for as correct.
7. No expenditure will be incurred without an officer's authority.
8. The Treasurer will present his accounts for the preceding month at each monthly Committee Meeting.

Appendix IX

Talbot House staff – June 1918

Name	Unit	Age	Religion	M/S	Date landing France	Civil Employment	Hometown
Pte. Evans E.	764 A.E. Co.	42	Welsh W.	M	10.11.16	Dept. Manager & Com. Traveller	London
Pte. Flynn P.	763 A.E.Co.	48	R.C.	S	18.12.15	Gardener	Cork
Pte. Moore W.	832 A.E. Co.	31	C.E.	M	19.03.17	Builder's Foreman	London
Pte. Pettifer A.	763 A.E. Co.	45	C.E.	M	08.11.14	Traveller	London
Pte. Ray S.E.	832 A.E. Co.	37	C.E.	M	19.03.17	Outfitter	Stockton on Tees
Pte. Rose A.	763 A.E. Co.	30	C.E.	M	16.12.16	Pianoforte maker	London
L/C Trower G.	2nd Royal Scots	35	C.E.	S	01.10.16	Clerk	Glasgow
Pte. Vokins C.	5th Army San. Sec. R.A.M.C.	23	C.E	S	19.02.15	Pharmacist	York
Pte. Willmott C.	748 A.E.Co.	29	Non	M	27.12.16	Actor	London

Appendix X

Talbot House Canteen

---

1. Smokers' Requisites

Matches	0.05 fr/box
	0.60 fr – 0.80 fr/packet
Cigarettes	
tins	
Abdullas	3.30 fr
Capstan	1.25 fr & 1.60 fr
Country Life	2.75 fr
De Reszke	12.50 fr
Gold Flake	1.30 fr
Three Castles	1.60 fr - 2.00 fr
packets/boxes	
Commanders	0.90 fr/packet
Greys	2.00 fr – 2.20 fr/box
Loyals	0.20 fr/packet
Players	0.25 fr/packet
Regiments	0.70 fr – 0.80 fr/ packet
Sweet Caporal	10.00 fr/box
White City	0.80 fr/packet
Woodbines	3.75 fr/box
A.G. papers	0.10 fr
Tobacco	
Tobacco	0.90 fr – 2.00 fr/tin
Fine cut tobacco:	
Nosegay	4.80 fr/lb
Nut Brown Shag	4.80 fr/lb
Unity Shag	1.25 fr/lb
Waverly	0.45 fr/packet – 0.80 fr/tin
Waverly Mixture	6.40 fr – 7.20 fr/lb
Tobacco pouch	0.80 fr

For pipe smokers:

pipe	1.00 fr – 2.00 fr
pipe cleaner	0.10 fr
pipe tobacco	
Boardmans	0.50 fr/packet – 8 fr/lb
British Oak	4.80 fr/lb
Chairmans	2.00 fr/tin – 8.00 fr/lb
Coblie Cut	4.00 fr/lb
Coolie Plug	4.00 fr/lb
Craven Mixture	2.60 fr/tin
Plug	4.00 fr/lb
Royal Seal	5.60 fr/lb
St. Julien	4.80 fr – 6.40 fr/lb
Three Nuns	2.70 fr/tin
Twist	3.20 fr – 4.80 fr/lb
Wrestler Plug	4.00 fr – 4.80 fr/lb
Cigars	0.25 fr – 0.35 fr/piece
	3.00 fr/case
Vegetas	1.40 fr/piece
Panatellas	15.35 fr/box

2. **Foodstuffs**

Tins

Apricots	0.85 fr
Pears	2.00 fr
Pines	0.75 fr – 0.90 fr – 1.25 fr
Pineapple	2.00 fr
Tomatoes	2.15 fr – 2.25 fr
Peas	1.50 fr
Sausages	1.60 fr – 2.00 fr
Prawns	2.30 fr
Salmon	1.10 fr – 2.05 fr
Lobster	1,80 fr/case
Herring	1.10 fr
Sardines	1.00 fr – 1.10 fr – 1.20 fr
Pilchards	2.00 fr

Spreads (tin)

Butter	3.80 fr
Apricot jam	1.70 fr
Honey	2.00 fr
Jam	1.70 fr
Marmalade	1.10 fr & 1.80 fr

Sundries

Corn flour	1.20 fr/packet
Sugar	0.50 fr/lb

Salt	0.15 fr – 0.25fr/packet
Currie powder	0.15 fr/packet
Custard powder	1.20 fr/packet
Golden syrup	1.40 fr/tin
Empire Relish	1.30 fr/bottle
Mustard	0.20 fr/tin
Pickles	1.30 fr – 1.50 fr/bottle
Sauce	0.75 fr – 0.85 fr – 1.00 fr/bottle
Oats	1.00 fr/tin
Oatmeal	1.00 fr – 1.30 fr/tin
Shredded wheat	1.00 fr – 1.10 fr – 1.20 fr/packet

3. Cake, Biscuits and Sweets

Cake	0.10 fr
Biscuits	
Fruit biscuits	0.60 fr
Packet	0.10 fr
Tin	2.90 fr & 6.50 fr
Caramel	0.20 fr
Nut toffee	0.20 fr
Toffee	0.15 fr/bar
	5.00 fr/box
Chocolate	
Bar	1.00 fr
Packet	6.00 fr – 7.20 fr
Box	5.40 fr
Chocolate wafer	0.20 fr
Pudding	2.50 fr – 2.60 fr
Christmas Pudding	2.50 fr
Spearmint	5.00 fr/box
Sweets	0.85 fr – 1.00 fr/bottle
French Nougat	0.20 fr

4. Drinks

Coffee	2.50 fr/packet
Café au lait	2.70 fr – 3.00 fr/tin
Canteen coffee	5.50 fr/bottle
Cocoa	0.90 fr/tin
	1.00 fr – 1.25 fr – 1.40 fr/packet
Cocoa & milk	2.20 fr – 2.35 fr/tin
Lemonade powder	1.50 fr
Lemon squash	2.25 fr/bottle
Milk	1.10 fr – 1.45 fr – 1.60 fr/tin
Soup	1.20 fr – 1.50 – 1.60 fr/tin
Symington soup	0.30 fr/square
Tea	2.50 fr/lb

5.   Simple Remedies

Aide-à-camp (snuff)	2.00 fr
Barkoff (cough tablets)	5.90 fr – 6.00 fr/tin
Beechams (headaches and colds)	1.60 fr/box
Enas & Salts (stomach)	3.15 fr/bottle
Health Salts	0.80 fr/tin
Vaseline	0.10 fr/tin

6.   Personal Hygiene

Carbolic	0.90 fr/bar
Soap	0.40 fr/tablet
	0.70 fr/bar
Toilet soap	0.40 fr/tablet
Coal Tar	0.60 fr
Lifebuoy	0.80 fr
Sunlight	0.70 fr – 0.80 fr/bar
Comb	1.20 fr
Hair brush	2.50 fr
Handkerchief	0.30 fr – 0.45 fr – 0.50 fr
Towel	1.10 fr – 1.30 fr – 2.25 fr – 2.35 fr
Shaving soap	0.75 fr – 0.80 fr – 1.25 fr – 1.40 fr
Shaving brush	1.50 fr
Tooth paste	1.25 fr – 1.30 fr
Tooth powder	0.60 fr – 0.70 fr
Tooth tin	0.70 fr
Brillantine	1.00 fr

7.   Clothing – Repair and Cleaning

Braces	1.60 fr/pair
Buttons	0.15 fr/packet
Bull dog buttons	0.15 fr/packet
Button stick	0.40 fr
Polish/paste (tin)	
Blacking	0.10 fr
Black Kiwi	0.60 fr
Dubbin	0.20 fr
Wrens polish	0.60 fr – 0.65 fr
Brown polish	0.10 fr – 0.60 fr
Boot polish	0.30 fr
Soldiers Friend	0.10 fr/tin
Boot brush	1.50 fr – 2.00 fr
Laces	0.30 fr/pair
Kaki Blanco	0.30 fr/packet
Saddle soap	1.10 fr – 1.30 fr/tin

8. **Miscellaneous**
    Candle   0.25 fr
    Playing cards   1.10 fr – 1.60 fr – 1.70 fr
    Christmas card   1.00 fr
    Writing pad   0.75 fr – 0.80 fr – 1.25 fr – 1.40 fr
    Pencil   0.40 fr – 0.80 fr
    Purse   1.50 fr
    Watch   8.00 fr

Bibliography

Archives

Talbot House Archives

Periodicals

De Poperingsche Keikop
Our Waifs and Strays
Point Three
Portsea Parish Church Magazine
The Challenge
The Le Touquet Times
The Toc H Journal
Twenty Years After

Books

Baron, B., *Half the Battle*, Toc H, London, 1922.
Baron, B., *Letters from Flanders*, The Centenary Press, London, 1932.
Baron, B., *Over There, A Little Guide for Pilgrims*, Toc H, London, 1935.
Baron, B., *The Birth of a Movement*, Toc H, London, 1946.
Bickersteth, J., *The Bickersteth Diaries 1914-1918*, Leo Cooper, London, 1995.
Brabant, F., *Neville Stuart Talbot 1879-1943, A Memoir*, SCM, London, 1949.
Brown, M. & Seaton, S., *Christmas Truce, The Western Front, December 1914*, Leo Cooper, London, 1984.
Burrage, A.M. (Ex-Private X), *War is War*, Victor Gollancz Ltd, London, 1930.
Chapman, P., *A Haven in Hell, Talbot House, Poperinghe*, Leo Cooper, Barnsley, 2000.
Chapman, P., *In the Shadow of Hell, Behind the lines in Poperinghe*, Leo Cooper, Barnsley, 2001.
Clayton, P.B., *Tales of Talbot House*, Chatto & Windus, London, 1919.
Clayton, P.B., *The Smoking Furnace and The Burning Lamp*, Longmans, Green & Co., London, 1927.
Clayton, P.B., *Plain Tales from Flanders*, Longmans, Green & Co., London, 1929.
Clayton, P.B., *Gen in Four Fyttes*, Toc H, London, 1931.
Clayton, P.B., *Earthquake Love*, G. Bles, London, 1932.

Clayton, P.B., *To Conquer Hate*, The Epworth Press, London, 1963.

Deneire, B., *A Peace of Flanders, Talbot House 1915-?, A personal story*, De Klaproos, Veurne, 1993.

Dumoulin, K., Vansteenkiste, S. & Verdoodt, J., *Getuigen van de Grote Oorlog*, De Klaproos, 2001.

Gosse, P., *Memoirs of a Camp-Follower*, Longmans, Green & Co., London, 1934.

Harcourt, M., *Tubby Clayton, A Personal Saga*, Hodder and Stoughton, London, 1953.

Haythornthwaite, P., *The World War One Source Book*, Arms and Armour Press, London, 1992.

Jones, D., *Bullets and Bandsmen, The story of a bandsman on the Western Front*, Owl Press, Salisbury, 1992.

Leonard, J. & Leonard-Johnson, P., *The Fighting Padre, Letters from the Trenches 1915-1918 of Pat Leonard DSO*, Pen & Sword, Barnsley, 2010.

Lever, T., *Clayton of Toc H*, John Murray, London, 1971.

Louagie, J. & Nolf, K., *Talbot House Poperinge – De Eerste Halte na de Hel*, Tielt, 1998.

Luard, K., *Unknown Warriors*, Chatto and Windus, London, 1930.

Macfie, A., *The Curious History of Toc H Women's Association, The First Phase, 1917-1928*, Crutched Friars, London, 1956.

Madigan, E., *Faith Under Fire, Anglican Army Chaplains and the Great War*, Palgrave Macmillan, Basingstoke, 2011.

Mansbridge, A., *Edward Stuart Talbot & Charles Gore*, J.M. Dent & Sons, London, 1935.

N.N., A Birthday Book, *Twenty-one years of Toc H*, London, 1936.

N.N., *Talbot House, Poperinghe, Concerning Toc H*, Marshall & Co., London, n.d.

Prideaux-Brune, K., *A Living Witness (A Personal Memoir of Philip Clayton)*, Toc H, Wendover, 1983.

Scott-Holland, H., *Gilbert Talbot, A Character Sketch*, All Hallows, London, 1933.

Snape, M., *The Back Parts of War: The YMCA Memoirs and Letters of Barclay Baron, 1915 to 1919*, The Boydell Press, Church of England Record Society, vol. 16, Woodbridge, 2009.

Talbot, L., *Gilbert Walter Lyttelton Talbot*, Printed for private circulation, Farnham Castle, 1916.

Talbot, N., *Thoughts on Religion at the Front*, Macmillan, London, 1917.

Wilkinson, A., *The Church of England and the First World War*, SPCK, London, 1978.

Woolley, G. & Clayton, P.B., *The Salient Facts*, All Hallows, London, 1931.

Index

GENERAL INDEX

Abeele *(Abele)*, 239

A la Poupée (Ginger's), xix, 72

All Hallows-by-the-Tower, xxiv, 75, 286, 309

Americans, 164, 191, 198, 204, 205, 210, 216, 237, 282

Amiens, battle of, 204

Anti-aircraft sections (Archies), 41, 102, 106, 108, 192, 209, 212

A.P.M., 171, 179, 181, 235

Armentières, 27, 178, 303, 304

Armistice, 193, 203, 221, 223, 226, 286, 291

Armstrong hut, 189, 191, 192

Army Chaplains' Department, 27, 155, 167

Arras, battle of, 130, 311, 327

Australia, xxi, 75, 230, 286, 303, 311, 321

Australians, 29, 95, 121, 150, 166, 198, 265, 279, 287, 320, 321

Avelgem, 224

Bailleul, 205, 299, 355

Baptisms, 130, 137, 155, 181, 279, 286, 287, 311

Baths, xix, 123

Beaulieu, 40, 50, 112

Beer, xix, xx, 58, 127, 236

Belgians, 43, 58, 59, 60, 61, 78, 179, 224, 305, 306

Bergues, 119, 301

Billiards, xxi, 84, 160, 162, 164, 180, 214, 228, 231, 239, 318, 319, 336, 358, 361

Boesinghe *(Boezinge)*, 41, 258

Boulogne, 48, 49, 80, 82, 83, 84, 88, 98, 134, 178, 299, 301, 364, 365, 368

Brandhoek, 335

Brielen, 68, 343

British Army

  Armies

    2nd, 70, 167, 322, 330, 355

    5th, 49, 96, 132, 359, 360, 364

  Corps

    II, 186, 188, 212, 359

    III, 84

    VI, 41

    VIII, 71, 85, 245, 358, 359

    X, 358

    XIV, 63, 71, 77, 88, 358

    XVIII, 133, 359, 360, 362

    XIX, 359, 360

    XX, 71

  Artillery units

    141st East Ham Heavy Battery, 110, 119, 120, 134, 142, 341, 342, 343

    146th Battery, 351

    154th Southampton Territorial Heavy Battery, 110, 345, 348, 362

    7th Belgian Field Artillery, 58, 59, 61

  Royal Army Medical Corps

    6th London Field Ambulance, 277, 348

    17th Field Ambulance, 27

    69th Field Ambulance, 95, 330

  Royal Engineers

    "P" Special (Gas) Company, 220, 311

  Royal Horse Guards, 64

  Divisions

    6th, xx, 27, 34, 36, 39, 40, 41, 44, 46, 50, 71, 99

    8th, 84

    14th, 241

    18th, 241

    20th, 71

29th, 53
38th, 228
39th, 228
48th, 364
49th, 41
55th, 228
Guards , 56, 71, 84, 239, 247, 275, 277
63rd Royal Naval Division, 46
Brigades
16th, xx
87th, 90
London Rifle Brigade, 277
Battalions
1st Bn The Buffs (East Kent Regiment),
25, 87, 302, 304, 306
1/16 London Regiment (Queen's
Westminster Rifles), 39, 43, 44, 130,
141, 277, 279, 358
8th Bn Bedfordshire Regiment, 25, 29
British Officers' Hostel, The, 72
British West Indians, 150, 155, 166, 253, 279,
287
Bruges *(Brugge)*, 193, 224, 322
Brussels *(Brussel)*, 58, 103, 217, 218, 331
Bus House, 348
Busseboom, 281

Calais, 178, 342
Cambrai, battle of, 158, 294, 354
Canada, xxi, 58, 61, 84, 230, 243, 280, 303,
316, 317
Canadians, 29, 57, 67, 78, 79, 87, 107, 150, 158,
253, 279, 287, 316, 317
Cape Gris-Nez, 114
Cassel, 70, 114, 142
Casualty Clearing Station No. 10 (Poperinge),
48
Casualty Clearing Station No. 17 (Poperinge),
69, 319
Casualty Clearing Station No. 64 (Proven), 160
Cat Farm, 342, 343
Cemeteries and Churchyards
Anneux British Cemetery, 281
Beacon Cemetery, 296
Blighty Valley Cemetery, 281
Buffs Road Cemetery, 296
Chocques Military Cemetery, 195, 296
Cross Roads Cemetery, 140
Deal Cemetery, 287

Duhallow A.D.S. Cemetery, 147, 281
Dunkirk Town Cemetery, 192, 324
Ecoivres Military Cemetery, 317
Godewaersvelde British Cemetery, 195, 281,
297
Grove Town Cemetery, 100, 281
Gwalia Cemetery, 136, 281
Hop Store Cemetery, 76, 326
Ipswich Old Cemetery, 76, 288
La Clytte Military Cemetery, 249
La Neuville British Cemetery, 96, 267
Larch Wood (Railway Cutting Cemetery),
194, 322, 323, 324
Lijssenthoek Military Cemetery, 44, 45, 48,
109, 136, 313
Mendinghem Military Cemetery, 290
Naval Trench Cemetery, 294, 297
Oak Dump Cemetery, 146
Oosttaverne Wood Cemetery, 122
Poperinghe Communal Cemetery, 59
Poperinghe New Military Cemetery, 59, 61,
91, 121, 122
Poperinghe Old Military Cemetery, 58
Portsmouth (Kingston) Cemetery, 48, 157
Potijze Burial Ground Cemetery, 45
Railway Dugouts Burial Ground, 122, 128,
221, 345, 349
Ramparts Cemetery (Lille Gate), 351
Rangemore (All Saints) Churchyards, 281
Reninghelst churchyard, 183
Sanctuary Wood Cemetery, 38, 39
Savy British Cemetery, 249
Stowmarket Cemetery, 296
St. Sever Cemetery, 276
St. Sever Cemetery Extension, 296, 297
Vlamertinghe Military Cemetery, 125
Wieltje Farm Cemetery, 202, 280, 313
Wytschaete Military Cemetery, 296
Ypres Reservoir Cemetery, 44, 45, 349
Censoring, 64, 85, 142, 151, 206, 210, 281
Challenge, The, xxiv, 94, 121, 204, 327
Chaplains, 27, 75, 76, 83, 87, 111, 131, 132,
148, 165, 169, 173, 216, 288, 289, 295, 327,
330, 349, 357
Chaplains' School, 116, 148, 167
Château Couthove, 119, 332, 333
Château La Lovie, 189, 190, 192, 193, 246,
292, 322
Château Reigersburg, 342

Chess, xxi, xxii, 214, 230, 252, 268, 311

Children, xx, xxi, 32, 39, 65, 68, 79, 100, 106, 107, 114, 123, 153, 157, 158, 159, 171, 200, 207, 245, 247, 255, 256, 257, 258, 259, 260, 261, 262, 263, 282, 303, 305

Chinese, 150, 222, 287

Christmas Truce, 272

Church Army, 39, 46, 58, 71, 132, 201, 216, 265, 291

Church of England's Men Society, 47, 50, 101, 102, 103, 106, 107

Church parades, 25, 40, 41, 62, 89, 112, 201, 281, 340

Church Times, The, 64, 204

Cinema, xxii, 94, 107, 127, 165, 168, 246, 251, 255, 273, 311, 343, 345, 361

Colet Court (London), 53

Community of the Resurrection, 27, 63, 100, 106

Concert Parties, xxiii, 165, 176, 198, 206, 207, 219, 222, 247, 248, 249, 251, 361

Concerts, xxii, 34, 43, 51, 56, 129, 176, 198, 206, 246, 247, 249, 250, 301, 314, 315, 358, 359

Conferences, 70, 75, 131, 132, 149, 164, 167, 169, 252

Confessions, 103, 111, 121, 175, 182, 279, 294

Confirmations, 27, 51, 62, 68, 76, 89, 94, 95, 101, 104, 112, 114, 128, 130, 137, 150, 155, 166, 185, 200, 201, 263, 277, 288, 289, 290, 312, 325, 345, 348

Courtrai *(Kortrijk)*, 218, 222, 225

Cyril's, 72, 132, 171

Daily Chronicle, 202

Daily Mail, 285

Daily Mirror, 285

Daily Telegraph, 202

Debates, xxi, xxii, 38, 51, 52, 103, 108, 251, 252, 253, 301, 311, 330, 336, 345, 358, 359, 361, 365, 368

Demobilization, 215, 218

Deserters, xx, 95, 141, 320, 330, 331

Dickebusch *(Dikkebus)*, 348

Dingley Dell, 189, 190, 192, 194, 196, 199, 200, 202, 322, 324

Direct Hit, The, 339

Dirty Bucket Camp, 25, 33

Dormy House, 342

Drunkenness, xx

Dunkirk, 104, 299, 321, 322

East Boldre, 81, 112, 138, 219

Elverdinghe *(Elverdinge)*, 25, 33, 68, 78, 135, 201, 335

Exeter College, Oxford, 25, 53, 203, 218

Expeditionary Force Canteens, 71

Fancies, The, xx, 34, 44, 48

Fantasia Farm, 68

Forward Cottage, 311, 316

Gallipoli, 321

Gamages, 300, 301, 318, 364

Gas, xx, 41, 43, 44, 45, 63, 89, 104, 131, 135, 155, 156, 169, 203, 230, 250, 260, 279, 284, 294, 311, 318, 343, 348, 350, 356

General Hospital No. 14 (Wimereux), 49, 78, 79

General Hospital No. 16 (Le Tréport), 25, 43, 53, 63, 70, 85, 109, 112, 287

Gordon House, 211, 220

Grousing circles, 254

Hamel, battle of, 198

Hazebrouck, 48, 299, 355

Hill 60, 29, 63, 121, 126, 136

Hooge, xx, 38, 160, 307

Hôpital Elisabeth, xx, 119, 332

Hussar Farm, 355

Illustrated London News, The, 62

India, 286

Ireland, 195, 214, 253, 286, 326, 328

John Bull, 337

Kemmel (Tubby's dog), 204, 208, 210, 215

Kemmel (village), 179, 285

Kemmel Hill, 181, 188, 210, 223

Kite Balloons, 116, 117, 191, 194, 199, 204, 207, 209

Kruisstraat, 342

La Boiselle, 84

Labour Corps, 222, 303

La Lovie aerodrome, 189, 190, 263, 332

Langemarck *(Langemark)*, 284

La Panne *(De Panne)*, 331
Lectures, 102, 112, 119, 129, 165, 166, 251,
    252, 253, 329, 354, 359, 361, 365, 368
Le Havre, 321
Le Touquet, 226, 291
Le Tréport, 25, 43, 47, 48, 63, 70, 335
Liber Vitae (Roll of Honour), 286
Lijssenthoek, xx, 48, 319
Little Hatchett (Beaulieu), 40, 53, 54, 81, 97,
    103, 112, 113, 114, 138, 141, 162, 163, 192,
    193, 196, 212
Little Talbot House, xxii, 153, 155, 156, 157,
    178, 181, 200, 216, 230, 262, 349, 351, 352,
    353, 354, 355, 359, 365, 368
London Opinion, 337
Loos, battle of, 66, 89, 287
Looting, xx

Marne, second battle of the, 198
Memorials
    1st Australian Tunnelling Company (Hill
        60), 121
    Pozières Memorial, 249, 259, 297
    Thiepval Memorial, 66, 96, 280, 288
    Tyne Cot Memorial, 105, 146, 296, 297
    Ypres (Menin Gate) Memorial, 147
    Vis-en-Artois Memorial, 297
Menin *(Menen)*, 223
Men's School, 291
Merkem, 179
Messines *(Mesen)*, 29, 178, 210, 294, 311, 322
Military Police, 27, 32, 128, 171, 259, 320, 321
Mirfield, College of the Resurrection, 63, 70,
    106, 137, 167, 215, 354
Mons, 66, 261, 303
Mont des Cats, 183

National Mission of Repentance and Hope, 94,
    95, 97, 100, 106
New Zealand, 181, 250, 263, 279, 303
Nieuport *(Nieuwpoort)*, 324
Nurses, 119, 263, 331, 332, 334, 335
Nutshell, The, xxiv, 30, 34, 56, 105, 122, 145,
    146, 155, 156, 330

Océan, l', 331
Officers' Club, The, 66, 70, 71, 72, 82, 85, 89,
    90, 102, 181, 275, 298, 306, 358, 359
Officers' Rest Station, 158

Officers' School, 291
Ordination, 93, 94, 103, 139, 226, 290, 291
Ostend *(Oostende)*, 217, 322
Oxford, 25, 27, 38, 53, 77, 93, 160, 162, 265,
    277

Passchendaele (*Passendale* - see: Ypres, Third
    Battle of)
Pearson's Magazine, 205
Pervijze, 324
Photographing, 68, 73, 107, 150, 247
Pilckem Ridge, 27
Pilots, 112, 322
Ploegsteert, 91, 126
Poperinghe *(Poperinge)*, passim
Portsea, 25, 30, 46, 53, 62, 66, 80, 97, 106, 107,
    108, 123, 128, 137, 145, 159, 160, 163, 179,
    206, 215, 282, 295
Potijze, 43
Prisoners of War Fund, 68, 131
Prostitution, xx
Proven, 119, 150, 160, 190, 193, 199, 200, 201,
    212, 355
Punch, 62, 204

Quiet Days (Chaplains), 116, 148, 167, 169,
    170, 173

Radinghem, 291
Railway Construction, 201, 203, 210, 222, 277,
    278
Railway Troops, 92, 119, 173, 194, 198
Reconstruction, 164, 165, 167
Recreation, xix, xx, 34, 39, 46, 51, 57, 83, 106,
    130, 186, 201, 338, 354, 358
Refugees, xix, 35, 72, 218
Rogerum, 44, 249, 250
Rouen, 27, 209
Rousbrugge *(Roesbrugge)*, 27, 124, 136
Roulers *(Roeselare)*, 211, 222, 223
Royal Air Force, 206, 322
Royal Navy, 46, 217, 286, 290, 322
Russia, 159

Shell shock, 95, 328, 331
Signal Schools, 102, 179, 182, 184
Sisters of Boesinghe, 258
Skindles (Hôtel de la Bourse du Houblon), xix,
    72, 132

Skindles Hotel (postwar), 71, 72
Somme, 66, 71, 88, 94, 97, 104, 116, 146, 279, 280, 294, 311, 321, 327
South Africans, 84
Souvenirs, xix, xxiv, 124, 218, 248, 276
Spectator, The, 142
Spying, xx, 303
Stationary Hospital No. 7 (Boulogne), 83, 88, 89, 90
St. Barnabas Hostel, 313
St. Eloi, 58, 80, 101, 348
St. Jan ter Biezen, 142, 143, 144
St. Jean *(Sint-Jan)*, 311, 355, 357
St. Julien *(Sint-Juliaan)*, 284
St. Omer, 94, 148, 164, 280, 291, 299
St. Quentin, 294, 321

Talbot House
    Billiard room, 84, 160, 162, 164, 180, 214, 231, 239, 318, 319, 358, 361
    Canadian Lounge, 125, 133, 134, 268, 289, 338, 362
    Canteen, xxi, xxiii, 30, 66, 133, 137, 142, 188, 199, 216, 231, 234, 239, 249, 250, 258, 289, 318, 358, 359, 362, 363, 364, 365, 368, 370-374
        Piano, xxi, 37, 42, 57, 143, 203, 214, 230, 231, 239, 257, 264, 314
    Chapel (ground floor), 179, 214
    Chapel (2nd floor landing), 32, 33, 34, 36, 40, 42, 43, 80
    Chapel (Upper Room), xxi, xxiii, 51, 52-53, 57, 63, 64, 65, 66, 68, 73, 80, 104, 106, 117, 121, 129, 131, 138, 140, 142, 144, 146, 148, 149, 151, 155, 160, 162, 166, 216, 217, 225, 230, 231, 235, 277-297, 304, 312, 316, 317, 318, 319, 326, 332, 338, 358
    Chapel ornaments
        Alms Box, 279
        Altar frontal, 66, 68, 277
        Altar hangings, 51, 52, 73, 162, 277, 289
        Army Chalice, 277
        Bible, 279
        Burse, 277
        Candelabrum, 277
        Candlesticks (black), 277
        Candlesticks (bedposts), 121, 140, 144, 152, 154, 279

Carpenter's Bench, xxi, 30, 31, 43, 51, 144, 277
Chalice, 277
Cherub's head, 279
Chimes, 282
Communicants' Roll, 77, 116, 159, 179, 208, 226, 279, 282, 286, 326, 332, 345
Communion Set (Uncle Ernest), 223, 277, 278
Confirmation chair, 277, 312
Crucifix (Canal Bank), 277, 278, 289
Crucifix (Portsea), 282, 283
Crucifix (slumming), 343
Crucifixion (Perugino), 115, 277
Font, 85, 137, 140, 155, 279, 286, 287, 312
Font stand, 140, 155, 279, 287
Harmonium (Major Street), 48, 57, 62, 64, 66, 67, 68, 99, 111, 148, 200, 246, 280, 282, 345
Harmonium II, 118
Last Supper, 80, 279
Missal, 279
Monk (carving), 146, 278, 279
Organ, 148, 186
Prayer desks, 195, 279
Pyx, 128, 345, 347, 348, 349
Sanctuary lamp, 289
Streamer, 279
Tubular bells, 184, 214
Veil (lace), 277
Virgin (carving), 279
Venez à Moi, 280
Wafer-box (N. Gammon), 278, 279
Wafer-box (stolen), 140, 142
Chaplain's Room, 93, 125, 166, 251, 252, 261, 269-271, 320
Church Hall, 94, 98, 101, 104, 245
Church Shop (Chaplains' Shop), 63, 142, 267
Concert Hall, xxi, xxiii, 29, 180, 181, 212, 214, 230, 243, 245, 247, 251, 272
Conservatory, 29
Drawing-room, 29, 266
Five Point Nine Room, 29, 242
Games rooms, xxi, 125, 133, 134, 231, 268, 289, 338, 362, 363
Garden, xxi, xxiii, 29, 30, 32, 33, 34, 43, 56, 57, 58, 62, 66, 68, 69, 73, 74, 76, 78, 94, 120, 122, 126, 129, 131, 132, 137, 139, 140, 151, 160, 168, 182, 212, 214, 219,

230, 231, 234, 235, 242-245, 249, 265,
    268, 289, 298, 302, 305, 307
    Aviary, 62
    Badminton Court, 56
    Cellar, 245
    Dovecot, 32
    Garden shed, xxi, 277
    Kitchen garden, 33, 56, 122, 243
    Summer House, 56, 137
General's bedroom, 153, 274, 275, 276
Grocery Bar, 365, 368
Hall, xxi, 29, 55, 78, 84, 230, 231, 234, 235,
    239, 243, 264, 324, 330, 332, 341
    Friendship's Corner, xxi, 237
    Notice board, 47, 230, 232-238, 243, 260,
    262
Kitchen, 29, 42, 50, 319, 320
Lecture rooms, xxi, 231, 329
Library, xxi, 63, 93, 137, 142, 151, 164, 166,
    168, 177, 213, 214, 216, 230, 232, 265-267,
    289, 338, 358, 359, 361, 362, 365, 368
Music room, 230
Newfoundland Lounge (see Canadian
    Lounge)
Reading-rooms, 32, 160, 273, 289
Recreation rooms, 39, 51
Supper Bar, 133
Tea Bar, 160, 359, 365, 368
Writing-rooms, xxi, 51, 82, 160, 231, 232,
    271-274, 289, 328
Talbot House companies
    Concert Party, 206, 207, 251
    Dramatic party, 169, 176, 235, 250, 251
    Orchestra, 129
Talbot House pets
    Bunter (budgie), 134
    Duchess (cat), 191
    Hunter (budgie), 134
    Jacko (magpie), 134, 135, 137, 138
Tanks, 198, 223, 225
Times, The, xxiv, 61, 168, 186, 285, 343
Toc H Journal, xxiv, 38, 162

Toc H League of Women Helpers, 314, 332
Toc H Mark I (Talbot House, London), 80,
    110, 226, 309, 313, 328
Toc H (movement), 27, 56, 62, 63, 66, 75, 77,
    93, 108, 109, 110, 121, 134, 137, 142, 162,
    286, 313
Treasury, The, 205, 206, 208
Typhoid, 58

Vélu, 146, 279
Venereal diseases, xx
Verdun, battle of, 53, 54, 56
Vlamertinghe *(Vlamertinge)*, 44, 330, 340, 345

Waifs and Strays Society, 68, 114, 259, 261,
    262, 263
Westminster Gazette, The, 142
Wytschaete *(Wijtschate)*, 210

Ypres *(Ieper)*, xix, 80, 163, 171, 178, 186, 210,
    220, 260, 277, 283, 294, 302, 318, 332, 341,
    345, 348, 349, 350, 351, 352, 355, 357
    Asylum, 342
    Canal Bank, 277
    Cloth Hall, 157, 356
    Lille Gate, 157, 211, 220, 250, 355, 356
    Lille Road (Rue de Lille), 157, 350, 351, 352,
    359, 362
    No. 10 Bridge, 345, 349
    Prison, 128, 168, 259, 261, 349, 350
    Rue de Dixmude, 349
    St Martin's Cathedral, 279
    Square, 220
Ypres, first battle of, 58, 160
Ypres, second battle of, 58, 311
Ypres, third battle of (= Passchendaele), 130,
    133, 178, 241
Ypres Salient, xx, 25, 30, 46, 110, 230, 250, 332

Zeebrugge, 322
Zillebeke, 38, 136, 342
Zonnebeke, 215, 222

INDEX OF PEOPLE

Adams, Harry, 145
Aked, Arthur, 295, 296
Albert I, King of the Belgians, 210, 331
Aldersey, T.O., 238
Allen, Mary Dorothy, 334, 335
Allenby, Edmund, 159
Anderson, F.I., 79, 82, 93 , 106, 291
Andre, Col., 165
Ashdown, Len, 47, 75, 77
Atkinson, Alfred, 295, 296
Avery, Wilfred P., 121

Bacon, Harry, 295, 296
Baggallay, 203
Bairnsfather, Bruce, 91, 126, 194
Balfour, Arthur, 38
Barber, G.T., 360
Barfield, Kenneth, 276
Barker, George, 260
Barker, John, 46
Barker, Reginald, 260
Baron, Barclay ('Barkis'), 38, 149, 162, 183,
    184, 245, 269, 347, 355, 356, 357
Barrs, Rfm., 252
Barry, F.R., 291
Batchelor, H., 115
Bates, Harold R., 39, 51
Battheu, Camille, 247, 248, 331, 342
Battheu, Jeanne, 247, 257
Battheu, Rachel, 257
Battheu, Simonne, 257
Battheu, Yvonne, 257
Beckh, Ronald, 286
Becket, Miss, 128
Bell, Peter, 288
Bell, Robert William, 36, 37
Benham, Harry, 145
Benham, Sgt., 346
Bennett, Jacob, 96, 97, 242, 288
Bentinck, Henry Duncan, 276
Berry, Walter H., 287
Beverley, Ted, 248
Bewlay, Herbert, 51
Bickersteth, Burgon, 240
Bickersteth, Julian, 137, 289
Bilton, R., 268
Blackhurst, L/Cpl., 360

Blomeley, Cyril, 112
Bostock, Allan, 287
Bottomley, John, 286
Bowes, Christine R., 177
Bowes, George Brimley, 137, 141, 150, 152, 153,
    168, 177, 255, 270, 359, 360, 361, 363, 364
Bradshaw, Cpl., 50
Brayfield, Harold, 248
Brent, Charles Henry, 165, 193
Brewer, 281
Brewster, Ronald, 104, 115, 125, 129, 130, 131,
    158, 250
Bridger, Herbert, 286
Brooke, Rupert, 38
Brown, Horace Manton, 290
Brown, Father, 301
Browne, Frederick H., 44
Browne, Leonard, 92, 93, 98, 100, 106, 107,
    112, 119, 122, 139, 141, 147, 151, 162, 201,
    298, 305, 306
Buchanan-Dunlop, Archibald, 272, 273
Buckworth, H., 238
Bullock, Rev., 63, 82, 84, 85, 86
Burgess, Arthur ('Titch'), 247
Burrage, Alfred McClelland, 267, 273
Burrow, Frederick G., 104, 105, 145, 146, 268,
    295, 296
Butt, 219
Buttery, Walter G., 288

Camerlynck, Alida, 27, 28, 66, 124, 189
Carver, Christian C., 135, 136
Castle, Sgt., 346
Cavan, Earl of, 62, 63, 64, 66, 70, 77, 85, 87,
    92, 267, 292
Chambers-Hunter, Charles, 51
Chaplin, Charlie, xix, 251, 344
Charlton, Edward, 43, 65, 198
Chase, 215
Chavasse, Noel, 286
Chesterton, G.K., 301, 310
Chilvers, G., 238
Chitnis, Bernice, 314
Chorley, J.K., 267
Clarke, J., 238
Clayton, Annie Blanch ('Nancy', wife of Hugh),
    36, 40, 42, 43, 53, 62, 65, 136

Clayton, Horace Ernest, 53, 85
Clayton, Hugh Byard, 34, 39, 48, 53, 113, 180, 192, 201, 206, 207, 214, 218
Clayton, Isabel (mother of Tubby), 26, 81, 113, 164, 175, passim
Clayton, Isobel ('Belle', sister of Tubby), 34, 39, 79, 113, 186
Clayton, Ivy, 53, 113
Clayton, Lt., 274
Clayton, Nancy (daughter of Hugh), 192, 193
Clayton, Philip Byard ('Tubby'), passim
Clayton, Reginald Byard Buchanan ('Guv.'), 32, 33, 34, 36, 40, 49, 50, 57, 64, 65, 89, 100, 113, 119, 160, 185, 191, 197, 199, 208, 218, 222
Clayton, Reginald John ('Jack'), 34, 65, 68, 91, 100, 110, 117, 135, 136, 144, 168, 207, 211
Clayton, Stuart, 91, 113, 136, 198, 203, 205, 208, 214
Coast, Sgt., 346
Coatbridge-Williams, Capt., 360
Coevoet, Marie-Madeleine, 124, 136
Coevoet, Maurice, xx, 27, 28, 124, 136, 188, 220, 225, 226
Cole, Arthur R., 195, 295, 296
Collins, E.H.D., 27
Colthurst, Alan St. George, 270, 293
Colwill, Aubrey, 69
Colwill, Miss, 69
Connell, J.C.W., 36
Cook, Harold, 92
Cooke, Mrs, 34, 65
Cooper, Percy V., 286, 295, 296
Corlett, John H.T., 44
Cornish, Alfred J., 248, 249
Corrie, BSM, 346
Cossey, Eliane ('Ginger'), xix, 72
Cox, Donald, 235, 337, 339
Cox, H.C., 235, 362
Cox, R., 238
Crawley, Sgt., 346
Crisford, Rev., 52, 277
Cunningham, Bertram Keir, 148, 162, 172, 194
Curtis, M., 265
Cutcliffe, 148

Dain, Capt., 134, 142
Darnell, John R., 288
Davey, A., 115

David, Bob, 116
David, Thomas, 116
Davidson, Randall Thomas, 75, 94, 288
Davies, Mrs, 62
Davies, P.M., 360
Davis, John W., 287
Dawkins, Guy, 96, 97, 267
Dawkins, Mrs, 267
De Keirsgieter, Emiel, 258
de Laveleye, Emile Robert Edouard, 58, 59, 60, 61
Dent, Leslie A., 111
Depage, Antoine, 331
Dodd, 137
Doggett, Frederick S., 45
Dooley, Phil, 248
Dowding, Owen, 246
Doyle, Arthur Conan, 41, 206
Du Calion, 249
Dulcken, Maj., 359
Duncan, A., 51
Dunford, F.H., 267

Eastwood, Cecil Mary, 162, 184
Edge-Partington, E.F., 163, 179
Edward, Prince of Wales, 77
Edward, Thomas, 354
Edwards, A., 238
Edwards, Herbert G., 45
Elgar, Edward, 249
Elisabeth, Queen of Belgium, 331, 332
Ellis, J., 238
Elwood, Rev., 355
Ensell, C.S., 71, 85, 87, 88, 90, 98, 101, 106, 110, 113, 116, 122
Evans, Eddie, 142, 212, 216, 251, 360, 369
Evans, Glyndwr D., 122
Evans, Percy, 286
Evans, W.R., 238

Farmer, Col., 205, 206
'Fatty', 64, 246
Field, James, 76, 288
Fielding, Maj.-Gen., 279
Finch, Capt., 176
Flamand, 80, 279
Flynn, Paddy, 195, 214, 216, 237, 369
Foch, Ferdinand, 193
Folkard, William L., 295, 296

Forrest, Archie, 130, 200, 202, 277, 279, 280, 311, 312, 313, 314
Forrest, Elizabeth, 313
Forrest, Harriet, 313
Fowler, John, 286
France, Dorothy, 334
Freeman, Bernard, 286
Frankau, Gilbert, 273
Fry, Mrs, 39, 53, 186, 234, 345

Gales, Frank, 145
Gammon, Newton E., 278, 279, 280
Gardner, Godfrey, 66, 67, 68, 96, 99, 280
Gasser, A.W., 238
George V, King, 249
Gethin, Charles, 251
Gibbs, Philip, 202, 220
Gibson, D., 238
Gibson, F., 238
Gilchrint, Geo., 238
Giles, Samuel, 267
'Ginger' (see Cossey, Eliane)
Glover, Horace A., 45
Godier, Sgt., 346
Godley, George, 36, 66, 74, 78, 79, 85, 89
Goldstone Farr, W., 115
Goodwin, Ralph Jonathan, xxii, 155, 157, 178, 181, 230, 350, 351, 354
Gosse, Philip, 35, 95, 330, 331
Grant, Charles W., 145, 146
Gray, Maurice, 286
Gray, Lt., 252
Green, Alfred, 286
Greenwood, Ernest, 290
Gregory, W., 238
Grenfell, Francis, 124
Griffin, 115
Griffith, John, 286
Gunn, R.F., 360
Gurney, Quintin E., 174, 176
Gwynne, Llewellyn Henry, 25, 50, 51, 55, 56, 63, 79, 86, 88, 94, 101, 116, 131, 165, 279, 290, 291, 325

Hackett, David, 286
Haig, Douglas, 82, 178
Haines, Oliver C., 91, 92
Hall, Sgt., 346
Hall, W.H., 128, 349

Hambling, Victor, 63, 70, 78
Hamer, Rev., 39, 41, 43
Hammond, Bombardier, 343
Hancock, Philip, 283
Hankey, Donald, 142
Hannam, Percy, 155
Harper, Edward, 115
Harris, A., 238
Harrison, George C., 107, 109
Harrison, Jack, 248
Harrison, J.I., 322
Hay, William, 51
Haynes, Bob, 238
Hayward, F., 238
Hayward, George, 238
Hazeldon, S., 248
Hazelhurst, David Thomas, 76, 288, 325, 326
Headley, Capt., 64
Henman, Sydney, 286
Henry, John, 141, 147, 318, 319, 320, 321
Herbert, Percy, 200
Higgins, 118
Higgon, Hugh, 119, 122, 126, 127, 128, 129, 131, 134, 142, 195, 196, 198, 199, 203, 340, 343
Hilker, Cpl., 200
Hill, Albert, 240
Hiller, C., 115
Hinde, George C., 45
Hoar, Ernest, 286
Hocking of Stockeny, A., 51
Hodge, Donald, 241
Hodge, Herbert, 241
Hodges, Daniel A., 122
Hodgson, Miles, 248
Holland, 215
Holliday, Fred, 248
Hollies, John, 76, 288
Hooper, Capt., 148
Hopkinson, Lt., 344
Hoptrough, Herbert C., 105, 145, 146, 155, 295, 297
Houlder, H.F., 160
Hoyle, Geoffrey, 286
Hubbard, Harold, 62
Hunter-Weston, Aylmer, 87, 98, 134
Hutchinson, Col., 129

Innes, Rose, 279
Irwin, Ronald, 170, 177, 186

Jago, Henry Harris, 259
Jeffrey, Fred, 145
Jenkins, Gwynne F., 290
Jenkins, Spr., 252
Jones, A. Llewellyn, 163, 164, 295
Jones, Sgt., 302, 346
Johnson, Q.M.S., 251
Johnston, Rev., 86
Jordan, George, 286

Kavanagh, Sgt., 346
Keir, John Lindsay, 32
Kelman, John, 361
Kennaway, Arthur, 286
Kerry, Charles, 288
Ketchem, Driver, 279
Keymer, Bernard William, 215
Kidd, Benjamin, 203
Kidd, Miss, 282
Kidd, W.A.T., 142, 151, 360
Kiddle, Col., 110
King, W.J., 322
Kingston, Charles R., 288
Kinloch-Jones, Rev., 39
Kipling, Rudyard, 107, 267, 315
Kirkland, 78

Lamaison, Wilfred, 286
Lang, Cosmo Gordon, 131, 243, 244
Lardner, R., 324
Law, E., 238
Law, H., 238
Law, J., 238
Lawrence, Basil, 293, 294, 295, 297
Laycock, Spr., 142, 153, 255, 360
Leach, W.E., 238
Leclercq, Madeleine, 171
Leclercq, Maria, 171
Lee, James, 157, 168, 186
Legg, Douglas, 216, 291
Le Mesurier, Thomas, 191, 192, 210, 322, 323, 324
Lewis, Edgar G., 45
Lloyd George, David, 234, 285
Leonard, Pat, 75, 166, 170
Leonard, Will, 284
Leroy, Marcel, 256
Lindley, W., 51
Lindsay, John Homer, 192, 193

Lister, John, 286
Locke, William Wellings, 135, 136, 279, 281
Lomas, Col., 222
Longman, F., 238
Longman, S., 238
Longridge, Tom E., 248
Lovell, Harold, 271
Lowman, 43, 65, 129, 360
Luard, Katherine Evelyn, 334, 335
Lubbock, George, 65
Lyle, N., 51

Macfie, Alison B.S., 49, 119, 120, 267, 331, 332, 333, 334
Macfie, A. Dorothea, 119, 120, 333, 334
Maclachlan, Ronald, 286
Maclaverty, Ella J.V., 334
Macmillan, John, 94, 131, 137, 288
Magrath, Charles J., 157, 178, 184, 185, 186, 187, 188, 189, 190, 192, 198, 204, 215, 349, 351, 352, 354, 355, 356, 357
Marsden, G., 51
Marshall, H.G., 360
Mary, Queen, 249
Masson, Geo., 115
Maxse, Ivor, 163, 360
May, Reginald, xx, 27, 28, 38, 358
Mayhew, Kenneth S., 135, 279, 281
McInnes, Sgt., 151, 152, 154, 157, 159, 235, 360
McNaught, Pte., 169
Mee, J., 238
Mellish, Edward Noel, 80
Merrifield, Lt., 248
Michelmore, Capt., 165
Miles, E., 115
Millar, Sgt., 360
Mitchell, Hannah Elizabeth, 68, 114, 259, 260, 262
Mitchell, Hannah Rosina, 260
Mitchell, William, 260
Monash, John, 198
Money, H.C., 167, 267, 354
Moore, W., 216, 369
Moorhouse, Jimmy, 151, 167, 171, 172, 181, 234, 319
Morley, Pte., 129
Morris, G.E., 238
Morris, Gilbert W., 279, 281
Morris, 'Monty', 266

Morris, Ralph, 239
Morrison, G., 238
Morrison, S., 238
Mottram, Ralph Hale, 273
Mumford, Cyril, 239
Murley, Harry, 112
Murray, Maurice, 132
Mursell, Sgt., 346

Nagle, Sidney E., 145, 147
Nancarrow, Stan, 145
Newton, George, 58
Nicholson, C.L., 50
Nicholson, John H., xxii, 336, 337
Nicholson, T., 115
Northcliffe, Lord, 285
Norton, 115
Norwood, John, 51

Officer, T.A., 64
Ogden, William, 295, 297
Ormond, Martin, 286
Orpwood, F., 51
Ostick, Frederick, 288
Overbury, 238

Padfield, Frank A., 48, 145
Pantin, Margaret, 107, 119
Parker, Leslie H., 358
Partington, Miss, 267
Paterson, Alexander, 108
Payne, Charles M., 57, 62, 145, 147, 278, 279, 281
Pead, Stan, 112
Pease, C.S., 139, 141, 143
Pershing, John J., 200
Pettifer, Arthur ('Gen'), 79, 89, 303-309, 369, passim
Pettifer, Arthur (Jr.), 153, 154, 304
Pettifer, Susan, 33, 307, 308
Pettifer, William, 153, 154, 304
Philby, Harold P., 75, 76, 325, 326
Phillips, Noel, 192, 196, 203
Pigott, Lt., 193, 267
Pike, F., 238
Pike, H.F., 125
Pike, J., 238
Plumer, Herbert, 70, 82, 167, 247, 291, 324, 325
Ponting, Herbert, 106, 107

Pope, Godfrey, 345
Popham, Rev., 191
Potter, Bert, 66, 108, 145
Powles, Mr, 175
Price, Capt., 130
Price, H.S., 36
Pridham, Harold, 156
Priest, F., 115
Prior, C.B., 267
Proudfoot, Sgt., 346
Pugh, Charles H., 279, 288

Quin, L/Cpl., 239
Quin, Pte., 239

Rackham, Richard Belward, 93, 198
Rawlinson, Henry, 167
Ray, Sid E., 216, 369
Redfern, Lt., 251
Reed, Guy, 286
Reed, Rev., 277
Rees, Hugh, 286
Rees, Timothy, 137
Rees-Mogg, Major, 165
Reid, Jimmy, 39, 47
Reid, Major, 210, 211
Renshaw, W., 115
Richardson, Bert, 248
Ridoutt, William A., 155, 157
Riley, Charles O.L., 95
Roberts, 283
Roberts, Lt., 218, 220, 222
Robinson, Lt., 37
Rogers, Harold D., 45
Room, Percy, 148
Rose, A., 181, 197, 214, 369
Rossall, Timothy, 286
Rowson, Cpl., 238
Ruddock, Richard, 51
Rudolf, C., 260
Rugg, L.H., 153, 360
Rushton, Cecil, 53, 88, 193, 194, 322, 323, 324
Russell, Cyril A.V., 286, 295, 297
Rydon, Lily, 293

Salisbury, Lord, 56
Salter, Harold, 145
Santy, Margareta, 257
Saye and Sele, Lord, 142, 143, 144, 148, 174, 192

Scott, Town-Major, 349
Seys, H., 171
Sheffield, Mr & Mrs, 279
Sheppard, Dick, 108
Shiner, Herbert, 110, 111, 116, 117, 119, 121, 125, 126, 127, 128, 129, 130, 136, 137, 144, 199, 345, 346
Sidney, Philip, 275
Smith, E., 51
Smith, Harry, 286
Smith, Herbert, 286
Southwell, H.K., 169, 172, 173
Stagg, Herbert, 104, 125, 131, 141, 147, 151, 158, 277
Stanton, Arthur Henry, 188
Stapleton, Eva Rose, 334
Stemp, L., 267
Stenning, Bernard C., 195, 279, 281, 295, 297
Stokes, H., 277, 279
Stone, Leslie E., 248, 249
Stone, William G., 140, 252
Stones, 118
Strachan, Capt., 171
Street, Edmund R., 48, 67, 99, 100, 280, 281, 290, 345
Stretton, George, 260
Strickland, Ernest H., 288
Stride, QMS, 346
Sweney, Brig.-Gen., 275

Talbot, Col., 279
Talbot, Edward Keble ('Ted'), 27, 39, 84, 100, 101, 105, 106
Talbot, Edward Stuart (Bishop), 27, 39, 51, 53
Talbot, Gilbert, xx, 38, 39, 77, 87, 160
Talbot, Gilbert (son of Neville), 162
Talbot, Lavinia, 39, 73, 206
Talbot, Neville S., passim
Talbot, Robert C., 287
Tandy, Arthur E., 122
Tanghe, Leonie, 171
Tannet-Walker, Col., 53
Temple, Frederick, 47
Thom, Rev., 205
Thomas, Arch, 252
Thomas, Frank A., 290
Thornton, Spr., 115
Tollemache, John, 51
Tomkinson, Frank, 115
Townley, Harry, 145

Trower, George, 212, 266, 267, 369
Turton, D.W., 161

Upton-Robins, George, 63, 217, 219, 220, 221

Van Cutsem, E.C.L., 167
Vanhove, Germaine, 171
Vanhove, Maria, 171
Vanhove, Theophiel, 171
Vermeulen, Cyriel, 72, 171
Victor, E., 215, 362
Vokins, Cecil, 63, 70, 87, 89, 90, 109, 117, 131, 142, 147, 151, 159, 199, 202, 203, 212, 214, 369

Wakefield, Lord, 80
Walker, Robert, 286
Wallace, Pte., 262
'Wallah', Corps Cyclist, 64, 246
Waller, John C., 315, 316, 317
Wardle, Joseph F., 281
Watson, George, 286
Watts, H.E., 360
Webb, Marshall W.T., 119, 326
Webb, Rev., 354
Webb-Johnson, Ethel, 334, 335
Webberley, 287
Webster, Bob, 248
Webster, R., 249
Wheeler, Rev., 39
Whiteman, Henry, 294
Wilhelm II, Kaiser, 46, 183, 251, 344
Wilkins, Frank, 112
Williams, Charles, 295, 297
Williams, Ernie, 155
Williams, Erskine, 109, 176, 246
Willmott, C., 214, 250, 251, 369
Wilson, Capt., 138
Wing, Vincent, 286
Winterbotham, Fatty, 107
Wood, A., 51
Woods, E.S., 215
Wootton, James W., 45
Wreford, J., 51
Wyard, James Arthur, 76, 288
Wyllie, William Lionel, 230

Yapp, Arthur, 234
Yeoman, R., 238
York, Sgt., 346